Mary Fletcher Hospital

first College of Medicine, now Pomeroy Hall

UVM campus, painted in 1907 by H. D. Nichols and printed by Paul Victorius, Inc., Charlottesville, Penn. *Far left:* the third College of Medicine, now the Dewey Building. Middle background: the Mary Fletcher Hospital. *Far right:* the first College of Medicine, now Pomeroy Hall.

The University of Vermont
College of Medicine

The University of Vermont

College of Medicine

by Martin Kaufman

Published by the University of Vermont College of Medicine

Distributed by the University Press of New England

Hanover, New Hampshire, 1979

To my wife

HENRIETTA

Foreword

WHAT FOLLOWS IS the true account, almost unbelievable at times, of the struggles of generations of dedicated physicians and others to establish and maintain a system of medical education in Vermont—one of the smallest of the states in size, population, and material resources. Beset by almost every imaginable difficulty from the time of its inception, the University of Vermont has nevertheless been training physicians since 1804, with the exception of the period between 1836 and 1853.

In the sixteenth and seventeenth centuries Vermont had few permanent inhabitants. Plagued by Indian raids and during the American Revolution by British invasions from Canada, the pioneers found that at times their existence was precarious. Added to these perils was the uncertainty that the titles to their lands were valid, for both New York and New Hampshire were claiming the right to grant tracts.

Nevertheless, frontiersmen did arrive in this beautiful but rugged state with its all too short summers, spectacularly beautiful autumns, and long, bitter-cold winters. Its mountains, hills, and valleys were covered with virgin forests so dense that until paths and rough roads could be hewn out, the earliest settlers had to pack in their household goods and supplies or drag them behind on sledges. (There was no grass or hay in this frontier land that would have provided sustenance for livestock.)

In the mid-summer of 1777, on the very day that Burgoyne was attacking Ticonderoga and Fort Independence, the founding fathers (many of them pioneers themselves) met in Windsor and adopted a constitution for the beleaguered but independent Republic of Vermont. Section 40 of this constitution states in part that "one grammar school in each county and one university in the state ought to be established by direction of the General Assembly." It is significant that "university" was used, rather than "college." The founders' intent was to give the citizens of Vermont access to broad areas of higher education.

After many delays a university was indeed established, in name at least, in 1791, the same year that Vermont joined the Union as its fourteenth state. The University was the twenty-fifth in the United States and the fifth oldest in New England. Largely because of the substantial support offered by Ira Allen, a resident of Burlington, the General Assembly voted to establish it in that community and assigned to it public lands set aside for higher education. In 1800 a president was elected and classes were started. Four years later, the first degrees were awarded. In 1804 John Pomeroy, a "doctor" who never attended a medical school but who had received his training through apprenticeship, was appointed to the faculty as Lecturer in Chirurgery and Anatomy. Pomeroy, who had been instructing students in the art of medicine since about 1800, received no stipend and conducted his teaching first in his home and later in a combined home and office on Water Street, now 164 Battery Street and still standing.

Although lacking in formal education, Pomeroy was an omnivorous reader of medical and other scientific books and was a highly regarded clinician and teacher. It became his dream to see a medical college established as part of the University, a dream that did not materialize until 1822 when the Trustees took the formal action necessary to organize a College of Medicine. The University of Vermont thus became the first state college or university to have a medical department.

Martin Kaufman's scholarly and fascinating history carries the the reader through the hundred and forty-eight years that followed. It is a tale of victories, defeats, near defeats, and challenges, and chiefly it is about the people involved. Survival of the College became a burning issue over and over again, but except for the period of 1836–53 the School was saved, often in the nick of time and always through the resolute determination and efforts of one or more committed individuals.

When I first read this quasi-epic narrative, the personalities that impressed me as most significant in influencing the course of events were: John Pomeroy, the pioneer with a vision; Benjamin Lincoln, the brilliant teacher, who succumbed all too soon to tuberculosis; Samuel White Thayer, the general practitioner from Northfield who reopened the School in 1853; Walter Carpenter who moved from Randolph to Burlington to aid Thayer in this enterprise and who years later encouraged Mary Fletcher to establish the first hospital in Vermont as a teaching institution affiliated with a College of Medicine; A. P. Grinnell, who expanded the student body at the expense of educational standards; Henry Crain Tinkham, who with the backing of Presidents Buckham, Benton, and Bailey met crisis after crisis stemming from the Flexner Report; and Ernest Hiram Buttles, who with the unified support of the faculty and of President Guy Winfred Bailey saved the School in the late 1930's during the last great battle to maintain accreditation, thus paving the way for the firm foundations of the fine educational institution we have today.

Scores of others, however—teachers, clinicians, investigators, administrators (Deans Kemp, Beecher, Brown, Wolf, Slater, Andrews and Luginbuhl), and, perhaps most of all, the people of Vermont—stood resolutely behind the School. They provided the resources and skilled planning that ensured the orderly development of a Division of Health Sciences for the education of health professionals, not only in medicine but in such allied fields as nursing and medical technology.

There were major roadblocks over the years: the small size and relatively small population of the state and especially the Burlington area, with consequent limited clinical facilities; the difficulties of obtaining and retaining gifted faculty especially in the earlier years, because they had to support themselves from students' fees; competition with early nineteenth-century proprietary medical schools, chiefly Castleton; meeting the standards of the accrediting agencies in the early twentieth century; and, of course, finding adequate financial support for what was and still is an expensive operation.

As one who has been fortunate enough to have been part of the scene for over half a century as observer and participant, I would be less than frank, however, if I did not stress my enormous pride in what our small school has been able to accomplish over the years and especially during the period of growth and enrichment since the early 1940's. Consistently, the major emphasis has been on training competent, skilled, and compassionate physicians and other health professionals, primarily for Vermont but to an appreciable extent for the nation as a whole, and to provide through our teaching hospital and ambulatory facilities highly skilled medical care.

Some developments of the last decade which cannot yet be seen in historical perspective have been touched upon rather lightly by the author. In recent years, investigative studies that were almost nonexistent until the late 1930's have played a significant role in the activities of the faculty and, to some extent, of the student body. Although handicapped by cutbacks in grant support, productive research has continued virtually unabated in all departments and has expanded greatly in several. To single out only a few of many fine programs in the Division of Health Sciences, Larry Weed's system of a "problem-oriented medical record" is revolutionizing the intelligent and effective delivery of medical care and is spreading rapidly throughout the medical world.

The federally funded National Lung Research and Demonstration Center established several years ago as the first in the nation has a statewide program, chiefly investigative and educational, involving not merely the Medical School but all hospitals in the state and public and private agencies as well. Among the current projects are intensive studies of pneumonia in community hospitals; of pulmonary emphysema, with emphasis on the education of patients and their families; of the dusty occupations (particularly wood-working); and of pulmonary fibrosis.

The life-saving programs in neonatology as developed by the departments of pediatrics and obstetrics-gynecology have reduced infant mortality not only in the Vermont area but wherever they have been duplicated. It gives me a thrill of vicarious pride to see a helicopter landing outside the hospital emergency suite, and delivering an isolette containing a tiny infant in deep trouble, and to know that it is already in good hands.

The University's Regional Cancer Center, also federally supported through the National Cancer Institute, concerns itself with malignant disease in not only the state of Vermont but also northeastern New York and northwestern New Hampshire. Its interdisciplinary orientation enables it to carry on a number of group protocol studies in the broad field of oncology.

The relatively new Department of Family Practice, most popular with our student body, is turning out practitioners well trained to cope with the ills of mankind in this complex age. Above all, it is heart-warming to observe the students today, young men and women with a sense of purpose in their lives. I realize that this is not unique for the UVM College of Medicine but I am happy and grateful that it is so evident here. Teachers and students alike are mindful of Chaucer's clerk: "gladly wolde he lerne, and gladly teche."

Burlington A. Bradley Soule, M.D.
April 1978

Contents

	Foreword by A. Bradley Soule	vi
	Preface	xvii
1.	John Pomeroy's Medical School	1
2.	The First Formal Medical College, 1821–1829	15
3.	Benjamin Lincoln and His "Reformed" College	29
4.	Every Man His Own Physician: Equal Opportunity and the Healing Arts	41
5.	Resuscitation of the Medical School	49
6.	Faculty Development, 1870–1886	61
7.	The Faculty and the Trustees, 1886–1900	74
8.	Development of the Physical Plant, 1829–1904	86
9.	Curriculum Development, 1870–1900	101
10.	Student Life, 1854–1900	113
11.	The Flexner Report and Its Aftermath	130
12.	From Tinkham to Jenne and Beyond	152
13.	The Forties	169
14.	From Medical College to Medical Center	189

15.   Students and Student Life in the Twentieth Century   211

16.   Only Yesterday   233

      Bibliography   257

      Index   265

Illustrations

Front endpaper. The UVM Campus in 1907

Back endpaper. The UVM Campus in 1976

1. Dr. John Pomeroy's home and office   8
2. The village of Burlington, ca. 1812   8
3. The building of the first College of Medicine, built in 1829; now Pomeroy Hall   24
4. The Faculty of the College of Medicine in 1865   59
5. The second College of Medicine Building, 1888   88
6. Fire destroying the Medical College Building, 1903   95
7. Laying the cornerstone of the third Medical College Building, 1903   97
8. The completed structure   97
9. The Mary Fletcher Hospital, 1899   98
10. The Hospital entrance, 1899   98
11. An operation at the Hospital in the early 1900's   99
12. Medical students of 1888   114
13. UVM's championship baseball team of 1891   123

14. President Matthew Buckham with the Faculty of the
    College of Medicine, 1904   131

15. Dean Jenne and professors, College of Medicine, 1933   139

16. Henry Crain Tinkham, Dean of the College of
    Medicine, 1898–1925   140

17. The Bishop deGoesbriand Hospital in the 1940's   174

18. The Entrance of the deGoesbriand Hospital   174

19. Dean Beecher and Dr. E. L. Amidon in MFH
    amphitheatre, 1942   175

20. Drs. H. A. Durfee, Sr., E. H. Buttles, and T. S. Brown,
    1943   181

21. Dean Beecher demonstrating the Beaumont surgical kit,
    1945   187

22. Dr. Paul K. French in the Old Men's Ward, MFH, 1946   187

23. The Class of 1950 in the MFH amphitheatre   188

24. Dean Brown and the Medical Faculty, 1951   188

25. Professors emeriti, 1951   190

26. Dr. Murdo G. MacDonald, '51, the City Physician, with
    senior medic Gerald Needleman, '53   190

27. Dr. E. L. Amidon, professor of medicine, lecturing in
    Hall A to the Class of 1955   195

28. Laying the cornerstone of the Medical Alumni Building,
    1958   198

29. Three deans, Drs. Beecher, Wolf, and Brown; the
    Medical Alumni Building on the way up   201

30. Members of the classes of 1960 and 1961 in the hallway
    of the Medical School   212

31. Dean Wolf and the Medical Faculty, 1960   213

32. The Class of 1936 whooping it up at a beer party several
    days before their graduation   213

33. Teachers of the Year, 1954–77   229

34. Dr. John H. Bland, Teacher of the Year, 1977   230

35. Pediatric awards for excellence in teaching, 1977   230

36. Dr. Ferdinand Sichel, professor of physiology, with
     students   247

37. Dr. Chester A. Newhall, professor of anatomy   247

38. Dr. Albert G. MacKay, professor of surgery   248

39. Dr. Wilhelm Raab, professor of experimental medicine
     with associates Gigee and Herrlich   248

40. Dr. Harold B. Pierce, professor of biochemistry   249

41. Dr. Durwood J. Smith, professor of pharmacology   249

42. Breaking ground for the Given Building; ceremony in
     Hall A   250

43. Air view of the campus showing the College of
     Medicine and hospitals, 1975   252-253

44. Dr. Bruce R. MacPherson '67, lecturing in the Given
     Building to the Class of 1979   254

Preface

THE HISTORY OF a medical school can be fascinating. The institution is alive, always changing. Professors come and go; deans arrive and depart in accordance with what seems a regular schedule. Students come to prepare themselves for their future profession, and while at school they add youthful exuberance to the scholarly atmosphere. The curriculum is periodically modified to fit the changing needs of the student, and of the society. To a large extent, the history of a medical school is the history of medicine during that period. Yet each school has its unique heritage, not only in terms of the names of the participants, but also in terms of how different people responded to similar forces.

Unfortunately, too often the written history of a medical school is terribly dull—more a collective biography than an institutional history. When I was first interviewed by the members of the History of Medicine committee of the University of Vermont, I insisted that I would focus on the institution, rather than on the faculty. I would write a biography of the School, rather than a collective biography of the professors. I am confident that I have succeeded in that respect. If I have failed to maintain a high level of interest, it is my fault, however, and certainly not that of the institution.

I was blessed with cooperation and assistance from many individuals. I am indebted to the Medical Alumni Association for the very generous financial support that made this work possible. I am also indebted to the members of the History of Medicine committee—T. D. S. Bassett, Samuel Hand, A. Bradley Soule, and Lester Wallman. Collectively and individually, they devoted a great deal of time and energy to the project. They read the manuscript at several stages, and they offered constructive criticism which improved both the accuracy and readability of the finished product. Dr. Bassett, the University archivist, provided access to the extensive collection accumulated over the years, and he and his staff were exceedingly helpful. Dr. Hand, chairman of the Department of History, provided office space, and material and moral support when needed. Dr. Soule, who played a major role in the College's recent history, was always able to answer the questions which arise in the course of historical research. In addition, Dr. Soule is responsible for preparing the excellent illustrations in the book. Finally, Dr. Wallman, chairman of the Committee, worked to iron out difficulties throughout the project.

In the course of the project I encountered many librarians and archivists whose assistance was crucial. They included David Blow, a member of the staff of the University archives and archivist of the Diocese. Also helpful was Connie Gallagher, of the Wilbur collection in the Bailey Library. I corresponded with numerous librarians and archivists, who provided information and copies of material in their collections. These included Mildred D. Bates of the Cummington Historical Commission, Gilbert J. Clausman of the New York University Medical Center, Graciela H. Coons of the College of Physicians and Surgeons of Columbia University, Ferenc A. Gyorgyey and Thomas G. Falco of the Yale Medical Library, Mary H. Hughes of the Bowdoin Medical Library, Joseph E. Jensen of the Medical and Chirurgical Faculty of the State of Maryland, Thomas Clark Pollock and Bayrd Still of the New York University archives, Judith A. Schiff of the Yale University Library, John D. Stimson of the New York Public Library, Alice D. Weaver and Denis Gaffney of the New York Academy of Medicine, and Richard J. Wolfe of the Countway Library of the Harvard Medical School.

I owe a debt of gratitude to Robert T. Brown and Peter S. Bulkeley, chairmen of the Westfield State College Department of History while this book was being written. They provided assistance when needed, and they helped to create an atmosphere conducive to the production of scholarly work.

These acknowledgments would not be complete without giving credit to Joseph Carvalho III. Not only did he prove to be an excellent research assistant, but he practically became a member of my family during the time we spent in Burlington.

Finally, I must thank my wife, Henrietta, without whose help this book would have been completed earlier, but who more than made up for that by presenting me with my second son, a Green Mountain Boy, born in Burlington during July of 1974.

Westfield, Massachusetts   M.K.
April 1978

Chapter One

John Pomeroy's Medical School

THE YEAR WAS 1772. Ira Allen, the youngest brother of Ethan Allen, came to northwestern Vermont. He had two specific objectives. He was to survey the lands claimed by the town of Mansfield, and he hoped to locate for himself and his brothers lands having commercial possibilities. Allen recognized that Lake Champlain would someday be a busy waterway, and he was especially impressed with the area around Burlington Bay, which offered an ideal location for a port. He and his brother, Heman, bought title to the land from the proprietors of the Burlington Township, and Ira set out to make a detailed survey.[1] Further progress had to wait, however, for the American Revolution was just a few years in the future.

During the War the citizens of Vermont wanted to be represented in the Continental Congress, but that proved impossible. Vermont had been claimed by New Hampshire as early as 1741 and by New York in 1764, and it was debatable whether Vermont was a state. As a result, Vermonters were forced to take unilateral action: in 1777 Vermont declared itself an independent republic. The young men of Vermont did participate in the war effort; the Green Mountain Boys, formed by Ethan Allen, figured prominently in the battles at Bennington, Ticonderoga, and Crown Point, among others.

In 1777 a constitution was prepared. One section provided that schools be established in each town, that one grammar school be organized in each county, and that "one university . . . ought to be established." The framers were thinking of a Yale or Harvard, developing out of British models and embracing the universe of learning or "science," as it was then called. The eighteenth-century univer-

1. The early history of Vermont can be developed from Samuel Williams, *The Natural and Civil History of Vermont* (Burlington, 1809).

sity prepared the sons of planters, squires, merchants, and other affluent aristocrats for a life in law, divinity, or business, and sometimes provided lectures on "physick" and other fields of science. By including a university as the capstone of its educational system, the infant state was asserting that it would one day be fully equipped to take its place in the society of developing states. Every colony from New Hampshire to Pennsylvania had one institution of higher learning, and so would Vermont.

As a frontier society, Vermont was, however, still preoccupied with survival, not science. The Vermont constitution was adopted at Windsor in July 1777 after General Burgoyne, with almost as many troops as the population of the new republic, had captured the forts at Ticonderoga and Mount Independence and routed the patriot rear guard at Hubbardton. Vermont remained exposed to British raids from the Lake Champlain forts, which cleared the Champlain Valley of settlers and threatened the upper Connecticut River Valley. Across the river in Hanover and relatively safe from attack, President Eleazar Wheelock in 1778 pointed out that Dartmouth College, then in its tenth year, could serve as Vermont's state university. Founded with English funds, the frontier college needed new support during the revolution. The assembly was able quickly and inexpensively to fulfill the wishes of the founding fathers by taking the New Hampshire institution "under the patronage of this state." But it was not to be quite so easy. New Hampshire protested the loss of land which occurred when Hanover and fifteen other border towns were annexed by Vermont, and in February 1779 the towns were returned to the control of New Hampshire.

Vermont wanted the protection of the United States, but its birth certificate was in question. New York claimed that it had provided government for the area calling itself Vermont and that a group of outlaws led by Ethan and Ira Allen had rebelled by declaring independence. The Allens had accumulated large tracts of land in northwestern Vermont by purchasing New Hampshire titles, and they were close to Governor Thomas Chittenden and the inner circle of the republic's rulers. Although New Hampshire also claimed the territory popularly known as the New Hampshire Grants, it had accepted the Crown's 1764 decision confirming New York's title, and was therefore out of the contest.

The State of Vermont survived, financed by the sale of Tory or wild lands. It boomed with the addition of 50,000 people from the south in the 1780's, but still could not implement the state university clause in its constitution. The settlers were preoccupied with lands, timber, and debts. When George Washington was inaugurated as president of the United States in 1789, many of the 85,000 people in the clearings of Vermont were close to starvation. According to one source, "more than a quarter . . . of the people" had "neither bread nor meat for 8 weeks."[2]

In any case, the Americans had to decide how their Union should be constituted before they could consider the admission of new states. In addition, the New Yorkers had to accept the validity of New Hampshire land titles and the fact of Vermont independence before Vermont could be admitted to the union. In 1791 the decision to accept Vermont into the United States was finally made. It was followed by the chartering of a state university.

Ira Allen knew it was good business to offer a full line of institutions to the buyers of his real estate. Consequently he promised a 4,000-acre endowment if the University of Vermont would be located in Burlington, the capital of his land empire. Ira's was the best offer; it was accepted and a university was incorporated. Burlington had potential for growth—shore position close to the well established Winooski Valley route, nearby water power, and, above all, the determination of Ira Allen.

In 1791, however, Burlington, with only 332 people, was relatively insignificant. Colchester, Ira Allen's home (population 137) was the county seat for Chittenden County, whose jurisdiction covered the area north to the Canadian border. Charlotte, the largest town in the county, was twice as large as Burlington. Throughout the state, money was scarce, prospects were uncertain, and village life, for which the University could prepare professionals, was only beginning. As a result, its Corporation was unable to launch the institution in the 1790's.

The stage was set for the arrival of Reverend Samuel Williams, who was to play a major role in the establishment of the University of Vermont. He had graduated from Harvard in 1761, and he became the protégé of Professor John Winthrop, succeeding his master as Hollis Professor at Harvard. Although at the pinnacle of success, he was about to face a crisis: a large sum of money had been entrusted to his care, and he was unable to account for it. Obviously convinced that he would be accused of theft, in 1788 Williams fled into the wilderness. Vermont was a perfect refuge—it was still independent.[3]

Williams, who settled in Rutland and founded the *Rutland Herald*, promoted that town as the seat of the state university. When Rutland lost to Burlington, he worked with Ira Allen and accepted a professorship at the University. Competition finally stirred the trustees of the University to hire a president and start teaching. The town of Middlebury maneuvered the legislature into holding its 1800 session at the Addison County courthouse and lobbied successfully for a second college charter. But Middlebury college was to remain a classical, Congregational one. At Burlington, on the other hand, the

2. Nathan Perkins, *Narrative of a Tour Through the State of Vermont From April 27 to June 12, 1789* (Rutland, 1964), pp. 21–22.
3. Julian Ira Lindsay, *Tradition Looks Forward* (Burlington, 1954), pp. 14–16.

aim was to develop a university. In 1804, when the Corporation granted its first degrees, it appointed John Pomeroy as lecturer in "chirurgy" and anatomy.[4] That action symbolized an expansion of the institution from a classical college to one with more diversified objectives.

At that time, in the late colonial and early national period, medicine was a trade, practiced by men who had little or no formal training. It has been estimated that of the 3,000 physicians who practiced in America during the colonial period, fewer than 400 had received medical degrees.[5] Since in the early years of the nineteenth century Vermont was still on the frontier, it is unlikely that any of the physicians in the state had formal medical training. The vast majority of the nation's practitioners and probably all of Vermont's physicians had been trained by apprenticeship. Boys were bound to their masters at early ages, often at 14 or 15. A legally binding indenture would be drawn up and signed by the master and the boy's father or guardian. The physician would agree to let the student "read medicine" in his library and would promise to train the boy for the successful practice of medicine. The apprentice would normally accompany his master on visits to the bedside of patients, and he would learn the trade by observing his master and by reading the books in his master's library. The boy would act as the body-servant of the physician, tending the horses, keeping the office clean, and even serving as bill collector.[6]

It was not a bad system if one considers that medical knowledge was limited, that only a handful of American colleges were in existence, and that they were too small to do much more than train a tiny percentage of the nation's physicians. If the preceptor (master) was well trained and if he had a genuine interest in improving the medical practice of the area, the students would receive an adequate education. Most preceptors, however, were themselves poorly trained products of the apprenticeship system, men with only a handful of books in their libraries, who were too busy to devote time to their students, and often had little scientific knowledge to impart.

Indications are that apprenticeship in Vermont was therefore inadequate. Dr. Benjamin Chandler, for instance, who practiced for many years in Fairfield, Vermont, and later in St. Albans, was trained in the 1790's by Ebenezer Marvin. According to his obituary, Chandler had received very little training from his master. Marvin had furnished his student "with nothing in anatomy, but Chesselden's little Compend—and textbooks in other departments were equally deficient." Yet even though he had received a rudimentary education, Chandler played a major role in the absence of better trained practitioners. He practiced among "a widely scattered population, where

4. UVM Trustee Minutes, August 13, 1804.

5. N. S. Davis, *Contributions to the History of Medical Education and Medical Institutions in the United States of America, 1776–1876* (Washington, D.C., 1877), p. 9.

6. For an excellent short description of colonial and early American apprenticeship, see Genevieve Miller, "Medical Apprenticeship in the American Colonies," *Ciba Symposia*, 8 (January 1947), 502–510.

roads were mere bridle paths" and cabins so distant "that a visit to a half dozen" patients "required a hard day's ride." According to tradition, on one instance he went so far into the wilderness to see a patient that he had to leave his horse and walk twenty miles, guided only by marked trees.[7]

Even John Pomeroy, who was to become a professor at the University of Vermont, had never attended medical school. He was born in Middleboro, Massachusetts, in 1764, and served in the state militia during the Revolutionary War. He was apprenticed to Dr. James Bradish, of Cummington. In 1787 the young physician migrated to Cambridge, Vermont, and after having developed what was reported to be a large practice, he moved in 1792 to the growing town of Burlington.[8] Yet in 1793 Pomeroy was frustrated by his lack of medical knowledge, and perhaps by his inability to "cure" the sick. In any case, he wrote to Lemuel Hopkins, of Hartford, Connecticut, complaining that he was "young & destitute in a great measure of Advantages in Physic."[9]

Hopkins responded by recommending the purchase of a number of books, including William Cullen's *First Lines* and John Brown's *Elements of Medicine*. Then Hopkins responded to several of Pomeroy's specific questions, including "how does the constitution become scrophulous" and "whether cancers differed from other complaints."[10] Considering the type of medical training given to the average American physician, most practitioners undoubtedly needed a more experienced acquaintance who could provide encouragement when required, and could answer questions that would naturally arise in the course of medical practice.

In 1792 a rural physician named Jacob Ruback wrote a letter to Pomeroy in which he commented on the practice of medicine on the frontier. He declared that "the Practice of Physick, is the most Disreputable Profession, of any now Extant." He complained that there were "too many young Practitioners . . . who are conceited enough to medle, with what they do not understand, and at the same time . . . impose their Ignorance upon the vulgar, for good Practice." Other physicians learned from experience that often it was impossible to cure the sick, and as a result many practitioners concluded that "all applications" were merely a "matter of Guess." The result was to reduce "in their opinion Empiricks, Quacks and old Granny's, to a level with good Physicians, & men of ability."[11] In those times it was easy for a practitioner to lose confidence as well as patients.

In addition, physicians were commonly considered mere tradesmen. Medicine was not much of a profession. After all, the physician had served an apprenticeship for no longer a period than the cobbler, the silversmith, and the blacksmith, and medicine did not attract

7. Vermont Medical Society, *Transactions, 1874, 1875* and *1876* (St. Albans, 1877), pp. 53ff. For Chandler's role as a preceptor, see John Loche Chandler, "Medical Education," *Buffalo Medical Journal*, II (September 1855), 218–219.

8. John W. King, "Dr. John Pomeroy and the College of Medicine of the University of Vermont," *Journal of the History of Medicine*, 4 (1949), 396.

9. Lemuel Hopkins to John Pomeroy, Hartford, Connecticut, December 6, 1793, John Pomeroy Papers, UVM Archives.

10. Ibid.

11. Jacob Ruback to John Pomeroy, Shelburne, December 25, 1792, Pomeroy papers.

the best students. Thomas Ruston, who had studied at Edinburgh, wrote his father that it would be difficult to earn a living as a physician, because he was "afraid that" medicine "will be but a traid" in Philadelphia.[12]

Physicians had a difficult time collecting their fees. Ruback noted that patients "are negligent to pay the Doctor." Attorneys and preachers collected their fees in advance, he declared, and the merchant only gave credit when he was certain that he would be paid. The physician, on the other hand, was "duty bound to go when called for," though he would have to wait until the patient "is able, or ready to reimburse him," which often meant a long time, "or Perhaps Never!"[13]

Pomeroy discovered fairly early how difficult it was to collect his fees. In April of 1796 he advertised in the *Burlington Mercury* that he had a "Universal assortment of Drugs and Medicines" for sale, and he offered them "on reasonable terms and credit," with a "generous deduction for prompt pay."[14] More than three months later Pomeroy announced that he was in the market for a number of horses, and that he wanted to pay for them with drugs. The advertisement continued that Pomeroy would "also be exceedingly happy to receive remittance from those a long time indebted for Medicine."[15]

All of this meant that the best qualified students would not dream of entering the medical profession. The compensation was limited and the prestige inadequate. In addition, the training given to physicians was rudimentary, and perhaps it had to be, considering the fact that anyone who called himself a physician could practice medicine. This was the climate in which the University of Vermont appointed John Pomeroy as lecturer in surgery and physic.

When the University's program was organized in 1800, the faculty consisted of one person—President Daniel C. Sanders, who had graduated from Harvard in 1788. Soon a tutor was appointed, and in 1804 Pomeroy received his appointment.[16] Pomeroy's appointment, however, was without compensation from the University. Although he was to give an annual course of lectures, he would be "supported by voluntary contributions from persons choosing to attend, whether students or practitioners."[17]

This was not an unusual arrangement. America's early medical schools were proprietary, meaning that the students paid their fees directly to the professors. The existence of the school depended upon its ability to attract enough students. If only a handful chose to attend classes, the professors would be forced to abandon the college as an unprofitable undertaking. The trustees of the University of Vermont obviously believed that medical education was important enough to have a place in the curriculum, but only as long as it was self-supporting. Yet the historian forms the impression that per-

12. Thomas Ruston to Job Ruston, Edinburgh, September 30, 1764, Ruston Papers, Library of Congress.

13. Jacob Ruback to John Pomeroy, Shelburne, December 25, 1792, Pomeroy Papers.

14. *Burlington Mercury*, April 1, 1796, p. 4, col. 3.

15. Ibid., July 8, 1796, p. 3, col. 4.

16. UVM Trustee Minutes, August 13, 1804.

17. House Journal, October 18, 1811, pp. 63ff, in Legislative History of the University of Vermont, p. 292, UVM Archives.

haps the trustees considered the appointment of Pomeroy as an inexpensive way to double the faculty, which in turn enabled them to argue for state support on the basis of the enlarged faculty.[18]

According to Samuel Williams, the "customary methods of education for the professions of divinity, law, or physic" were "extremely deficient; and do not promise either eminence, or improvement." Williams, who had helped to found the University, declared that "The body of the people seem to be more sensible of this defect, than professional men themselves."[19] John Pomeroy, however, *was* devoted to the advancement of the profession. As early as 1797 he requested that all the physicians in Chittenden County assemble at Gideon King's Tavern, in Burlington, to establish a medical society.[20] Perhaps Pomeroy was trying to emulate the physicians of Rutland and Bennington counties, who in 1784 had formed the "First Medical Society in Vermont," and those of Windham, who in 1794 had incorporated the "Second Medical Society."[21]

In any case, that the "Third Medical Society of Vermont" was not established until December 29, 1803, indicates that very few physicians responded to Pomeroy's call. When it was finally organized in 1803, Pomeroy was elected president, an office he held until 1813, when the Society was reorganized.[22] The Society tried to regulate medical practice by drawing a distinction between the qualified physicians, who were admitted to the society, and the "empirics," who continued to treat the ill. Candidates for membership in the Society were examined by the censors and were expected to demonstrate a knowledge of "the theory of anatomy, animal functions in their natural and diseased state and of the remedies in general use both simple and compound."[23]

In addition to his efforts to professionalize the practice of medicine, Pomeroy was happy to assist young practitioners and students. In 1806 he loaned a number of books to William Beaumont, who was studying with Dr. Benjamin Chandler. Beaumont, who later was to become world famous for his studies of the process of digestion, in 1812 was licensed to practice medicine by the Third Medical Society, and his diploma was signed by John Pomeroy and his son, Cassius Pomeroy.[24]

Finally, Pomeroy worked to develop a medical college at the University of Vermont. In 1804, as noted, he was appointed lecturer in surgery and physic. Three years later he was elected as a trustee of the University, and in less than two years it seems that he had managed to convince the trustees to grant medical degrees to qualified students. On August 17, 1809, the trustees voted that the degree of Bachelor of Physic could be granted to "any person who has been licensed to practice physic by any Medical Society established by law, and has attended two courses of lectures, delivered by the pro-

18. See for instance, the plea for funds in ibid.

19. Samuel Williams, *The Natural and Civil History of Vermont* (Burlington, 1809), II, 388.

20. *Burlington Mercury*, March 10, 1797, p. 2, col. 4.

21. Lester J. Wallman, "Early History," in *Vermont Society Handbook: Vermont, 1813–1963* (Rutland, 1963), pp. 13ff.

22. Minutes of the Third Medical Society of Vermont, December 29, 1803, Wilbur Collection, UVM Library.

23. Ibid., January 3, 1804.

24. Jesse S. Myer, *Life and Letters of Dr. William Beaumont* (St. Louis, 1912), pp. 18, 29–31.

*University of Vermont
College of Medicine*

1. Dr. John Pomeroy's
home and office, 164
Battery St., earlier
known as Water Street,
Burlington. In this
building Dr. Pomeroy
lived and taught medi-
cal students as early as
1804. William Beau-
mont visited here.
Photograph about
1930.

2. The village of Bur-
lington in 1812 as
rendered by David
Blow and Lanny
Scopes in Bygone
Burlington, Bur-
lington, the Bicenten-
nial Committee, 1976.
No. 6 is Dr. Pomeroy's
house; No. 32 is the
college building later
known as The Old
Mill. No. 33 marks the
approximate location of
the first Medical Col-
lege Building, not yet
built. Reproduced with
permission of the Bur-
lington Bicentennial
Committee.

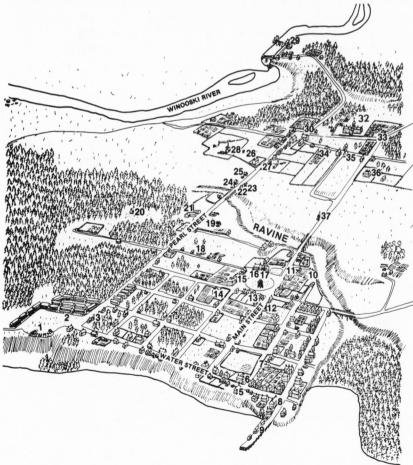

fessor of medicine. Upon receiving their recommendations, the trustees would grant the degree.[25]

It is likely that the decision to develop procedures for the awarding of medical degrees was made *after* one student had fulfilled every qualification. According to the *Vermont Centinel*, Truman Powell delivered an inaugural dissertation "on the use and action of Mercury on the human system." Then the trustees voted to confer an honorary degree on Pomeroy and what had to be an earned degree of Bachelor of Medicine on Truman Powell.[26] Thus as early as 1809 the University turned out its first medical graduate, even though a formal program of studies had not yet been established, and the faculty consisted of John Pomeroy, who was not a medical graduate.

In 1811 the faculty of the University was expanded. A professorship of chemistry and mineralogy was established, with instructions "to analyze . . . all fossils, minerals and which may be discovered within the limits of this State, and who shall be accommodated with a laboratory within the college for that purpose."[27] The addition of a professor of chemistry made it possible to expand the medical course, now that someone would be available to teach medical chemistry and pharmacy. No appointment was made, however, until 1814.

In 1813 Pomeroy sought to improve medical education by opening a new front in his private war against empiricism in Vermont. He sought to organize a state medical society which would be able to regulate the practice of medicine in the state. The act to incorporate the Vermont Medical Society, adopted by the legislature and signed into law in November 1813, gave the society the right to act as a licensing agency. Local societies would be established in the various counties, and the local censors would examine all applicants for medical licenses. Only students who studied medicine for three years and who passed the examinations would receive a license to practice. When the state society was formed, the Third Medical Society of Vermont dissolved, to be reconstituted as the Chittenden County Medical Society. Pomeroy, who had been president of the local society since its birth in 1803, was elected president of the newly organized county society.[28]

At its meeting on July 9, 1814, the Vermont State Society established a committee to develop a list of books to be studied by students preparing for licensing examinations. Pomeroy, Benjamin Chandler, and Selah Gridley, of Castleton, were named to the committee.[29] In October 1814 they recommended that a "strict examination" be required of all students, based on Cheselden's anatomy, Haller's physiology, Huxham on fever, Cullen's practice, Brown's elements, and Wilson and Thomas on the theory and practice of medicine. In addition, students would undergo examination on

25. UVM Trustee Minutes, August 17, 1809.
26. *Vermont Centinel*, August 18, 1809, p. 3, cols. 2–4. UVM Trustee Minutes, August 16, 1809.
27. Ibid., January 1, 1811.
28. Act to Incorporate the Vermont Medical Society, in Third Medical Society of Vermont, Minutes, November 13, 1813. See also Wallman, "Early History," *Vermont Society Handbook*, pp. 13ff.
29. Vermont Medical Society, Minutes, July 9, 1814, Wilbur Collection.

Smellie's obstetrics, Cullen and Thatcher on materia medica, and Benjamin Bell's surgery.[30]

Although the state medical society had made a fine start, the University of Vermont was in the midst of chaos produced by the War of 1812. In the summer of 1813, "large quantities of arms, belonging to the United States, were deposited in the university building without the consent of the faculty, or the corporation." The result was "much injury to the building," with fences being destroyed and a great deal of commotion interrupting teaching and learning. Then in March 1814 the trustees were informed that the army wanted to rent the building of the College, "intimating that, if they did not consent" the army would forcibly take possession. Obviously aware that they had little choice in the matter, the trustees decided to yield. On March 24 they suspended instruction and dismissed all the salaried officers of the College. Federal troops occupied the building from March 1814 to April 19, 1815, disrupting the normal operations of the University.[31]

Pomeroy had been trying to develop a strong medical college; he was to find that the military occupation of the University made his job more difficult. He had been trying to convince Jairus Kennan, who had graduated in 1804, to return from New York. Kennan apparently had lectured at the University in 1813, but when the army took control of the college building, he went to New York. On March 18, 1814, Kennan replied that he was willing to work to "raise the reputation of the college, and to promote the establishment of a medical school." He was willing to devote all his time "to assist in the accomplishment of these objects—to labor night and day and to encounter any difficulties which it was possible to anticipate." "But," he continued, "I never dreamed of having a regiment of soldiers to oppose." He noted that the proposed college would be "extremely useful to Medical Students," although he predicted correctly that it would not be profitable to the professors. If he were practicing medicine in Burlington, he said, he "might depend on that for support, and continue to deliver lectures." He decided against returning, however; he thought he would feel "very much like a professor in a dead college."[32] When the term began in the fall of 1814, it was obvious that Kennan had reconsidered, for he and Pomeroy constituted the two-man faculty.[33]

Pomeroy was happy at his ability to continue the medical lectures in total disregard of the military presence at the University. In what must have been a moment of exultation, he wrote to Selah Gridley. Although Pomeroy s letter cannot be located, Gridley's response enables us to understand exactly what Pomeroy had written. Gridley replied, for instance, that he was happy to learn "that time makes no diminution of your Zeal, for the establishment of medical instruc-

30. Ibid., October 17, 1814.

31. Zadock Thompson, *History of Vermont, Natural, Civil, and Statistical* (Burlington, 1842), II, 145.

32. Jairus Kennan to John Pomeroy, New York City, March 18, 1814, manuscript in John Pomeroy Papers. Kennan's letter to the Corporation, July 22, 1815, ibid., only makes sense if he taught at the University prior to 1814.

33. *Burlington Gazette*, October 17, 1814, p. 4, col. 3.

tion at Burlington, for the honour and for the benefit of the State."
Gridley also expressed satisfaction at learning that Kennan would
be lecturing on chemistry and mineralogy, noting that "his performances will be respectable, that the apparatus although it will not
admit of a brilliant shew, will be sufficient for all that can be expected, or need be required." Gridley agreed with Pomeroy's statement
that "it will be essential to have an able and expert Lecturer on anatomy, accompanied by demonstration," and he noted that John Le-
Comte Cazier, who had been working with Gridley at Castleton,
"is much animated with the hope of assisting as professor of anatomy." Gridley suggested deferring anatomy lectures until January,
when Cazier would be available. "At that time," the Castleton physician declared, "information may be given to all parts of the State,
& young gentlemen will be in readiness. Travelling may be convenient in sleighs. Subjects may as easily be preserved, and perhaps
obtained."[34]

The year 1814 was a turning point in Pomeroy's career as a medical
educator. Before that time his lectures were given rather informally
in his office. According to his son his office was a beehive of activity,
with his students learning anatomy by dissection, and assisting him
in tending to the "small hospital of invalids" located there.[35] In 1814,
attracting a class of twelve students, he rented a building on Water
Street (now Battery) and turned his informal lectures into what had
the markings of a full-fledged medical college.[36]

Just before the beginning of classes, however, Jairus Kennan became ill, and Pomeroy called on his second son, John N. Pomeroy,
to replace him. His son had assisted Kennan in an earlier course, and
had attended chemical lectures given in New York City by John H.
Griscom at Columbia College and William James MacNevin, at the
College of Physicians and Surgeons.[37] It seems that Pomeroy's chemical lectures were well received, both by the medical students and
by the "citizens and ladies of Burlington" who attended. According
to one account, the only problem developed when Pomeroy announced that he would make nitrous oxide and administer it to a
student. A large crowd gathered to see what was to be an early
experiment with anaesthesia. The subject decided that discretion was
the better part of valor, however, and at the last minute declared
that the professor had better find another guinea pig. After unsuccessfully trying to convince a member of the audience to volunteer,
Pomeroy decided to take the gas himself. He climbed onto a table
and directed a student to administer the gas. When it was starting
to take effect, Pomeroy shocked the audience by arising "and with
an exhibition of muscular power unguided by reason, grasped the
timid student who had well-nigh made the lecture a failure, and
forced him under the seats." According to the account, "when quiet

34. Selah Gridley
to John Pomeroy,
Castleton, October
8, 1814, Pomeroy Pa-
pers.
35. Abby Maria
Hemenway, *Ver-
mont Historical Ga-
zetteer* (Burlington,
1867), I, 629.
36. Henry C. Tink-
ham, "History of the
Medical Department
of the University of
Vermont," manu-
script in Tinkham
Papers, UVM ar-
chives. H. Edwin
Lewis, "The History
of the Medical De-
partment of the Uni-
versity of Vermont,"
*Vermont Medical
Monthly*, 5 (Septem-
ber 1899), p. 265. A.
P. Grinnell, *History
of the Medical Depart-
ment of the University
of Vermont, An Intro-
ductory Address de-
livered before the Med-
ical Class, Thursday,
March 4th, 1880*
(Burlington, 1880),
p. 4.
37. John N. Pom-
eroy, "Sketch of the
Life of John N. Pom-
eroy," John Pomer-
oy Papers. *Diction-
ary of American Bio-
graphy* (1943), VIII,
7. *Medical Register of
New York, 1873–74*
(New York City,
1874), pp. 333–334.

had been restored, the remaining few of the audience who possessed sufficient courage to remain, loudly applauded the lecturer."[38]

In 1815 John LeComte Cazier, of Castleton, accepted Pomeroy's offer to become an assistant in anatomy, which in effect gave the Medical School a three-man faculty.[39] Then Pomeroy managed to convince his colleagues on the Board of Trustees to allow the medical professors full use of university facilities. The trustees, however, were far from enthusiastic about the prospects of the School. They granted the use of four rooms and allowed the chemistry professor a salary of five hundred dollars, none of which they would have to pay themselves. The professor was "to receive from the Students of the University and others, who may attend his lectures," three hundred dollars, "at his own risque." Pomeroy "individually, assumed the payment" of the remaining two hundred dollars.[40] It seems that Pomeroy was so elated by his successful term of 1814 that he was convinced enough students would attend lectures in 1815 to finance the entire undertaking.

The Medical School was still informal. In the fall of 1815 Pomeroy lectured on the practice of medicine and surgery, but Cazier's lectures on anatomy did not start until January 1, 1816, and another course of anatomical and chemical lectures began on March 14, 1816. On January 17, 1816, Jairus Kennan died of "a pulmonary complaint."[41] This eliminated one of the three members of the faculty, a devastating blow to the hopes of John Pomeroy. Kennan's death was but one of a number of disappointments to Pomeroy—his son Cassius had died in March 1813; he had been intending to follow in his father's steps. Pomeroy initiated correspondence with prospective professors of chemistry and mineralogy, but he had a difficult time finding a competent physician who was willing to take on added duties as a medical professor.[42] He might have been able to call on his second son, John N., who had taken over when Kennan became ill back in 1814, but by this time the son had chosen a legal career and was studying law with Judge Daniel Farrand and Charles Adams.

In January 1817 Pomeroy resigned "that part of his office" pertaining to anatomy and physiology, and Cazier was appointed professor of anatomy and physiology, "without any salary from the Corporation until an appropriation for that purpose shall be made by them."[43] In August of the same year Cazier was appointed professor of chemistry, also without compensation from the University.[44]

Early in January 1818 the trustees publicly announced their intention "as speedily as possible to perfect the medical establishment attached to the University, and to render it so respectable as to invite the attention of medical students in this part of the Country."[45] By that time, however, it had been decided to establish a medical

38. Grinnell, *History of the Medical Department*, p. 5.

39. John LeComte Cazier to John Pomeroy, Castleton, June 21, 1815, Pomeroy Papers.

40. UVM Trustee Minutes, July 27, 1815.

41. *Burlington Gazette*, December 29, 1815, p. 3, col. 4; January 19, 1816, p. 3, col. 2.

42. The letter from James Dean to John Pomeroy, Windsor, February 5, 1816, Pomeroy Papers, is probably related to the vacancy in chemistry.

43. UVM Trustee Minutes, January 3, 1817.

44. Ibid., August 15, 1817.

school in Castleton, headed by Selah Gridley and with John LeComte Cazier among others on the faculty. This development shattered Pomeroy's dream of developing a medical institution at Burlington. From 1818 to 1821 the city's newspapers did not include any announcements of Pomeroy's medical lectures, and he apparently suspended his work so as not to interfere with events at Castleton.

Meanwhile, Cazier informed Pomeroy that he had consented to participate in the Castleton venture on the condition "that it shall not interfere with arrangements at Burlington . . . for my assistance there." Although Cazier thought that "the distance of the two places almost precludes the possibility of a rivalship," later events were to prove him wrong.[46]

Although only a few records of these early years of "Pomeroy's medical school" are available, the journal of Erastus Root provides some excellent descriptive information. Root had studied with Dr. Willard Arms at Brattleboro, and in the fall of 1815 he set out for Burlington to study under John Pomeroy at the University of Vermont. Root described in his journal how the damage done by the soldiers in the War of 1812 had been repaired, noting that "two study rooms in the upper story" of the University building "have been converted into a medical hall, a chemical hall, museum, &c."[47]

He described Pomeroy as "a man of vivacity, his appearance manifests a strong mind and penetrating genius." Several days later he watched Pomeroy reduce a fractured thigh bone, "according to Benjamin Bell's principles." On October 25 Pomeroy lectured on the analysis, physiology, and pathology of the blood, and according to the student, Pomeroy's opinion was similar to that of Benjamin Rush, namely that "there is but *one fever*." Pomeroy's theory was that "fever" and local inflammation take on for the most part the same disease action, tho' perhaps in different degrees." He prescribed "the same cold applications and antiphlogistic regimen" in the treatment of both fever and local inflammation.[48] One surviving letter, however, indicates that Pomeroy disagreed with Rush on the value of blood-letting. While the Philadelphia professor advocated bleeding the patient for virtually every ailment, Pomeroy believed that the lancet had "been abused lately" and that it "never fails to injure the constitution." The physician, he declared, "can hardly commit a worse error than to take away blood unnecessarily."[49]

Root's journal indicates that Pomeroy had his students read extensively in the leading medical works of the day, which was obviously necessary, since the state society required specific knowledge from those works. Root finished Dobson's Edinburgh system of anatomy on October 27 and began William Buchan's *Domestic Medicine*. On October 30 he was diligently reading Cooper on the joints, and he continued to study Buchan, along with a metaphysical work on

45. *Northern Sentinel* (Burlington), January 2, 1818, p. 2, col. 4.
46. Cazier to John Pomeroy, Castleton, January 9, 1818, Pomeroy Papers.
47. Erastus Root, "A Journal of the most remarkable proceedings, studies and observations," October 12, 1815, Pomeroy Papers.
48. Ibid., October 16, 19, 25, 1815.
49. John Pomeroy to Dr. Bond, Burlington, July 1819, Pomeroy Papers.

the mind. Pomeroy, when he lectured, offered a great many practical observations that supplemented what the students were getting from their books. In view of Pomeroy's long years of medical practice, his suggestions undoubtedly proved invaluable to his students.[50]

In November, Pomeroy took his students to Westford, a journey of eighteen miles, to watch him amputate the leg of a lady who had fallen from a horse. The fall resulted in a fractured tibia and fibula, with ulceration. According to Root's journal, the trip was over rocky terrain; the party had to walk more than half the way because of roots and rocks in the roadbed. When they arrived in Westford, Pomeroy succeeded in amputating the leg in less than three minutes. He dressed it in another five minutes and prepared for the most difficult and dangerous part of country medical practice, the journey back on the roads of northwestern Vermont.[51]

In summary, it seems that Pomeroy's medical school was relatively successful if one considers the level of medical training given the students. He was a busy practitioner, but he obviously took the time to instruct his students. He guided them through the works of the leading medical writers of the day, and perhaps most importantly he provided practical suggestions based on years of observation.

The basic problem was that to a large extent he was alone in trying to provide a medical education to the students of Vermont. The trustees of the University offered little assistance, being willing only to provide rooms in the college building and to appoint professors only when guaranteed that the appointments would be accompanied by no financial remuneration. In a revealing letter, Daniel C. Sanders, who had been the first president of the University, wrote to Pomeroy that the "College ought to, and would flourish, if its counsels were not those of idiots or madmen." Sanders went on to declare that it would have been difficult to find more unqualified trustees, even if lack of ability were the primary criteria.[52] Sanders' bitterness was related to the fact that when the Calvinists gained control of the Board, they removed him, a Unitarian; his two successors were both staunch Calvinists. Pomeroy also was a Unitarian, which may help explain why the trustees were hesitant to help him develop a complete medical school. In any case, by the time the trustees seemed willing to underwrite a medical school, the Castleton Medical College had already been organized, and that institution undoubtedly attracted students who would have attended Pomeroy's classes, had the trustees decided to establish a complete medical institution.

50. Root, Journal, October 27, 30, 31, 1815.

51. Ibid., November 8 to 10, 1815.

52. D. C. Sanders to John Pomeroy, Medfield, Massachusetts, March 27, 1821, Pomeroy Papers.

Chapter Two

The First Formal Medical College, 1821–1829

BY 1820 Burlington had grown from a small frontier village to a town with a population of 2,111. The year before, the English reformer Frances Wright had visited the area while touring the United States. "The site of the flourishing town of Burlington is one of singular beauty," she declared. The location especially impressed her, with the blue waters of Lake Champlain bounded on one side by the Green Mountains of Vermont and on the other by the Adirondacks of New York. She marveled that less than forty years earlier "the ground now occupied by this beautiful town . . . was a desert, frequented only by bears and panthers."[1]

The architectural setting was less prepossessing. A small cluster of wood-colored houses, interspersed with the brick homes of the prosperous, such as "Admiral" Gideon King and "Dr." John Pomeroy, constituted the main hamlet of Burlington Bay, focused on the wharf. From Water Street, the Main Street led up the slope to Court House Square, bordered by an inn, Samuel Hickok's store, the *Burlington Sentinel* printing shop, the post office, and the courthouse, which was built in 1802.

From the Square the traveler could take a road south to Shelburne, east to Montpelier, or north by heading for the Unitarian Church and then up Pearl Street and over the hill to the falls of the Winooski. The northward detour avoided the steep pitch of Main Street. Freight wagons climbed Pearl Street past the large houses of the Loomis family, Eleazar Deming, and others of the commercial community, with Moses Catlin's home on the hill above the College. Years later it would become the site of the Mary Fletcher Hospital.

1. Frances Wright, *Views of Society and Manners in America* (New York, 1821), p. 220. The following description of Burlington is from the unpublished background material prepared by T. D. S. Bassett and David Blow, of the UVM Archives.

At the third terrace on top of the hill was the College building, flanked by the substantial frame dwellings of John Johnson, Surveyor General of Vermont, on the turnpike, and former president Daniel C. Sanders' and Alvan Foote's to the north. The trader could stop at Tuttle's store before deciding whether to go straight down the hill past the elegant Tuttle house, soon to fall into the hands of Governor C. P. Van Ness, or to pay a call on President Haskel on upper College Street, or continue to what had recently been "Hurlburt's Corners," a small collection of shops, dwellings, and a tavern on Pearl Street.

There was no "front campus," as it came to be known after the 1830's, but rather several houses inside the rectangle and various private owners of "pieces," hayed each summer and perhaps cultivated. The turnpike forked at Johnson's house, with a road heading for Pearl Street across the present campus. Those who planned colleges wanted to find a secluded academic grove on the edge of town. Reminiscent of the medieval cloister, the American college could not afford to complete a quadrangle and had to depend upon one all-purpose building. The University was a mile from the dock and a mile or so from the falls—as quiet and attractive a spot as could be found on the main roads.

During the postwar depression a medical college was a luxury that the University trustees would not and possibly could not support. Now, in 1821, the first steps were taken to establish a full-fledged medical school in the town of Burlington. On March 21 the trustees appointed a committee to determine whether the local practitioners were willing to join the faculty of the University. The following day the committee reported that the "Medical Gentlemen" of Burlington had "consented to receive appointments, if thought proper by the Corporation." After an adjournment for dinner, the trustees voted to appoint Nathan Ryno Smith professor of anatomy and physiology, William Paddock as professor of botany and materia medica, and Arthur Livermore Porter as professor of chemistry and pharmacy.[2] None of the professors was to receive any compensation from the Corporation; they would support themselves through the sale of lecture tickets to their students.

Although John Pomeroy was still listed in the University catalog as professor of surgery, he was not to serve. When the lectures began in the fall of 1822, Pomeroy was not on the faculty.[3] At this point the historian must reconstruct the scene, with very little help from the sources. Since Pomeroy remained a member of the faculty, it seems likely that the trustees expected him to teach surgery when the course began. Perhaps Pomeroy, who was devoted to the cause of medical education in Vermont, consented to step aside when Nathan Smith, one of the nation's leading physicians, expressed an

2. UVM Trustee Minutes, March 21, 1821; March 22, 1821.
3. The *Northern Sentinel*, May 24, 1822, p. 3, col. 1, lists the faculty, omitting Pomeroy's name.

interest in joining his son on the faculty. After all, the success of the College might be ensured by the participation of Nathan Smith, who had organized medical schools at Dartmouth and Yale and was the most prominent medical educator of his day.[4]

The trustees had appointed a faculty, consisting of the veteran Nathan Smith and three local physicians who were willing to become medical educators. Paddock and Porter were recent graduates of the Dartmouth Medical School, Paddock graduating in 1815 and Porter in 1818. The appointment of Smith's son, Nathan Ryno Smith, was perhaps the most important. As a young boy he had assisted his father in surgery, and he was experienced in spite of the fact that he was only 23 years old when appointed to the Vermont faculty. In 1817 he received his bachelor's degree from Yale, and in 1820 he moved to Burlington to practice medicine. Almost as soon as he arrived, he agreed to become professor of anatomy and physiology, but his major role in the development of the Medical School was to convince his father to join the faculty.

In April 1822 Porter began a course of chemical lectures, after he had "incurred considerable expense in completing his apparatus with a view to the medical course in the fall." Next month the *Northern Sentinel* announced that the regular course of lectures would begin in September, and described the history of medical education at the University. "The disasters which have befallen the University" had always "prevented the complete organization of a Medical Faculty," the *Sentinel* asserted, "until the past year." The disasters began when the trustees fell deeply into debt by financing the construction of the College building. Then came the military occupation of the College during the War of 1812. Finally, it was necessary to make repairs when the army evacuated the building following the war. By the spring of 1821 the Corporation owed ten thousand dollars and had little hope of repaying it. The president resigned and only two students appeared for the freshman class. Since then, however, a public campaign had raised enough money to repay the debt and the officers of the University looked forward to better days, as symbolized by the forthcoming medical lectures.[5]

On August 15, 1822, several weeks prior to the beginning of the course, the trustees voted to appropriate thirty-five dollars to renovate the Philosophical Hall and the adjoining room, "for the accommodation of the Chemical apparatus." These were to be the only expenses incurred by the Corporation in establishing the Medical College. Then the trustees voted to give the president the authority to grant medical degrees "to such persons as shall attend the Medical Lectures, and are recommended by the Medical Professors & lecturers in the University."[6] In effect, the trustees had appointed the professors and given them complete autonomy, which was to be

4. See the *Northern Sentinel*, March 29, 1822, p. 3, col. 1, for the announcement of Smith's position at the University. Pomeroy was *not* devoted to the Austin administration. See, for instance, the records of his financial disputes with the trustees, in UVM Trustee Minutes, August 15, and December 30, 1817, and August 12, 1818. From the latter date to 1821 he did not attend any meetings of the Board of Trustees. See also James Murdock to Francis Brown, Burlington, August 14, 1818, Dartmouth College Library.

5. *Northern Sentinel*, March 29, 1822, p. 3, col. 1; May 24, 1822, p. 3, col. 1. See also Zadock Thompson, *History of Vermont*, II, 146.

6. UVM Trustee Minutes, August 15, 1822.

expected, considering the fact that the faculty and not the Board of Trustees was taking the financial risk. The trustees had spent a mere thirty-five dollars, and they were more than willing to provide free rooms to the medical students, since the academic class would not fill the College building. Board was offered for one dollar per week.[7]

The first few years of the Medical School are best described in the correspondence of Nathan Smith. When the lectures began in September 1822, over fifty students enrolled. With a great deal of satisfaction, Smith informed Mills Olcott, of Hanover, that the School "flourishes well so far." The students, he said, were "all good & true men." He was pleased that no other college had ever started with a larger enrollment.[8] In January 1823 Smith again wrote to Olcott, this time from New Haven. He continued to teach at Yale while spending the fall term in Burlington and the winter in Brunswick, Maine, helping to develop the Bowdoin Medical College. Smith informed Olcott that Porter was studying chemistry with Professor Benjamin Silliman at Yale. Though Smith had been able to write earlier that Porter "succeeds well in his lectures & gives great satisfaction to those who attend," the young chemist recognized that he had a lot to learn.[9]

Smith noted in the letter: "We are making every attempt to build up the College & Medical School at Burlington & so far the prospect is quite flattering." He was convinced, however, that for the College to survive, state support was needed. Smith was preparing to petition the Vermont legislature for aid; he said that he had "a long string of reasons why the medical school of the state should be located at Burlington in preference to any other place."[10]

In March he once again wrote to Olcott, this time from Maine. Satisfied with the progress of the Bowdoin institution, he declared: "The next thing which I wish to effect is to place the medical school at Burlington on as good a foundation" as the one at Brunswick. "To do this," he said, "the legislature of Vermont must be pressed into service."[11] In April 1823 he wrote to George C. Shattuck, a leading Boston physician, happily announcing that the school at Brunswick "is now established. The next year," he went on, "will decide the fate of the school in Burlington. We made a very good beginning last year, and if no untoward circumstances occur I think it will live." Smith asserted that along with Harvard the four schools he had helped to establish—Dartmouth, Yale, Bowdoin, and Vermont— would be "as much as New England will bear." "A medical school," he said, "does more toward ameliorating conditions of mankind than any other institution, as the knowledge acquired in them is of more practical importance."[12]

On August 14, 1823, the success of the institution was signaled

7. *Northern Sentinel*, August 23, 1822, p. 4, col. 3.

8. Nathan Smith to Mills Olcott, Burlington, September 29, 1822, Dartmouth College Archives.

9. Ibid.

10. Smith to Olcott, January, 1823, Dartmouth College Archives.

11. Ibid., March 14, 1823.

12. Smith to George S. Shattuck, Brunswick, Maine, April 18, 1823, Yale Library.

by the first medical commencement. M.D. degrees were conferred upon four students—Moses Chandler, Elijah Cooper, John Moody, and Elisha Moore—all of whom had taken their first courses at other colleges. Having completed their second course at Vermont and having submitted their dissertations and been examined by the faculty, they were recommended for the degree.[13]

In 1823 plans for the next year's course of lectures were completed. Nathan Ryno Smith, Porter, and Paddock were to continue as professors. Nathan Smith, who apparently could not spend much time in Burlington, would teach only the theory and practice of medicine, leaving surgery to Pomeroy—who, however, resigned his professorship in July of 1823.[14]

Pomeroy's resignation might have been related to a division within the Burlington medical profession which made Nathan Ryno Smith and John Pomeroy leaders of different factions. Back in 1813 a state medical society had been established, and the Third Medical Society of Vermont became the Chittenden County Medical Society. Relations between the state and local society were amicable until John Lyman was expelled from the Chittenden County Medical Society for "having procured premature labor" in one of his cases. He appealed to the Vermont Medical Society, which reversed the decision. Many members of the county society were outraged that the state society dared question a decision of the local. A special meeting was called; it was voted to secede from the state society and reestablish the Third Medical Society. John Pomeroy was elected president of the secessionist majority; Nathan Ryno Smith and the minority decided to maintain the Chittenden County Society. The result was a bitter dispute between the factions. In a communication to the *Northern Sentinel*, Smith noted that not one of the secessionists had "received instruction at public seminaries." The Third Society responded by asking if proof could be given for the assertion that college training was superior to private work under a preceptor.[15] Pomeroy was in a quandary. He was a professor at the University of Vermont Medical School and at the same time leader of a group that included no medical graduates and was asserting that medical colleges were not beneficial.

In July, just a few weeks after the dispute flared into the open, the Medical College advertised its fall course. James Kent Platt, who had graduated from Middlebury in 1812 and was a member of the Royal College of Surgeons, replaced Pomeroy as professor of surgery.[16] It is difficult to determine whether Pomeroy had resigned or was removed. The following month the trustees formally accepted Pomeroy's "resignation" and announced Platt's appointment.

In the final analysis, Pomeroy's departure was probably beneficial to the College. It would have been embarrassing for him to be work-

13. UVM Trustee Minutes, August 13, 1823. *Northern Sentinel*, August 15, 1823, p. 3, col. 1.

14. Daniel Haskel to John Pomeroy, UVM archives.

15. *Northern Sentinel*, June 20, 1823, p. 3, col. 1; June 27, 1823, p. 3, cols. 1–2; July 4, 1823, p. 2, col. 4, p. 3, col. 1. See also Wallman, "Early History," in *Medical Society Handbook*, pp. 15–16.

16. *Northern Sentinel*, July 18, 1823, p. 3, col. 4; August 22, 1823, p. 3, col. 1. UVM Trustee Minutes, August 14, 1823.

ing alongside Smith and other medical graduates who looked down on the veteran physician because of his lack of formal training. One can imagine Pomeroy's anger at the young whippersnappers who questioned his qualifications and forced him into retirement as a medical educator—and, of course, who were eroding his position as the grand old man of the Burlington medical profession.

The 1823 course of lectures was just as successful as those of the 1822 term. A total of fifty-five students enrolled, including thirty-five from Vermont, ten from New York, seven from New Hampshire, two from Canada, and one from Connecticut.[17] In August 1824 the trustees awarded M.D. degrees to thirteen men, all of whom had completed two full courses of lectures, presented their dissertations, and survived examination by the faculty.[18] The University of Vermont was well on its way to success. It was able to attract large numbers of students from upstate New York and nearby New Hampshire as well as from Vermont. Since the success or failure of a medical college could be measured by enrollment, the University had survived quite well its first two years of medical lectures.

Prior to the second commencement, however, disaster was to hit the young institution. On the first day of the regular academic term, May 27, 1824, the University building was destroyed by fire. According to the newspapers, it was one of a series of fires and the work of an arsonist. After fires were reported also in the house of President Daniel Haskel, the culprit was caught. "After a vigilant search it was pretty well ascertained" that the fires were the work of a "servant girl," who confessed her guilt.[19]

The trustees met on June 1 to take action that would ensure the continuation of the University. A public subscription was started to raise money to rebuild the College, and by August 1824 the citizens of Burlington had raised $8,362.50, enough to guarantee its continued existence.[20] The loss to the Medical School had been relatively insignificant. Arthur Porter, however, lost about one hundred dollars worth of chemical apparatus, and the professors would have to locate a hall large enough for the next session's work. For a while there was some doubt about the continuation of the University itself, and the success of the subscription drive. Nathan Ryno Smith wrote that he and Porter were thinking of leaving Burlington for New Haven or elsewhere, and soon after the fire Porter applied for a position at West Point. Within a few days, however, he was able to write that "There is little doubt but the college will shortly be rebuilt."[21] Having decided to remain, Porter helped raise additional funds, and on June 11, 1824, he announced that he would give a course of chemical lectures, with the proceeds used "to repair damages sustained by the late fire."[22]

Now that the financial problems were being overcome, it was nec-

17. University of Vermont Catalogue, 1823, UVM archives. *Northern Sentinel*, November 21, 1823, p. 3, col. 2.

18. UVM Trustee Minutes, August 11, 1824.

19. *Northern Sentinel*, May 29, 1824, p. 3, col. 1; June 4, 1824, p. 2, col. 4.

20. UVM Trustee Minutes, June 1 and August 10, 1824.

21. Nathan Ryno Smith to George C. Shattuck, Burlington, November 13, 1824, Yale Library. A. L. Porter to Mills Olcott, Burlington, June 7, 1824, Dartmouth College Archives.

22. *Northern Sentinel*, June 11, 1824, p. 3, col. 3.

essary to publicize the upcoming course of lectures. The *Northern Sentinel* noted "that the destruction of the College building will, in no respect, interrupt nor impede the usual Medical Lectures. The property belonging to the Medical Department sustained little injury, and that loss will be replaced." In August, when the medical course was announced, students were assured that "the loss sustained by the Medical Department in the conflagration was trifling."[23] Nathan Ryno Smith "erected" a building, at the expense of the faculty; the professors announced that it was "conveniently situated, and will be equally spacious and convenient as the Medical Hall which was destroyed . . . by the late fire." The building was an emergency measure, and it was hardly satisfactory. In December the *Northern Sentinel* noted that before the next course of lectures "a commodious building will be provided exclusively" for the medical department.[24]

The third session of the college, which began in September 1824, attracted fifty-three medical students.[25] There were several faculty changes. Nathan Smith no longer taught the theory and practice of medicine. The death of James Kent Platt, professor of surgery, left a vacancy in that position. Joseph A. Gallup, a well-known Vermont physician who had served on the faculty at Castleton, taught theory and practice and materia medica.

Gallup had written an excellent study of epidemic disease in Vermont, and he had been active in the early days of the Vermont Medical Society.[26] He was noted for his role in medical disputes, and when he resigned his Castleton position, he is reported to have said that "deceptions have been palmed upon him," that "rights and perquisites . . . have been surreptitiously taken away," and that the trustees had "truckled with a neighboring institution, to deprive him, as well as the students, of their well-merited and legal honors."[27] With Gallup teaching medicine, Nathan Smith (the father) continued as professor of anatomy and physiology and Arthur L. Porter remained as professor of chemistry and pharmacy.

In September 1825 the trustees received a proposal from the Troy Medical Institution, in New York. That "college" was having trouble obtaining a charter from the New York legislature. Since the institution could not legally confer degrees, the professors suggested an affiliation with the University of Vermont. In effect, the University's trustees would grant degrees to the graduates of the Troy institution, and receive graduation fees. It was a tempting offer, one which promised to increase the treasury of the University as well as double the number of medical graduates. On October 8 the trustees voted to grant medical degrees to graduates of the Troy Medical Institution, as long as they were "educated in acquiescence with the rules and usages of Medical Colleges of the United States." The alliance apparently fell through; there is no evidence that the trustees conferred

23. Ibid., June 25, 1824, p. 2, col. 4; August 6, 1824, p. 3, col. 3.

24. Ibid., August 27, 1824, p. 2, col. 4; December 10, 1824, p. 2, col. 4.

25. UVM catalogue, 1824.

26. Joseph A. Gallup, *Sketches of Epidemic Diseases in the State of Vermont, from its first Settlement to the year 1815* (Boston, 1815).

27. *Northern Sentinel*, May 14, 1824, p. 3, col. 1.

28. UVM Trustee Minutes, October 8, 1825. See also Original Correspondence from Troy Medical College, in Trustees File, UVM Archives. Also David L. Cowen, *Medical Education: The Queens-Rutgers Experience, 1792–1830* (New Brunswick, New Jersey, 1966), p. 34.

29. William Sweetser, Jr., "On the Treatment of Cynancha Trachealis," *New England Journal of Medicine and Surgery*, 10 (January 1821), 1–16. *New England Journal of Medicine and Surgery*, 9 (January 1820), 11–15; 12 (October 1823), 438; 14 (January 1825), 56–65.

30. *Northern Sentinel*, August 26, 1825, p. 3, col. 4. Nathan Smith to George C. Shattuck, Brunswick, Maine, April 12, 1825, Yale Library.

31. *Northern Sentinel*, July 1, 1825, p. 4, col. 4. UVM Trustee Minutes, May 12, 1825, September 13, 1825.

32. UVM Trustee Minutes, January 3, 1828.

any degrees upon Troy graduates. Then, in 1827, the New York State assembly enacted legislation nullifying medical diplomas granted by out-of-state colleges to students who studied in New York institutions. The law was aimed at Rutgers and the University of Vermont.[28]

From 1825 to the early 1830's the turnover of faculty was high. In May 1825 Nathan Ryno Smith resigned to move to Philadelphia, where he was to play a role in founding the Jefferson Medical College. Several years later he helped to organize the University of Maryland Medical School, and he was the foremost medical educator in Maryland for nearly fifty years. Nathan Smith no longer would be on the Vermont faculty, a decision he had made earlier and which was not related to his son's resignation. Paddock died, and Porter resigned as professor of chemistry and went to work for the Dover Manufacturing Company, in New Hampshire. Gallup taught for just one term.

These men were replaced by several young physicians who were beginning to receive recognition for their research and writing. William Sweetser, Jr., of Boston, who had graduated from Harvard in 1815 and had received his M.D. degree from the same college in 1818, was appointed professor of the theory and practice of medicine, a position he held from 1825 to 1832. Sweetser had published the results of his research in the *New England Journal of Medicine and Surgery*, and in 1820 and 1823 he was awarded the Boylston Prize of the Massachusetts Medical Society, a much-coveted honor for the best medical dissertation. In 1820 he received the prize for a study of the treatment of croup, and in 1823 he won the same honor for his examination of the "functions of the extreme capillary vessels in health and disease."[29]

In 1825 John Bell was appointed professor of anatomy and physiology, just after he had been awarded the Boylston Prize for his study of the effect of vaccination against smallpox. He received M.D. degrees from Dartmouth and Bowdoin; while at Bowdoin he worked closely with Nathan Smith, preparing one of Smith's works for publication.[30] Bell brought his "valuable Anatomical Museum," which was attached to the University for the purpose of demonstrating anatomy to his students. For some unexplained reason, however, Bell resigned prior to the beginning of the 1825 session; William Anderson, an Englishman who graduated from Middlebury in 1823, was selected as a last-minute replacement.[31]

In 1828 the trustees voted to dissolve the connection between Anderson and the University, "owing to his residence out of the State & difficulty of communication between him and the other members of the Medical Faculty, & other causes."[32] Specifics of the problem are lost, but George W. Benedict, the new professor of chemistry, cast some light on the matter in a letter written on April 10, 1828.

He wrote that the Board had concluded that "they could very well dispense with the further services of that troublesome compound of meanness, rascality & anatomical skill call[ed] William Anderson of Troy," and the board "voted to tell him so." "He hung like a dead weight to our heels," Benedict declared. The chemistry teacher concluded by noting that "Anderson being a foreigner has given a bad odor to the name with us."[33]

In the winter of 1826 Sweetser began extracurricular work on behalf of the University. He announced that he would give lectures on physiology to "interested ladies and gentlemen," to raise money for the "erection of a suitable building for medical lectures," which he declared was "now absolutely demanded to place the Medical Institution on a sure and respectable foundation." He promised that he would avoid technical terms, and that his lectures would be "intelligible to every one." There would be two lectures a week, for a period of five weeks, with tuition being fifty cents a lecture, or two dollars for the entire course. In the fall of 1827 land was donated to the University by E. T. Englesby, a prominent citizen, and construction began on what was to be the first permanent home of the Medical College.[34]

The exterior of the building was completed in the fall of 1828, and some of the rooms were finished in time to allow their use in the session which began in September of that year. The expenses of construction were met with the money accumulated by Sweetser and that solicited by George Benedict, who acted as agent for the trustees in a public subscription.[35] With the medical classes in a new building and classes continuing in spite of deaths, resignations, and internal dissent, there could be nothing but optimism about the future of the Medical College of the University of Vermont.

That optimism was reinforced by the addition of Benjamin Lincoln to the faculty. He had received his bachelor of arts degree from Bowdoin in 1823, and he was awarded an M.D. from the same college in 1827. He served as demonstrator of anatomy for both Nathan Smith and John Doane Wells, and he had studied with George C. Shattuck in Boston. Just prior to accepting his position in Burlington, Lincoln received honorable mention for the Boylston Prize. He was a lecturer at the University of Vermont in 1828, and in 1829 he was elected professor of anatomy and surgery. With Benedict, a classical scholar who was truly devoted to the University; Sweetser, whose star was rising in the American medical profession; and Lincoln, who showed great promise, the University's faculty was stable, even if undermanned.

During these early years there were no formal admission requirements. Anyone interested in hearing the medical lectures could enroll, pay a three-dollar matriculation fee, and purchase lecture tickets.

33. George W. Benedict to Erastus C. Benedict, Burlington, April 10, 1828, Benedict Papers, UVM Archives.

34. *Northern Sentinel*, January 27, 1826, p. 3, col. 4; November 2, 1827, p. 3, col. 1.

35. George W. Benedict to Joseph Torrey, New York, April 7, 1829, Benedict papers.

3. The first College of Medicine, built in 1829; now somewhat altered in appearance, with the cupola removed, and known as Pomeroy Hall.

The cost of one set of tickets was forty dollars, the money going directly to the professors. In 1825 each of the four members of the faculty received ten dollars from each student who enrolled. Since the average enrollment was about fifty, each professor received approximately $500 as compensation.

It was one thing to attend lectures, another to earn an M.D. degree. In the summer of 1824 the faculty, following accepted practices of the day, developed an elaborate set of regulations and requirements. In order to be admitted to the final examination, a student had to produce "satisfactory certificates" demonstrating that he was of good moral character and had studied medicine for at least three years with a preceptor. In addition the candidate had to attend two full courses of medical lectures, the last at the University of Vermont. Then the student had to submit a dissertation "upon some medical subject." Finally, he was required to pay an eight-dollar graduation fee directly to the treasurer of the University. After having fulfilled these requirements, the candidate would undergo an examination before "at least two of the medical faculty" and any other University officials who wished to attend. If he was successful, the faculty would recommend that he be awarded the M.D. degree. Physicians who had practiced medicine for five years did not have to attend two courses of lectures. After completion of one course, submission of a dissertation, and payment of the graduation fee, they would be examined by the faculty.[36]

The medical course was ungraded. Students who attended the College for two terms would have to sit through the same lectures on surgery, anatomy, physiology, and so on, rather than having basic courses preliminary to advanced ones. The practice of repeating the same lectures over two separate courses was a throwback to the days when books were scarce and expensive and only the professors had access to the medical writings of the day. It must have been especially frustrating for the young medical student, who most likely received a cursory preparation in his preceptor's office. When he arrived in Burlington to attend medical lectures, he might find himself overwhelmed at having to hear four lectures a day, covering the entire spectrum of medical science, much of which was completely over his head.

Repeating the same lectures over two years encouraged students to migrate from one college to another, so they would benefit from the teachings of different professors. Frederick Waite found, for instance, that more than two thirds of the nongraduates of the medical college at Woodstock, Vermont, eventually graduated from some other institution.[37] Since every college required two courses of lectures for graduation, and since the schools were in direct competition for students, the professors planned their schedules to make it

36. Medical Faculty to the Corporation, August 12, 1824. Corporation to the Medical Faculty, October 1824, UVM Archives. UVM Trustee Minutes, August 14, 1824.

37. See comments in J. L. Hills, manuscript history of the Medical College, UVM Archives, p. 39.

possible for students to transfer to or from other colleges. It was possible, then, to attend one institution in the fall and another in the spring; the student could complete his two courses in a period of eight or nine months. The Berkshire Medical Institution in Pittsfield, Massachusetts, scheduled its term from June to September; the course at the University of Vermont began in September and ended in December; and Castleton began in January and continued to March or early April.

In the 1820's the length of the lecture term varied according to the wishes of the professors. In 1825 the course at the University of Vermont ran for twelve weeks; in 1828 and 1829 it lasted fourteen weeks. If, as in the case of Nathan Smith, a professor had to move to another institution, the schedule was arranged to allow that teacher to complete his course in six or eight weeks of intensive lecturing. Dissection was not required, but students who wished to learn anatomy through dissection were able to do so on payment of an additional fee to the professor of anatomy, who would provide subjects.

The University of Vermont was free from the traditional problems resulting from grave-robbing to provide anatomical material. A great many colleges were constantly faced with attack by irate mobs of local citizens, in the aftermath of the "desecration" of a local cemetery.[38] That the University was able to maintain good relations with the community most likely indicates that very few students chose to dissect, that the professors got their anatomical material from New York or Canada, or that the College obtained bodies of transients or paupers. As long as the graves of local citizens remained untouched, the medical professors were assured of the wholehearted support of the community.

It is difficult to reconstruct the medical lectures, although several sources provide a glimpse into what the students at the University were taught. Isaiah Whitney, a student in Nathan Smith's course in 1822, kept notes that clearly indicate the type of medical practice taught by the professor of theory and practice. Smith devoted some time to the classification of disease according to the functions affected. Then he described the symptoms of various diseases and prescribed treatment. It is clear that Smith was a firm exponent of "heroic medicine," emphasizing blood-letting and the administration of large doses of emetics and cathartics to purge the body of waste material. For apoplexy, Smith recommended that his students "bleed copiously from the arm" and "apply leeches to the head." He suggested letting intermittent fever "cure itself," but remittent fever required "an emetic and cathartic to cleanse the stomach and bowels," along with "opium and bark as in intermittant." Smith encouraged his students to use the lancet and leeches in blood-letting, and he

38. For information on body-snatching see Martin Kaufman and Leslie L. Hanawalt, "Body-Snatching in the Midwest," *Michigan History*, 55 (Spring, 1971), 23–40; Frederick C. Waite, "Grave-Robbing in New England" *Bulletin of the Medical Library Association*, 33 (July, 1945), 272–294. See also Linden F. Edwards, "Resurrection Riots during the Heroic Age of Anatomy in America," *Bulletin of the History of Medicine*, 25 (March–April 1951), 178–184.

prescribed the leading drugs of the day, including laudanum, nux vomica, and opium.[39]

The writings of William Sweetser, professor of theory and practice from 1825 to 1832, reveal that he, too, placed great emphasis on heroic medicine. In an essay on the treatment of croup, Sweetser demonstrated that like Smith he was a follower of Benjamin Rush. Sweetser began his essay with the declaration that without blood-letting, croup would always prove fatal. "In a child from two to six years," he said, "from five to eight ounces of blood taken at once, would be pretty full bleeding." He recommended taking blood from the vein on the back of the hand, but noted that "more certain reliance" could be placed, if necessary, "on the jugular vein." He admonished his readers to wipe up the blood, or the physician would make a terrible impression on the friends and relatives who might be watching the operation. In the event that the initial bleeding failed to bring relief, Sweetser recommended trying again and again, if the "strength of the patient would admit," until the symptoms disappeared. He prescribed local blood-letting, by the use of leeches, and emetics, such as ipecac, to cleanse the stomach. The bowels should be kept clear, he said, by the administration of a cathartic, especially calomel. If necessary, he recommended a blister, but not on the neck, as that was where leeches had to be applied. Sweetser demonstrated a familiarity with the leading medical authors of the past and present, including Hippocrates, Galen, Cullen, Van Swieten, and Rush, but it is clear that he was a firm advocate of the precepts of heroic medicine.[40] He was in line with the accepted medical practices of the day, even though these practices had been discredited in Europe and would soon be partially rejected in the United States.[41]

In 1822 the medical students at the University established the Medical Society of the University of Vermont, which subsequently played a major role in the process of medical education at the University. By pooling their resources, the students were able to develop a library. In addition, the Society provided a forum for discussing and debating the medical issues of the day. It most certainly added to what they were receiving in the lecture hall, and it allowed for the formal and open discussion of diseases, treatments, and problems facing the young physician. Elaborate rules were developed, making the members accountable for being tardy or absent and for being unprepared to discuss the subject of the day. All members of the medical class were invited to join the Society, but only about half of the students participated on a regular basis.[42]

The members of the Society discussed specific diseases and treatments, and they debated whether "theoretical or Practical knowledge" was "most advantageous to the student of Medicine." (They

39. Notes taken by Isaiah Whitney from lectures given by Nathan Smith, 1822, UVM Archives.

40. William Sweetser, Jr., "On the Treatment of Cynancha Trachaelis," *New England Journal of Medicine and Surgery*, 10 (January 1821), 2–8; 14 (January 1825), 57.

41. For information on the rise and fall of heroic medicine, see Martin Kaufman, *Homeopathy in America* (Baltimore, 1971), pp. 1–14, 110–113; Richard H. Shryock, *Medicine and Society in America: 1660–1860* (Ithaca, 1962), pp. 72–76.

42. Medical Society of the University of Vermont, Original Act of Incorporation, 1825, UVM Archives. Medical Society of the University of Vermont, Records, September 13, 1823, in Recordbook, 1822–31, UVM Archives. In 1831 the library of the Society contained 68 volumes; see List of Books Belonging to the Library of the Medical Society of the University of Vermont, Novem-

ber 12, 1831, Medical
Society Papers,
UVM Archives.
43. Medical Soci-
ety of the University
of Vermont, Rec-
ords, October 16, 30,
1824; November 13,
1824; October 29,
1825.
44. Ibid., Septem-
ber 28, 1827; Sep-
tember 23, 30, 1828.
45. Ibid., Novem-
ber 11, 25, 1828.
46. Ibid., Septem-
ber 28, 1830. See
Charles P. Daggett
to Benjamin Lincoln,
September 27, 1830,
Lincoln Papers,
Countway Library,
Harvard Medical
School.

decided that practical knowledge was more advantageous.) They argued whether "all diseases arise from local causes," deciding in the
affirmative. The students came to the conclusion in one discussion
that nature did not provide a specific remedy in the case of every
disease. Then, after what must have been a most illuminating discussion, by a vote of 16 to 8, the students decided that "the practice
of medicine" had been "beneficial to mankind."[43]

Beginning in 1827, each member of the Society was required to
participate in the discussion, and one of the members would present
a dissertation. Also beginning in 1827 members of the medical faculty
were present for the meetings of the Society, adding knowledge and
experience to the discussion and debates. In 1828 the society voted
to establish an "anatomical cabinet," and Benjamin Lincoln, the
young professor of anatomy and surgery, donated "some preparations of bones."[44]

In what must have been an interesting meeting, on November
11, 1828, the Society debated whether abortion was justified to "save
the reputation of the parties," and two weeks later, on November
25, the students decided that a physician was justified in deceiving
his patient. The minutes of the latter meeting indicate that after the
members voted in the affirmative, the President, Sweetser, "decided"
in the negative.[45] In 1830, just after the professors expelled a student
on suspicion of having taken part in an abortion, the students debated whether it was "morally justifiable to procure abortion in any
case excepting to save the life of the mother." The debate resulted
in an affirmative vote, 17 to 8.[46]

With a new building, with young and dynamic professors like
Sweetser and Lincoln, and with a forum for student discussion of
medical issues, the University of Vermont's Medical College had survived its birth and infancy and moved into adolescence.

Chapter Three

Benjamin Lincoln and His "Reformed" College

DURING THE 1820's the state of Vermont had three medical colleges. Castleton had been established in 1818; the University's Medical College was organized in 1821; and in 1827 Joseph Gallup founded the Clinical School of Medicine at Woodstock. The existence of three such institutions resulted in a fierce competition for students which threatened to reduce standards at all three schools. The Vermont Medical Society tried to resolve the problem. As early as 1821 the Society's "censors" went to Castleton to assist in the examination of candidates for medical degrees.[1] That could have been an important precedent, but Castleton was the only institution to request the presence of censors. Generally, the proliferation of medical schools eliminated the major role of medical societies as the faculties took over the function of medical examiner, theoretically ensuring that physicians were qualified to practice medicine.[2]

The Vermont State Society, however, was not to disappear without making an attempt to bring about cooperation with the colleges. In 1823 the Society suggested a merger of the schools at Burlington and Castleton which would have eliminated competition before it became destructive.[3] The following year, 1824, the Society attempted to raise standards for membership in the county societies. All candidates for admission to county societies had to have a knowledge of philosophy and botany, and a preliminary education "preparatory to admission to the colleges of the state." In addition, the Society demanded that all candidates attend at least one course of lectures at some medical college.[4]

1. Vermont Medical Society, Minutes, October 12, 1821, October 10, 1822, Wilbur Collection, University of Vermont Library.

2. For a theoretical analysis of the relations between colleges and societies, see William G. Rothstein, *American Physicians in the Nineteenth Century: From Sects to Science* (Baltimore, 1972), chapter VI.

3. Frederick Clayton Waite, *The First Medical College in Vermont: Castleton, 1818–1862* (Montpelier, 1949), pp. 68–69.

4. Vermont Medical Society, Minutes, October 15, 1824.

In 1825 the members of the Vermont Society debated the problems facing the profession, and after some discussion they adopted a committee report charging the colleges with reducing the requirements for admission. The committee report noted "the scant requirements and professional acquisitions" of candidates for medical degrees and licenses. Not only did the colleges reduce standards, but in the 1820's the requirements for an M.D. degree were less than was "formerly required to obtain" the M.B., a bachelor's degree awarded by the earliest medical schools. The report continued by declaring that the reduction of standards tended "to depreciate the reputation of the profession and prove ultimately injurious to the community." The Society responded to the challenge by adopting five resolutions and sending copies to the medical societies and colleges in the adjoining states. Members of the Vermont society hoped to initiate action that would encourage the cooperation of colleges and societies in bringing about a general improvement in the quality of medical education.[5]

The five resolutions were in the form of suggested standards for medical education and licensure. A candidate for a medical license would be required to present evidence that his preparatory education was sufficient for admission to the freshman class of any college in the state. Others could be admitted only after passing an entrance examination. Students with a B.A. degree would have to study three full years with a licensed practitioner. Those who did not possess the degree would have to work four years with his preceptor. Every candidate for a license to practice medicine would have to attend at least two courses of medical lectures, be over twenty-one years of age, and possess certificates attesting to his good moral character. In addition, the Society recommended that the colleges award bachelors degrees, with the doctorate reserved for those who had successfully practiced medicine for at least seven years.

The members of the Vermont State Society recognized that if colleges and societies in other states refused to adopt the reforms, they could not be enforced in Vermont without driving students to low standard schools in other states. As a result, the members of the Society decided that the reforms would be enforced in Vermont only if other societies and colleges adopted them.[6]

When other state societies considered the Vermont plan, they agreed that medical reform was needed, but they could not agree on the specific proposals. The Massachusetts Medical Society thereupon called a convention at Northampton, to enable delegates from the colleges and societies of New England to discuss specific ways of bringing about the needed reforms. In June of 1827 delegates from the medical societies of Connecticut, Maine, Massachusetts, and New Hampshire, and representatives from Bowdoin, Brown, Dartmouth, Harvard, and the Berkshire Medical Institution converged on North-

5. Ibid., October 14, 1825.
6. Ibid.

ampton. The Vermont Medical Society was not represented. Joseph Gallup, President of the Society, did send a letter expresssing interest in the outcome.[7] The University of Vermont was not represented, either, probably because no one wanted to go. After all, the dean, George W. Benedict, was not a medical educator, and of the other professors, William Sweetser was young and had extensive duties at both Bowdoin and Burlington, and William Anderson had proved to be troublesome and lived in New York State.

After what must have been a great deal of discussion, the delegates decided that every medical student and candidate for a license to practice medicine should either hold a B.A. degree or provide evidence of having a good English education, including a knowledge of Latin, geometry, and natural philosophy. In addition, it was agreed that candidates for medical licenses had to attend at least one course of medical lectures and be able to pass a thorough examination in anatomy, physiology, surgery, theory and practice of medicine, materia medica, chemistry, and midwifery. The requirements on preliminary education were to go into effect on July 4, 1829.

When the representatives returned to their respective colleges and societies, discussion ensued on the local level. The medical schools at Bowdoin, Brown, Dartmouth, and the University of Vermont all voted to give unqualified support to the proposals. Yet the evidence indicates that there was little real improvement. If the University of Vermont increased its standards, the result would only strengthen Castleton and Woodstock, which did not send delegates to the Northampton convention and did not raise their standards. Even Harvard, which was considered the best medical college in New England, made no changes as a result of the conference, at least not until 1833, and those reforms were abandoned in 1840.[8] According to Whitfield Bell, Yale was the only institution to increase its requirements as a result of the Northampton convention. When that resulted in decreased enrollment and when other colleges did not follow her lead, the faculty was forced to return to the lower standards of the past.[9]

In 1831, in spite of the failure of the Northampton conference, the University of Vermont embarked on a far-reaching series of medical reforms intended to provide an example for others. Motivated largely by competition with Castleton, the faculty of the University, and especially Benjamin Lincoln, hoped to prove that a college *could* raise its standards and increase its requirements without suffering decreased enrollment and ultimate self-destruction.

This competition began as early as 1821, when the officers of the Castleton institution tried to develop plans to destroy the newly established Burlington college. In December 1821 the Castleton trustees organized a Board of Fellows and granted the title of fellow to forty-

7. For a detailed description of the meetings, see Byron Stookey, "Origins of the First National Medical Convention: 1826–1846," *Journal of the American Medical Association*, 177 (July 15, 1961), 123ff. See also *Proceedings of a Convention of Medical Delegates, Held at Northampton (June 20, 1827)* (Boston, 1827).

8. Minutes, Harvard Medical Faculty, October 5, 1833, May 2, 1840, May 29, 1841, Countway Library.

9. Whitfield Bell, Jr., "The Medical Institution of Yale College, 1810–1885," *Yale Journal of Biology and Medicine*, 33 (December 1960), 175. For more on the effects of the Northampton Convention, see Martin Kaufman, *American Medical Education* (Westport, Conn., 1976), chapter V. The University of Vermont may have raised its standards, for there *was* a reduction in the number of students after 1829, as indicated by the decrease in numbers of graduates, from 16 in 1829 to 9 in 1830 and then to 6 in 1831.

10. Waite, *The
First Medical College
in Vermont*, pp. 68–
69.

11. Benjamin Lin-
coln to Faculty, Uni-
versity of Maryland,
Burlington, March
21, 1833, Lincoln
Papers, Countway
Library. He was of-
fered a permanent
position, but he re-
fused. See Nathan
R. Smith to George
Shattuck, Baltimore,
May 18, 1831, Shat-
tuck Papers, Massa-
chusetts Historical
Society; and Richard
Wilmot Hall to Ben-
jamin Lincoln, Balti-
more, April 8, 1833,
Lincoln Papers.

12. Kelly and Bur-
rage, p. 503. For a
biographical account
of Lincoln, empha-
sizing his years at
Burlington, see
Lester Wallman,
"Benjamin Lincoln,
M.D. Vermont Med-
ical Educator," *Ver-
mont History*, 29
(October 1961),
196–209.

13. Lincoln to
Shattuck, Bur-
lington, April 6, 26,
1831, Shattuck Pa-
pers. For a detailed
description of Lin-
coln's plans see Lin-
coln to Shattuck,
May 1, 1831, ibid.

one physicians. In effect that was an attempt to deprive the University of potential students by connecting the leading preceptors in the state to Castleton. Then, in October 1823, the trustees voted to change the name of the institution from the Castleton Medical Academy to the Vermont Academy of Medicine. Frederick Waite, historian of the Castleton school, suggests that this action was taken as a result of competition with the University, in the expectation that the state name would be more attractive to students than the name of a relatively small town.[10]

As the years passed, the competition between Castleton and Burlington grew more intense. In 1830, for instance, when Benjamin Lincoln returned to Burlington after having lectured at the University of Maryland, rumors spread through Vermont that he had been rejected as a permanent member of the Baltimore faculty. Lincoln believed that the rumors were "industriously circulated" in the state, "with the most malicious intent."[11] When Lincoln went to lecture at Bowdoin, "his opponents in Vermont sneered at him for deserting, like any rat, the sinking ship at Burlington."[12]

Lincoln decided to make a thorough reform of medical education at the University of Vermont. Possibly his decision was based on his personal experiences at both Burlington and Baltimore. The University of Maryland medical school was a large, impersonal institution with over 250 students, many of whom were totally unqualified. As a typical medical school of the day, its only admission requirement was the ability to pay the fee. In any case Lincoln had a great deal of optimism, and he believed that human nature was basically good. He believed that if the University reformed by admitting only qualified students and providing them with thorough training, the best students would seek out his school, and the citizens of Vermont would soon learn to patronize the graduates of the Burlington institution.

As early as 1831 Lincoln informed George Shattuck: "I have taken up arms against what I conceive to be certain *abuses* in the system of public medical Instruction, & that (in my own opinion) I am now in the attitude of a determined *Reformer*." "Our teachers think too much of their *own* purses," he declared, and "they think too much of the means of magnifying their *own praise* & of inculcating their own particular dogmas." The professors, he said, "think too little of the real good of their pupils & think far too lightly of the responsibility which rests on their shoulders as the protectors of the Public against Quacks." Lincoln described what he could do to bring about reform. "I can withhold my name from all Diplomas except such as are earned by Study instead of money alone." His colleagues, he said, referring to Benedict and Sweetser, "are engaged in a like spirit," although Lincoln confided that neither of them "yet knows how far I intend to push my endeavors."[13]

Lincoln already had spent a great deal of money in his drive to reform medical education. He had made about three thousand dollars at the University of Maryland, and he used that to pay his debts and purchase books for the College library. "I have faith enough in the ultimate success of my plan," he said, "to feel assured that by this casting my bread upon the waters I shall find it again with interest—before many days." "Still for the present," he noted, "the sacrifice is great, & there is a chance of utter failure in the end. We shall require much more of our pupils . . . than is required by any other school." Lincoln concluded by asking Shattuck for a loan of two hundred dollars to help finance reforms at the Burlington college. The Boston physician sent Lincoln the money.[14]

Before he was through, Lincoln spent a great deal in his attempt to improve the entire program at the University. In addition to purchasing books for the library, he renovated the anatomical theatre, constructed a room attached to the museum, and purchased preparations and plates which were made available to the students. Then he hired John Delamater, well known for his teaching at Bowdoin and elsewhere, at a salary of $300.[15]

In the fall of 1831 Lincoln learned that Theodore Woodward, dean of the Castleton school, had tried to convince four Canadian students to leave the University and enroll at Castleton. It seems that the four Canadians had called on George W. Benedict, dean of the Burlington college, but since they had attended their first courses at McGill College, in Montreal, Benedict could not assure them that the McGill tickets would be considered as evidence of having attended a first course of lectures. The students agreed to stay in Burlington while Benedict waited for information on the standing of McGill. Meanwhile, the students wrote to Woodward to inquire whether Castleton would accept McGill lecture tickets. Woodward responded by sending one of his private students, Cornelius Orms, to talk with the Canadians and to offer them reduced rates if necessary.[16]

Lincoln was outraged when he learned from one of the Canadians, Cyril Coté, that Castleton had sent agents to entice his students away by admitting them without checking on their credentials and by offering discounts. He decided against publicizing the unethical activity of his competitor; but the episode strengthened Lincoln's determination to effect a substantial reform of medical education. Obviously convinced that justice would ultimately prevail, Lincoln was encouraged to continue his drive to improve the quality of education.

In spite of everything, Lincoln's program at the University resulted in disaster. When prospective medical students learned that they were expected to pay their bills in cash rather than in promissory notes, and when they discovered that they would be expected to study and demonstrate their medical knowledge, they "stayed away

14. Ibid.
15. *Burlington Free Press*, March 4, 1831, p. 3, col. 2; June 10, 1831, p. 3, col. 3. *Burlington Sentinel*, July 8, 1831, p. 4, col. 1.
16. See Benjamin Lincoln, *Hints on the Present State of Medical Education and the Influence of Medical Schools in New England* (Burlington, 1833), appendix, pp. 1–3. Also Benjamin Lincoln, *An exposition of certain abuses practiced by some of the medical schools of New England* (Burlington, 1833).

in droves."[17] Enrollment statistics bear this out. In the fall of 1828 forty students attended the medical lectures at the University of Vermont. By 1832 the number had dwindled to fourteen.[18] Since the College depended upon student fees for support, the decrease in enrollment made it even more difficult for Lincoln to develop and maintain an adequate faculty. After one term, for instance, it was impossible to retain John Delamater. The fourteen students in 1832 paid a total of $400. If three quarters of that went to pay Delamater, little was left to be divided among Lincoln, Sweetser, and Benedict. Significantly, Sweetser resigned in 1832. Much as he advocated medical reform, he would not devote his time and energy to so few students that his living expenses could not be met.

George C. Shattuck, Jr., was one of the fourteen students who attended the University in the fall of 1832. He had been sent by his father for private instruction with Benjamin Lincoln, who had been a student of the elder Shattuck. The young man wrote a number of letters to his father, in which he described the situation at the University during the crucial year when Lincoln was trying to effect a reform of medical education. In one letter Shattuck described how the introductory lectures were heard by a tiny group of six students, along with two or three local citizens "who took pity in our loneliness and came up from the village." He commented on how Lincoln devoted much more time to his students than did the other professors, not because of the "laziness" of others, but because of his enthusiasm for the education of his pupils. The young Bostonian compared the program at Burlington with that at Woodstock and Castleton, where the professors gave only rudimentary courses and provided nothing resembling individualized instruction. Those who enrolled at Burlington, on the other hand, had to have "ready money," and they knew that eventually they would have to pass "a severe examination." In what was a hint of things to come, Shattuck noted that Lincoln was suffering from a bronchial hemorrhage and that Sweetser had blistered the professor and prescribed a little medicine. Within ten days Lincoln had missed three lectures.[19]

Lincoln impressed the entire medical class with his diligence, enthusiasm, and willingness to devote hour after hour to the needs of his students. The younger Shattuck noted that the professor's lectures were exceptionally valuable—better, in fact, than any offered in Boston. Every member of the class seemed to consider Lincoln "something superior to what we commonly meet with."[20] Yet while he was trying to improve medical education in Vermont, Lincoln was also struggling to maintain his health. In the fall of 1832 he had several attacks of "bleeding from the Lungs"; they were so debilitating that he was unable to hold recitations in the evening. In a let-

17. Tom Bassett, "Training Medics in Early Vermont," *Chittenden*, 4 (July 1973), 29.

18. James Marsh to Joseph Torrey, Burlington, February 14, 1829, Marsh Papers, UVM Archives. Lincoln to Shattuck, Burlington, August 26, 1832, Shattuck Papers. In 1833 and again in 1834 only four M.D. degrees were conferred, indicating that classes in 1833 numbered from 10 to 15.

19. George C. Shattuck, Jr., to George C. Shattuck, Burlington, August 19, 28, 1832, Shattuck Papers.

20. Ibid., October 14, 1832.

ter to the elder Shattuck, he sadly stated that when he resumed the recitations, he would have to limit them to one hour per evening![21]

When the 1832 term ended, Lincoln must have been terribly discouraged. His reforms had driven students to other institutions, and his efforts were destroying his health. In the spring of 1833 he decided to publicize his attempts to improve medical education; in the process he would describe the abuses practiced by Theodore Woodward and others in the struggle to attract more and more students. In March, Lincoln published a series of letters in the *Vermont Statesman* and the *Northern Sentinel*. He described how Woodward had sent an agent to convince the four Canadian students to enroll at Castleton. He documented his assertions by publishing depositions from the students involved.[22] In the process, he explained the problems facing medical education, and suggested his remedy. He said that he had never intended to publicize the situation, but since Sweetser had resigned his position, it appeared that the University of Vermont would have to suspend lectures for at least one term. Thus his letters and the ensuing pamphlets would not be considered as advertisements for his medical class.[23] Originally, Lincoln simply sent a statement of facts to the newspapers. Woodward responded, however, with letters of his own, denouncing Lincoln's allegations as "the smut of a blackguard" and accusing the Burlington professor of attacking his competition as a means of advertising his next course of lectures. Woodward claimed that Lincoln was rejected at Baltimore and he insinuated that Lincoln's incompetence had destroyed the Medical College at Burlington. When Lincoln began lecturing in Burlington, the class numbered between fifty and sixty students, but in 1831, according to the Castleton professor, Lincoln found himself "dealing out" his "droppings to a pretty little class of fifteen students, and in 1832 to the still smaller number of 12."[24]

Interestingly, Woodward confessed to everything. He admitted that he had sent an agent to Burlington and he pointed to the "pitiful condition" of the University as evidence that Lincoln "had never, verbally or by letter, directly or indirectly, done one single act . . . to build up" his school "or add to its prosperity." "I try to induce students to seek instruction at the Vermont Academy of Medicine," Woodward said, "and desire to accommodate and please them when they come. . . . I write letters, send out circulars and agents to give the necessary information to medical students." He declared that he could not possibly feel "justified in pursuing the lazy, indifferent course" that Lincoln had followed. Lincoln was well qualified to be "a professor in a school without scholars, lecturing to the naked walls of a College, pretending to practice," but having "no patients." He concluded by predicting that Lincoln's attack on Castleton would

21. Lincoln to Shattuck, Burlington, September 30, 1832, Shattuck Papers.

22. Lincoln, *Hints on the Present State of Medical Education*. Depositions of Cyril Coté, November 23, 1832, Lincoln Papers. See also Coté to Lincoln, August 12 and November 10, 1832, January 15 and September 1, 1833; and Theodore Woodward to Cyril Coté, Castleton, August 11, 1831: Lincoln Papers.

23. Lincoln, *Hints on the Present State of Medical Education*, p. 8.

24. Ibid., appendix, p. vi.

be considered "the convulsive struggles of a disappointed, neglected, and evil-minded nincompoop."[25]

In his letters and his pamphlets, Lincoln deplored the fact that medical students were so poorly educated. He declared that it was impossible for scientific medicine to be learned by "those whose whole education is included in being able to 'read, write and cypher.'" In addition to the problems of preliminary education, he noted that the term of apprenticeship was too short. Three years "is less than is required for the apprentice to learn the 'Art and Mystery' of the Smith or the Joiner." Apprentices in other fields studied for a period of seven years, but in order to be qualified to practice medicine, to cure or to kill, students were required to devote only three short years to their studies. The Burlington professor complained that "the profession" was filled with "illiterate men." Under the present system of medical education, he declared, "illiterate men, in great numbers," including some "grossly, and criminally ignorant" were able to enter the profession. The preceptors did not examine students as to their preliminary education, and the medical schools were interested only in collecting fees from anyone who wanted to attend lectures. It was commonly known, he said, that "of all the methods of getting a livelihood invented by Yankee ingenuity, no one secures its object so effectually and with so little expense of Mental Labour as 'turning Doctor.'"[26]

Lincoln's solution was simple. The colleges had to ensure that students were fully prepared to study scientific medicine, and they could do so only by restricting admission to those who had an adequate preliminary education. After that, schools must provide a thoroughly scientific course of medical studies, concluding with a difficult final examination. Lincoln was convinced that when the people learned how other institutions were disregarding the public interest by accepting illiterates and turning them into physicians after a rudimentary course of studies, the inferior colleges would be forced to close their doors, and diligent students would attend "honorable" colleges like the University of Vermont.[27]

In the fall of 1833, contrary to Lincoln's expectations, the University managed to hold its regular course of medical lectures. Although William Sweetser had resigned to devote more time to his duties at Bowdoin, he consented to teach seven-week courses on the theory and practice of medicine and on obstetrics. Rather than dividing the proceeds of the term, however, he insisted on receiving a salary of $300.[28] The term began on August 12, 1833, continuing for fourteen weeks. Lincoln, Sweetser, and Benedict were the faculty. As indicated, the response was again discouraging: no more than fifteen students attended the 1833 lectures.

In the early spring of 1834 Lincoln's health deteriorated, and he

25. Ibid., appendix, pp. vii–viii. Nathan Ryno Smith wrote a note to Lincoln on April 12, 1833, which began "Dear 'Nincompoop.'" See University of Maryland Anatomical Class to Benjamin Lincoln, Baltimore, April 12, 1833, Lincoln Papers.

26. Lincoln, *Hints on the Present State of Medical Education*, pp. 13–15. Lincoln also attacked Joseph Gallup, of Woodstock, accusing him of illegally creating a college and affiliating with Waterville College in Maine so that he could legally grant degrees. See Waite, *Story of a Country Medical College*, p. 76; *Burlington Sentinel*, February 28, March 14, 21, 28, April 4, 18, 1834.

27. Lincoln to Shattuck, April 1, 1834, Shattuck Papers.

28. See William Sweetser to Lincoln: Boston, May 6, 1833; Brunswick, May 12, 1833; and Boston, May 20, 1833; Lincoln Papers.

returned to his family home in Dennysville, Maine. He apparently had some hope that a rest would restore his health and enable him to continue with his work. George Shattuck, Jr., wrote: "Never did a man labor with less regard to self than has Dr. Lincoln during his residence in Burlington. His object has been to raise the standard of medical education in this part of the country," he noted, and "his strenuous efforts . . . have met with little cooperation from those amongst whom his labors have been performed." According to Shattuck, things were beginning to look brighter when Lincoln was forced to leave Burlington. He would have had a private class of eight in the summer of 1834, which meant that a larger class could have been expected to enroll in the fall session.[29]

On May 29, 1834, George W. Benedict wrote to Lincoln, bemoaning the fact that "Providence seems to have terminated for the present & I fear forever the plans you had in view for future action in *this place* for the promotion of sound Medical Education." Benedict then told Lincoln that he had intended to suggest that he would continue fund-raising, but without a commission, if the trustees agreed to assume the debt of the Medical College, pay salaries to the professors, and eliminate the student fees, thus releasing the professors from the influence of the students. In addition, the elimination of student fees would have attracted many more students, in spite of the fact that they would be expected to study and demonstrate that they deserved to receive medical degrees. Benedict concluded: "I know not however what to do in the matter of the med. school" with Lincoln in Maine and Benedict the only professor remaining with the College.[30]

On June 23, 1834, Lincoln wrote to inform the trustees that "in consequence of ill health" it was "improbable . . . that I shall ever be able to resume the duties of the office which I now hold in the University." As a result, he resigned his chair of anatomy and surgery.[31] There was no course in the fall of 1834. Benedict had been unwilling to "place anyone else" in Lincoln's rooms or let anyone else use Lincoln's apparatus.[32] In August the trustees, after discussing the Medical College, were in favor of having it continue. By then Benedict had proposed that the trustees take possession of the medical building and assume the debts of the faculty, which amounted to over two thousand dollars. The trustees hoped that the College could be saved, but they were unwilling to assume the debt. As a result, they tabled the proposal to the next meeting of the Corporation.[33]

The failure of the trustees to take action meant that Benedict had to recruit professors to join a faculty that was in debt, and it was certain that enrollment would be so small that it would hardly pay the expenses of the professors. Benedict tried, nevertheless, to keep

29. George C. Shattuck, Jr., to Miss E. Shattuck, May 6, 1834, Shattuck Papers.

30. G. W. Benedict to Benjamin Lincoln, Burlington, May 29, 1834, Lincoln Papers.

31. Lincoln to the Corporation, Dennysville, Maine, June 23, 1834, Pomeroy Papers.

32. Benedict to Lincoln, Burlington, October 5, 1834, Lincoln Papers.

33. UVM Trustee Minutes, August 8, 1834.

the College alive. He asked Lincoln for his opinion of Joseph Marsh, who had graduated from Dartmouth back in 1830. He also asked whether Edward Elisha Phelps, of Windsor, would be a "good choice for the anatomical & surgical chair."[34] Phelps had studied at Dartmouth and graduated from Yale in 1825, where he worked under Nathan Smith. He had spent some time in the South assisting in a survey of the Dismal Swamp canals and studying the botany of the region.

In October 1834 James Marsh wrote to Lincoln. Marsh had been president of the University from 1826 to 1833, and he was professor of intellectual and moral philosophy. He mentioned a physician who had recently arrived in Burlington, a German named Bernard Heineberg. It seems that Heineberg, a graduate of the University of Bonn who received his medical degree at Goettingen, had come to town in the hope of becoming a member of the medical faculty. He was disappointed to learn that the fall class had been canceled because of Lincoln's illness. Marsh believed that Lincoln would have "been greatly pleased with him & most probably would have contrived to find work & some means for him to support himself." According to Marsh, Heineberg was "a fine fellow extremely ardent in the pursuit of science," whose "scientific notions and notions of the profession" were "entirely coincident" with Lincoln's.[35]

Heineberg would have made a fine addition to the medical faculty. He was familiar with the works of the leading physicians of the past and present, as evident in a letter he wrote to the *Burlington Free Press*. In giving medical advice to the citizens of Burlington, Heineberg quoted Hippocrates, Celsus, Boerhaave, and Friedrich Hoffman, among others.[36] It is likely that he was better prepared to practice medicine and to teach it than any other physician in Vermont.

On February 26, 1835, Benjamin Lincoln died of tuberculosis at the age of 32.[37] It seems that Benedict and others had hesitated to make appointments to the medical faculty until they were certain that Lincoln was unable to return to his work. One reason may be that as the last remaining medical professor, Lincoln had held title to the Medical College building and its land, along with most of the apparatus. On August 31, 1835, George Benedict informed the trustees that "he felt obliged to purchase" from Lincoln's heirs "all his right and title" to the building and the land. The chemistry professor did so to prevent the removal of the apparatus and the sale of the building, which would have meant the immediate and complete end of medical teaching at the University.[38]

Now that the building was legally owned by Benedict, the trustees could proceed with the appointment of a new faculty. Surprisingly, in spite of the glowing endorsements, Heineberg was passed over

34. Benedict to Lincoln, Burlington, October 5, 1834, Lincoln Papers.

35. James Marsh to Benjamin Lincoln, October 30, 1834, Lincoln Papers. *Burlington Free Press*, November 21, 1834, p. 3, col. 2, for an advertisement by Heineberg, "Recently from Germany, and professionally educated in the Universities of that Country." His obituary was published in the *Free Press*, July 3, 1878, p. 3.

36. *Burlington Free Press*, December 12, 1834, p. 2, cols. 4–6.

37. For Lincoln's obituary see ibid., May 15, 1835, p. 2, col. 5.

38. George W. Benedict to the Corporation, August 31, 1835. Benedict papers, UVM Archives.

by the trustees, even though in August 1835 they had granted him an honorary medical degree and he had offered a toast at the commencement dinner of that year.[39] His obituary indicated that he "was a faithful friend and a frank foe," "without guile, of absolute honesty." That sounds like the description of a man with a sharp tongue, who could have made enemies among the trustees. In addition there was in Burlington a growing nativist movement, and a German immigrant might not be attractive in a nationalistic America. Also, Heineberg may have been unacceptable for religious reasons. A religious census recorded that he was not a Christian, and although there is no direct evidence that he was Jewish, he had Jewish descendants. In any case, in September of 1835 the trustees appointed Joseph Marsh professor of theory and practice of medicine and Edward Elisha Phelps professor of anatomy and surgery. There seems to have been no doubt of the ability of Marsh to do a creditable job, but according to Benedict some members of the Corporation were afraid that Phelps was unable to deliver a good lecture, as "he has naturally a very thick tongue."[40]

The medical lectures began on March 9, 1836, continuing for fourteen weeks. The faculty consisted of Marsh, Phelps, and Benedict. Phelps taught anatomy, surgery, and physiology; Marsh lectured on the theory and practice of medicine, materia medica, pharmacy, and obstetrics; and Benedict taught natural philosophy and chemistry.[41] This was the last course of medical lectures at the University until the 1850's. There is no indication of the size of the class, but it is likely that the lectures attracted only a handful of students. When the University canceled its fall course of 1835, Castleton responded by adding one, doubling its total enrollment, and reducing the number of potential students for the University's spring course. The enrollment at Burlington had been low all during the 1830's, making it difficult to find qualified teachers. While Castleton and Woodstock were attracting forty, fifty, and more students, and while the Castleton and Woodstock faculties received from four to five hundred dollars compensation for their work, the professors at the University of Vermont lectured to empty benches, for a total compensation of one hundred dollars or less. The failure of the University to compete can be easily seen in the commencement records. In 1835 the Medical School had no graduates; in 1836 one student was awarded an M.D. degree. Then the Medical College ceased its operation.

Medical teaching at the University might have been salvaged. Benjamin Lincoln had returned to Burlington after having rejected lucrative offers from the University of Maryland. He was too dedicated to the cause of medical reform to remain affiliated with a large medical school that accepted unqualified students. Had he remained

39. UVM Trustee Minutes, August 4, 1835. *Burlington Free Press*, August 7, 1835, p. 2, col. 3.

40. UVM Trustee Minutes, September 3, 1835. Benedict to Lincoln, Burlington, January 24, 1835, Lincoln Papers. The lectures were not given until March 1836, to allow time for advertising and to give Benedict a chance to recover from a crippling attack of rheumatism. Benedict to I. R. Chadbourne, Burlington, September 13, 1835, Lincoln Papers. See also Myron Samuelson, *The Story of the Jewish Community of Burlington, Vermont* (Burlington 1976), pp. 41–42.

41. *Burlington Free Press*, January 22, 1836, p. 3, col. 2. *Burlington Sentinel*, February 19, 1836, p. 4, col. 3. The advertisements continued to appear in the *Sentinel* until March 18, after the beginning of the course.

in Baltimore and a traditional medical educator taken control of the program at Burlington, the program could have been salvaged by the use of traditional methods of attracting students.

On the other hand, if Lincoln had survived to continue his quest for the ideal medical college, it is possible that his work would have ultimately proved successful. After all, the prospects were bright for a larger class in 1834, which might have been the predecessor of still larger classes, with the best students coming to Burlington rather than going to schools that were not as interested in producing scientific physicians.

Finally, if Benedict had made his proposal to the trustees to place the faculty on salary and eliminate student fees, that might have enabled the College to continue as the only "reformed" medical college in the United States. Yet Benedict only *suggested* the plan, in a letter to Lincoln, and there is no evidence that he made it in the form of a recommendation to the trustees.

At any rate, none of this came to pass. Lincoln died before he could realize his elusive dream; the trustees were never placed in the position of having to accept or reject Benedict's plan; and the outcome was that the University's Medical School was closed from 1836 to 1853.

Chapter Four

Every Man His Own Physician:
Equal Opportunity and the Healing Arts

AT ITS AUGUST 1836 meeting, as noted, the University's Board of Trustees had discussed the problems of financing the Medical College. George W. Benedict had presented the Corporation with a request for additional support. Though the Medical Building was situated on donated land and a campaign had raised over eight hundred dollars, these contributions had not been sufficient to complete construction. Back in 1827 or 1828 the faculty had met the additional expenses by issuing a promissory note to Ozias Buell, the contractor. Then, the inadequate income of the College prevented repayment. After the 1836 course of lectures, the faculty still owed $1,755.91.[1] In effect, there was a lien on the medical building.

In addition, the heirs of Benjamin Lincoln presented a claim for $978.77, representing the expenses Lincoln had incurred in renovating the building and including the cost of erecting a small building "for the purposes of the Anatomical professor & other professors" and the purchase of some additional land. Benedict feared that the building might be attached, or that Lincoln's valuable collection of anatomical preparations might be sold by the heirs. As a result, Benedict had given one Theodore Lincoln his personal note, in exchange for the deed to Lincoln's property which remained in the building. Now, in August 1836, Benedict asked the trustees to reimburse him. If the trustees agreed to assume the debt of the medical faculty, he would respond by transferring the property to the University. The Corporation would be able to spare itself the cost of developing new laboratory facilities, and in the event that they decided

1. "Statement of the Condition of the Medical College (so called) & its Properties," August 1, 1836, Trustees File, UVM Archives.

2. Ibid.
3. By the fall of 1838 arrangements had been made which satisfied the heirs of Ozias Bull and G. W. Benedict. See Benedict to Erastus C. Benedict, Burlington, October 25, 1837, Benedict Papers; UVM Trustee Minutes, August 4, 1837, and August 2, 1838.
4. UVM Trustee Minutes, August 4, 1836.
5. John Wheeler to Samuel Fletcher, Burlington, October 28, 1836, Dartmouth College archives.
6. Wheeler to Hatch, January 1837, quoted in Lindsay, *Tradition Looks Forward*, pp. 213–214. This must have been in Wheeler's letter-books, which are not in the University Archives and could not be located.
7. Wheeler to Hatch, April 18, 1837, quoted ibid., p. 214. See also material on Hatch in Kaufman Folder, UVM Archives.

to continue the Medical School, the trustees would not have to construct a new building.[2]

When the trustees met on August 4, 1836, they indefinitely postponed consideration of Benedict's proposition.[3] At the same meeting the board voted to ask the medical professors (Phelps, Marsh, and Benedict) to "prepare a code of laws for the government of their Department" to present to the Corporation at some later date.[4] The trustees did not want to abandon the Medical School, but they were either unwilling or unable to finance it.

Meanwhile, President John Wheeler was trying to develop the faculty, so that medical teaching could resume as soon as possible. In October 1836 he wrote to inquire about the moral and professional attainments of Dr. Luther V. Bell, who apparently had been recommended for a position on the faculty.[5] Early in 1837 Wheeler wrote to ask Dr. Horace Hatch, of Norwich, Vermont, who had received his medical degree from Dartmouth in 1817, to take control of the Medical College. The offer seems to indicate that of Phelps, Marsh, and Benedict, none was willing to act as medical dean. In any case, Wheeler told Hatch that Phelps approved of Lincoln's plan to keep the School open all year, and to require the students to pass examinations in all preparatory subjects. Wheeler also informed Hatch that the trustees had considered a proposal to pay the professors regular salaries, but he noted that "no plan has been matured." Finally, Wheeler indicated that Hatch could develop a large and extensive practice in Burlington.[6]

On April 18, 1837, Wheeler again wrote to Hatch, who apparently replied that he was too old to participate in a long-term project to revitalize the Medical College. Wheeler responded with the suggestion that Hatch "seize the lamp & transmit it to another." Hatch did not suggest anyone else who might have been able to rekindle the lamp at the University of Vermont, but he did move to Burlington, where he practiced medicine for twenty more years.[7] Wheeler's inability to attract a medical dean signaled the end of the University's first Medical School.

The failure to resume classes was a blow to the cause of medical reform, yet was only one of a series of setbacks in the campaign to improve or maintain the caliber of the medical profession and to protect the public from unskilled practitioners. As early as the turn of the century, unqualified practitioners were increasing in numbers. They included not only those whose apprenticeship was inadequate, but also those with absolutely no medical training. Samuel Thomson, a New Hampshire native, played a major role in encouraging practice by untrained individuals. The son of a small farmer, Thomson spent his early years working in the fields. At a young age he became aware of the use of botanic medicine. He learned the properties of various plants from an "old lady by the name of Benton" who provided medical care for the rural population of the area.[8] As he grew older, he continued to study the medicinal properties of vegetable life; soon he was treating the illnesses of his family and his neighbors. He was so successful as a practitioner that he decided to abandon farming and devote all his time to medical activities. Convinced that he possessed a God-given power to cure the ill, he concluded that formal training was not necessary. As he wrote: "If I possessed such a gift, I had no need of learning, for no one can learn that gift." Thomson went to the nation's capital, patented his "system" for curing the ill, and set out to spread the word of his great discovery.[9]

Basically, Thomson believed that disease was caused by the reduction of body heat. In order to cure the patient, he would administer remedies that increased the temperature, cleansed the system, and provided sustenance. The stomach was purged with lobelia (Indian or wild tobacco), which caused the patient to vomit; then Thomson prescribed capsicum (cayenne pepper), which was virtually guaranteed to increase body heat, particularly in the mouth.[10] In addition, Thomson urged the extensive use of steam baths; his followers were soon to be called "steamers" or "steam doctors."

Thomson decided to help "make every man his own physician." He began to sell "family rights" to anyone who wanted to practice medicine according to his system. For twenty dollars one could purchase the right to be a Thomsonian practitioner, along with a set of books describing the new system of medical practice. From 1820 to 1840 Thomsonianism spread throughout the country; a great many people were willing to pay twenty dollars to become physicians.[11]

Significantly, Thomsonianism developed precisely during the period of Jacksonian democracy. It was a time when the common man was emphasized. It was argued that the common man had common sense and so could do anything or be anything, whether it meant practicing medicine, becoming a military officer, or governing himself. Since the common man had common sense, formal medical training was unnecessary. Thomson provided the common man with a guide to medical practice. The Thomsonians were most prevalent in rural areas, providing medical care for farmers and their families. The increasing number of botanical physicians resulted in a distinct threat to the organized medical profession. The Thomsonians promised their patients a more humane treatment than the orthodox physicians, who practiced bloodletting, and the growth of Thomsonianism helped to demonstrate the inadequacy of traditional practice. Of course, it also posed a severe economic threat to the medical profession.[12]

The effect of Thomsonianism and the botanic practice on the Ver-

8. Samuel Thomson, *A Narrative of the Life and Medical Discoveries of Samuel Thomson, containing an account of his System of Practice, and the Manner of Curing Disease with Vegetable Medicine, upon a Plan Entirely New* (5th ed., St. Clairsville, Ohio, 1829), p. 7.

9. Ibid., pp. 7–28.

10. Samuel Thomson, *Thomsonian Materia Medica* (12th ed., Albany, 1841), pp. 58off. See also Phillip D. Jordan, "The Secret Six: An Inquiry into the Basic Materia Medica of the Thomsonian System of Botanic Medicine," *Ohio State Archaeological and Historical Quarterly*, 53 (October–December 1943), 347–355.

11. For more on Thomsonianism see Alex Berman, "The Thomsonian Movement and Its Relation to American Pharmacy and Medicine," *Bulletin of the History of Medicine*, 25 (September–October 1951), 405–428, (November–December, 1951), 519–538.

12. See Joseph F. Kett, *The Formation of the American Medical Profession* (New

mont medical profession can be seen from the history of medical licensing in the state. In 1818 and 1819 members of the Vermont Medical Society discussed the need to suppress quackery; they petitioned the legislature for the passage of a bill "promoting the interests of the profession and the good of the community." A law was passed in 1820 prohibiting physicians and surgeons from using the legal process in collecting bills unless they were members of the state or local medical societies or licensed to practice by a supreme court justice, after examination by two physicians.[13] The bill was weak, authorizing practice by unqualified individuals but not allowing them to sue to collect fees. As some physicians declared, that type of law prevented the larceny but not the murder!

In October 1838 the legislature repealed the 1820 act. During the debate in the state senate it became obvious that the botanics played a major role in the struggle. Most of the advocates of repeal were supporters of Thomsonianism. One senator declared that the botanic physician ought to "enjoy the same rights with other citizens of this State." He continued by exclaiming that there was more quackery "in the ranks of regular practitioners than in those of Thomsonians." Some legislators who were not advocates of Thomsonianism supported repeal because the earlier law protected the physician rather than the public. Incompetent physicians continued to practice and the medical colleges continued to produce more and more of them. Because the 1820 bill had failed to protect the public, these legislators were willing to place "the Thomsonian and Regular physician upon the same grounds, and then let the people employ whom they please."[14]

The development and success of Thomsonianism clearly represented a setback to the cause of orthodoxy, as the regular practitioners failed in their attempts to protect the interests of the public and the profession. As noted earlier, members of the Vermont State Society had encouraged the merger of the state's medical institutions, but to no avail. Having failed to prevent the proliferation of the colleges and the corresponding decline in standards, the Society's initiative resulted in a convention in Northampton, but again no substantial improvement came about. Finally members of the Society acknowledged their ineffectiveness by failing to hold *any* meetings from 1830 until 1841. The County Societies once again set their own standards, which undoubtedly were further lowered. When the State Society reconvened in 1841, it sought to broaden its base—by reducing standards. No longer would the society rely upon examination by censors, and no longer would it depend on the local societies to send delegates to its meetings. Basically, all college graduates and members of county societies who desired to join the State Society were welcome to do so.[15]

Haven and London, 1968), chapter IV.

13. *Vermont Laws* (1820), pp. 27–28. Vermont Medical Society *Transactions, 1864* (Woodstock, 1864), pp. 16–17.

14. *Acts and Resolves passed by the Legislature of the State of Vermont, 1838* (Montpelier, 1838), pp. 13–14. *Burlington Sentinel*, October 22, 1838, p. 1, cols. 1–3, 5.

15. Minutes, Vermont Medical Society, October 15, 1841, Wilbur Collection, Bailey Library, UVM.

Clearly the medical profession was not respected by the citizens of the state of Vermont.[16] After all, the orthodox physicians practiced heroic medicine, with its emphasis on the use of the lancet and the administration of large doses of harsh drugs. Medicine was almost synonymous with barbarism. Physicians also came in for a great deal of criticism because they tried to use the legislature to provide protection from the competition by Thomsonians. Finally, the medical profession was roundly condemned for robbing graves to provide material for dissection.

The proliferation of the colleges resulted in an increase in body-snatching. In the spring of 1796, for instance, Dartmouth announced the formation of a medical college, and less than two months later the New Hampshire legislature passed a law against body-snatching. Since Dartmouth was only one mile from Vermont, it posed a threat to the sanctity of cemeteries in the state. In 1804 the Vermont lawmakers enacted legislation "against disturbing the remains of the dead." The penalty was a one-thousand-dollar fine, one year of imprisonment, or a public whipping of not more than "39 stripes."[17]

In 1828, with three medical schools operating within the state of Vermont, the 1804 act was amended to increase the penalty to three years at hard labor or a one-thousand-dollar fine.[18] Even before the passage of the 1828 act, the practice of grave-robbing began to affect the public relations of the colleges. The citizens of Woodstock, for instance, opposed the chartering of a medical school there, because of their fear of body-snatching. In 1829 the head of the college assured Woodstock residents: "We will not use or suffer to be used . . . any human body that may have been disinterred hereabouts." Since Woodstock was only thirteen miles from the New Hampshire border, it is doubtful that the citizens of that state rested undisturbed.[19]

A number of cases of grave-robbing or threats of body-snatching found their way into the columns of the Vermont newspapers. In 1818 rumors spread that the remains of Samuel E. Godfrey, a murderer who was executed at Woodstock, were coveted by the "resurrectionists." The Northern Sentinel noted that "it is well known that great exertions were made by several persons from various directions, to procure the subject for dissection." "Such were the means used and the deceptions practiced, to obtain the deceased" that friends of the murderer had to resort to deception to protect his body. A large piece of wood was put into a coffin, which was carried by "armed men" and left in a barn several miles from town. Presumably the body-snatchers would be searching the woods for possible grave sites, while the real "corpse" was "deposited" in a "suitable place."[20]

In 1824 it was discovered that a grave in Poultney had been dese-

16. This is typical. See, for instance, Edward Atwater, "The Development of the Medical Profession in a Frontier Economy: Rochester, New York (1812–1860)," paper presented before the American Association for the History of Medicine, Montreal, Canada, May 4, 1972; and Martin Kaufman, American Medical Education: The Formative Years, chapter IV.

17. Frederick C. Waite, "Grave Robbing in New England," Bulletin of the Medical Library Association, 33 (July 1945), 272–293. Acts of Vermont, 1804, p. 58.

18. Acts of Vermont, 1828, pp. 5–6. For more on the place of grave-robbing in the history of American medical education, see Martin Kaufman and Leslie L. Hanawalt, "Body-Snatching in the Midwest," Michigan History, 55 (Spring 1971), 23–40.

19. Waite, "Grave Robbing in New England," p. 274.

20. Northern Sentinel, April 10, 1818, p. 3, col. 1.

crated by the "resurrectionists." It was naturally assumed that the body had been taken to Castleton. According to the *Sentinel*, "Owing to the reports of similar outrageous acts having been perpetrated in the neighboring towns, the excitement . . . was very great." Three Castleton students were arrested, but they were released because of insufficient evidence.[21]

The public considered body-snatching immoral as well as illegal, and people generally held the medical profession responsible whenever a grave site was found to be empty. Not only did the physicians threaten their patients through the administration of heroic medicine and not only did some physicians rob graves to secure anatomical material, but a few physicians were willing to purchase bodies from underground sources, so to speak—with no questions asked. In 1828, for instance, it was discovered in Edinburgh that William Burke and William Hare had committed sixteen murders, with the intention of selling bodies for anatomical study. Burke and Hare had plied their victims with liquor until they lapsed into unconsciousness; then they smothered them and sold their bodies to a local surgeon. Burke was found guilty, largely on evidence provided by Hare, who was given immunity in exchange for turning state's evidence. In 1829 Burke was hanged before a crowd estimated at from twenty to thirty thousand people.[22] Three years later the *Burlington Sentinel* reported two more cases of "that almost incredible crime, 'Burking,'" this time in London.[23] Disclosures like these added to the public mistrust of the medical profession, which seemed to encourage murder.

In 1830 Vermont had its first major body-snatching case. This resulted in the so-called "Hubbardton raid." It seems that when a grave in Hubbardton was found to be empty, a crowd of three hundred men gathered. "In three divisions, one led by the sheriff of the county," they marched to the Castleton medical school. They surrounded the medical building and demanded that they be allowed to search the premises. While the dean delayed them by declaring that he had lost the key, a student walked "leisurely" through the crowd with a package hidden under his overcoat. Finally a delegation was allowed to search the building. Someone discovered a loose nail in the floor; when the boards were removed they found the body of a woman, who had been decapitated. The body could not be immediately identified, but when the sheriff promised that no arrests would be made, the dean had the student retrieve the woman's head.[24]

The only publicized case of body-snatching in Burlington occurred in March 1834. A Woodstock student, John F. Daggett, was convicted of breaking the law by disturbing the remains of the dead and was

21. Ibid., March 19, 1824, p. 3, cols. 1–2.
22. A fine description of the case is in Howard W. Haggard, *Devils, Drugs, and Doctors* (New York and London, 1929), pp. 154ff.
23. *Burlington Sentinel*, January 13, 1832, p. 3, col. 3.
24. "Grave Robbing in New England," pp. 286–287.

sentenced to three years in prison.[25] Local citizens undoubtedly feared that local graves were being disturbed, and these fears were heightened when Benjamin Lincoln publicly defended anatomical dissection. In February 1830 in the first of a series of anonymous letters to the *Sentinel*, the writer, who undoubtedly was Lincoln, declared that "The manner, in which bodies are now obtained for the use of students of anatomy is an improper one." Thus every member of the society had the common fear "of finding the graves of our friends robbed of the remains." Even with grave-robbing, however, the medical schools could not get enough cadavers, meaning that the people were suffering from the *"effects of ignorance of anatomy."* The writer declared that anatomy students risked arrest by snatching bodies, but if they did not resort to grave-robbing, they would be "ignorant of anatomy." In subsequent letters the author urged the passage of anatomy laws similar to one in Massachusetts which provided the medical schools with bodies of paupers and criminals. In addition he advocated public lectures on anatomy, so that the citizens would be aware of the need for anatomical knowledge, both for themselves and for their physicians.[26]

On March 5, 1830, Lincoln announced that he would give such a series of lectures. Possibly because of the morbid curiosity of the public, Lincoln found the hall packed. He had to issue tickets and repeat the lectures to allow everyone to have an opportunity to learn about anatomy.[27] Although Lincoln tried to encourage the people to recognize the need for anatomical knowledge among physicians, there was virtually no drive to repeal the law against grave-robbing, or to bring it more into line with the needs of the profession.

There is very little information on sources of cadavers used at the University of Vermont, but a recent biography casts some light on the matter. In June of 1828 Lincoln asked a young Harvard Medical student, Edward Jarvis, to serve as demonstrator of anatomy at the University of Vermont. Jarvis accepted the offer; he would do the dissecting, and Lincoln would share with him his extensive knowledge of anatomy and physiology. Jarvis arrived in Burlington in late August, and immediately Lincoln set him to work procuring cadavers. "After some close brushes with law enforcement officials," Lincoln sent Jarvis to New York City, Philadelphia, Baltimore, and Washington, D.C. He failed to purchase cadavers in the first two cities, but in Baltimore he managed to contact "the resurrection man" and arrange for the purchase of two cadavers. He packed them in barrels, and they accompanied him on the stage and boat trip back to Vermont.[28] Jarvis, incidentally, was later to become world famous as a pioneer in the use of medical statistics, and as an expert in the treatment of the mentally ill.

25. Waite, *Story of a Country Medical College*, pp. 90–92. Citizens of Burlington to the faculty, Woodstock Medical College, March 25, 1834, Vermont Historical Society, Montpelier.

26. *Burlington Sentinel*, February 5, 1830, p. 2, col. 4; February 12, 1830, p. 2, cols. 3–5; February 19, 1830, p. 2, cols. 5–6, and p. 3, cols. 1–2.

27. Ibid., March 5, 1830, p. 3, col. 2; March 19, 1830, p. 3, col. 5.

28. Gerald N. Grob, *Edward Jarvis and the Medical World of Nineteenth Century America* (Knoxville, 1978), p. 42.

In any case the public had an intense fear of the medical profession, even though some individuals considered their own physicians to be above suspicion. The failings of the profession can be seen by the growth of Thomsonianism, the repeal of the medical license laws, and the failure to enact a workable anatomy law. The cessation of the Medical School at Burlington must be seen as one of these failures, for it was precipitated by an honest attempt to upgrade the profession by training scientific physicians. Raising standards at the University of Vermont directly resulted in the closing of the School.

Chapter Five

Resuscitation of the Medical School

As early as 1840 Dr. Samuel White Thayer, of Northfield, unsuccessfully tried to convince the trustees to revive the Medical School. Thayer, a young physician who had graduated from Woodstock in 1838, wanted to become a professor at the University, and he saw fertile ground, since Castleton had temporarily suspended operations in 1838 and 1839. In 1841 the death of Joseph Marsh, still listed in the catalogue as professor of the theory and practice of medicine, and the resignation of Edward Elisha Phelps, who became professor of materia medica and therapeutics at Dartmouth, destroyed any hope that the College would be revived.[1] Neither Marsh nor Phelps had done any medical teaching since 1836.

Thayer was not one to give up easily, however, even when his proposal for the revival of the Medical School was summarily rejected in 1840.[2] In the spring of 1842 he presented a formal petition, signed by some of the leading names in the medical profession, including Valentine Mott, Granville Sharpe Pattison, and Martyn Paine, all members of the faculty of the University of New York.[3] Once again, Thayer's request was refused, with the trustees apparently deciding that a defunct Medical College was better than one whose weakness might prove to be a continuing embarrassment.

It is interesting to speculate why New York professors would encourage medical teaching in Burlington, especially at a time when reviving the College could adversely affect the income of other institutions. One explanation involves an understanding of the history of medical education in New York. The medical department of the University of New York, established the previous year, 1841, was

1. Phelps remained on the Dartmouth faculty until 1871, as professor of materia medica from 1841 to 1849 and as professor of the theory and practice of medicine from 1849 to 1871.

2. The proposal was not even recorded in the Trustee Minutes.

3. H. Edwin Lewis, "History of the Medical Department," *Vermont Medical Monthly*, 5 (September 1899), 267. Grinnell, *History of the Medical Department*, p. 9. The petition could not be located by me.

competing with the old and respected College of Physicians and Surgeons, which attracted large classes of medical students. It is possible that the faculty at the University of New York hoped to become more competitive by affiliating with the University of Vermont. If this theory is correct, the New York professors hoped to teach a fall or spring term in Burlington, with a winter course being held in New York. Such an arrangement would attract more students to the University of New York, for it would be possible to attend one term in Burlington and a second in New York, thus receiving a medical degree in slightly more than eight months of study.

Such a plan might be considered unethical, but it was in character. When in 1846 the National Medical Convention met in New York, for instance, Martyn Paine condemned it as a plot to "cripple the College" by raising standards.[4] This would indicate that the University of New York found it possible to compete with the more established institutions by reducing requirements and lowering standards. If the convention resulted in a nationwide set of standards, all the prospective medical students in New York would attend the College of Physicians and Surgeons, which had higher standards but also more prestige. If this analysis is correct, the New York faculty represented a total repudiation of the work and ideas of Benjamin Lincoln. If Thayer's petition implied the importation of a New York faculty and the development of a low-standard school in Burlington, the trustees were justified in refusing to revive the Medical College.

Nevertheless, in 1852 attempts were once again made to revive it. In that year Dr. Levi W. Bliss of Bradford petitioned the trustees to "resuscitate" the Medical Department. Bliss offered to buy or rent the old building from the Corporation, which meant that the University not only would have no financial investment, but for the first time would profit from medical teaching in Burlington. In addition, Bliss promised to supply the College after the faculty was fully organized.[5] It was a tempting proposal!

When President Worthington Smith received the petition, he met with ex-president John Wheeler and Professor George W. Benedict. They decided to ask Thayer to organize the faculty. Since Thayer had shown a great deal of enthusiasm back in the early 1840's, if he were still interested he would be the ideal one to develop a faculty. When the proposal was presented to the trustees, it was tabled to a committee consisting of Wheeler, John N. Pomeroy, and Henry P. Hickok, a manufacturer and banker.[6] On March 29, 1853, the committee reported that it had spoken with Bliss and Thayer, and with Thayer alone, and that in order to perfect the "relations" between the faculty and the trustees, it had corresponded with the presidents of Harvard and Dartmouth. Moreover, the committee had received letters testifying to the good character of the professors. Finally, the

7. UVM Trustee Minutes, March 29, 1853.
8. Ibid.
9. Ibid., March 30, 1853.
10. Grinnell, *History of the Medical Department*, p. 10.
11. Lewis, "History of the Medical Department," p. 268.
12. Ibid.
13. UVM Trustee Minutes, June 19, 1854.

committee recommended the establishment of a new Medical College at the University.[7]

The agreement between the Corporation and the medical faculty provided for the professors to determine arrangements for instruction, salaries, and teaching duties, as long as the faculty did not "charge the corporation with any pecuniary liability whatever." The trustees would allow the faculty to use the Medical College Building, including the museum, the chemical apparatus, anatomical plates, and the books that formerly belonged to the medical library.[8] In effect, the faculty would be independent of University control; instruction would be in University buildings, and the trustees would award degrees to the medical graduates. The faculty would collect tuition from the students, pay all bills, and distribute the income to the professors.

On March 30 the trustees appointed the medical professors, who presumably had been chosen by Thayer. The faculty consisted of Thayer as professor of surgery, Bliss as professor of anatomy, Ezra L. Carr of Castleton as professor of chemistry and pharmacy, and Orrin Smith of Montpelier as professor of the theory and practice of medicine.[9] Thayer had found it difficult to recruit a faculty, for local physicians were reluctant to have their names affiliated with what might be a faltering institution. Not many were willing to be associated with "an adventure which promised nothing but failure."[10]

Within a few months Thayer had to reorganize the faculty. Just one week after having accepted the chair of chemistry, Carr informed Thayer that he had had second thoughts about the financial arrangements, and had decided against gambling on the success of the institution. Rather than receiving a share of the proceeds, which might be very little, he insisted on a salary. Since that was impossible, Carr was dropped from the list of professors.[11]

Thayer corresponded with Horace Mann, the great educational reformer, to inquire whether he would be willing to lecture on chemistry. Mann suggested writing to Harvard's professor Agassiz, who recommended Henry Erni for the position. Erni had been an assistant to Benjamin Silliman at Yale, and in 1853 he was a traveling lecturer for the Massachusetts Department of Education. Erni consented to join the faculty, after receiving Thayer's assurance that he would receive $200 for his services, part of which would be contributed by the medical faculty, with the rest provided by the trustees, as compensation for teaching in the academic department of the University.[12] Interestingly, when Thayer asked the trustees to approve the appointment of Erni to the medical faculty, the trustees refused. Recognizing the value of a professor of chemistry and natural philosophy, especially one so highly recommended, they appointed Erni to the academic department, at a salary of $500 a year.[13]

4. N. S. Davis, *History of the American Medical Association, from its organization up to January, 1855* (Philadelphia, 1855), pp. 24, 28–31.
5. William A. R. Chapin, *History: University of Vermont College of Medicine* (Springfield, Massachusetts, 1951), p. 33. Lewis, "History of the Medical Department," pp. 267–268.
6. Lewis, "History of the Medical Department," pp. 267–268; UVM Trustee Minutes, January 7, 1853.

Thayer had a difficult time finding a local physician who was willing and able to teach obstetrics and the diseases of women and children. When no one could be located, Orrin Smith consented to teach obstetrics. Now it was necessary to find a professor of theory and practice, to replace Smith. Horatio Nelson, of Plattsburgh, New York, was offered the chair, but after having accepted, he insisted upon teaching surgery. This resulted in another change, with Nelson teaching surgery and Thayer lecturing on the theory and practice of medicine. Finally, just when everyone seemed satisfied, Levi Bliss, whose proposal had brought about the revival of the School, resigned his position as professor of anatomy. It may be that Bliss had become discouraged about the prospects of a School with so many individualists on the faculty and decided not to fulfill his obligation to provide the needed supplies. In any case, this resulted in Thayer having to teach anatomy and physiology. Edward Kane of Plattsburgh was appointed to teach the theory and practice of medicine, as well as pathology. In a final move, it was necessary to appoint a professor of materia medica and pharmacy because of the withdrawal of Carr and because Erni would not be a full-time member of the medical faculty. Walter Carpenter, who resided in Randolph, Vermont, was appointed to this chair.[14] At that point the faculty consisted of Thayer teaching anatomy and physiology, Carpenter teaching materia medica and pharmacy, Kane teaching the theory and practice of medicine and pathology, Smith teaching obstetrics and obstetrical jurisprudence, Nelson teaching surgery, and Erni teaching chemistry.

Except for Erni, the faculty consisted of inexperienced men who were unknown in their specialties. They were all general practitioners, and not one was a professional medical educator. Kane and Smith were graduates of the University of Vermont, Kane in 1824 and Smith in 1831. Nelson had graduated from New York University and like Kane had practiced in Plattsburgh. Thayer had graduated from Woodstock in 1838 and served as demonstrator of anatomy from 1837 to 1841.[15] After that, he settled down as a general practitioner in Northfield, Vermont. Carpenter had studied at Fairfield, New York, and had graduated from Dartmouth in 1829. He settled into a medical practice in Randolph. The most qualified member of the faculty was Henry Erni. He had studied at the University of Zurich, had been assistant to Benjamin Silliman at Yale's Analytical Laboratory, and after leaving Yale had taught at Eastern Tennessee University, in Knoxville. Then he worked as a traveling science lecturer for the Massachusetts Department of Education.[16] Even though he was only 32 years old when he joined the Vermont faculty, he was the only member with scientific experience and, other than Thayer, the only one with prior teaching experience.

14. Ibid., August 4, 1853, June 19, 1854. Lewis, "History of the Medical Department," pp. 268–269.

15. Vermont Medical Society, *Transactions, 1883* (Montpelier, 1884), p. 78.

16. Wyndham D. Miles and Louis Kuslan, "Washington's First Consulting Chemist, Henry Erni," *Records of the Columbia Historical Society of Washington, D.C., 1966–1968* (Washington, D.C., 1969), pp. 158–162.

Not one of the members of the faculty practiced medicine in Burlington, which probably indicates that Thayer could not convince local physicians to participate in what had to be considered a risky venture. Aware that the first medical school at the University had closed for lack of students, the opinion within the local profession was that the new college was also doomed to failure and that the professors would receive little financial reward for their time and energy. Within a few years, however, both Thayer and Carpenter were to move to Burlington, where they developed extensive medical practices.

As Thayer's career continued, he was to become the grand old man of the profession, "almost idolized by Burlingtonians." A familiar sight in town was Thayer driving in his "very low phaeton." He was notoriously careless about his financial condition, for he was not one to demand payment from his patients.[17] Carpenter, who was Thayer's partner for a period of four years, was a large man noted for his keen sense of humor. Though he was "an inveterate smoker," when asked if tobacco injured the brains, his reply always caused a laugh: "No, because a man who uses tobacco has no brains."[18]

The first term of the Medical School began in February 1854. It is uncertain how many students enrolled for the course of lectures, but based on the fact that seven students were granted degrees that year and that normally about one third of the students in any school would receive the degree in any given year, it is possible to estimate that about twenty students came to Burlington to take advantage of the first course of medical lectures in the city since 1836.

The School had a great many more problems, which initially threatened to destroy it. For instance, after the first term the faculty decided it needed more material for anatomical dissection. One of the professors was sent to New York City to purchase cadavers. Most of the College's treasury was entrusted to that "gentleman," but according to several sources, he "never returned to report the result of his mission."[19] It is likely that the culprit was Horatio Nelson, the professor of surgery. Several sources note that he failed to return to Burlington for the second term, although still a member of the faculty.[20] The college had a balance of only seven dollars and twenty-five cents, and no cadavers.

At this point Walter Carpenter stepped forward. He assumed all the obligations of the institution, enabling the course to continue. Thayer played a major role also by consenting to teach surgery as well as anatomy and physiology.[21] A fund-raising campaign was organized to pay the operating expenses of the College. Thayer and Carpenter each subscribed $250, and Thayer's wife held a fair and bazaar which raised another $450.[22]

Another problem facing the School was the inexperience of the

17. *Vermont Alumni*, 20 (April 1941), p. 158.

18. Ibid. See also *Alumni Weekly*, 4 (March 25, 1925), p. 353.

19. Grinnell, *History of the Medical Department*, p. 12. Vermont Medical Society, *Transactions*, *1893* (Burlington, n.d.), pp. 244ff. Lewis, "History of the Medical Department," p. 269.

20. W. A. R. Chapin, *History: University of Vermont College of Medicine*, p. 34. Lewis, "History of the Medical Department," p. 269.

21. Vermont Medical Society, *Transactions*, *1893*, pp. 224ff. Lewis, "History of the Medical Department," p. 269.

22. Grinnell, *History of the Medical Department*, p. 12.

faculty. During the first term, for instance, the students learned that one of the professors was reading his lectures from a well-known medical text. The students purchased copies of the book and kept them handy during lectures, "occasionally interrupting the professor by informing him that he had left out a word."[23]

Statistics indicate that the University's medical college reopened at a difficult time, even when established institutions were adversely affected by prevailing economic conditions.

Attendance at Woodstock went down from 91 in 1853 to 65 in 1854, and enrollment at Castleton was reduced to 62 in the fall of 1853, which represented that school's smallest class since 1831.[24] Yet the students did *not* come to Burlington in 1854, 1855, or even in 1856. In 1854 no more than twenty students heard lectures at Burlington; in 1855 the attendance went down, with only three graduates in that year, indicating a total enrollment of ten or fifteen students. Statistics indicate a general decrease in the number of students in 1855, which most likely represents an economic change in New England rather than an increase in competition. In 1854 the ten New England schools graduated a total of 194 students; in 1855 that had been reduced to 131, with decreases at nine of the colleges and an increase of one graduate at Yale.[25]

Interestingly, 1853 to 1856 were relatively prosperous years, at least compared with the depression of 1857 to 1860. It could be that potential students looked at the country-wide prosperity and decided not to be "mere" physicians, since it was possible to make so much more money in real estate, business, or western lands. This hypothesis might help explain the general decline in students, in the absence of an increase in standards or an economic setback to decrease enrollment.

The faculty had a problem with the University's Board of Trustees. Low enrollment and the theft of the treasury deprived the faculty of the financial resources necessary to keep the medical building in repair. In August 1855 the trustees applied pressure to the faculty to keep its part of the agreement, which guaranteed use of the Medical College Building only if the faculty kept it in good condition. On August 2 the trustees directed the executive committee of the board to enforce the provisions of the contract regarding "the repairs of the Medical Building," and they gave the committee the power to annul the contract for "the nonfulfilment of said provisions." In addition, the committee was authorized to change the agreement, if necessary, to provide for the rental of the Building to the faculty, rather than having the faculty keep it in repair.[26]

The records of the trustees do not indicate how the difficulty was resolved, but in 1857 the Building was still in disrepair. The faculty

23. Ibid.
24. Frederick Waite, *Story of a Country Medical College*, p. 133. Waite, *The First Medical College in Vermont*, pp. 160–161.
25. Waite, *Country Medical College*, p. 155.
26. UVM Trustee Minutes, August 2, September 7, 1855.

was barely making ends meet—student fees were used to purchase supplies, with what was left over providing compensation to the professors. In his president's report, Calvin Pease noted that "Some attention has been given to the matter of raising funds" to erect a fire-proof library, and "for the repair of the Medical College building." A subscription was started in the spring of 1857, with the hope of raising $20,000. Pease said that "nearly half of the whole sum was raised."[27] In August 1857 the *Free Press* endorsed the fund-raising campaign. The editor declared: "The medical school cannot go on without a reparation and improvement of the building devoted to it." "Students will not be attracted by the comfort and conveniences at present afforded by that building."[28]

In his 1858 report Pease noted that only $12,000 had been subscribed, as opposed to the goal of $20,000. The problem, he declared, was the "financial trouble which covered the Country and the world," namely the panic of 1857.[29] In his report for the next year, Pease described what happened when it became clear that the fund-raising campaign was doomed to failure. He asked each subscriber to "pay a certain percentage" of his pledge, "for the benefit of the Med. Department unconditionally." The medical professors managed to raise some money from other sources, and "the ladies of Burlington" put on a fair and costume party to benefit the College. Pease was determined to repair the Medical Building as soon as possible. He was concerned about the needs of the medical faculty, but he was also convinced that the success of the Medical School improved the academic department of the University by adding to the faculty a professor capable of teaching the natural sciences.[30] If the Medical College was forced to close because of insufficient funds to repair the Building, the University would have lost its chemistry professor, whose primary support came from the Medical College itself.

The total expense of repairing the Building was $4,000. It was a complete renovation, including the construction of rooms in the rear and the addition of a third story. By 1858 the Building had a much larger amphitheatre and more dissecting rooms. It was a tremendous improvement over the "plain brick structure of two stories" that was constructed for the medical faculty back in 1829. According to the *Free Press*, the citizens of Burlington were proud "of this edifice, and justly, too, for it was erected almost entirely at their expense."[31]

In 1855, possibly resulting from an inability to provide enough cadavers, the faculty established a surgical and medical "clinique," to give the students more than book learning. According to the catalogue of the following year, "a large number of patients availed themselves of this charity last term." The students were able to observe several amputations, the removal of tumors, the dressing of fractures

27. Calvin Pease to the Corporation, August 4, 1857, Trustee File, UVM Archives.

28. *Daily Free Press*, August 21, 1857, p. 2, col. 1.

29. President's Report, August 3, 1858, Trustee File.

30. Ibid., August 3, 1859. *Daily Free Press*, March 4, 1859, p. 2, col. 1.

31. *Daily Free Press*, September 29, 1858, p. 2, col. 2; August 10, 1859, p. 2, col. 3.

and lacerations, and a number of specific operations. Reportedly, the clinic received patients from other parts of Vermont, from the northern section of New York, and even from Canada.[32]

The 1859 catalogue described the course thoroughly, although some of the rhetoric should be disregarded, for the catalogue was intended to attract students. It is likely, however, that the course descriptions approximated reality; if a school were *too* deceptive, word would spread to the preceptors of the region, who would discourage their students from attending lectures at that school. According to the catalogue, anatomy was taught with the use of plates, preparations, and dissections of the "recent" subject. Dissection was not required, but any student who wanted to dissect would be provided with cadavers, at cost. Medicine and materia medica were taught with an emphasis on "the actual state of practical medicine." The professor intended to "dwell upon the important art of physical diagnosis" and to describe the changes "occurring in different diseases." In addition, the professor would try to give a "succinct account" of the physical and chemical properties of every drug in the pharmacopeia, including the "preparation, adulteration, dose and mode of administration, and their physiological and therapeutic action."[33]

Surgery was taught with the help of specimens, plates, and casts, and students would learn to use all the instruments and the "modern surgical appliances." The catalogue declared that "All important operations will be performed upon the *cadaver* in the presence of the class," and the students would be able to observe operations at the college clinics. Obstetrics and the diseases of women and children were taught "by the aid of a manikin, plates, and models." The professor exclaimed in the catalogue that he would "demonstrate the mechanism of labor (the basis of successful and scientific midwifery practice) with such accuracy that no student is excusable who fails to master it properly."[34] In physiology and pathology, the professor promised to "give a course of as complete and scientific instruction" as possible, by means of "experiments, microscopical illustrations, and plates." Physiology was taught by demonstrations and experiments on living animals. Chemistry and pharmacy emphasized toxicology and urine analysis, as well as physiological chemistry.[35]

In addition to the clinics and the regular term, the professors offered a private course of instruction, in two terms of three months each. The two or three professors who remained in Burlington would participate. In 1856, for instance, Thayer and Erni provided lectures and demonstrations, and they held recitations. The winter term was devoted to practical anatomy and microscopy, along with private dissections. The cost was ten dollars per term, plus the cost of anatomical material. The private courses were important for those stu-

32. *Catalogue of the Officers and Students of the University of Vermont, 1855–1856* (Burlington, 1855), p. 29.

33. UVM Medical Department, *Catalogue and nineteenth annual announcement, 1859,* pp. 5–6.

34. Ibid., p. 6.

35. Ibid., p. 7.

dents whose preliminary education was deficient, who needed more personal instruction than was given during the regular course of lectures. Students who were especially diligent and who could afford to remain in Burlington for an additional three months might also have taken advantage of the private classes. The quality of instruction was far superior to that of the regular session, which consisted of impersonal lectures and demonstrations, and observing operations from the upper seats of the amphitheatre, where the patient was often surrounded by so many assistants that it was impossible to see anything.[36]

It has been suggested that the preliminary course enabled students who had not studied for three years with a preceptor to fulfill the requirements for graduation. A student enrolling in the preliminary course would receive credit for a year of study, with one of the medical professors listed as his preceptor. During the 1850's about 25 percent of the class took the preliminary course, and eighteen of the sixty-two students in 1858 had professors listed as their preceptors. As late as the 1890's the catalogues show that about fifteen percent of the students had the "Medical Faculty" as their preceptor, and they came from other states than Vermont.[37]

From 1854 to 1870 there was a large turnover in the medical faculty, and some professors who were recruited were far superior to those of the first two terms. This was to be expected, as initially Thayer had not been able to recruit on the basis of qualifications but was limited to appointing those willing to take a chance by affiliating with the University. After the first few years, when the existence of the college was no longer in doubt, it became possible to improve the quality of the faculty.

In 1855 David Sloan Conant became professor of surgery. Conant had studied at Dartmouth, and he went to Bowdoin with Dr. Edmund R. Peaslee as demonstrator of anatomy. After graduating from Bowdoin in 1851 he went to New York City, where he gave private lectures in anatomy. In 1854 he took control of the Mott Street Cholera Hospital. From 1855 to 1865 he was professor of surgery and anatomy at Bowdoin while also serving as professor of surgery at Burlington.[38] Conant was a professional medical educator rather than a local practitioner who consented to lecture on medical subjects.

From 1857 to 1865 R. Cresson Stiles was professor of physiology and pathology. He had received his Bachelor's degree from Yale in 1851, and in 1854 he was awarded a medical degree by the University of Pennsylvania. Stiles completed his medical education by studying in Europe. While serving on the faculty at Burlington, he was a professor at the Berkshire Medical Institution, in Pittsfield, Massachusetts. After the Civil War he moved to Brooklyn, where he was twice elected president of the King's County Medical Society.[39]

36. University of Vermont Catalogue, 1855–56, p. 32.

37. J. L. Hills, "History of the Medical College," pp. 59b–64, UVM Archives. UVM Medical Department, *Catalogue and Nineteenth Annual Announcement, 1859.*

38. Kelly and Burrage, pp. 242–243.

39. Ibid., pp. 1105–1106.

Joseph Perkins also joined the faculty in 1857. He had studied with two of Vermont's leading physicians, Joseph Gallup and Selah Gridley. In 1821 he received his degree from the University of Pennsylvania. He settled down to practice at Castleton, and for many years he was professor of materia medica and obstetrics at the Vermont Academy of Medicine. When he joined the faculty of the University in 1857 he moved his extensive private museum and apparatus to Burlington. Perkins was professor of materia medica and therapeutics at the University from 1857 to 1858, and from 1858 to 1868 he was professor of obstetrics.[40] He continued to reside in Castleton, and he offered private classes there which were approved by the faculty as a preliminary course of lectures.

In 1865 John Ordronaux joined the faculty. He was one of the most qualified men in his field, medical jurisprudence. In 1850 he received his medical degree from Dartmouth, and in 1852 he received a law degree from Harvard. He was professor at Dartmouth 1864–1908, and he was one of the peripatetic lecturers of the day, teaching at Boston University Law School 1872–92 and at Columbia College Law School 1860–97. He taught physiology and medical jurisprudence at Burlington 1865–73. Given his extensive legal background, he was far better qualified to teach medical jurisprudence than the physicians who taught the subject at most other schools. Ordronaux was known to be eccentric. He slept "with his head in a bandbox to outwit the bats," and he disinfected his paper money with camphor. In warm weather he drank and served his own concoction, consisting of diluted phosphoric acid, tincture of gentian, sugar, and ice water. In addition, he was reportedly the inventor of a "glycerine tonic" sold commercially from Utica.[41]

In 1866 Alpheus Benning Crosby joined the faculty. The son of the well-known Dixi Crosby, a long-time member of the medical faculty at Dartmouth, he had completed both his undergraduate and medical training at Dartmouth, receiving his medical degree in 1856. From that year to 1861 Crosby served as demonstrator of anatomy at Dartmouth. During the Civil War he erected the first complete military hospital on the modern "pavilion plan." Crosby served as professor of surgery at the University of Vermont 1866–72 and from 1868 to 1877 he held the same position at Dartmouth.[42]

In 1868 Edward Swift Dunster, editor of the *New York Medical Journal*, signed on as professor of obstetrics. Dunster was a professional medical educator, teaching at Dartmouth, the University of Michigan, the Long Island Medical College, and the University of Vermont. He had taken one course of lectures at Dartmouth, and in 1859 he graduated from New York's College of Physicians and Surgeons.[43]

Taking two typical years, 1858 and 1868, one can clearly see improvements in the faculty. In 1858 the faculty consisted of two Bur-

40. Kelly, *Cyclopedia of American Medical Bibliography*, II, 267.

41. *Dictionary of American Biography*, XIV, 50–51. His fear of bats may have been appropriate. Twice in a three-week period, the author and his family found bats swooping through their Burlington home.

42. *National Cyclopedia of American Biography*, IX, 98.

43. Kelly, I, 267–268.

lington residents, Thayer and Carpenter, along with Perkins, Conant, and Stiles. By 1868 Thayer and Carpenter had been joined by Dunster, Crosby, and Ordronaux. In either year the faculty was respectable. Although none of the professors had an international reputation, they were capable educators who were a great improvement over the earlier period, when teaching was done by busy practitioners in their spare time.

Throughout this period the Vermont Medical Society continued to send delegates to sit in on examinations at the state's medical schools, and the delegates consistently reported that the University offered a satisfactory course of medical studies. In 1864, for instance, Dr. E. A. Knight reported that "all the Candidates underwent a most thorough and rigid examination," one which "reflects great credit on Students and Professors."[44] In the following year the delegates reported that they were especially pleased "with the readiness and correctness of the answers given to questions by the Professors, and by ourselves . . . showing that the teaching had been thorough and practical." The two physicians noted that the answers made it apparent "that the Students had been taught to exercise their reason and judgment, and not to rely on their memory alone." The delegates

44. Vermont Medical Society, Minutes, June 1, 1864, Wilbur Collection, UVM Library.

4. *The Faculty of the College of Medicine in 1866.* Seated, left to right: *Perkins, Carpenter, Thayer.* Standing: *Ordronaux, Seeley, Crosby.*

45. Vermont Medical Society, *Transactions, 1865* (Burlington, 1865), p. 5.

46. Student enrollment has been determined from annual catalogues, financial figures from UVM Medical Department Cash Book, 1866–1875, UVM Archives.

went on to compare the college with "City schools," and though they noted that facilities were lacking for teaching the specialties, "its present graduating class will not suffer in comparison with city graduates, in knowledge required by the general practitioner of Medicine and Surgery."[45]

Although Burlington's only hospital, run by the Sisters of Providence, was not accessible to the College, its Medical School had survived the early years of its rebirth. The college at Woodstock collapsed after its 1856 session and Castleton closed its doors in 1862, but the University of Vermont Medical College remained open, the only medical school in Vermont to do so. By 1859 the School could boast of a class of eighty-two students; by 1865, eighty-nine students. By 1868 the School was a profitable concern, paying $440.83 to each of the six professors, after meeting all expenses incurred in purchasing supplies—obviously a great improvement over the days not so long before when the faculty had $7.25 in its treasury and could neither pay the faculty nor purchase cadavers.[46]

Chapter Six

Faculty Development, 1870–1886

IN 1871 the medical faculty consisted of six professors. Samuel White Thayer taught anatomy, Walter Carpenter lectured on the theory and practice of medicine, John Ordronaux taught physiology and medical jurisprudence, A. B. Crosby demonstrated surgery, Edward Swift Dunster taught obstetrics and the diseases of women and children, and Peter Collier, a Yale graduate who was a member of the academic faculty, taught chemistry. As dean from 1854 to 1871, Thayer had been responsible for recruiting students, advertising, maintaining the financial records of the College, and coordinating the activities of the professors.

In 1871 Thayer, Dunster, and Crosby all had to be replaced. Because of illness, Thayer could not keep up his teaching or administrative duties; Dunster and Crosby both resigned, presumably to devote more time to more lucrative positions elsewhere. Thayer's loss was the most serious, for it was difficult to find a competent dean who lived in Burlington. Walter Carpenter was too busy with his medical practice to assume the duties of dean, and as the only member of the faculty other than Thayer and Carpenter, who resided in town, Peter Collier was forced into the position by default. To forestall the embarrassment of having a medical dean without a medical degree, President James B. Angell, who was Collier's brother-in-law, presented him an honorary degree at the 1870 commencement.[1] Collier was later to achieve recognition for his work in scientific agriculture. From 1872 to 1876 he was first secretary of the Vermont State Board of Agriculture, and from 1877 to 1883 he was a chemist with the United States Department of Agriculture. In 1887 he became direc-

1. J. L. Hills, "History of the Medical College," pp. 99, 104, UVM Archives. See also UVM Trustee Minutes, August 1, 1871. The biographical information in this chapter is, unless otherwise indicated, from standard biographical directories.

tor of the New York State agricultural experiment station at Geneva.[2]

William Darling replaced Thayer as professor of anatomy. Darling was a leading anatomist, and his presence at Burlington added to the prestige of the Medical School. A graduate of the University of Edinburgh, he received an M.D. degree from New York University, where he served as demonstrator of anatomy from 1845 to 1853. From 1856 to 1866 he was in Europe, attending lectures and clinics in London, Edinburgh, Glasgow, and Paris; while in England he was elected fellow of the Royal College of Surgeons. In 1866 he became professor of anatomy at New York University, a position he held until his death in 1884. From 1871 to 1884 he held the same position at the University of Vermont.

Darling was described by one of his colleagues as a "letter perfect anatomist." He possessed all the attributes expected of a Scotsman, being exceptionally frugal and terse. He reportedly lived on bread, crackers, and milk during the week, gorging himself on Sundays at the Van Ness House at the expense of his colleagues. Darling showed no mercy with the student who "thought he knew and didn't," and the one "who knew he didn't know and tried to bluff it through." In one instance, a student was asked what organ passed through the foramen magnum, the opening at the base of the skull through which the spinal cord passes into the spine. The student, bluffing, said, "the esophagus." Darling exclaimed: "Yours does, ye dam' fool, and if God ever gave ye any brains, they've all run down it into your guts!" It was reported that during his Saturday morning quiz Darling asked 300 questions in 60 minutes.[3]

Dunster was replaced by Albert Freeman Africanus King, of Washington, D.C. King was named "Africanus" by his father, Dr. Edward King, who was deeply involved in the back-to-Africa colonization movement. King graduated from the National Medical College in 1861, and in 1865 he received another medical degree, this time from the University of Pennsylvania. He was at Ford's theater on the night President Lincoln was shot, and he joined two other physicians in a desperate attempt to save the life of the Great Emancipator.[4] Later, King was to achieve recognition and some notoriety for his scientific work. In 1882 he wrote a paper on the prevention of malarial disease and another that established the relationship between mosquitoes and malaria. This was more than a decade before Ross was able to confirm the theory, made possible by Lavaran's discovery of the malarial parasite. King's ideas on malaria, however, did not indicate a great scientific mind. He put forward a number of other "hypotheses, usually fantastic, one on the origin of cancer being especially so."[5]

When King joined the Burlington faculty, he was only 29 years old. He was professor of obstetrics from 1871 to 1914, when he died. He was also professor of obstetrics at Columbian University in Wash-

2. Obituary in the *American Journal of Sciences*, 1896.

3. John Brooks Wheeler, *Memoirs of a Small-Town Surgeon* (New York, 1935), pp. 166ff. *University Cynic* (student newspaper), May 16, 1883, p. 20.

4. Carl Sandburg, *Abraham Lincoln: The War Years* (New York, 1939), IV, 287. James A. Bishop, *The Day Lincoln Was Shot* (New York, 1955), pp. 215–217.

5. See *Popular Science Monthly*, September 1883, for his work on malaria. *Dictionary of American Biography*, X, 381.

ington, D.C., from 1871 to 1914, and from 1879 to 1894 he was medical dean at that institution.[6] In 1871 Benjamin Howard replaced Crosby as professor of surgery, lecturing until 1875.

In 1873 John Ordronaux resigned as professor of physiology and jurisprudence to become New York's Commissioner in Lunacy. The faculty decided that it was an excellent time to increase the number of medical professorships without decreasing the income of the remaining teachers. "Two half-chairs" were established, one for a professor of materia medica and general pathology and the other for physiology and microscopic anatomy. Henry Dwight Holton, of Brattleboro, was appointed professor of materia medica and pathology, and Marshall Calkins of Springfield, Massachusetts, professor of physiology and microscopic anatomy.[7]

Holton had studied medicine with John H. Warren of Boston and Valentine Mott in New York, and in 1860 he graduated from New York University. In 1867 he moved to Brattleboro, where he developed an extensive practice. He became active in the public health movement, serving as president of the American Public Health Association in 1902. In addition, he was a member of the Vermont State Board of Health from 1900 to his death in 1917. He published several papers in the *Transactions of the A.M.A.*, including ones on diphtheria and "Apparatus for Dislocated Clavicle."[8] From 1873 to 1890 Holton was a member of the University's Board of Trustees. As will be seen, his role on the board as well as on the faculty placed him in some difficult positions. According to a colleague, Holton's only weakness was a "desire to appear familiar" with every subject. His ignorance was sometimes apparent to his audience. He constantly used Latin quotations, but often at the wrong time and in the wrong context.[9]

Marshall Calkins graduated in 1848 from the Worcester Medical College, in Massachusetts, and attended Union College, where he received a bachelor's and master's degree. After serving as an intern at the Pennsylvania Hospital, he settled in Springfield, Massachusetts. He served as professor of physiology at the University of Vermont from 1873 to 1879.

In 1875 Benjamin Howard resigned as professor of surgery and was replaced by James Lawrence Little, of New York City. Little had graduated from New York's College of Physicians and Surgeons, after having studied with Willard Parker, one of the leading surgeons in the country. From 1863 to 1867 he was Parker's assistant at the College of Physicians and Surgeons, and from 1868 to 1878 he was lecturer on operative surgery and dressings at the same institution. Little was professor of surgery at the University of Vermont from 1875 to his death in 1885. During a portion of this period, from 1880 to 1882, he was professor of clinical surgery at New York University, and from 1883 to 1885 he was professor of surgery at New York's Post-

6. *UVM Notes*, XI (March 1915), 7–8. Columbian University later became the George Washington University School of Medicine.

7. John Ordronaux to Matthew Buckham, Burlington, June 27, 1873, UVM Trustee Files.

8. See *UVM Notes*, XIII (February 1917), 13–14.

9. Wheeler, *Memoirs of a Small-Town Surgeon*, pp. 172–173.

Graduate Medical School. Little was big: he weighed 250 pounds. Despite a defective early education that left him largely ignorant of the rules of grammar, he was a good surgeon who "could express his ideas clearly and forcefully." [10]

By the 1870's medical specialism had started to develop on a large scale, at least in the major cities. As scientific knowledge proliferated, it was no longer feasible for the professors to teach their own classes and at the same time hurry through lectures on the specialties which touched on their areas. This was certainly obvious to Ordronaux, Little, Darling, and Holton, who had either attended school in New York or taught at city schools where specialists taught their specialties. In 1875 the faculty decided to improve the quality of education at the University by bringing in specialists to teach short courses in recently developed areas that were hardly touched upon in the traditional curriculum, at least at country medical schools. The specialists were appointed to the faculty as lecturers of special subjects, and they came to Burlington for periods of two or three weeks. They lectured and held clinics, providing short, basic courses in the various specialties. According to John Brooks Wheeler, who came to the University in the 1880's, the training received was inadequate for someone who might be called upon to provide specialized work, but it enabled the country practitioner to know when a specialist was needed and what kind to call. [11]

The lecturers on the special subjects were very well qualified. In the first year, for instance, they included D. B. St. John Roosa, professor of the diseases of the eye and ear at New York University; Stephen M. Roberts, professor of the diseases of children in the Woman's Medical College of New York; Robert W. Taylor, professor of dermatology at the same institution; George P. Fowler, assistant to John C. Dalton at New York's College of Physicians and Surgeons; and the relatively unknown Ashbel P. Grinnell, who lectured on the diseases of the heart and lungs. [12] These professors served without pay from either the University or the medical faculty, but were compensated by the fees of patients referred to them for examination. Rural Vermont had so very few specialists, except for the untrustworthy traveling ones, that when it was announced that a New York professor would be at the University of Vermont, a great many patients would appear on the scene, providing payment for the professors and material for the clinics.

In 1875, the year of the arrival of the first special lecturers, Peter Collier was in the midst of intrigue. As noted, Collier was a professor in the academic department but also lectured in the Medical School, and from 1871 to 1874 served as medical dean. He had steadily moved away from the academic life and into state service. He was secretary of the Vermont State Board of Agriculture, Mining, and Manufactur-

10. Ibid., pp. 170–171. See also UVM Medical Department, *26th Annual Announcement, 1879* (Burlington, 1878), p. 6.

11. UVM Medical Faculty Minutes, May 22 and June 30, 1875, UVM Archives. Wheeler, pp. 164–165.

12. See *23rd Annual Announcement, 1876* (Burlington, 1876).

ers, and he was often away at scientific meetings. In 1875 he was appointed Vermont's Commissioner to the Vienna Exposition. Some members of the faculty seized upon this as an opportunity to rid themselves of one who had become removed from traditional academic pursuits. The faculty informed the trustees that it was impossible to locate "a competent instructor for a temporary engagement," which was necessary because of Collier's "ill-health" and "his absorption in other occupations." On July 10 the medical professors urged the trustees to take Collier off their hands, so that they could seek a full-time professor of chemistry.[13]

Three days later Collier appeared before the board to discuss his relations with the University. The board subsequently voted to hire an assistant to take over his duties while he was in Vienna, and then concluded that "the Faculty, acting in connection with the Executive Committee" of the board, would have "entire control of the Department of Chemistry, and its Professor," and would be empowered to make any needed changes.[14]

According to the *Democratic Sentinel*, a Burlington newspaper, President Matthew Buckham wanted to remove Collier because of his opposition to Buckham's attempt to have the faculty support the reappointment of the postmaster, G. G. Benedict, a trustee who was editor of the *Free Press*.[15] Since Collier had been a leader in an attempt to remove the State Agricultural College from the University and from Burlington, he had very few supporters on the Board of Trustees. By 1877 the trustees had decided "that the best interests of the University" required Collier "to tender his resignation as Professor of Chemistry in the Academic and Medical Departments of the University." If he had not resigned by August 4, he would be fired.[16] The *Democratic Sentinel* reported that the trustees refused to allow Collier to read his defense, and the newspaper declared: "It will be hard to make our plain people believe that faculty and trustees have acted other than as a pack of jesuit-minded Calvinists."[17]

In 1878 the medical faculty recommended the appointment of Rudolph A. Witthaus to replace Collier as a full-time professor of chemistry and physics. Witthaus had received his undergraduate training at Columbia College, in New York City; after having earned a Master's degree, he had attended one course of medical lectures at the Bellevue Hospital Medical College, then spent a year in France studying at the Sorbonne and at the Collège de France. In 1875 he received his medical degree from New York University, and the following year he became associate professor of chemistry and physiology at that school. He served in this capacity until 1898, when he joined the faculty of the Cornell Medical College. Witthaus was an expert on toxicology, and he was often called to testify at murder trials. He was author of several books, including *Essentials of Chem-*

13. President's Report of 1875, Trustee File, UVM Archives.
14. UVM Trustee Minutes, July 13, 1875.
15. *Democratic Sentinel*, June 30, 1877, p. 3, cols. 1–2.
16. UVM Trustee Minutes, July 25, 1877.
17. *Democratic Sentinel*, August 4, 1877, p. 3, cols. 1–3.

istry and *Manual of Chemistry*, as well as *Laboratory Guide to Toxicology*. Witthaus remained on the University faculty from 1878 to 1900, and he provided excellent training to his students. In 1879 the delegates of the Vermont Medical Society reported that they were pleased with the students' proficiency in chemistry, as "it is a notable fact that generally students have evinced a woeful deficiency in this important branch." Two years later the delegates noted that in the examination in chemistry, "generally the great horror and bugbear of the green room," the students were quite proficient.[18]

Also in 1878 Ashbel P. Grinnell joined the regular medical faculty, as professor of physiology and microscopical anatomy. Although he had a very limited background, Grinnell had served as a special lecturer at the University since 1875 and dean since 1877. He graduated from the Bellevue Hospital Medical College in 1869 and apparently settled in Burlington in anticipation of a position in the Medical School. Back in 1871, with Thayer ill and Carpenter ageing, President Buckham had insisted that if the Medical School was to continue, it would be necessary to attract "some young physician" who would "take up his residence" in the city. Buckham had concluded that the School could not exist without a medical dean living in the area.[19] Grinnell's initial appointment as a special lecturer was apparently to give him some teaching experience prior to his formal appointment to the medical faculty.

In 1877, while still a part-time lecturer, Grinnell was elected dean when Carpenter, who had replaced Collier as dean in 1875, declined to serve longer. Perhaps it was poetic justice for Grinnell to replace Marshall Calkins as a regular member of the faculty, for in 1877 Calkins had objected to paying Grinnell for serving as dean. Calkins had declared that Grinnell accepted the position knowing there was no compensation, and that Grinnell had proven himself incompetent as a physician, as evidenced by Grinnell's medical treatment of Calkins' wife. When the faculty voted on the motion to compensate Grinnell, Calkins was alone in his opposition. The following year, Calkins resigned.[20]

Grinnell was bright and energetic. He was an excellent lecturer, both amusing and instructive. He used a great many anecdotes to hold the interest of his audience, and became one of the most popular members of the faculty. Not only did he teach physiology and anatomy, but he also served as dean or acting dean for nineteen of the twenty-one years from 1877 to 1898. In addition, he was secretary of the medical faculty from 1877 to 1890.[21]

In June 1880 Walter Carpenter submitted his resignation as professor of the theory and practice of medicine, effective at the end of the next term. In his letter to the trustees Carpenter recommended that he be replaced by a "Vermont man." He declared: "The experi-

18. Vermont Medical Society, *Transactions, 1879* (St. Albans, 1879), p. 100. *Transactions, 1881* (Montpelier, 1881), pp. 33–34.

19. President's Report of 1871, Trustee File, UVM Archives.

20. See UVM Medical Faculty Minutes, June 23, 1877, and June 24, 1878.

21. Wheeler, pp. 171–172. Thayer was dean from 1881 to 1882, and President Buckham was elected dean in 1883 and 1884. See UVM Medical Faculty Minutes, November 20, 1882, and June 20, 1883.

ence of the past leads me to believe that the only true prosperity of State Institutions like this are to be obtained by having the prominent men of the State among its faculty." Carpenter concluded by recommending the appointment of Henry D. Holton, the professor of materia medica and pathology, a man "who has already done something towards" the school's "prosperity, and who is today well and favorably known."[22] In making this recommendation, he bypassed the medical faculty and upset his colleagues. The medical faculty had traditionally discussed candidates, taken a formal vote, and submitted its nomination to the board, for an automatic confirmation. To prevent the trustees from selecting Holton before the entire faculty had an opportunity to discuss the vacancy, the professors voted to inform the board that the medical faculty had postponed consideration of a successor to Carpenter until a later meeting.[23]

On June 21, 1881, the faculty nominated Grinnell to replace Carpenter. There were no other nominations, although Holton did not cast his vote.[24] When the trustees met in the morning of June 28, Thayer presented the recommendation of the faculty, and Carpenter, speaking in favor of Holton, presented supporting letters from a number of Vermont physicians. It was a difficult decision for the trustees, especially since Holton had been a member of the board since 1873 and Grinnell was a comparative newcomer to Vermont. The trustees sent a delegation to discuss the problem with the medical faculty. There is no record of the meeting, but it is obvious that with the exception of Holton himself, the medical faculty stood solidly behind Grinnell.[25] By the time the medical faculty reconvened after lunch, Thayer had received a note from President Buckham informing him that Grinnell had been elected to the chair of theory and practice. Holton then arrived at the faculty meeting and announced that he would support Grinnell and remain loyal to "the interests of the College."[26]

In the midst of the trouble the faculty debated whether to elect Walter Carpenter to emeritus status. The professors received a communication from Samuel White Thayer, Carpenter's former partner and long-time colleague, who declared that "circumstances have come to our knowledge which lead us to suspect" Carpenter's "loyalty." Undoubtedly the information was that Carpenter had gone directly to the trustees with his recommendation that the faculty nomination of Grinnell be overruled. The minutes of the medical faculty contain no information as to the specifics of the discussion, as the faculty voted to expunge it from the minutes and the secretary did so by removing two pages from the Minute Book. Carpenter had to wait until 1891 before finally being elected to the emeritus status denied ten years earlier.[27]

The dispute had been between Carpenter and the faculty, but the

22. UVM Medical Faculty Minutes, June 25, 1880.

23. Ibid., June 28, 1880.

24. Ibid., June 21, 1881; UVM Trustee Minutes, June 27, 28, 1881.

25. UVM Trustee Minutes, June 29, 1881.

26. UVM Medical Faculty Minutes, June 27, 1881. The faculty secretary described the entire situation under the date of June 27, even though much of it occurred on the 28th and 29th.

27. Ibid., June 28, 1881. UVM Trustee Minutes, June 22, 1891.

other professors must have doubted Holton's loyalty, for he did not withdraw his name when the faculty voted to nominate Grinnell. On June 23, 1883, A. F. A. King, the professor of obstetrics, spiced up a meeting with "some remarks respecting Prof. Holton's relations with the Faculty." A general discussion ensued, but no record was kept of the specifics.[28] In 1886 Holton and the trustees virtually declared war on the medical faculty by appointing a professor who was *not* recommended by the faculty.

In December 1884 the faculty was shocked by the death of William Darling, the professor of anatomy. On January 7, 1885, the medical faculty gathered to select a replacement. James L. Little, the professor of surgery, suggested that each member of the faculty present candidates. King suggested Ambrose Loomis Ranney, who had taught a short course in neurology in 1884 and again in 1885 and was well liked by the students. King also suggested William Beverly Towles, of the University of Virginia. Echoing the sentiments of Carpenter, Holton declared that he preferred a "Vermont man," and he mentioned Leroy Monroe Bingham, who was demonstrator of anatomy at the University for five years and was attending surgeon at the Mary Fletcher Hospital. Little said that he preferred Ranney, but he suggested several other possibilities. Grinnell expressed himself in favor of a local man if one could be found who was better qualified than others. He mentioned Thayer's son, Charles Paine Thayer, who had been adjunct professor of anatomy since 1883, and Henry Crain Tinkham, the demonstrator of anatomy who had the full support of the student body. After the general discussion, Grinnell nominated Thayer, and King nominated Ranney. When the ballots were cast, Ranney received four votes and Thayer had one: Ranney was elected to replace Darling, as a lecturer for one term.[29]

Ranney was a fine selection. He also replaced Darling as professor of anatomy at New York University and at the Post-Graduate Medical School. The *University Cynic*, then a student magazine, expressed satisfaction at the choice of Ranney. According to the *Cynic*, Ranney had "given the utmost satisfaction as a teacher, scholar, and gentleman. His lectures are thorough . . . on those branches which are . . . most vital . . . to the physician." In addition, Ranney's lectures were so informative that a number of local physicians had regularly attended his course.[30]

The selection of Ranney went very smoothly, perhaps encouraging the faculty to forget the problems that had developed when Carpenter's successor was named back in 1881. Later the same year, however, a dispute erupted which threatened the very existence of the College. The trouble began when James Lawrence Little died on April 4, 1885. The medical faculty held a special meeting on April 23, and Grinnell moved the election of J. Williston Wright, of New

28. UVM Medical Faculty Minutes, June 23, 1883.

29. Ibid., January 7, 1885.

30. *University Cynic*, April 1, 1885, p. 141; (May 14, 1884), p. 19.

York City, for a trial period of one year. Wright was unanimously elected as a last-minute replacement.[31]

Wright had attended one course of lectures at Geneva, and in 1866 he graduated from New York's College of Physicians and Surgeons. He was demonstrator of anatomy at the Woman's College of the New York Infirmary, and in 1877 he became professor of obstetrics and the diseases of women and children at New York University. The *Cynic* declared on June 10 that Wright "had already ingratiated himself into the hearts of the students." "His lectures are concise and to the point," the writer exclaimed, and "as an operator he is careful and certain."[32]

On June 23 the medical faculty voted to recommend the permanent appointment of Wright as professor of surgery. Holton was the only member of the faculty to vote against it.[33] When the Board of Trustees met on June 30, the situation was complicated by the fact that Holton presented letters from "a large number of Vermont physicians" who supported Leroy Monroe Bingham. Dean Grinnell, appearing before the trustees, declared that "it would be necessary to look outside of Vermont for a man possessing the standing, experience and National reputation desired." After hearing the testimonials on behalf of both Wright and Bingham, the board proceeded to the election. When the votes had been counted, Bingham had eight and Wright had six.[34] In spite of the opposition of the medical faculty, the trustees elected a "Vermont man" as professor of surgery.

On the following day the trustees attempted to placate the faculty by proposing to divide the chair of surgery into two professorships, one a chair of didactic surgery and the other of clinical surgery.[35] If the professors accepted the proposal, they would have been able to appoint Wright, although Bingham would still remain on the faculty. Yet it would have increased the total number of professorships, and since each full professor received a share of the receipts of the College, it would have meant a reduction in compensation for every member of the faculty. The professors decided to reject the proposal and accept the appointment of Bingham, at least for the moment.[36]

In the fall of 1885 Ranney resigned as professor of anatomy, after just one term. When the medical faculty met to fill the vacancy, the discussion shifted to the power of the faculty to select a replacement, in light of the fact that just three months earlier the trustees had ignored the faculty's nomination. The executive committee of the board assured the professors that the actions of the past June "would not probably ever be repeated," and that the power to nominate replacements would continue to rest with the faculty, with this one exception." A. F. A. King then nominated William B. Towles, of the University of Virginia. J. Henry Jackson, who had been appointed professor of physiology back in 1883, moved that King be sent to

31. UVM Medical Faculty Minutes, April 23, 1885.
32. *University Cynic*, June 10, 1885, p. 32.
33. UVM Medical Faculty Minutes, June 23, 1885.
34. UVM Trustee Minutes, June 30, 1885.
35. Ibid., June 30, 1885.
36. Ibid.

Philadelphia to locate other candidates, and then to discuss the matter with Towles personally. The faculty voted to elect Towles, "provided that Dr. King reported favorably after meeting him." By mail from Buffalo, Witthaus voted against the proposal, expressing his opinion that only the trustees had the power to fill vacancies, and that "any attempt on the part of the medical faculty to in any way fill the existing vacancy in the chair of anatomy would be entirely illegal and without authority."[37]

King later reported that he had met with two potential replacements in Philadelphia, but each had declined the position. He apparently was joined by Holton; together they met with Towles and offered him the position. They said that they preferred a "lecturer from Philadelphia," but since they had been refused by two professors, they decided that "further delay" would not have enabled them to find a suitable Philadelphian.[38]

Toward the end of April 1886, just before the opening of the course of lectures, the *Burlington Independent* published an editorial which indicated that trouble was brewing over the appointment of Bingham. The editor noted that Bingham was one of the best local physicians, but he hoped that the trustees have not "elected a man incompetent to fill the place." The editorial declared: "It may be true that he is not a successful talker," but predicted that "if he fails it will be more likely to be for want of wind than brains."[39] That was the first indication of any problem over the selection of Bingham.

Early in May, Bingham presented four clinical lectures at the Mary Fletcher Hospital. After the lectures the students were in an uproar. They claimed that he had paid little attention "to antiseptic treatment," and thus showed his inexperience. The dissident students began to circulate a petition calling on Bingham to resign and the trustees to offer the position to Wright, who had satisfied everyone the previous year. The petition was signed by all but one of the 140 medical students, who decided to boycott Bingham's classes until the faculty and trustees accepted their demands.[40]

The question naturally arises whether the medical faculty played any role in instigating the student boycott. Apparently some believed that to be the case. President Buckham, for instance, told the students that they should not become involved in a faculty affair. When the medical faculty met on May 11, Bingham himself stated that he was convinced that Grinnell was "innocent of having incited the students to the circulation of the petition, or had anything to do with it." He declared, however, that he had learned that "much of the work done with the students had been performed" in the offices of Jo Hatch Linsley, instructor in physiology, and Henry Crain Tinkham, instructor in anatomy. In any case, the faculty informed the students

37. Ibid., September 3, 1885.
38. Ibid.
39. *Burlington Independent*, April 30, 1886, p. 4, col. 4.
40. UVM Medical Faculty Minutes, May 11, 1886.

that it was their "unanimous desire" that the students listen to Bingham's lectures on surgery.[41]

When Bingham's regular course of lectures began on the 10th, very few students attended. During the first week he lectured before six to ten students.[42] On May 13 a letter to the editor of the *Burlington Free Press and Times* explained that the boycotting students wanted to be instructed by men of "national ability," who were generally acknowledged as experts in their fields. Two years before, James Lawrence Little had been professor of surgery, and he was very well known in medical circles. When he died, Grinnell was told by prominent New Yorkers that the best man for the position was J. Williston Wright, who had been hired for a one-year trial period. Wright's course at Burlington was "pronounced by professional men the best ever given in this college." In spite of the fact that the faculty had recommended the appointment of Wright, the trustees elected Bingham, "without even a trial."[43]

The *Free Press*, published by G. G. Benedict, a member of the Board of Trustees, supported the faculty and the trustees in the matter. Other local newspapers, however, were sympathetic to the students. The *Burlington Clipper*, for example, declared that it was unprecedented for the trustees to appoint Bingham without a trial period, and stated that "the medical college cannot maintain its reputation throughout the country on local talent." The next week the *Clipper* predicted the "final and complete disruption of the college," caused by the trustees, who "are very good and 'nice' gentlemen" but who "hold themselves so aloof from the world that a majority of them don't even know who is president of the United States."[44] The *Burlington Independent* agreed with the *Clipper*. The editor declared that the trustees had made a "serious mistake last year when it elected an untried, inexperienced man." In addition, the appointment of Bingham turned the once harmonious medical faculty into "a divided house," since the other professors had supported J. Williston Wright.[45] The only solution to the impasse was Bingham's removal.

Since the faculty had endorsed Wright the previous year, the professors were happy to see Bingham forced out of his position. They had publicly taken a stand in support of Bingham continuing at the College, but the students undoubtedly knew that the faculty, with the exception of Holton, fully supported their boycott. Some of the students left Burlington because of the chaos that threatened to disrupt the year's course of lectures. The ones who remained gathered on May 13, held a parade through the city, and attended a mass meeting, at which they gave "3 groans" for Bingham, "3 more for Dr. Holton . . . and 3 cheers for the rest of the faculty." When the boycott lasted ten days and threatened to prevent the completion

41. Ibid.
42. *Burlington Free Press and Times*, May 11, 1886, p. 8, cols. 2–3.
43. Ibid., May 13, 1886, p. 5, col. 3.
44. *Burlington Clipper*, May 13, 1886, p. 3, col. 2; May 20, 1886, p. 3, col. 2.
45. *Burlington Independent*, May 14, 1886, p. 4, cols. 1–2.

of the course, the faculty decided that they had supported Bingham long enough. They decided to take action by submitting the student petition to the trustees, who were already under a great deal of pressure. After all, their decision to appoint Bingham had led to the entire situation; it also seems that "the business interests of the city" were in favor of the students. "Church St. did not want to lose the dollars which medics spent each year."[46]

The faculty asked the president to call a special meeting of the board. At that meeting, on May 20, the students requested an opportunity to substantiate their charge that Bingham was incompetent. Then Grinnell presented the petition from 139 students, requesting Bingham's resignation. He stated that the medical faculty had earlier decided that the request could not be granted, but now the faculty had voted to refer the petition to the trustees.[47] The trustees had caused the trouble by hiring Bingham; now they had to resolve it by removing him.

It was obvious that Bingham had to go. The very existence of the College was threatened by the boycott and by the publicity given Bingham's real or imagined incompetence. Yet the trustees certainly could not appear to be giving in to the demands of the student body. Seeking some way of firing Bingham without appearing to have surrendered to student pressure, they began by adopting a resolution admitting that the students had the right to petition for resolution of "any well founded grievance" but declaring that the demand for the resignation of Bingham was "so dictatorial and offensive in manner" and the boycott of Bingham's classes was "so like lawlessness and violence" that the board could not consider the petition of the students.[48]

Then the board adopted a resolution expressing confidence in "the capacity and qualifications of Professor L. M. Bingham." Finally, the trustees appointed a committee, which apparently requested Bingham's resignation while making it appear that he had voluntarily decided to do so. His resignation was immediately accepted.[49] The medical faculty convinced Wright to resume his chair, and on June 1, 1886, the trustees appointed him professor of surgery.[50]

Just two days after the trustees had accepted Bingham's resignation, Henry D. Holton resigned as professor of materia medica and pathology. He had used his influence to convince the trustees to appoint Bingham in the first place, and he was angry that the trustees had thrown Bingham "to the medic student wolves."[51] Holton had opposed the interests and wishes of the medical faculty back in 1880 when Carpenter had recommended him for his own position. Now, after having played a major role in convincing the trustees to overrule the nomination of the faculty, he was *persona non grata* with the medical professors. Moreover, the students knew of his relationship with

46. Hills, "History of the Medical College," pp. 86ff.
47. UVM Trustee Minutes, May 20, 1886.
48. Ibid.
49. Ibid.
50. UVM Trustees, "Record of the Proceedings of the Executive Committee of the Corporation," June 1, 1886, UVM Archives.
51. Hills, "History of the Medical College," p. 88a.

Bingham; had he continued, his students would have had little respect for him. In his letter of resignation Holton declared that he had hoped that the faculty would adopt an advanced curriculum, but "the adoption of any such progressive policy by the present Medical Faculty seems to be chimerical." He declared that since his "continuance in that faculty may be construed as endorsing their present avaricious policy," he must submit his resignation.[52]

The *Burlington Independent* concluded its coverage of the incident by noting that the students were attending their classes, with the exception of about twenty who did not return to Burlington when the boycott ended. "The experiment of making this a 'Vermont College' with Vermont professors, has been costly and unsuccessful," the editor declared, "and will not be soon repeated." The newspaper asserted that there was no way for a Vermont school to have national prestige with Vermont professors alone, regardless of how experienced they happened to be.[53]

On June 15, 1886, the medical faculty voted an amendment to the agreement between the faculty and the trustees, providing for the appointment of professors "on nomination of the Medical Faculty."[54] The trustees refused to allow the faculty that right, however, even though it had been disastrous to do otherwise in 1886. The trustees adopted a resolution providing that "if the Medical Faculty concur," the trustees would appoint professors, but if the trustees rejected the first nomination, the faculty would make another one, and if the trustees rejected that one, they could appoint a professor "without such nomination, if deemed advisable." The minutes of the trustees noted, however, that the "Medical Faculty declined to concur."[55] The year ended with the faculty and the students triumphant, having seen Bingham resign and Wright appointed to replace him. Yet the relationship between the medical faculty and the University was still largely undefined, and it would continue to be so until the early years of the twentieth century.

52. Holton to Buckham, Brattleboro, May 22, 1886, trustee file, UVM Archives.

53. *Burlington Independent*, May 28, 1886, p. 4, col. 1.

54. UVM Medical Faculty Minutes, June 15, 1886.

55. UVM Trustee Minutes, June 29, 1886.

Chapter Seven

The Faculty and the Trustees, 1886–1900

IN SPITE OF the problems with the trustees, by the 1890's the College was well established. Enrollment was high, and the faculty was experienced and dedicated. A. P. Grinnell, the dean, taught the theory and practice of medicine. William Beverly Towles, who was also affiliated with the University of Virginia, taught anatomy; obstetrics and the diseases of women and children was handled by A. F. A. King. Rudolph A. Witthaus was professor of chemistry and toxicology. J. Henry Jackson taught physiology and microscopic anatomy. A local and relatively obscure physician, Julius Hayden Woodward, taught materia medica and therapeutics.

When J. Williston Wright resigned in 1889, he was replaced by Abel Mix Phelps of New York City. Phelps was extremely well qualified. He was a native of Vermont who had received his medical degree from the University of Michigan in 1873. In 1880 he went to Europe to further his education. He made a grand tour, studying surgery with Schede at Hamburg, Esmarch at Kiel, Von Volkman at Halle, Billroth at Vienna, and Thiersch at Leipzig. While in Hamburg, Phelps organized the orthopedic department at the Allgemeines Krankenhaus. When he finally returned to the United States, he was appointed professor of surgery at New York's Post-Graduate Medical School, serving there from 1887 to 1902. From 1890 to 1900 he held the same position at the University of Vermont.

It was a respectable faculty, in many ways similar to the situation several decades earlier. It included several undistinguished Vermont men—Grinnell, Jackson, and Woodward—who were joined by professional medical educators from the cities—King, Witthaus, Towles, and Phelps. In addition, a number of well known specialists came to Burlington during the term to give short courses and hold clinics. In 1890, to take one year, the faculty was well represented at international gatherings. Jackson and Phelps attended the annual meeting of the British Medical Association, and King joined his two colleagues at the International Medical Congress held in Berlin. At the latter meeting Phelps read a chapter on his own work—"The Present Status of Phelps' Operation in the Treatment of Clubfoot."[1]

In 1892 the faculty made a number of significant changes in the curriculum. They extended the term from five to six months and eliminated the preliminary term. In addition they abolished the "private" courses in urinary analysis, histology, pathology, bacteriology, physical diagnosis, and practical obstetrics, and included them in the regular program required for graduation.[2]

The faculty voted to appoint men to teach the new courses. In effect the "instructors" who had been handling laboratories and recitation sections and who lectured in the absence of the professors would play larger roles as "adjunct professors." Each full professor selected the adjunct in his field. Thus Jacob C. Rutherford became adjunct in obstetrics, Henry Crain Tinkham in anatomy, John Brooks Wheeler in surgery, James N. Jenne in materia medica and therapeutics, Charles S. Boynton in chemistry, and Jo Hatch Linsley in physiology.[3]

Each professor was scheduled to give fifty lectures, with each adjunct presenting an additional twenty-two. Since Towles could not be in Burlington for the entire course, Tinkham delivered fifty-seven lectures on anatomy and Towles the remaining fifteen. The two men divided the student fees.[4] Tinkham had an exceptionally full schedule —he had been demonstrator of anatomy since 1884 and continued in that capacity. On September 15, 1893, Towles became ill while delivering the first lecture of the session at the University of Virginia, and he died the same day. The Vermont faculty rewarded Tinkham for his years of service and reduced expenses by letting him give the entire course of lectures in anatomy. They voted to compensate him by paying him $800, about $500 less than the salaries of the full professors. Two assistant demonstrators of anatomy were appointed so that Tinkham could devote more time to his lectures.[5]

The following year, 1894, Tinkham was appointed full professor, permanently filling the vacancy left by the death of Towles. That same year Woodward resigned as professor of materia medica, and in 1895 his adjunct, James N. Jenne, was elected to replace him.[6] These were important precedents, leading to inbreeding and a static approach to medical education. Previously, the faculty had sent to New York or elsewhere for a young man who was highly recommended by professors at New York University, the College of Physicians and Surgeons, or some other leading medical school. Both Tinkham and

1. *Burlington Free Press and Times*, July 17, 1890, p. 4, col. 3.
2. UVM Medical Faculty Minutes, July 6, 1892. For a description of curriculum development, see below, Chapter 9.
3. Ibid., July 8, 1892, July 11, 1892.
4. Ibid., July 11, 1892.
5. Ibid., October 26, 1893.
6. Ibid., July 25, 1894; June 24, 1895.

Jenne had moved from instructor to adjunct, and finally to professor. No attempts were made to find the best qualified men who were then available. It would not be many years before the faculty would consist of "Vermont men": graduates of the University or those whose only experience had been at Burlington.

In 1897 the professors adopted a four-year graded curriculum, which necessitated an increase in faculty. The course, which was to begin the following year, required the seven full professors, adjunct professors in surgery, obstetrics, practice, and materia medica, recitation instructors in chemistry, histology, and pathology, a laboratory instructor in urinalysis, a demonstrator of anatomy, and instructors in physical diagnosis, practical surgery, and practical obstetrics.[7] Thus the faculty expanded from six in 1853 to a total of twenty-two in 1898, the increase being due to the bacteriological revolution, which resulted in the need for specific courses in histology and pathology, and to a renewed emphasis on clinical work. Because of the growth of medical and scientific knowledge and the emphasis on laboratory work, it was impossible for the same person to teach anatomy and physiology, for instance, as had been the case in the past. With a four-year graded course, which included laboratories and recitations, six or seven professors could not possibly handle everything.

In the late 1890's trouble began again among the faculty, commencing with the marital problems of Professor Witthaus. In October 1896 his wife found him in a restaurant with a young lady named Kate de Vivo and shortly thereafter divorced the chemistry professor. Later, this former wife claimed that he had tried to poison her. She was about to depart for Europe, and Witthaus had given her a bottle of "medicine." When the contents were analyzed, poison was present. Witthaus, it may be noted, was a specialist in toxicology who was constantly being called upon to testify in murder cases. Nothing came of his wife's claims, but early in 1898 they found their way into the columns of the Burlington newspapers.[8]

Less than a year later the entire college community was up in arms over the role of Grinnell. The problem began at the June 22, 1898, meeting of the medical faculty, when it came time for the annual election of officers. Grinnell, who had served as dean from 1874 to 1877 and again from 1880 to 1898, left the meeting just prior to the election, apparently aware that his colleagues had decided to replace him. Tinkham unsuccessfully tried to convince Grinnell to return to the meeting; the election had to be held that day or a quorum would not be present, for Witthaus, Phelps, and Jackson were going to leave Burlington the next morning, and Jenne had already "gone to the war." The professors decided to hold the election, however, in the absence of the dean. When the votes were counted, Henry Crain Tinkham had been elected dean of the medical faculty.[9]

7. Ibid., June 23, 1897.

8. *Burlington Free Press and Times*, January 25, 1898, p. 6, col. 5; January 26, 1898, p. 2, col. 1.

9. UVM Medical Faculty Minutes, June 22, 1898. See also unidentified newspaper clipping in Grinnell Papers, UVM Archives.

Two days later, on June 24, the *Burlington Free Press* announced that Grinnell had "retired" as dean. The following edition, however, included a letter from Grinnell, declaring that he did not "retire." "My successor was elected as dean," he exclaimed, "without my knowledge and without consultation with me."[10]

When the students learned that Grinnell had been removed from his position, they rushed to his support. As far back as 1885 they had described their respect for Grinnell in the *Cynic*, which had declared, "To know him is to love him." "He is, indeed, a friend to the student." "We love him, we revere him, and we trust him."[11] On June 25, 1898, the students held a "red hot" meeting. After a number of speeches condemning the professors, the students prepared a petition endorsing Grinnell. Then they marched to Grinnell's house, shouting, "What's the matter with Grinnell?" and responding, "He's all right." When Grinnell came out to thank them for their support, he was greeted by a round of applause. Finally, the students dispersed, again marching through town, chanting, "What's the matter with Grinnell?"[12]

It is interesting to speculate why the faculty decided to relieve Grinnell of his duties as dean. He had held the office since the 1870's, and during his administration the enrollment had increased from 51 in 1874 to 171 in 1881, and then to a record high of 238 in 1897. Since the dean's job included advertising the course of study, corresponding with prospective students, and handling the day-to-day business of the College, Grinnell was largely responsible for the increase in professors' salaries from $600 in 1875 to $2100 in 1897.[13] According to Dean Joseph Hills, of the College of Agriculture, Grinnell was a perfect dean of a proprietary medical school. He admitted everyone who applied, kept the benches filled, and maintained very low standards.[14] The age of the proprietary school was ending, however. Now was a time of medical reform, with the Association of American Medical Colleges trying to bring about a general improvement in standards. It was a time for the Medical Department of the University of Vermont to advance or disappear. That was the reality in an age of state board examinations; if the School could not provide a quality education, the students would fail to pass the state boards and could not be licensed to practice. The result would be a decrease in enrollment and the collapse of the College. Since Grinnell had expressed his opposition to the six-month term, declaring that he wanted to continue to teach the way he had in the past twenty years, it was obvious to his colleagues that his usefulness had ended. He had done his job very well when that meant attracting poorly qualified students. Now he had to be eliminated.

Financial considerations were also a factor. Grinnell, who was responsible for the financial operations of the College, had been lax

10. *Burlington Free Press and Times*, June 24, 1898, p. 5, col. 2; June 25, 1898, p. 5, col. 2.

11. *University Cynic*, June 10, 1885, pp. 32–33.

12. *Burlington Free Press and Times*, June 26, 1898, p. 5, col. 6. See also *Burlington News*, June 25, 1898, in Grinnell Papers. There seem to be no existing files of the *News* anywhere in Vermont, although it was one of the longest-lasting newspapers in the city's history.

13. Enrollment figures from annual announcements; financial figures from UVM Medical Department Ledgers, 1879–90, 1890–98: UVM Archives.

14. Hills, "History of the Medical College," pp. 68–69, UVM Archives.

by allowing students to pay their fees whenever they had the money, rather than insisting on payment in advance. Furthermore, he was lenient with lecture tickets, even giving them to students who were far behind in their payments. Grinnell assumed that the students would eventually pay, or even if they did not, they would at least fill the benches, making it possible for him to boast in 1898 that the Medical College ranked "6th in this country in point of numbers." [15]

The net effect of Grinnell's policies was an increase in attendance and a corresponding financial loss to the members of the faculty. For example, the students who were enrolled in 1896 left bad debts totaling $825. Students in the next year owed $430, which had not been paid as of the end of 1898. Then, and perhaps most significant, in 1898, the year Grinnell was replaced as dean, 32 students, 15.2 percent of the class, owed a total of $2,234.16. That meant a reduction of over three hundred dollars in the salaries of each of the seven full professors. [16] An analysis of the financial records makes it easy to understand why the students loved Grinnell and the professors opposed him.

The Grinnell situation was complicated by the question whether the trustees should take complete control of the Medical Department or let it remain virtually autonomous. Even though the age of the proprietary school was nearly over, the Medical College at Burlington had only a nominal affiliation with the University. In the future, medical education would be more expensive, requiring endowments and closer connections to leading Universities. For the College to remain in existence, it had to raise entrance requirements and increase standards, knowing this would decrease enrollment. Yet expenses would continue to rise, with more professors and better laboratory facilities needed in the future. Medical educators certainly knew that to be the case, and President Buckham recognized that closer university affiliation was required.

In 1897 the trustees and the faculty each established committees to consider the future relations between the College and the University. At its 1898 meeting the trustees decided to get a legal opinion on whether they had the "right to assume full control of the Medical department." [17] Thus, while the professors were taking an unpopular action in replacing Grinnell as dean, the trustees were preparing to assume complete control of the College.

The summer and fall of 1898 was filled with intrigue. Grinnell and his friends were busy rallying support for him, and they apparently blamed King, Phelps, and Witthaus, the out-of-state professors, for his removal. One of Grinnell's leading advocates was Dr. W. Seward Webb, of Shelburne, a member of the Board of Trustees as well as chairman of the board of the Rutland Railroad Company. Webb, who had married into the Vanderbilt family, worked hard to under-

15. Ibid., p. 69. For examples of Grinnell's financial dealings, see UVM Medical Department Ledger, 1890–98, pp. 12, 13, 29, 32, 57, 112, 114, 153, 208, 213, 215, 224, 226, 298, 331, 338, 341, 342, 392, 404, 411, 425, 427, 473, 474, 475, 477, 489, 491, 492, 522.

16. Figures developed from ibid., 1890–98.

17. UVM Medical Faculty Minutes, June 17, July 1, 1897. UVM Trustee Minutes, June 29, 1898.

mine the decision of the professors. He sent letters to influential trustees and alumni. Meanwhile, the faculty tried to figure out what they could do to protect their position. Dean Tinkham, new to the office, did not know *what* to do but was convinced that something had to be done. He wrote A. F. A. King for advice, since King had been dean of the faculty at Columbian University. The obstetrics professor told Tinkham to relax. There was no reason for panic, he said, and "no danger of the Med' school receiving any injury to its 'vitals.'" He declared that "there is no more reason *now* to go wild over the machinations of Dr. Grinnell than there was last summer. It is much better to ignore him and his 'eagle-screams.'" King predicted that if Grinnell thought he could "oust me or Witthaus or Phelps," he would find himself in the battle of his life. In conclusion, King hoped that Tinkham "and the New York Profs. would just keep quiet."[18]

The next course of lectures seemed to go along nicely, although according to one observer "suspence pervaded the college atmosphere" and the "students were uneasy."[19] There was no sign of trouble until March 30, when Grinnell completed his course with a lecture on the situation at the College. Then he and his wife prepared to spend a week in New York. A rumor spread that he had resigned to accept a position in that city, but when interviewed by a reporter, he denied the rumor. According to the *Free Press*, "almost the entire class gathered at the railroad station to shake his hand. Mrs. Grinnell was presented with some beautiful roses, and as the train moved, Grinnell "recognized the cheering by appearing on the car platform and bowing his acknowledgments." After the train had departed, the students "marched around the park and up Church Street, cheering vociferously for Dr. Grinnell and asserting in no uncertain terms that he was all right."[20]

Almost immediately, trouble developed. Grinnell had terminated his course three weeks ahead of the schedule that had been prepared the previous year, and just before the last lecture, he had informed the executive committee of the faculty that he "would deliver his lectures in the usual time and cover his entire subject as he had done in the previous 20 years."[21] After he departed, the committee directed James N. Jenne, professor of clinical medicine, to complete his course. When Grinnell learned that Jenne had taken his class without his permission, he filed a formal complaint. In response to his letter the faculty established a committee, consisting of King and Jackson, to investigate the facts of the matter.[22]

The committee report was lengthy, running to fifteen typewritten pages. It exonerated Jenne, noting that the executive committee had directed him to complete Grinnell's course. The report continued, however, by examining Grinnell's failure to fulfill his obligations to

18. King to Tinkham, Washington, D.C., November 17, 1898, King file, Tinkham Papers, UVM Archives.

19. *Vermont Medical Monthly*, 5 (1899), 277ff.

20. *Burlington Free Press and Times*, March 31, 1899, p. 5, col. 2.

21. *Burlington Clipper*, July 8, 1899, p. 5, col. 2.

22. UVM Medical Faculty Minutes, May 18, 1899.

the University. In effect, by refusing to teach his class until April 21 he had defaulted on his agreement to teach his course as directed by the faculty. The committee had learned that in his concluding lecture Grinnell had devoted one full hour to "addressing a revolutionary harrangue to the students." The committee concluded that Grinnell had "assumed a position of hostility to the government of the school" and that his complaints were "lacking in sincerity of statement of fact, and are made in a spirit of rebellion against the proper authority of the Faculty."[23]

Now that Grinnell's charges had been dismissed, the faculty set up a new committee, consisting of King, Jenne, and Tinkham, to investigate Grinnell's conduct and "report on any alleged spirit of insubordination and antagonism which is subversive of the order and good government of this Medical School."[24] King withdrew from the committee, which obviously was established to find evidence to warrant Grinnell's removal from the faculty. Some of the professors could not wait, however, and at meetings of June 7, 12, and 14, they discussed a motion to request Grinnell's resignation. Each time, they decided to postpone action until they had more substantial evidence upon which to act.[25]

On June 9, Jo Hatch Linsley, who taught pathology and bacteriology, resigned from the faculty. Although he refused to discuss the matter with the press, his decision was obviously related to the fact that his preceptor, Grinnell, was being drummed out. Moreover, Linsley had benefited from Grinnell's financial policies—in 1880 he was not required to pay fees (no explanation was recorded in the ledger). The loss of Linsley was significant—he was one of the early students of bacteriology, having studied under Koch in Berlin. He had been pathologist to the Post-Graduate Medical School, and in 1898 he had established the Vermont Laboratory of Hygiene as a demonstration of the use of the laboratory in medical practice.[26]

Five days later, on the 14th, Jenne wrote to Tinkham, asking: "What do you hear if anything of our 'committee' and of the movements of 'our friends the enemy.'"[27] That Jenne asked Tinkham about the "committee" indicates that although he was supposed to be a member, the work of the "committee" was being done by Tinkham. Finally, at the faculty meeting on June 21, 1899, and with Grinnell in attendance, Tinkham read his "committee" report. First, it noted that Grinnell had held the office of dean for so long that he believed that he "owned" it. Then it reported that Grinnell had given students "the false impression that the Faculty had treated him in an unfair and unjust manner in exercising its unquestionable right to make its own selection of a Dean." The report stated that Grinnell had tried to enlist the aid of the students by declaring that he had made enemies when he reprimanded a colleague who had "abused" a stu-

23. Ibid., June 1, 1899, and attachments.

24. Ibid.

25. Ibid., June 7, 12, 14, 1899.

26. *Burlington Free Press and Times*, June 9, 1899, p. 5, col. 5. *National Cyclopedia of American Biography*, XV, 370. See also UVM Medical Department Ledger, 1879–90.

27. Jenne to Tinkham, St. Albans, June 14, 1899, Jenne Folder, Tinkham Papers.

dent. The report concluded that Grinnell was hostile to the interests of the College, that he had tried to agitate the students against other professors, and that he should be removed from his position as professor of theory and practice.[28]

After hearing Tinkham's report, Jackson moved that "in view of the apparent hostility of Dr. Grinnell towards the Faculty and towards its policy; it is the sense of this Faculty that the interests of the school are jeparized by the continuance of Dr. Grinnell as a member of the Faculty." When the vote was taken, Grinnell abstained and the other six professors voted in favor of his resignation.[29]

At that same meeting Tinkham moved an amendment to the college by-laws which would make it possible to remove Grinnell from the faculty even if he did not resign. The amendment, which was adopted, provided that "in case of dissatisfaction with any member of the Faculty," he "may be requested" to resign "by an affirmative vote of at least five members of the Faculty." If he failed to resign "within two days after service of such request in writing," a statement explaining the reasons for the request would be forwarded to the president of the University, for submission to the trustees.[30]

When the faculty met on the 23rd, Grinnell was asked if he had any response to the resolution adopted two days earlier. He declared that he had none. In accordance with the recently adopted amendment, a committee was directed to present the request to President Buckham, for submission to the Board of Trustees. After that action had been taken, the professors voted that Grinnell be paid 28/40ths of the dividend, since he had only delivered twenty-eight of the assigned forty lectures.

Three days later when the trustees gathered, they were informed that they could assume complete control of the Medical Department, since "either party to the existing contract . . . had the legal right to terminate the same, at will." The board in turn established a committee, which included Dr. Webb, to handle "the whole subject of the relations between the University and the Medical Department, and of any grievances that may be presented."[32] Everything was now in the hands of that committee. John Henry Jackson analyzed the comments of Benjamin Franklin Fifield, a member of the board and a supporter of Grinnell, and concluded that the faculty would find Fifield "acting as the keenest of lawyers in favor of his client." Fifield would admit that Grinnell "may not have filled his hours," but he would ask about the other professors, "notably Prof. Witthaus." Jackson predicted that an attempt would be made to appoint a new faculty, "under the immediate control of the university," with Grinnell as dean. Jackson reported to Tinkham that Linsley "is making much effort to support the ex-dean, and all his friends are working . . . to break down our charges and carry out the above programme."[33]

28. "Report of Committee appointed May 31 to investigate conduct of Prof. Grinnell," Grinnell Papers.

29. UVM Medical Faculty Minutes, June 21, 1899.

30. Ibid.

31. Ibid., June 23, 24, 1899.

32. UVM Trustee Minutes, June 26, 1899.

33. Jackson to Tinkham, Barre, July 15, 1899, Jackson file, Tinkham Papers.

The trustee committee held two meetings. At the second, on September 22, they heard statements from the two sides. The committee finally decided that the University had to assume complete control of the Department, and it suggested that the professors submit their resignations.[34] The following day the entire faculty resigned, presenting a letter expressing their hope that "this course will contribute to settle the present difficulty with regard to the retirement of Dr. Grinnell, and further lead to the Medical School becoming an integral part of the University, on the same basis as the other several departments." The letter concluded by declaring that the professors "*confidently hope* that in the reorganization of the Medical School, and in the selection of future Professors in years to come, the Medical Faculty will have . . . a voice in nominating candidates for any chair that may be vacant," as well as control over the general "management and direction of the courses of study." The letter was signed by the entire executive faculty—Grinnell, Tinkham, King, Jackson, Phelps, Witthaus, and Jenne.[35] With the resignation of the faculty there was no longer doubt about the right of the trustees to "take possession of the building and property of the Medical Department in the name of the University."[36]

Since it was too late to reorganize the faculty completely, and fearing that a drastic change would result in a significant decrease in enrollment, the trustees decided to reappoint the entire faculty for a one-year period. An attempt was made to eliminate Phelps, who had expressed a desire to resign, and Grinnell, who was not wanted by the other professors. The vote on an amendment to that effect resulted in a tie, 4 to 4, and so was defeated.[37] On October 20 President Buckham issued a public statement explaining the situation. He said that the entire faculty had been reappointed for the "ensuing year," so the "Medical Department may maintain as close a continuity as possible with its honorable past," and so "alumni and undergraduates may feel assured that no radical or revolutionary measures are contemplated in their dealing with the department."[38]

It appears that Grinnell had won: after all, the professors had failed in their attempt to remove him from the faculty. Yet the trustees did not support any of Grinnell's claims. On November 20, for instance, the executive committee of the board elected Tinkham dean of the medical faculty, and when Grinnell petitioned for a larger share of the proceeds than was awarded him by the faculty, the trustees refused to take action, declaring that "the determination of the matter . . . belongs to the Medical Department."[39]

On January 4, 1900, the faculty approved the schedule for the ensuing term; once again Grinnell protested. He declared that he was "unwilling that lectures continue after the month of March."[40] In spite of the fact that the College had developed a graded course

Tinkham Papers.

34. UVM Trustee Minutes, October 6, 1899.

35. UVM Medical Faculty Minutes, September 23, 1899.

36. UVM Trustee Minutes, October 6, 1899.

37. Ibid.

38. *Burlington Free Press and Times*, November 4, 1899.

39. UVM Trustees, Record of the Proceedings of the Executive Committee, November 20, and 24, 1899, UVM Archives.

40. UVM Medical Faculty Minutes, January 4, 1900.

consisting of 4 six-month terms, Grinnell insisted that the longer course was unnecessary. He wanted to retain the traditional four-month course.

In June 1900 the *Vermont Medical Monthly* published an editorial on the situation. The author noted: "For some time past rumors have been current to the effect that all or nearly all of the old faculty were to be dropped. Ridiculous stories concerning the incompetency of individual members of the faculty have been circulated, and though every bit of the so called information thus far promulgated has come from unofficial sources, it has served to create great uncertainty and much conjecture as to the ultimate outcome." Speaking for the alumni, the editor expressed his hope that "as many as possible of the old faculty should be retained." It would be ridiculous, he declared, to replace the faculty with strangers "who must necessarily lack the sentiment and sincerity which only comes from long association and experience in certain lines of work," and that such a change "will be unjust and certainly react to the detriment of the Department."[41]

The editor proceeded to discuss the various professors. Phelps and Witthaus had resigned, effective at the end of the 1900 term. Since the two men had extensive "metropolitan duties" and had "grown away from the institution," their work in Burlington had not been their major interest. Therefore, in spite of their prestige, their resignation "may have its good results after all." The editor credited Grinnell with placing the College "in the front rank of medical institutions." In addition, he noted, Grinnell's lectures were exceptionally popular. Students had found that he was not "infallible, perhaps, but always helpful, with scientific, up to date suggestions, criticizing where his extensive experience warranted, or commending where his judgment approved." He concluded that the "majority of the alumni" wanted Grinnell to continue as professor of the theory and practice of medicine.[42]

Then the editor commented on the work of the professor of obstetrics. "We have no fear of contradiction," he declared, "when we make the statement that Dr. A. F. A. King is one of the foremost teachers of obstetrics, not only in America, but in the whole world. . . . His withdrawal from the chair of obstetrics would certainly cripple the institution." Finally, the editor noted that Tinkham was a valuable member of the faculty. He had "been closely identified . . . with the success of the college." He was "full of enthusiasm for his subject and exceptionally capable as a teacher." "Dr. Tinkham has no equal as a lecturer on anatomy," the writer concluded, and "to place a new man in the exacting chair of anatomy at this particular crisis, would certainly handicap the Department."[43]

At the end of the 1900 course of lectures the trustees once again had to consider the question of reorganizing the medical faculty,

41. *Vermont Medical Monthly*, 6 (June 1900), 168–169.
42. Ibid., p. 169.
43. Ibid., pp. 170–171.

since in the previous year the professors had been appointed for only one term. Once again there was a great deal of lobbying in favor of Grinnell. Dr. Webb, who had helped the former dean retain his position, sent personal letters to his friends on the board, urging Grinnell's reappointment.[44]

When the trustees met on July 11, the executive committee recommended the appointment of Tinkham, Grinnell, and King, and the establishment of a committee, consisting of Buckham, King, and Tinkham, to "consider the reconstruction of the Medical Faculty." The recommendations were adopted, guaranteeing some continuity by appointing Tinkham, King, and Grinnell to the faculty.[45] Now that the trustees had given Grinnell a vote of confidence, quite different from the cavalier treatment he had received at the hands of his colleagues, he decided to resign.

On July 25 the special committee presented their report to the trustees. The recommendation was for the appointment of Jackson as professor of physiology, Jenne as professor of materia medica and therapeutics, John Brooks Wheeler as professor of surgery, and Horace L. White, of New York, as professor of chemistry. Wheeler and White would be appointed for one-year probationary periods. The committee requested more time to find a competent professor of theory and practice, the most important chair in any medical college, to succeed Grinnell. The report was accepted.[46]

After a search King learned that Aloysius O. J. Kelly, who had been instructor in clinical medicine at the University of Pennsylvania, might be interested in joining the faculty. Kelly's background was impeccable. He had received his undergraduate training at La Salle College, and in 1891 he was awarded a medical degree from the University of Pennsylvania. From 1892 to 1894 he studied with leading European physicians, and since 1894 he had been on the faculty at Pennsylvania and served as director of laboratories at the Philadelphia Polyclinic. During 1903–1907 he was to become editor of *International Clinics*, and from 1907 to 1911, when he died at the age of 40, he was to be editor of the *American Journal of the Medical Sciences*.

He was difficult to recruit, however, because he insisted on three conditions. First, he demanded that the University "inaugurate improvement in teaching medicine" by reducing the number of lectures and instituting practical clinical work. He advocated the use of "clinical conferences," in which several students would examine a patient, make a diagnosis, and prescribe treatment, after which the professor and his students would discuss the diagnosis and the treatment. For the first time, students would become active in the process of medical education at Burlington, rather than simply absorbing material through attendance at lectures and reading books. Kelly said that he required at least twenty beds "under his absolute control . . .

44. Webb to G. G. Benedict, New York City, July 9, 1900, Trustees File, UVM Archives. For more on the machinations on both sides, see the F. N. Baylies Folder, UVM Archives.

45. UVM Trustee Minutes, July 11, 1900.

46. Ibid., July 25, 1900. See also report of the committee, in Trustees File.

continuously throughout the year." Finally, he demanded that no "incompetent men be graduated, no matter what their social, political, or professional backing." King informed Kelly that "as far as practicable" his provisions would be accepted.[47] A. O. J. Kelly was then appointed professor of theory and practice.

The problems of the period from 1898 to 1900 had been solved. Grinnell, who represented the old proprietary system, had been replaced by a well educated professor who was committed to reform. For the College to remain in existence, men like Grinnell, who thought in terms of numbers of students, had to be eliminated in favor of men like Kelly, who thought in terms of quality education. With the appointment of Kelly the University's Medical School came into the twentieth century with a great deal of hope for the future. Although the experienced and prestigious New Yorkers—Darling, Wright, Phelps, Little, and Witthaus—were gone and replaced by "Vermont men," the School had taken a significant step toward repudiating its proprietary past.

47. King to Buckham, Washington, D.C., November 1, 1900, King Folder, Tinkham Papers.

Chapter Eight

Development of the Physical Plant, 1829–1904

AS NOTED EARLIER, the Medical College Building had been constructed in 1829 to house the University's first medical school. From 1836, when lectures were discontinued, until the 1854 reorganization of the Medical Department, the Building was used by the chemistry professor. In 1854 the Corporation allowed the medical professors to reoccupy the building on condition that they keep it in repair. Low enrollment and the resulting financial problems made that difficult if not impossible; yet the trustees insisted that the faculty maintain the property.[1]

President Calvin Pease decided that renovation of the Building was necessary to maintain the Medical College and at the same time ensure the presence of a professor capable of teaching natural science without the Corporation having to pay his entire salary. Pease directed a campaign that raised enough money to remodel the Building. The work began in 1858; by the following year a third story had been added, the amphitheatre had been expanded, and the Building could accommodate more students in greater comfort than ever before.[2]

By 1875, however, the Building was "very much in need of repairs" and the faculty asked the trustees to help in making improvements that would "seem necessary to preserve the Building from decay."[3] Since the faculty was supposed to keep the building in repair, the trustees made no response to the request. In 1879 the faculty invited an architect to suggest plans for renovating the Building; after his presentation the professors established a building committee, consisting of Carpenter and Grinnell, who were directed to discuss the

1. Above, Chapter 5.
2. Ibid.
3. A. P. Grinnell to Matthew Buckham, Burlington, July 9, 1875, Trustee File, UVM Archives.

matter with the Board.[4] Once again the trustees provided no assistance, but this time the faculty decided to raise its own funds to finance the renovation.

In June 1880 the committee reported that it had paid a total of $2,116.81 for renovations, which included the installation of gas in the museum, the laboratories, and the lower lecture room. A public subscription raised $1,957.38, which left only $159.43 to be paid by the faculty.[5] The improvements were only a stop-gap measure, however. Increasing enrollment made necessary a larger building. In 1874 the Medical Department had a class of 51. In 1877 enrollment had increased to 90. Four years later, in 1881, 171 students attended medical lectures.[6] Much of this increase was due to Grinnell's enthusiastic search for prospective students. When the Building had been expanded back in 1858, enrollment was no more than 60; it had therefore tripled in less than twenty-five years.

In June 1881 the faculty discussed the need to increase the number of seats in the amphitheatre.[7] It was decided not to make any renovations, however—possibly because the trustees would not finance them and the public would not donate again after so little time had elapsed. The situation did not improve. In reporting the 1883 commencement, a local newspaper noted that "the limits of the present building" had been reached and "it has become a serious question as to what shall be done for the accommodation of the next class and succeeding classes." The matter was crucial, the editor wrote, "and the friends of the department hardly know what to do."[8]

It did not take long for a public-spirited citizen to respond. John Purple Howard, a local philanthropist, offered to buy the Underwood property on the north side of the College Green and "convert" it into a medical building. Once the residence of Harry Bradley, president of the Rutland and Burlington Railroad, it had been purchased and renovated by Levi Underwood. Howard's proposal included converting the old Medical Building into a gymnasium. The executive committee of the Board of Trustees voted to accept the offer provided that the medical faculty would transfer to the University all rights to the old Building and agreed to spend at least $250 a year to maintain the new building and its grounds.[9] When the faculty accepted those provisions, work on the new building began.

On November 28, 1883, the *University Cynic* reported that a mansard roof and cupola were in place. The walls of the top floor had been raised an additional half story, to provide enough room for the seats inside the amphitheatre, which would hold some 350 students. The *Cynic* stated that the "renovated structure will be a great improvement upon the old building in comfort as well as in convenience," but it predicted that if the enrollment continued to increase, "even this enlarged structure" would "be all to small."[10] By the end

4. UVM Medical Faculty Minutes, June 26, 1879.

5. Ibid., June 26, 1877, June 9, 1880.

6. Figures developed from the Medical College catalogues.

7. UVM Medical Faculty Minutes, June 3, 1881.

8. Unidentified newspaper clipping. UVM Medical Faculty Minutes, 1875–93, p. 113.

9. UVM Trustees, Record of the Proceedings of the Executive Committee, September 29, 1883.

10. *University Cynic*, November 28, 1883, p. 97.

11. Ibid., February
27, 1884, p. 143. See
Burlington Free Press,
March 7, 1884, p. 3,
col. 2, for reports of
the inaugural exer-
cises for the "new"
building.

12. *University
Cynic*, March 19,
1884, p. 155.

13. UVM Medical
Department, *31st
Annual Announce-
ment* (Burlington,
1883), pp. 4–5.

of February the museum had been moved into the new Building
and preparations were being made for the start of the 1884 course,
to begin early in March.[11] After the start of the course the *Cynic*
described the new building, emphasizing the roomy accommodations. The editor noted, however, that "considerable complaint" had
been made about the seats in the amphitheatre. Only a few had been
cushioned, and the *Cynic* declared that if they all were to be "so
fixed it would add much to the comfort of the students."[12]

The new Building was described in the college catalogue as "a substantial brick structure" with seating capacity for 350 students. It
had a "thoroughly appointed and commodious Laboratory of Practical Chemistry," and a dissecting room three times as large as the
one in the old Building with "all the modern conveniences and com-
forts." The structure included a "reading room," where students
could "consult the current medical literature and journals of the day."
The Building was heated by steam and was well ventilated.[13]

After the professors moved in, however, they began to wonder

*5. The second College
of Medicine, acquired
in 1884 by gift of John
Purple Howard, Bur-
lington philanthropist.
This was the former
residence of Lieutenant
Governor Levi Under-
wood, situated on the
site of the present
Dewey Hall. It re-
quired extensive alter-
ations to make it suita-
ble for use as a medical
building.*

if they had made a mistake in agreeing to the provisions of Howard's donation. First, they were worried about the "possibility of a rival school getting possession of the old building." President Buckham informed the trustees of the anxiety among the medical faculty, recommending that some action be taken to "set their minds at rest." In response the board voted to amend the agreement between the Corporation and the faculty by adding a stipulation restricting the old Building "to some use other than for a Medical School or Department."[14]

Then the professors realized that the accommodations in the new Building were so far from ideal that immediate alterations were required. The sources do not indicate exactly what the problems were, but after the 1884 term the Building "received a thorough renovation."[15] The situation must have been intolerable, for the professors took the unprecedented step of spending $4500 of their own money, reducing their salaries from $2000 in 1884 to $800 in 1885.[16] The faculty then voted to initiate a fund-raising campaign, with the proceeds to be divided—each full professor to receive $1125 and each holder of a "half-chair" to receive $562.50. The rationale was that the "repairs were permanent in their nature, and more for the future benefit of the school than for the present advantage of the Medical Faculty, as now constituted." Therefore the current professors should not bear the burden of paying for the renovation. The professors apparently decided that it was worth while to approach Howard, who had paid for the earlier remodeling. Dean Grinnell was directed to see if Howard wished "to participate in the liquidation of the indebtedness" of the faculty.[17] There is no record of Howard's response.

In 1879 a hospital opened which would soon develop into a teaching institution loosely attached to the School. The developments leading to establishment of the hospital had begun in 1876. Influenced by their family physician, Walter Carpenter, two of Burlington's prominent citizens—Thaddeus R. Fletcher and his wife, Mary—expressed a desire to endow a hospital with part of their estate. After they both died, their daughter, Mary Fletcher, who herself suffered from tuberculosis, decided to push ahead with the plan. Encouraged by Carpenter, she donated a total of $150,000, one third of which was to be used for the construction of the hospital, with the rest to provide for the continuing support of the institution.[18] The hospital was named by Miss Fletcher in honor of her mother, Mary.

Carpenter was placed in charge of the entire project. He formed a corporation and secured a charter. Then the Board of Directors, with Carpenter as President, hired a Boston architect, W. P. Wentworth.[19] The medical faculty was asked to participate by making specific recommendations for the organization of the medical and surgical staff, and to make suggestions for the construction of the medical and

14. President's Annual Report, June 1884, President's Reports File, UVM Archives. UVM Trustee Minutes, June 25, 1884.

15. *University Cynic*, April 1, 1885, p. 140.

16. Figures developed from UVM Medical Department Cash Book, 1875–1890, UVM Archives.

17. UVM Medical Faculty Minutes, June 26, 1885.

18. Mary Fletcher Hospital Board of Directors, Minutes, December 6, 1876, Administrator's Office, MFH.

19. Vermont Medical Society, *Transactions, 1893* (Burlington, 1893), pp. 224ff.

surgical wings. The professors developed a plan for construction and then made specific suggestions for the staff. Carpenter would serve as physician-in-chief, with James Lawrence Little as surgeon-in-chief. There would be two attending physicians, one of them Grinnell, and two attending surgeons, including Leroy M. Bingham. There would be three consulting physicians, including A. F. A. King, and three consulting surgeons, including Samuel White Thayer and Henry J. Holton. The Board of Directors voted to approve all the recommendations made by the medical faculty; the proposed medical and surgical staff was appointed.[20]

Construction was completed in January 1879. The building was located on the hill east of the campus, on the site of the former Catlin residence. The center of the hospital was an impressive four-story building, which included offices, two "large pavillion Wards," and rooms for private patients. In a separate building, connected to the offices and wards by a corridor, was a large operating room in the center of an amphitheatre seating nearly 200 persons. There also was "an anaesthetizing and a recovery room, opening into the amphitheatre." For post-mortem examinations the hospital had "a Pathological room" with about one hundred seats for students to observe the examinations. To the rear of the buildings were a vegetable cellar, a "dead house," a barn, and a stable. The thirty-five acres surrounding the hospital were to be used as farmland, to provide food for the patients.

The total cost of construction was 50 percent higher than expected. Purchase of the land took $25,000, and the construction cost $50,000. Miss Fletcher paid the difference and then increased the endowment to $110,000, which would provide an income of $7000 a year to pay for "the running expenses of the hospital."[21]

The Mary Fletcher Hospital was formally dedicated on January 22, 1879. It was a significant occasion, not only to celebrate the completion of a teaching hospital for the Medical College, but to dedicate the first nondenominational hospital in the state of Vermont. The main address was given by D. B. St. John Roosa, the prominent New York opthalmologist and one of the College's special professors. He noted the philanthropic work of Mary Fletcher, who also gave Burlington a public library. Then he described the significance of the Hospital in medical education. "A hospital *is* a medical school," he exclaimed. "If our lawyers go wrong we may lose our property; if our doctors go wrong, we may lose our lives. How are they to go right?" he asked. The answer was simple—through "experience." "How shall they get this experience?" The response was simple: "Generally, in hospitals."[22]

In his memoirs John Brooks Wheeler described the public attitude toward the Mary Fletcher Hospital. When he became a member of

20. UVM Medical Faculty Minutes, June 23 and 24, 1877. MFH Board of Directors, Minutes, August 20, 1877.

21. UVM Medical Department, *26th Annual Announcement, 1879* (Burlington, 1878), p. 10. *Burlington Free Press and Times*, January 23, 1879, p. 2, col. 1.

22. *Burlington Free Press and Times*, January 23, 1879, p. 2, col. 1.

the surgical staff in 1883, "people had not become hospital-minded." As with hospitals elsewhere, it was considered as a place for strangers and paupers to die. When Wheeler arrived, the institution was only five years old and "fifteen patients were considered a pretty good number." During the college term, when surgical clinics were held and prominent specialists came to Burlington, the number of patients increased. At all other times the Hospital was practically empty. Eventually "the 'horror of a hospital' and the dread of experimentation" subsided and "the number of patients gradually increased." At that point "more room had to be provided."[23]

The College now had a teaching Hospital, which helped it compete with city schools for students. In the early years, however, the Hospital did not provide enough experience. Only when the specialists came to town were there enough cases to observe. The Hospital would not admit anyone suffering from a contagious disease, and it had no maternity ward. Moreover, neither patients with chronic ailments nor those suffering from mental or nervous disorders were considered "suitable subjects for admission." The Hospital was for surgical cases and for short-term medical ones.[24]

In 1885 the Hospital's medical committee recommended the addition of a lying-in ward, but no action was taken by the Board of Directors. In 1887 the directors voted to build another pavillion ward and a maternity ward, and a committee was appointed to develop specific plans. When the committee reported, however, it recommended the construction of a new pavillion ward and an "isolating ward" for contagious diseases, but it declared that more time was needed to study the feasibility of a maternity ward.[25] Perhaps the directors hesitated to provide obstetrical care because of moral questions. Since the Hospital was a public charity, they might have feared that a free lying-in ward would sanction illegitimacy. It was not until well into the twentieth century that the Hospital finally added a maternity ward, and then only because it was required if the College was to remain in existence.

In 1882, responding to a desperate need for well prepared nurses, the directors decided to establish a training school. As a result of the introduction of antiseptic techniques and the use of anaesthesia, surgery had become safer and more effective than ever before. By the 1870's and 1880's, hospitals were more acceptable because they were no longer places where paupers and strangers went to die, or pesthouses where diseased patients were isolated. And there was a corresponding need for a larger number of well-trained nurses. Society no longer could depend on the uneducated, often drunken Sairy Gamp characters of the past. In 1873 Dr. Susan Dimock, Marie Zakrzewska's assistant at the New England Hospital for Women and Children, began a training school based on the German dea-

23. John Brooks Wheeler, *Memoirs of a Small Town Surgeon*, p. 180.

24. *Burlington Free Press and Times*, March 16, 1882, p. 3, col. 4.

25. Mary Fletcher Hospital Board of Directors, Minutes, May 11, June 1, 1885; January 5 and 17, 1887.

conness system. That same year the Bellevue Hospital training school was established, following the methods developed in England by Florence Nightingale. The Bellevue experiment was followed by others at the New Haven Hospital and the Massachusetts General Hospital.[26] Nine years later, in 1882, the Mary Fletcher Hospital began its program to train professional nurses.

The thirteen students who enrolled in the first class were to receive their training from some of the best medical men in Vermont, including several instructors in the University's medical department. Hiram Atwater, instructor in obstetrics and diseases of women and children at the Medical School, taught the care of lying-in women and infants. A. J. Willard, instructor in chemistry and toxicology, taught the "general conduct of nurses and their duties in emergencies," as well as "the inspection of discharges from the body." A. P. Grinnell taught anatomy and physiology to the student nurses. William B. Lund, an attending surgeon at the Hospital and instructor of materia medica and therapeutics at the College, taught hygiene, the administration of remedies, and care of the helpless. Leroy A. Bingham, also an attending surgeon, taught surgical nursing and dressings, as well as cupping and leeching, two remnants of the age of heroic medicine. Finally, Mrs. Laura J. Waite, the head nurse, gave lessons on practical instruction at the bedside and preparation of food for the sick. Nursing students had to be between the ages of 20 and 40, provide certificates of good health and moral character, and pay the ten dollar fee in advance.[27]

President Buckham spoke at the opening of the training school on May 3, 1882. He noted that "Fiction and the Drama have represented the Nurse as one of the most repulsive of our species, ignorant, insolent, thievish, gluttonous, bibulous, garrulous, the dread of young mothers, the bugbear of children, the horror of doctors, the loathed of all mankind, and yet apparently one of those necessary evils with which it has pleased an inscrutable Providence to afflict mankind." He predicted that the training school would serve three purposes. It would "supply an immediate and pressing want of our own State, that of competent nurses for private families." In addition the School would "do something toward training a class of professional nurses." Finally, it would "furnish women who are adapted to it, an honorable and remunerative employment."[28] With these three objectives the Mary Fletcher Hospital Training School began its first course.

With the Hospital providing some clinical experience for the medical students, with the training school preparing "a class of professional nurses," and with the new Medical Building opening in 1884, the School had at least for the present solved the physical problems involved in providing a medical education. In 1890, though, when

26. For trends in nursing history, see Lavinia L. Dock and Isabel M. Stewart, *A Short History of Nursing* (New York and London, 1938), pp. 146ff; and Elizabeth M. Jamieson and Mary F. Sewall, *Trends in Nursing History* (4th ed., Philadelphia and London, 1954), pp. 297ff.

27. Mary Fletcher Hospital Training School for Nurses, *Announcement, 1882* (Burlington, 1882).

28. *Daily Free Press and Times*, May 4, 1882, p. 3, col. 2.

enrollment exceeded 200, the faculty decided that better accommodations were needed. Specifically, the professors hoped to raise enough money "to erect in the near future a building to be devoted exclusively to the teaching of anatomy, physiology and pathology."[29] When Grinnell appeared before the trustees to plead for additional funds, he received little attention. The matter was referred to a committee, which did not even submit a report. One of the members of the committee, however, George G. Benedict, editor of the *Free Press*, responded by publishing an editorial calling on philanthropic citizens to donate money to help the Medical School attain excellence.[30]

In 1892 Grinnell once again appeared before the board. He described "the urgent needs of the Medical Department, especially for additions and larger lecture rooms." The following year the scene was replayed, this time with some success. The trustees agreed that the lecturers on special subjects be provided with additional accommodations "in the new science building to be erected," as long as rooms were not needed for students in the academic department of the University.[31]

In June 1893 the faculty established a committee, consisting of King and Witthaus, to propose specific changes to improve the facilities, and to "ascertain whether and how the required funds can be obtained." They reported that it was necessary to renovate the Building and to provide additional laboratories and one more recitation room. President Buckham had informed them that although the University could not pay for any renovations, the Corporation might be able to loan $5,000 at a "high interest rate"—between 6 and 8 percent. They recommended that the money be used to provide more laboratory facilities in the basic sciences. Their recommendation was accepted.[32]

In January 1894 the *University Cynic* reported that the Medical Building had been "quite extensively repaired during the vacation." "Four of the Grecian pillars on the porch have been removed, which makes a decided improvement in the looks." In addition, the lecturer's platform in the amphitheatre had been elevated and the laboratory had been enlarged. Now the laboratories would accommodate "about three times as many students as formerly." In any case, even if the laboratories in the Medical Building were still inadequate, the Williams Science Hall was under construction, and when it was completed the medical students were "to be supplied with ample accommodations for laboratory work."[33]

In January 1897 the *Cynic* noted that nearly 200 students had matriculated in the Medical Department. It declared that "the time was fast advancing when a new building will be necessary" to accommodate the ever-increasing number of students.[34] In June of that same year the medical faculty set up a committee, consisting of

29. UVM Medical Faculty Minutes, June 20, 1890. *Burlington Free Press and Times*, July 17, 1890, p. 4, col. 3.

30. UVM Trustee Minutes, June 25, 1890. *Burlington Free Press and Times*, July 17, 1890, p. 4, col. 3.

31. UVM Trustee Minutes, June 27, 1892; June 26, 1893.

32. UVM Medical Faculty Minutes, June 6 and 23, 1893.

33. *University Cynic*, January 13, 1894, p. 147. UVM Medical Department, *42nd Annual Announcement, 1895* (Burlington, 1895), p. 6.

34. *University Cynic*, January 25, 1897, p. 141.

Grinnell, King, and Witthaus, to confer with the trustees about the need for additional room for laboratories. Again, nothing was done to solve the problem, but the trustees *were* willing to discuss the future relations between the Medical Department and the Corporation, with a view to having the University take over complete control of the Medical School.[35] This explains why the trustees were so hesitant to help the School—increasing enrollment meant additional compensation for the professors and no monetary benefit for the University.

By the first few years of the twentieth century everyone had agreed that the Medical School needed a new building, one that would include the laboratory facilities essential for modern scientifically oriented medical education. The *Vermont Medical Monthly* noted that with the four-year graded course and its numerous lectures, recitations, and laboratories, the "old building had been taxed to its utmost, and it has been found necessary to establish several laboratories outside of the building proper."[36] In December 1903 the problem was resolved: a fire destroyed the Medical Building.

The fire began about eleven o'clock in the morning of December 3, while the members of an obstetrics class were in the amphitheatre waiting for the arrival of Clarence H. Beecher, the instructor. "There was always smoking in the ten minutes' interval between lectures," and according to John Brooks Wheeler, "somebody's cigar stub fell through a crack" in the boards under the seats, landing in a pile of "college catalogues and other pamphlets" which were stored there.[37] "One of the students noticed a tiny column of smoke coming from a crack in the floor beneath the seats" and he turned to ask "who was under the seats smoking." By the time he could get an answer, the "blaze was in sight." "A hasty scramble followed." The fire alarm was activated and while waiting for the fire engines the students formed a bucket brigade. "When the fire department arrived upon the scene everything seemed to go wrong." It took a long time to connect the hoses to the hydrants, and then it was discovered that the steamer was out of order. It took thirty minutes before a substantial stream of water "could be poured into the burning building." Then the pressure was so inadequate that the water "barely reached the sills of the second story windows."[38]

When it become obvious that the Building was going to burn to the ground, the students and professors tried to rescue the valuables— the books from the library, specimens from the museum, and a large number of cadavers. The cadavers were "shrouded in old matting, carpeting or anything that would cover them," and they were carried out the rear to an empty barn in the back. When the fire reached the chemical laboratory there were several explosions. At about 3:30

35. UVM Medical Faculty Minutes, June 14, 1897; June 17, July 1, 1897.

36. *Vermont Medical Monthly*, 8 (June 23, 1902), 169–170.

37. Wheeler, *Memoirs of a Small Town Surgeon*, p. 183.

38. *Burlington Daily Free Press*, December 3, 1903, p. 1, cols. 2–3; p. 4, col. 1.

6. *Fire destroying the second Medical College Building, December 3, 1903.*

in the afternoon, after having burned for over four hours, the fire was extinguished. All that remained were the four walls.[39]

There were few tears shed. The Building was hopelessly outdated, and many observers noted that the fire had performed a service, especially since the Building was insured. The student yearbook, *Ariel*, described the fire in the fashion of Finley Peter Dunne's "Mr. Dooley." According to Dooley, there were a lot of precautions against fire. For instance, when the boys smoked between classes, "there wuz shthrict rules against their shwallering so much as a cigarette shtump fur fear av sottin' things afoire." Then, there was "a fassit in th' fur corner av th' cillar, an another wan at Mrs. Lee's, within a quarther av a moile." When the fire started, the alarm was set; nineteen minutes later "th' grand band-wagon" came over from the fire station "wan square away." Then, the firemen lined up, called the roll, gave each other the "brotherhood grip," and stood at attention while the chief read the by-laws of the Fireman's Union.[40]

Finally the chief decided to get to the business at hand, putting out the fire. First the firemen smashed all the downstairs windows, to make a good draft. Then they were ready to start pouring water on the fire, but they found that the steamer was broken and "squitin' wather in ivery diriction at oncet." At that point in the proceedings, someone thought of the "poor corpses up in th' dissecting room" and how they might "be wantin' a brith av frish air." This resulted in a "grrusome procission av shtiffs" being evacuated from the building. Finally Mr. Dooley commented on the "poor doctors" who were watching the fire. "They shid a tear, now an' agin, fur appearance's sake," while they quietly discussed whether brownstone or white marble should be used in the *"new* Midical College Building."[41]

That same afternoon the medical faculty met at President Buckham's house to arrange for temporary quarters. Buckham offered the use of recitation rooms in the college buildings. Joseph Hills, dean of the department of agriculture, and George H. Perkins, dean of the department of natural sciences, offered the use of rooms "occupied by them, so far as it was possible." On behalf of the directors, Buckham offered the use of the Hospital's amphitheatre. Other meetings were held on the following two days; finally it was decided to use the chemical laboratory in the Old Mill, the Hospital amphitheatre, and the "old Vilas house" on the corner of Pearl and Prospect. Thus the Medical School was able to resume classes less than one week after the fire had completely destroyed the Medical Building.[42]

On April 8, 1904, the trustees instructed Tinkham to have preliminary plans drawn for construction of new accommodations. Later that month a fund-raising campaign began. The *Vermont Medical Monthly* asked alumni to donate from $25 to $50 to help pay for the new building.[43] In July the trustees approved the construction of a

39. Ibid. See also Wheeler, p. 184.

40. *Ariel*, 18 (1905), 253–254.

41. Ibid., pp. 255–256.

42. For Tinkham's description, see UVM Medical Faculty Minutes, June 20, 1904. See also *Burlington Free Press*, December 3, 1903, p. 1, col. 3; December 4, 1903, p. 5, col. 6.

43. UVM Trustees, Record of the Proceedings of the Executive Committee, April 8, 1904. *Vermont Medical Monthly*, 10 (April 26, 1904), p. 93.

7. Dean Henry Crain Tinkham speaking at the laying of the cornerstone of the third Medical School Building, 1904.

8. The completed structure, now known as Dewey Hall. This photograph was taken about 1960.

University of Vermont
College of Medicine

9. The Mary Fletcher
Hospital in 1899. Left
to right: *Main build-*
ing (Fletcher House);
first amphitheatre (la-
ter replaced by the
Surgical building and
amphitheatre); and the
nurses' home (de-
stroyed by fire in
1948).

10. The Hospital
entrance in 1899.

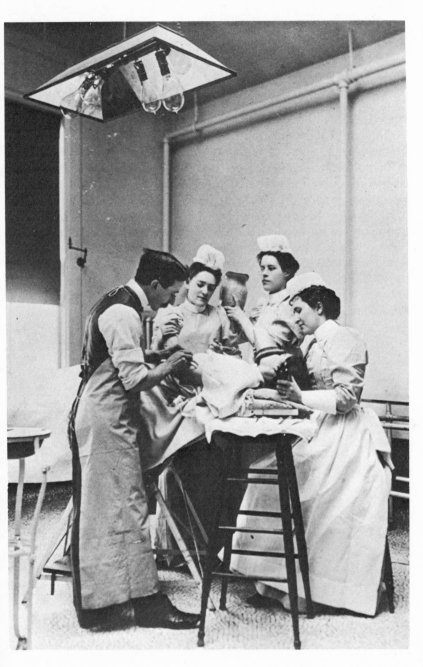

*11. An operation in the
Mary Fletcher Hospi-
tal in the early 1900's.
Dr. Frank Norris,
Edith Kinsley, R.N.,
Mary Monroe, R.N.,
Minnie Hollister,
R.N.*

44. UVM Trustee
Minutes, July 4,
1904. UVM Trustees,
Record of the Pro-
ceedings of the
Executive Commit-
tee, July 25, 1904.

45. *University
Cynic*, July 8, 1905, p.
50. For description
of the new building
see October 8, 1904,
p. 113.

new and completely modern building, costing $80,000, provided that the medical faculty agreed to pay 4 percent interest on a loan of $30,000.[44] On August 25 the contract for the new building was awarded to the Champlain Manufacturing Company, with completion set for May 1, 1905. The new building was to be large enough to accommodate the medical class easily, and it was to have adequate laboratory facilities in the basic sciences. The building was dedicated on June 27, 1905, on Alumni Day. It was planned to hold the ceremonies on the steps of the main entrance. Unfortunately, "shortly after four o'clock gathering clouds foretold a shower" and the exercises were moved to the second floor amphitheatre. The ceremonies included speeches by President Buckham, Dean Tinkham, and Dr. J. H. Woodward, as well as a major address by A. F. A. King on the history of the Medical School.[45] When classes began, the Medical School was located in a thoroughly modern building for the first time in its recent history. The School had moved from one side of the College Green to the other, and had gone through two buildings. As it entered the modern era, it had a building that was suited for the laboratory approach to medical education.

Chapter Nine

Curriculum Development, 1870–1900

IN 1873 members of the Vermont Medical Society heard Dr. Edward
S. Peck, of Burlington, present a paper on "Modern Medical Education." Peck totally disagreed with the traditional system, which
forced students to sit through the same lectures in two different
terms, and he predicted that the quality of education would substantially improve if a graded system were adopted. He called for the
study of anatomy and other basic sciences in the first term, followed
by a year of advanced subjects—theory and practice, obstetrics, and
surgery. For the first time there would be order to the curriculum.
No longer would the lectures be too advanced for half the students
and too simple for the rest.[1]

No action was taken on Peck's suggestions, but at the same meeting of the Society a significant step was taken to improve the relationship between the Society and the University. After a conference with
some of the professors, the Society unanimously adopted a resolution
authorizing the president to attend final examinations and to sign
diplomas.[2] This was important for both the Medical School and the
Society, for it allowed the Society to influence the professors to reform their methods, and it meant that a diploma from the University
would be more valuable, representing the approval of the Society
as well as the faculty.

In specific terms, however, there was little change in the program
at the University. Students in the Medical Department continued
to sit through two courses of lectures and then present themselves
for examination before the faculty. There were no entrance requirements, except that each student was to have studied with a preceptor

1. Vermont Medi-
cal Society, Minutes,
June 26, 1873.

2. Ibid.

for three full years. As indicated earlier, that did not ensure that students came prepared, for many preceptors were happy to have an apprentice who would clean the office and tend to the horse. A number of students were apparently admitted to the program without having served their three years as long as they also enrolled in the preliminary private course.[3]

Once admitted, students were exempted from other rules. The faculty met several times each year to vote on requests for special consideration. In 1875 the professors voted to sell tickets to a student who instead of paying in cash presented a promissory note, "satisfactorily endorsed." They also voted to allow this student to take final examinations, even though he had attended only one course of lectures. The student thus favored had practiced medicine for seven years and attended lectures in a dental school. In other cases the faculty voted to hold diplomas until students reached the age of 21 or until they had studied three full years with a preceptor.[4]

Because of low standards and the willingness of professors to waive regulations when petitioned to do so, it was inevitable that some graduates would prove incompetent. This was demonstrated in 1875 when the president of the Northern New York Medical Association called attention "to a notorious case of malpractice by the use of morphia." Gilman E. Baldwin, the doctor, had graduated in 1873. The professors apparently had waived some of the requirements for him, since an investigatory committee reported that the faculty had granted Baldwin a degree "under misapprehension of the law."[5]

In 1876 the faculty was forced to evaluate the entire program. A committee representing several American medical schools decided to call a convention of all schools in Philadelphia in June 1876. Headed by John B. Biddle of the Jefferson Medical College, the committee hoped to initiate reform of the medical curriculum. Previous attempts at reform, like the Northampton conference of 1827, had failed because of fear that raising standards in some schools would drive students to low standard schools. The University of Vermont was invited to send delegates to the Philadelphia meeting, and Henry D. Holton, professor of materia medica and pathology, was appointed to represent the faculty.[6] The meeting was attended by representatives of fewer than half of all medical colleges, and the University of Vermont was the only New England school to send a delegate.[7] After the election of officers, a committee was established to develop agenda. Holton was appointed to that committee, along with Eli Geddings of the Medical College of South Carolina and Samuel Gross of the Jefferson Medical College. Then the delegates decided that reform of medical education was so crucial that they would hold annual meetings, and that this convention would be considered as

3. See Martin Kaufman, *American Medical Education: The Formative Years*, chapter 7, for a thorough description of the traditional system.

4. UVM Medical Faculty Minutes, April 7, 1875, May 20, 1876.

5. Vermont Medical Society, *Transactions, 1874, 1875, and 1876* (St. Albans, 1877), pp. 403–404.

6. UVM Medical Faculty Minutes, May 20, 1876.

7. *Medical Record*, 11 (July 1, 1876), 432–434.

the first of a "provisional" Association of American Medical Colleges.[8]

The delegates discussed whether to condemn the "beneficiary system" of giving scholarships to fill empty benches and to attract students who might have attended competing institutions. Colleges offering "beneficiaries" were able to advertise large classes, which symbolized success, and recover financial losses by collecting matriculation and graduation fees. The delegates decided that the "indiscriminate use" of beneficiaries was unjust and except in unusual cases should be eliminated.

The delegates also debated whether there should be a minimum period between enrollment and graduation. That was a serious question, for many students were attending two terms in the same year and graduating from medical school nine months after the beginning of their first course. After some debate the delegates voted that no college could graduate a student who had enrolled for his first course during that year, or within fifteen months of entrance.

In another decision the delegates expressed their support for a graded curriculum, to replace the traditional nongraded one. The professors voted to retain graduation fees, even though some considered them detrimental, since professors could benefit financially by passing unprepared students. The first meeting of the Association of American Medical Colleges was valuable, promising to bring about cooperation in raising standards. It remained to be seen, however, if the colleges would really improve, and if reform was possible without the cooperation of all, including those not represented at the meeting.

In June 1877 the Association met in Chicago. Once again the University of Vermont sent a delegate, Adrian T. Woodward, the special professor of the surgical diseases of women. When the constitution of the Association was prepared, Woodward signed it and thus signified that the University of Vermont was committed to reform.[9] Later that same month the faculty revised the regulations of the Medical Department and adopted a provision stating that the "requirements for graduation shall be identical with those described in the By-Laws of the American Medical College Association."[10]

As long as the Association did not insist upon immediate reform, the professors could be firm supporters of increased requirements. At its 1878 meeting, however, the Association moved from oratory to action. The delegates decided that member institutions had to raise standards, probably assuming that the public would recognize the advantages of engaging doctors who were graduates of the better schools. In any case, in 1878 and 1879 the delegates voted to require members of the Association to lengthen the term from sixteen to twenty weeks. Moreover, they began to discuss the possibility of adopting a uniform, graded curriculum.[11]

8. Association of American Medical Colleges, *History of Its Organization* (Detroit, 1877). The following description of the 1876 meeting is developed from this source.

9. Ibid., p. 11.

10. UVM Medical Faculty Minutes, June 23, 1877.

11. See Kaufman, *American Medical Education*, chapter 9, for a description of the developments surrounding the history of the Association of American Medical Colleges.

As soon as the Association became more militant, the professors at Burlington began to have second thoughts about their involvement in the reform movement. On June 24, 1878, the faculty voted to correspond with the secretary, Leartus Connor, "regarding our relations with the American College Association."[12] It can be assumed that the faculty hesitated to lengthen the term when other colleges in New England would continue with the traditional sixteen-week courses. In 1879 the convention of the Association began with the announcement that Dartmouth had to withdraw from membership, since it was unable to lengthen its term.[13] Now Vermont, if it remained a member, would be the only reforming institution in New England.

At that 1879 meeting, in early June, the delegates discussed the possibility of requiring preliminary examinations and whether member institutions could offer a three-year graded course of studies. By late June the faculty at Burlington had come to the conclusion that it could not remain in the Association. With no other New England school raising standards, it was obvious that adopting a three-year course, lengthening the term to twenty weeks, and requiring preliminary examinations would reduce enrollment and destroy the College. On June 25, 1879, the professors voted that since the University's Medical Department "cannot comply with all the present by-laws & regulations" of the Association, it was forced to withdraw from membership.[14] The University was in good company—at the same time New York's College of Physicians and Surgeons and the Bellevue Hospital Medical College resigned from membership, actions undoubtedly related to the fact that New York University continued to offer the traditional two-year course, with sixteen-week terms.[15]

In 1876, the year of the founding of the Association of American Medical Colleges, the Vermont state legislature had adopted an "Act to Regulate the Practice of Medicine and Surgery in the State of Vermont." The act required state and local medical societies to establish boards of censors, to examine aspiring practitioners of medicine, surgery, or midwifery, and license those who were qualified. The act did not apply to several categories of physician, however, and that made it virtually inoperative. First, it provided that possession of a medical diploma was evidence of qualification, regardless of the standards of the college or the training of the individual concerned. Moreover, the bill did not apply to the practice of dentistry, or to midwifery practiced by women in their home towns. Finally, those who had practiced in Vermont for the past five years were exempt from the provisions of the law.[16]

This type of legislation was typical of the period. Assuming that physicians who had graduated from medical college were qualified

12. UVM Medical Faculty Minutes, June 24, 1878.

13. A.A.M.C., *Proceedings, 1879* (Detroit, 1879), p. 8.

14. UVM Medical Faculty Minutes, June 25, 1879. A.A.M.C., *Proceedings, 1880* (Detroit, 1880), p. 7.

15. A.A.M.C., *Proceedings, 1880*, pp. 6–10.

16. Vermont Medical Society, *Transactions, 1878* (St. Albans, 1879), pp. 69ff.

to practice medicine, legislators usually stipulated that a diploma was evidence of qualification. Because of the low quality of medical education, however, possession of a diploma meant very little. After all, the "physician" might have bought his diploma from one of the many diploma mills in operation at the time, and even if he had graduated, he might be totally unqualified to practice medicine: he might have been graduated so that his preceptor would continue to send apprentices to that school, for example, or so that the professors could collect the graduation fee. Moreover, the law protected no one from the "class of frauds commonly known as traveling quacks, who migrate from place to place." [17]

At the 1876 meeting of the Vermont Medical Society, the president, Dr. L. C. Butler, reported that he had attended the commencement at the University of Vermont. He was upset at the low quality of the graduates, and he declared that "in this mid-day of science and progress, a good preliminary education is absolutely essential to the success and usefulness of the practitioner of medicine." Dr. S. S. Clark, who was present at the final examinations, "deplored the lamentable deficiency in the preliminary education of some of the students." He concluded his report by presenting resolutions providing that every practitioner require his apprentices to have either "a good Academic education" or "a qualification sufficient to enter a Vermont college," demonstrated by possession of a certificate signed by a majority of the Board of Censors or a diploma from some accredited school or college. The resolution went on to direct the censors to prepare and publish a list of examination questions and to administer examinations to students who wanted to become apprentices. [18]

The resolution was intended to deal with the problem of inadequate preliminary education. If the censors were to enforce this requirement, it would result in better prepared apprentices who, when enrolled in the University's Medical Department, would be able to derive more benefit from the lectures. Unfortunately, by 1879 amendments turned Vermont's medical license law into a farce. Recognizing this, the Society voted that since the medical practice act was inoperable and "useless as a protection against fraud and imposition in medical practice," it should be repealed. At first the Society decided not to elect any censors, as provided in the act, but then reconsidered and decided to try to improve the situation "by a more complete enforcement of the license law." [19]

The reform movement in Vermont had clearly failed to achieve its purpose. Yet as the years passed, the faculty at the University slowly and steadily moved toward higher standards. Though they had decided against some specific proposals of the Association of American Medical Colleges, several professors hoped to upgrade medical education in Burlington without driving students elsewhere.

17. A. P. Grinnell and H. Edwin Lewis, "History of Medical and Surgical Practice in Vermont," in William T. Davis, ed., *The New England States: Their Constitutional, Judicial, Educational, Commercial, Professional, and Industrial History* (Boston, 1897), III, 1452–71. For a description of the national developments in terms of licensing, see Richard H. Shryock, *Medical Licensing in America* (Baltimore, 1967).

18. VMS, *Transactions, 1874, 1875, and 1876*, pp. 411–414.

19. Ibid., *1879* (St. Albans, 1879), p. 6; *1893* (Burlington, 1893), pp. 25–26.

In May 1880 James Lawrence Little suggested acceptance of the provision against graduating students who had completed two courses
in the same year. The next month the faculty agreed to adopt the
requirement of the Association that no student could be graduated
unless there were a fifteen-month period between his first enrollment and the completion of his second course.[20] In effect the University was adopting an important part of the program of the Association. The professors could not, however, lengthen the term to
five months or require three courses of lectures for graduation.

On June 21, 1881, Henry Holton proposed that the Medical Department require preliminary examinations for admission to the program.
Although his motion was defeated, the faculty established a three-
man committee to "consider the advisability" of requiring such an
examination. The three reform-minded professors were appointed
to the committee—Holton, Witthaus, and Little. Two days later
Witthaus suggested a change in the procedures for administering
final examinations. Rather than have all the professors examining
students in the same lecture hall, on an assembly line basis resembling musical chairs, he proposed to have each professor in a separate
room.[21] The faculty adopted the new system, enabling the professors
to devote more time to examining each student.

In the same year, 1881, the relations between the Vermont Society
and the University began to deteriorate. There is no explanation in
any of the sources. Samuel White Thayer, dean of the Medical Department, moved to rescind the resolution which since 1872 had affiliated the two organizations. The members of the society unanimously supported Thayer's motion, indicating that everyone present
knew why it was no longer necessary or mutually beneficial for delegates of the Society to be present for final examinations.[22] The professors soon recognized, however, the importance of restoring good
relations with the Society, or at least encouraging preceptors to send
their students to Burlington rather than to Hanover or elsewhere.
In 1882 Grinnell, the secretary of the Medical Faculty, informed the
members of the Vermont Society that the faculty wanted delegates
to be present at both the final examinations and commencement.
The Society agreed to the request and voted to establish a committee
to "consider the subject of having more intimate relations" with the
College. When the committee reported in favor of sending delegates
to the examinations, it provoked a great deal of discussion, with
Holton, Grinnell, and Jackson all participating in the debate before
the report was finally approved.[23]

In 1883, when the delegates appeared for the examinations, it became apparent that the professors wanted the Society to approve
the graduates but not to participate in the examinations. When Dr.
E. F. Upton appeared, he was informed that the examinations were

20. UVM Medical
Faculty Minutes,
May 18 and June 25,
1880.

21. Ibid., June 21
and 23, 1881.

22. VMS, Minutes,
October 12–13, 1881.

23. VMS, *Transac-
tions, 1882*
(Mont pelier, 1882),
pp. 151–154.

being held at the same time in seven different rooms. Upton could only sit in on a few examinations, which upset him. Although the professors informed him that he would be able to examine the students, no more than one fourth of the candidates appeared before him. He reported that the ones he saw were "of average credit to both teachers and students." Upton concluded that he was there to listen and not to participate. He questioned the need to send delegates when the faculty did not want them to "interfere."[24]

Upton's complaints apparently resulted in some improvement in the following years. In 1884 the delegates reported that they were given "every facility . . . to test the abilities of the candidates." They noted that final examinations were considered to be of the utmost importance, as indicated by the fact that only 101 of the 124 candidates were awarded degrees.[25]

In 1882 the faculty added an optional third course. Students who wanted a graded curriculum could be examined on materia medica, physiology, and chemistry at the end of the second year. They would then be able to devote their third term to studying surgery, medicine, and obstetrics, in preparation for examinations in those fields. In effect the professors offered an optional graded course, with "special examinations in the elementary departments," for students who preferred not to digest six subjects in their second year.[26]

In this same year the professors made two significant changes in the program. First, they decided not to require a thesis for graduation. Most medical theses were inadequate, for students worked on them while preparing themselves for final examinations and while attending numerous lectures each day. Secondly, in a major change the professors decided to offer more practical instruction. That must have been a welcome addition to the students, whose medical education largely consisted of sitting through lectures and keeping up with readings. In the traditional method of medical education it was possible for someone to graduate without ever having seen a live patient. Beginning in 1883 the College offered optional practical courses in anatomy, urinary analysis, toxicology, physical diagnosis, microscopy, minor surgery and bandaging, and examination of the eyes and ears. The intention was to "more perfectly" drill students in "the actual performance of the various methods of diagnosis and treatment employed by the physician."[27] A great many students took advantage of these private practical courses, and by 1884 Witthaus had 45 students in urinary analysis and Grinnell had more than 75 in physical diagnosis.[28]

In 1883 Witthaus proposed that no student be graduated "who shall be reported totally deficient in any department." His motion was defeated by a vote of five to two, with Jackson and Witthaus being opposed by Darling, King, Holton, Little, and Grinnell. Then in 1884

24. Ibid., *1883* (Montpelier, 1883).
25. VMS, Minutes, October 15, 16, 1884.
26. UVM Medical Department, *Twenty-Ninth Annual Announcement, 1882* (Burlington, 1881), p. 14.
27. Ibid., *30th Annual Announcement, 1883* (Burlington, 1882), pp. 11ff.
28. *University Cynic*, 2 (May 14, 1884), 19.

Witthaus moved that the next graduating class be examined in writing. This also was defeated by his colleagues, who preferred a short oral examination. Witthaus entered a protest against the graduation of a student who was "totally deficient in one branch," obviously his own specialty—chemistry. After discussion it was decided that once the faculty had voted to pass a student, no professor could refuse to sign his diploma.[29]

Although Witthaus had failed in his attempt to prevent the graduation of students who were "totally deficient" in one subject, in that same year, 1884, the professors took the first steps toward a major curriculum revision. Alfred Mitchell, secretary of the medical faculty at Bowdoin, wrote to ask if Vermont and Dartmouth would cooperate with Bowdoin in extending the course to five months.[30] Now in 1884 it seemed possible to reform *with* the competition.

About the same time that the faculty began to consider the implications of cooperative reform, the trustees established a committee to attend final examinations and discuss with the medical faculty the possibility of requiring entrance examinations and improving the course of study. The professors directed Grinnell and Jackson to correspond with Dartmouth and Bowdoin and to consult with the trustee committee.[31]

Grinnell and Jackson reported back to the faculty in June 1885, noting that Dartmouth had agreed to require three years of medical study with a preceptor, to demand that each student attend two courses of study, with at least fifteen months between the beginning and the graduation, to require a preliminary examination and a written final examination, and to require dissection. The majority of the Dartmouth faculty, however, was opposed to lengthening the term to twenty weeks, "not because we do not fully appreciate its desirability, but because we do not see how we can do it as present situated."[32]

In May 1885 Alfred Mitchell and Henry Gerrish, the members of the Bowdoin faculty who met with delegates from Vermont and Dartmouth, reported that "neither Dartmouth or Burlington were prepared to act with us." They also noted "the extraordinary delay of the Secretary of the Burlington school in replying to communications of this School and the assumption of superiority" by Grinnell and Jackson.[33]

When Grinnell and Jackson reported back to the Burlington faculty, the discussion centered on the possibility of the University lengthening its term to twenty weeks. Finally the professors decided to go ahead with the Bowdoin plan. They did not bother to notify the faculty at the Maine school. Perhaps the Vermont professors intended to make their institution appear to be the only "reforming" one in New England, even while Grinnell continued to recruit students

29. UVM Medical Faculty Minutes, June 20, 1883; June 19, 20, 1884.

30. Ibid., June 20, 1884. Records of the Bowdoin Medical Faculty, June 1880 and May 27, 1884.

31. UVM Trustee Minutes, June 23, 1884. UVM Medical Faculty Minutes, June 21, 1884, January 7, 1885.

32. UVM Medical Faculty Minutes, June 23, 1885.

33. Records of the Bowdoin Medical Faculty, May 1885.

who were not qualified by the new standards. In any case, Bowdoin's faculty decided that even though the Burlington professors had not acted with the expected "courtesy" in announcing a twenty-week term, there was now no obstacle to Bowdoin's "making a similar advance."[34]

When the UVM medical faculty approved the requirements for graduation, they included two twenty-week terms, fifteen months between the beginning and the end of the course, presentation of evidence that students had studied "practical anatomy," and written and oral examinations before the faculty and the examiners of the state medical society.[35] Preliminary examinations were not required, and the course was not graded. It was a laudable beginning but clearly a half-way measure. The professors had lengthened the term to five months without ensuring that the students were capable of benefiting from the lectures and without grading the program to make it more educationally sound.

Five years later, in 1890, the faculty decided to require three full courses of lectures.[36] In doing so, the professors were in step with the movement to reform American medical education. In 1890 the Association of American Medical Colleges reconstituted itself after having been dormant since 1882. At approximately the same time, a number of states established state licensing boards, which required examination of all applicants. For the first time a premium was set on providing high-quality education. Graduates of schools that continued to offer fast and easy degrees would be unable to pass the board examinations.

The AAMC required three years of study in medical school, with the annual term at least six months long. Moreover, the Association required laboratory work in chemistry, histology, and pathology, and all students had to pass oral and written final examinations. In addition, member schools would no longer be able to enroll students who could not pass an entrance examination that included the translation of easy Latin prose, tests in mathematics and physics, and the writing of a short composition in good English. College graduates were exempted from this requirement.[37]

By 1893 fewer than 10 percent of the schools had two-year courses of study. Four colleges—Pennsylvania, Harvard, Michigan, and the Chicago Medical College—offered four-year courses; significantly, their enrollment had increased. In 1894 the Illinois Board of Health, which had pioneered in examining applicants for licenses, reported that 96.3 percent of the colleges required at least three years of study. That was a drastic change, for in 1880 only 26.8 percent of the schools required more than two years of work.[38] In 1894 the members of the Association voted to extend the requirements to a four-year course, effective with the graduating class of 1899.[39] The trend was

34. UVM Medical Faculty Minutes, June 23, 1885. Records of the Bowdoin Medical Faculty, August 22, 1885.

35. UVM Medical Faculty Minutes, June 26, 1885.

36. Ibid., June 27, 1890. Dartmouth and Bowdoin advanced at the same time. See records of the Bowdoin Medical Faculty, August 1890.

37. *Journal of the American Medical Association*, 14 (June 7, 1890), 829–830.

38. Ibid., 20 (January 7, 1893), 24; 22 (March 17, 1894), 393–394.

39. Dean F. Smiley, "History of the Association of American Medical Colleges, 1876–1956," *Journal of Medical Education*, 32 (July 1957), 516. Association of American Medical Colleges, *Report of the Committee on Syllabus* (Chicago, 1895), p. 10.

apparent. Future schools were to have four-year graded courses of study, which would prepare students for the board examinations required of all applicants for licenses.

In 1890, at the same time that the professors at the University voted to require three full terms for graduation, they decided to require entrance examinations of students who had not completed a three-year high school course. Before being allowed to matriculate, such students had to pass examinations in arithmetic, grammar, geography, orthography, American history, English composition, and elementary physics. Students who failed in one or more of the areas, however, were allowed to make up their deficiency during the first year of medical school. Students were given the choice of taking special examinations for the medical school, administered by a board appointed by the medical faculty, or taking the regular entrance examinations, administered by the University. The University's announcement noted that although the preliminary term was still optional, it was taking on a larger role. Students were "earnestly advised to attend, as they are thus better prepared to comprehend the lectures in the Regular Course."[40]

The following year, 1891, Witthaus proposed a "scheme" for grading the course of study, and he submitted a detailed schedule "demonstrating the feasibility of a plan." After listening to his arguments, the professors voted to adopt a graded system as soon as possible.[41] Not only was a three-year course required for graduation, but students would no longer have to sit through the same lectures in each term. The first year would be devoted to the basic sciences; during the next year students would add to their knowledge, preparing for the practical work of the third year—medicine, surgery, and obstetrics.

The improvement in standards, as exemplified by the three-year course and the entrance examinations, brought about a slight decrease in enrollment. In 1890 the Medical Department had enrolled 203 students. The following year, surprisingly, attendance increased to 210. By 1892, however, there had been a reduction to 190, and then to 188 in 1893. The *Burlington Free Press* erroneously reported in February 1892 that although it had been "supposed that the change in curriculum" would decrease the enrollment, "this has not been the result." Rather than reducing attendance, the newspaper declared, the increase in standards had "attracted to this institution a more thoroughly educated class of young men."[42] It seems likely, however, that the enrollment figures indicate that the "reform" was not drastic. After all, students who had completed a three-year high school course would continue to matriculate, and others could enroll even if they were unable to pass the entrance examinations. Perhaps some students who otherwise would have enrolled for medical lec-

40. UVM Medical Department, *38th Annual Announcement, 1891* (Burlington, 1890), pp. 15–16, 19.
41. UVM Medical Faculty Minutes, July 10, 1891.
42. Figures taken from the annual announcement of the Medical Department and *Burlington Free Press and Times*, February 20, 1892, p. 5, col. 3.

tures went elsewhere rather than take an examination which they almost certainly would have failed.

In 1892 the faculty received a letter from the Secretary of the Association of American Medical Colleges, describing the requirements for membership—the three-year graded course, the six-month term, and the entrance examinations. A Vermont faculty committee which prepared the schedule for the following year presented *its* report—providing for an extension of the term to six months, with the course being graded, as required by the Association.[43] The professors voted to accept the report and to approve the schedule. Interestingly, the committee had discovered a way to develop a graded course without reducing the income of the professors. The preliminary term and the private courses were abolished, and the practical courses were integrated into the regular program. Needless to say, tuition was increased. In the future, instruction in urinary analysis, histology, pathology, and bacteriology, along with practical work in physical diagnosis and demonstrative obstetrics, were required for graduation. In 1894 the faculty voted to establish a practical course in surgery, taught by John Brooks Wheeler. The faculty was enlarged to meet the new situation, as described in the previous chapter. The special professors continued to come to Burlington to hold clinics and to lecture on their specialties, but their lectures were required only for advanced students.[44]

In 1895 the faculty sanctioned a plan to improve the graded course. First-year students would be "made to dissect as much as possible." They also would be assigned laboratory work in histology. Second-year students would be assigned to laboratory work in urinalysis and pathology, and if necessary they would complete their work in anatomy. Third-year students would be assigned to classes in physical diagnosis, practical surgery, and demonstrative obstetrics. No student would be permitted to take courses ahead of his class. Furthermore, the committee recommended that formal medical clinics be held on Wednesday mornings at the Mary Fletcher Hospital. The first nine weeks would include clinics in theory and practice, and the next nine weeks would have clinics under the direction of the professor of materia medica and therapeutics.[45]

In 1896 the professors discussed the possibility of requiring four years of study, which would put the college fully in line with the standards of the Association of American Medical Colleges. As indicated earlier, members of the Association were to have a four-year course effective for the graduating class of 1899. After a discussion, the faculty voted to increase the length of the course to four years, "and to extend the graded system of instruction beginning with the session of 1898."[46] Thus the University of Vermont was only two

43. UVM Medical Faculty Minutes, June 9 and 16, 1892.
44. UVM Medical Department, *40th Annual Announcement, 1893* (Burlington, 1892), pp. 4, 6–8, 9–11. UVM Medical Faculty Minutes, July 11, 1894.
45. UVM Medical Faculty Minutes, June 29, 1895.
46. Ibid., July 2, 1896, June 14, 1897.

years behind the members of the Association in expanding its program to four years. Finally, in 1899, the faculty instructed the dean to apply for admission to the Association, now that the college was able to comply with its requirements for membership.[47]

The University's Medical School had come a long way in a relatively short time. In 1902 H. Edwin Lewis, writing in the *Vermont Medical Monthly*, boasted of the faculty, the graded curriculum, the clinical advantages, and the extensive laboratories. Lewis exclaimed: "No student is expected to attend the clinics until he has finished the first two years work, and is competent to understand what he sees." Just a few years earlier, the only laboratories had been in anatomy and urinalysis. Now there were laboratories in chemistry, histology, physiology, pathology, and bacteriology, and they were compulsory, not optional, as had been the case. A few years ago, he said, the School had had seven professors and a few adjuncts. Now, in the first years of the twentieth century, it had seven professors, eleven special professors, four adjuncts, nine instructors, and five laboratory instructors, for a total of thirty-two faculty members.[48]

Furthermore, Lewis noted changes in the grading system. Until 1901, he said, students had been graded entirely on final examinations. That was a problem, for many good students were unable to pass "creditable examinations or demonstrate their actual knowledge under the excitement, embarrassment, or anxiety of a final test." Now students received grades for every recitation and were examined every two months. The recitation marks comprised 50 percent of the grade, with the rest depending on performance on the final examination.[49] A four-year graded course was certainly far superior to the traditional system, which required students to sit through the same lectures for two years. In effect, by 1905 the University of Vermont's Medical Department had entered the modern era. It had an expanded faculty, a new building, an improved curriculum, and membership in the reform-minded Association of American Medical Colleges. The College had entered the world of the twentieth century.

47. Ibid., May 18 and June 1, 1899.
48. H. Edwin Lewis, "The Medical Department of the University of Vermont," *Vermont Medical Monthly*, 8 (June 25, 1902), 154–156.
49. Ibid.

Chapter Ten

Student Life, 1854–1900

FROM 1854 TO 1900, 1822 students graduated from the School of Medicine at the University of Vermont, and the vast majority were poorly prepared. Joseph Hills analyzed the student rolls from 1854 to 1894 and found that only 2.8 percent or 43 of the 1497 graduates in those forty years had bachelor's degrees when they began their formal medical training.[1] Indeed, a comparison with other New England institutions indicates that the University's Medical School had the lowest percentage of college graduates. In 1900, after the faculty had been requiring entrance examinations of all students who did not have a three-year high school background, only 5.9 percent of the students held college degrees, as compared with 16.4 percent at Yale, 17.5 percent at Bowdoin, 19.7 percent at Dartmouth, and 28.4 percent at Harvard.[2]

The students who came to Burlington were from a wide geographical area. An analysis of the enrollment from 1881 to 1888 indicates that of the 1511 students who attended classes at the University, 412 (27.3 percent) were from Vermont. The next largest group came from New York, with 325 students (21.4 percent). Massachusetts provided 183 students (12.1 percent), while Maine sent 129 (8.5 percent), and New Hampshire 120 (7.9 percent). The others came from a scattering of states and from nearby Canadian provinces.[3]

The enrollment statistics seem to indicate that much of the increase in out-of-state attendance was related to transportation improvements which made Burlington more accessible. For instance, the number of students from New York State increased from 7 in 1875 to 19 in 1876, and then to a high of 58 in 1884. There was a significant

1. J. L. Hills, "History of the Medical College," p. 91, UVM Archives.

2. Developed from the *Bulletin of the American Academy of Medicine*, 5 (June 1901), 349–486.

3. Figures taken from annual announcements, 1881–88.

increase from Massachusetts, from 2 students in 1877, 10 in 1878, and 22 in 1881. Between 1877 and 1882 there was an increase in students from Maine and New Hampshire, with the Maine students increasing from one in 1877 to twelve in 1882, and the numbers from New Hampshire rising from four in 1878 to fifteen in 1880.[4] The consolidation of railroad networks, the adoption of standard gauge, the improved credit structure, and the expansion of national media for advertising all encouraged the development of a national market for medical institutions as well as for industrial goods.

4. Ibid.
5. Hills, "History of the Medical College," p. 94. President Buckham's report to the trustees, 1886–87, UVM Archives.

Low standards attracted many students to the University; there were no "scholastic barriers to attendance," and it was notoriously easy to graduate. In his report to the trustees in 1886–87, President Buckham noted that "a large number of those" in the medical course "are quite illiterate."[5] This may partially explain why a large number of UVM Medical College graduates had difficulty passing their board exams. Indeed, when statistics became available at the turn of the

12. *Medical students of
1888.*

century, they indicated that the Vermont graduates had a higher percentage of failure than students in the other medical schools of New England.[6]

Although in 1871 the trustees had decided to admit young women to the various programs at the University, the medical faculty remained adamantly opposed to their admission. In 1878, when the professors were faced with the problem of the admission of women and "colored students," they tabled and in effect defeated a motion allowing females to attend lectures on midwifery, but they voted to admit Negro students to the medical lectures. In 1891 a woman apparently applied for admission, but the professors refused to sell her lecture tickets.[7] Thus during the nineteenth century and into the twentieth, the student body at the Medical School was composed entirely of men.

In his autobiography John Brooks Wheeler compared Vermont students with those at Harvard. The Harvard students were better educated than the boys who came to Burlington, he said, at least in terms of preliminary education. He noted that "the Vermont boys" were mostly "farmers' sons whose only schooling had been obtained in their native villages." There were "brains enough among the Vermonters," Wheeler declared, "but, as a class, there was less education and though most of them worked hard (harder, I think than the average Harvard student) they were not used to studying and it did not come easily to them." On the whole, however, Wheeler concluded, "they were a good lot of students, intelligent and industrious, and for that period of medical education, they became a very satisfactory lot of graduates."[8]

After having purchased their lecture tickets, the students prepared for the "rush for seats" in the amphitheatre. Since seats were allocated on a first-come, first-served basis, students who wanted the best seats in the lower rows began to line up twenty-four hours before the first day of classes. According to Lyman Allen, a member of the class of '96 who later joined the medical faculty, the students who participated in the annual rush for seats came well prepared, with food, drink, cushions, and blankets. Years afterward he likened it to "bleacherites waiting for the opening of the gates before a World Series game."[9] In 1898 the faculty tried to put an end to the long line of students by refusing to allow them into the Medical College Building until the opening day of the session. Thirty students entered the building, however, and announced their intention to stay through the night. When the janitor informed them that they would have to leave when the building was locked for the night, he was roundly hissed. Finally, after an unsuccessful try at petitioning Dean Grinnell to let them stay, the students left for the evening. Undoubtedly, the rush for seats was merely delayed until the following day.[10]

6. See report in the *Bulletin of the American Academy of Medicine, 1899–1905.*

7. UVM Trustee Minutes, October 31 and August 2, 1871. UVM Medical Faculty Minutes, May 16 and June 27, 1878; June 19, 1891.

8. John Brooks Wheeler, *Memoirs of a Small-Town Surgeon* (New York, 1935), pp. 180–181.

9. William A. R. Chapin, *History, University of Vermont College of Medicine* (Springfield, Mass., 1951), pp. 118–119. *University Cynic,* February 27, 1884, p. 143.

10. *Burlington Free Press,* January 6, 1898, p. 5, col. 3.

The annual course traditionally began with an introductory lecture by a designated member of the faculty. After the lecture, the students often would request a copy of his address so they could publish it for others to read. In 1857 the introductory was given by Henry Erni, the professor of chemistry. Erni described the physician's need for scientific training. "The era of a truly rational system of medicine" was approaching, and he predicted that every student in the near future would need a thorough acquaintance with "Natural Science, as the only sure and true basis to build upon." Since medical students tended to pay more attention to practice, surgery, and obstetrics—practical training for the future physician—Erni defended the place of chemistry in the medical curriculum. He noted that "some professional men of the 'old school'" considered chemistry "an idle and useless handmaid of medicine," often sneering at "the revelations of a microscope applied to physiology or pathology." Erni said that every disease was attended by chemical changes and that the profession had advanced from the time when physicians ascribed "supernatural forces to medicines," to the present day, when it was known that the effect of a medicine was directly related to its chemical properties. Finally, Erni pointed to the scientific developments of the day— the telegraph, the "art of daguerreotyping," electrotyping, friction matches, and "the illumination of our houses with gas." He described how scientific developments had improved the practice of medicine, emphasizing "that blessing to suffering humanity, the application of Ether and Chloroform."[11]

The following year the introductory address was delivered by R. Cresson Stiles, professor of physiology and pathology. Like Erni, he defended his specialty against condemnation by physicians "of the old school." He admitted that physiologists had "not yet been as fruitful of practical results" as those responsible "for the discovery of the remedial effects of Opium, Quinia, Iron, or any of the invaluable weapons with which we successfully combat disease." He explained that the science of physiology "is yet in its infancy," since the microscope was not in general use until the nineteenth century and the sciences of physics and chemistry had not developed until recent times.[12]

In 1876 the introductory address was given by Peter Collier, professor of chemistry, who eloquently described the role of the medical professor. "Before us is a crowd of young men about to engage in combat with the great destroyer," he exclaimed. The students had come to the faculty, "as to an armorer," in the hope of becoming better prepared "for their crusade." He declared confidently that "The armory of Chemistry is full." Collier proceeded to advise the students, in keeping with introductory addresses of the day. He told the students to pay careful attention to their own health. "Do not

11. Henry Erni, *Introductory Lecture, Delivered before the Medical Class of the University of Vermont, May 12th, 1857* (Burlington, 1857), pp. 6–9, 11–14.

12. R. Cresson Stiles, *An Introductory Lecture to the Course of Instruction in the Medical Department of the University of Vermont, February, 1858* (Burlington, 1858), pp. 5–6, 9–10.

forget yourselves," he said, "in the assurance that by thus caring for yourselves, you are able the more effectually to care for your fellows." He noted that medicine was a practical profession—"no half-way knowledge will suffice. Ignorance or carelessness on *your* part," he exclaimed, "means *death* to those who have placed their life in your hands." He informed the students that their most powerful allies in the struggle against disease "are the forces of nature." He warned against closing their minds to new ideas, for new developments were revolutionizing the practice of medicine. Finally, he admonished the students to believe in God.[13]

In 1877 the introductory was given by Marshall Calkins, professor of physiology and microscopic anatomy. Calkins emphasized the duties of both the physician and the student. He warned his audience not to waste "precious time in useless frivolities," and he urged the students to "work systematically, perseveringly and faithfully." The medical student, he said, could not let his attention be diverted from his work, as he would soon be a physician and thus vital to the health and welfare of mankind. "When plague and pestilence walk abroad in the land," he declared, the physician is expected "to brave the danger and to be successful in cure."[14]

J. Henry Jackson gave the introductory in 1883. He warned the students that it was unusual for a physician to be financially successful. He told how Valentine Mott advised his students to have two pockets—"a large one to hold the insults, and a small one to hold the fees." Then, after warning against charlatans and imposters, he offered some valuable suggestions. "A methodical use of your time will prove of great advantage to you as students," he said. "Correct habits, punctuality, patient attention, careful reviews, thorough dissections, regular hours for study," all were necessary for success in medical school, and success in medical school meant greater likelihood for success in practice. Like Collier, he declared that students should not neglect their health—"though the pale, sickly student may win the prize in college, it is the strong, vigorous one who will win most prizes in life."[15]

After the introductory lecture the work of the term began. Students would spend five or six hours a day in the amphitheatre, listening to lectures and observing demonstrations. Until the 1890's, when the recitation system was adopted, "instruction was almost wholly from didactic lectures." According to Winfield Scott Nay of the class of '73, the Saturday morning clinics were useless: "only minor operations were performed in the presence of the class . . . with little chance for observation; bacteriology was not taught and asepsis was . . . unknown in surgical procedures." Examinations consisted of "the recognition of drugs, dosage, and minor surgery, and the treatment of a few diseased conditions prevalent."[16]

13. Peter Collier, *Opening Address delivered before the Medical Class of the University of Vermont, Thursday, March 9th, 1876* (Burlington, 1876), pp. 4–7, 11–12.

14. Marshall Calkins, *An Introductory Address delivered before the Medical Class of the University of Vermont, Thursday, March 8, 1877* (Burlington, 1877), pp. 12, 15ff.

15. J. Henry Jackson, *An Introductory Address delivered before the Medical Department of the University of Vermont, March 1st, 1883* (Burlington, 1883), pp. 3, 7–8.

16. *Alumni Weekly,* March 25, 1925, October 31, 1928, quoted in Hills, "History of the Medical College," p. 66.

Many students prepared for sitting on the hard wooden benches of the amphitheatre by "blowing up air cushions or arranging feather pillows" on the seats.[17] The ten or fifteen minutes between classes or before the day's lectures were riotous periods. Before the professor arrived, a student might be "passed up" to the last row of the amphitheatre. The ordeal would begin when a student was settling down in a front row seat. Suddenly he would feel strong arms on his shoulders and he would be lifted in the air. Then he would be passed over the rest of the students until he was unceremoniously deposited in the last row. It was understood that once a student took "the ascent passively," he did not have to undergo the ordeal again. On the other hand, a student who struggled to prevent his removal would be "passed up" again and again, until he learned to accept his fate stoically.

Once Frank C. Lewis, class of '02, made the mistake of resisting his classmates while they were trying to pass him up to the last row. When it was about to happen again "he began a vigorous objection." "He struck bravely out from the shoulder," and according to newspaper accounts, "his prowess against odds is recorded upon the bruised visage of more than one of the men in his vicinity." Henry Crain Tinkham, the professor of anatomy who replaced Grinnell as dean in 1898, entered the room "as Lewis was making his ascent." When the noise had subsided, he suggested that "whatever physical exercise the students cared to take they take it previous to lectures." When interviewed by a reporter, several students predicted that it would not be the last time Lewis would undergo the ordeal.[18] In another instance, Lyman Allen described one strong student who "crooked his legs under the board bench." "When he was passed up the entire bench went with him."[19]

When a classmate arrived in the amphitheatre after a lecture had begun, he was "greeted" in a manner calculated to embarrass him and perhaps encourage him to be on time in the future. While the student was trying to get to his seat without attracting the professor's attention or disturbing the class, the students would begin to tramp slowly until he was seated. Tramping on wooden floorboards would always focus attention on the tardy classmate. In 1884 the students' newspaper, the *University Cynic* noted that tramping "may have been funny at first, but it seems childish to continue it longer to the annoyance of both the speaker, and those who desire to hear what is being said." The following year, however, the *Cynic* seemed to approve of tramping: "As we usher our tardy classmates to their respective seats, with that harmonious discord of t-r-a-m-p, t-r-a-m-p, and seat them with a heartiness that would do justice to the serfs of the Czar."[20]

L. W. Flanders, a member of the class of '85, described how the

17. L. W. Flanders, in *Vermont Alumnus*, 2 (January 10, 1923), 85–86.

18. Unidentified newspaper clipping, Grinnell Papers, UVM Archives.

19. Cited in Chapin, *History, University of Vermont College of Medicine*, p. 120.

20. *University Cynic*, April 23, 1884, p. 7; May 20, 1885, p. 20.

students kept themselves occupied during the ten-minute intermission between classes. "We were a riotous crew," he declared. The break between classes was "full of incident," including "flying missiles" like blocks of wood, notebooks, blackboard erasers, and once a "good, big, soft, hot 2-inch thick 2 pound poultice."[21] In 1884 the *Cynic* described the result of the "riotous" activity: "The windows of the lower lecture room look as though *a western cyclone* had passed through them." It was simply "the result of the contact of a few stray rubbers and overshoes with the glass." The *Cynic* concluded by asking "who are the students who are to '*toss up*' to see who pays the damages?"[22]

When the graded system went into effect in 1892, it separated the course into beginning and advanced students, often leading to open battle between the classes. Once, in 1896 or 1897, a fight developed between first- and second-year men. The second-year men had been taking chairs from the room where first-year men had recitation. Ultimately this resulted in a lack of chairs and a corresponding lack of comfort. Finally, when a second-year man entered the room and tried to take another chair, the first year men objected and "a lively scrap began. The second year men soon came to the rescue of their classman, and in a few minutes between 40 and 50 men were hard at it." "No ill-will was shown on either side," but during the scuffle "collars and neckties were thrown about the room, trousers were ripped and a few noses were battered." Other students and the professors were "attracted to the room by the noise and all enjoyed the sport." After ten minutes Patrick McSweeney, who was about to lecture, called "time up" and the "boys quieted down." By the end of the "scuffle," only 5 of the 20 chairs in the room "remained whole."[23]

Even during the classes, the medical students were a riotous bunch. They tried to play practical jokes on the professors; in 1885 they managed a good one on William Darling, the professor of anatomy. Darling had a skeleton hanging from the amphitheatre ceiling by a cord attached to a ring in the top of the skull. Before the professor arrived to lecture, the students lowered the skeleton, put a stovepipe hat on its head, tied a valise to its right hand, and placed a burning cigarette between its jaws. Then they returned it to the ceiling. Darling called for the janitor to lower the skeleton; when he did, "the two stood face to face, the living and the dead." "Lightning played from the professor's eyes . . . he shuffled around the grotesque figure, muttering as he went . . . then the storm broke." "Ye're a set of idle loons! Ye're not pious enough for meenisters, ye haena brain enough for lawyers, so your parents sent ye up here to be made into doctors, and its narthing but damned nonsense a' the time." Then Darling began to quiz the class, and when the students could not answer his questions, he declared that "a little o' the time spent to dec-

21. *Vermont Alumnus,* 2 (January 10, 1923), 85–86.
22. *University Cynic,* February 27, 1884, p. 43.
23. Unidentified newspaper clipping, Grinnell Papers.

oratin' my skeleton had better been pit intil the study of anatomy."[24]

Whenever a pathological specimen was passed around during class, it would invariably return to the professor filled with toothpicks. In one instance a professor passed around a "saucer of gall stones," but by the time the saucer had completed its trip around the amphitheatre its contents had been removed. The professor became so upset that he took off his coat and threatened to "lick the entire class." Since the professor had been light-heavyweight boxing champion of his college, the students returned most of the gall stones.[25]

Most of the students chewed tobacco, and cuspidors "were part of the standard equipment of the amphitheatre," strategically positioned so there was one for every three or four students. The students did not normally smoke during class, but if the lecture was dull or poorly presented they would let the professor know by shifting their feet, smoking, or in some cases leaving the amphitheatre.[26]

There were many interruptions in the regular routine, enabling the students to get some exercise or to get away from the amphitheatre and the books. For instance, the students were welcome to spend time in the Young Men's Christian Association. At the beginning of each school term, there was a reception for students and faculty at the YMCA. The *Cynic* noted in 1884 that the YMCA was "about the pleasantest place in the city for a student to spend his leisure hours." Also, the medical students were normally invited to special services at local churches; in 1883 it was reported that "nearly every member of the class" attended.[27] Toward the end of each term, the faculty held a reception for the students. In 1899 the party was held at Tinkham's residence, with 175 students in attendance. It was a catered affair, with entertainment.[28]

The medical students were a musical lot. John Brooks Wheeler noted in his autobiography that singing was a common pastime for the students, "especially when several of them walked the streets together in the evening." He recalled one song addressed to the faculty, with humorous verses for each professor. Wheeler, however, could only remember one verse, dedicated to Walter Carpenter:[29]

Oh! Here's to Prof. Carpenter, Jolly old man,
    Vive La Medicine!
He teaches us Practice, beat him if you can!
    Vive La Medicine!
Oh! Vive la, Vive la Medicine!
Cholera Morbus, apples green,
Calomel, Ipecac, Rhubarb, Quinine!
    Vive La Medicine!

One song has been preserved by F. J. Henry, who attended medical lectures in 1883:[30]

24. *Alumni Weekly,* 4 (March 10, 1925), p. 318.

25. Chapin, *History, University of Vermont College of Medicine,* p. 120.

26. Ibid., p. 119.

27. *University Cynic,* January 16, 1884, p. 119; April 1, 1885, p. 142; *May* 16, 1883, p. 20.

28. *Burlington Free Press and Times,* May 15, 1899, p. 5, col. 5.

29. Wheeler, *Memoirs of a Small-Town Surgeon,* p. 181.

30. F. J. Henry Scrapbook, UVM Archives.

I know full well this form of mine
    Is but a monad cell,
And pubulum and blastoderm,
    Within each tissue swell.
But while my heart and nerves and lungs
    Are subject to my brain,
Each pulse will thrill, each nerve impart
    My love for Mary Jane.

CHORUS

My darling Mary Jane
My Mary Jane so true.
I die a death with every breath
I draw when far from you.

Let HOLTON prate and vindicate
    Verad Vird, good and strong,
While GRINNELL still on quinine pill
    Extolls both loud and long.
And KING the ladies' favorite,
    Describes each pelvic plane,
While I am here my thoughts are there
    Where dwells my Mary Jane.

CHORUS

Prof. LITTLE, with his trenchant knife,
    Can cut with steady hand,
And DARLING entertains the class
    With his quotations grand.
But ready knife and brilliant phrase
    Being naught to me but pain
While I am far away from home,
    And from my Mary Jane.

CHORUS

Let MORTON with his Neurolem
    and talks of reophore
While JACKSON slays from day to day
    of canines half a score;
And RUTHERFORD, with his silver thread,
    Ligates each portal vein,
My thoughts still turn in dreamy muse,
    To my sweet Mary Jane.

CHORUS

Let Sal Rochelle and Sal Prunelle,
     With other sirens burn,
While I of WITTHAUS' cupric salts
     And acids strive to learn,
But when with sheepskin in my hand
     I leave old Galen's fame,
I'll spend less nights with phlebolites,
     And more with Mary Jane.

CHORUS

In 1878 the students of the preliminary term organized a "club for the discussion of subjects relating to the study and practice of medicine."[31] In effect this was the beginning of the medical fraternity system at the University. On December 21, 1880, Delta Mu, the first formal medical fraternity at the University, was established with nineteen charter members. It was organized primarily to provide students with formal quiz sections in the almost total absence of recitation in the old didactic program of the Medical School. The fraternity never had more than forty members, even when the total enrollment exceeded two hundred. Over the years the fraternity was well represented on the medical faculty. For instance, the charter members of 1880 included Charles S. Caverly, who was to be professor of hygiene after 1903, and James N. Jenne, who was to succeed Tinkham as medical dean.[32] Little is known about initiation into Delta Mu, but in 1884 the *Cynic* declared that "it requires a man of iron will to pass without flinching, the terrible ordeal" of initiation into this fraternity.[33]

In 1884 the fraternity men came into conflict with the rest of the medical students when the members of Delta Mu decided to control the election of class officers by casting a bloc vote for a slate of candidates. The secret was revealed, and the rest of the medical class responded by voting for an opposing slate. When the class met to make plans for commencement, the Delta Mus managed to convince the other students to approve an invitation which omitted the names of the class officers, except for the President and the Valedictorian. According to the *Cynic*, "The society men very naturally feel that they have in a measure *got even* for their defeat in the organization of the class."[34]

In 1889 another medical fraternity was organized at the University— the Alpha chapter of Phi Chi. In 1893 Delta Mu and Phi Chi were joined by a third fraternity when an informal organization, the Alpha Delta Sigma society, amalgamated with a national medical fraternity, Alpha Kappa Kappa. According to the *Free Press*, Alpha Kappa Kappa "bids fair to become one of the most powerful societies in the United States," having chapters at Dartmouth, Yale, and New York's College

31. *Burlington Free Press and Times*, December 18, 1878, p. 3, col. 1.

32. *Alumni Weekly*, 5 (October 21, 1925), 38, 41–42.

33. *University Cynic*, January 16, 1884, p. 119.

34. Ibid., April 23, 1884, pp. 7–8.

of Physicians and Surgeons, with another chapter in process of formation at the University of Michigan.[35]

In the late 1870's the medical students became involved in organized athletics. In 1878 the local newspaper reported that a "'very hotly contested' football game" was played between the freshman class and the "Medics." The report noted that "the participants seemed to enjoy the promiscuous rolling through the mud and wet grass, which is one of the necessary consequences of the game." The medical students, however, were outmatched. "The Freshies were younger, lighter and more active than their opponents, having them, on this account, at a decided disadvantage." The final score was not noted by the *Free Press*, but the reporter declared that "The Medics played well and have no reason to be ashamed of the gallant fight they made."[36]

In 1883 the medical students organized a baseball team, which finally "disbanded for the season after a course of uninterrupted vic-

35. *Burlington Free Press and Times*, April 23, 1893, p. 5, col. 3.

36. Ibid., May 27, 1878, p. 3, col. 3.

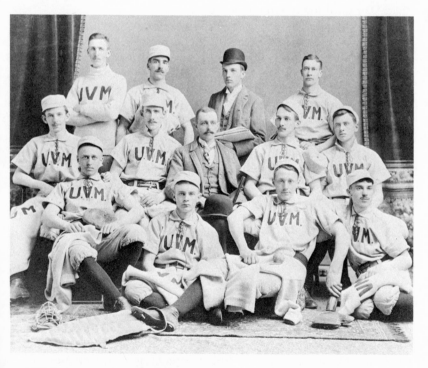

13. *UVM's famous baseball team of 1891.* Left to right, back row: *Thomas C. Cheney '91; Carlisle Ferrin, Medic '91; Er-* *nest Morgan '91; J. Clark '91.* Middle row: *Joseph D. Allen '93; Thomas C. Hill, Medic '93; Frank L. Moore '90; Lyman* *Allen, Medic '93; Joel Allen '92;* Front row: *Ralph W. Stewart '93; Charles H. Hogle '91; Bert W. Abbey '91; Charles E. Lamb '93.*

37. *University
Cynic*, May 16, 1883,
p. 21; June 6, 1883, p.
33.
38. Ibid., June 6,
1883, p. 32.
39. H. K. Bork-
land, "Something
about the History of
Athletics at the Uni-
versity of Vermont,"
*Vermont Alumni
Weekly*, 10 (October
22, 1930), 55.
40. *University
Cynic*, June 10, 1885,
pp. 32, 34.
41. Chapin, *His-
tory, University of
Vermont College of
Medicine*, p. 121. *Bur-
lington Free Press*,
May 1, 1890, p. 1, col.
4.
42. Chapin, *His-
tory, University of
Vermont College of
Medicine*, p. 121. See
University Cynic,
May 15, 1890, pp.
18–19, for caustic
remarks on the
medics.

tories." The team defeated the Rock Points, the Academics, the Mes-
sengers of Winooski, and Middlebury, and rolled up a score of 41
to 7 against the Vermont Episcopal Institute.[37] When the Medics defeated "the Winooski Club" by a score of 26 to 17, there was a fight
between the two teams. The *Cynic* expressed the hope that "the people of Burlington who witnessed the base-ball game . . . will hold the
Medical students in *no wise* responsible for the disgraceful fracas that
occurred on the grounds during the game. Any one having any chance
for observation could easily see where the trouble originated."[38]

The following year, 1884, the University organized a Field Day to
encourage physical fitness among the students. The program included running, jumping, vaulting, and bicycle riding, and the medical
students "captured the majority of the awards."[39] In 1885 there was a
second Field Day, with disastrous results. The *Cynic* reported that
several students practicing for the events were "quite badly" hurt,
"one so much so that he had to go to the hospital." The medics
won the tug of war on Field Day.[40] That was apparently the last
Field Day until the twentieth century.

In 1889 the medics and academics came into conflict over control
of the University's baseball team. The academics had always played
the major role in the organization, since the medical students did
not arrive on campus until March; by then the schedule had been
arranged and managers appointed. Since there were more medics
than academics enrolled at the University (a situation that continued
to 1901 when an increase in standards reduced the Medical College
enrollment), the medical students demanded complete control of the
baseball team. Finally it was decided that they would play a game,
with the winning team to be given control. "Suddenly three new
medical students matriculated and began training for the team, but
they did not bother to attend many lectures." In spite of their help,
when the game was played the academics won by a score of 19 to
4. The *Free Press* reported that "the medical students were out en
masse, and even while their opponents were knocking out run after
run, retained their spirits, and kept their banners waving."[41] "The
Medics grudgingly accepted the verdict," and the academics won
control of the team.

Two medics played on the University team that year, but there was
"marked coolness between the two groups." After the game with
Dartmouth, the conflict resumed. "Crowds of Medics and Academics
were battling up and down Church Street; eggs and potatoes flew
through the air, and many were the black eyes, and torn or stained
coats to be seen in the college halls for the next few days."[42] Before
bestowing the diplomas that year, Dean Grinnell mentioned the disappointment of those who had failed the examinations, and then

he noted the "obstacles encountered in baseball by the class as a whole."[43]

Even though the academics retained control of baseball, a number of medical students continued to play. During the 1890s, the medical faculty often reduced tuition for the baseball players. In 1892, for instance, the professors voted to reduce fees by 50 percent for Ernest Richmond, the second baseman, and for Lawrence Ignatius Kinsella, who later was called the "Babe Ruth" of the team.[44] Kinsella, incidentally, never received a medical degree from the University, despite the fact that he was listed as a student from 1892 to 1894. Perhaps the explanation for his failure to graduate is to be found in the faculty response to a request from Lyman Allen, who was the first baseman in 1894 and 1895. Allen asked for an abatement of all fees for members of the team. In response to Allen's request the professors voted to contribute $100 to the team, to be credited to the reduction of fees. The donation had one condition, however—"that the members of the medical class shall not be called upon to sacrifice their medical studies to the interests of base ball by absenting themselves from the lectures."[45] Other medical students whose fees were abated by the faculty included the pitcher, Erasmus Arlington Pond, and the third baseman, James H. Naylor, both of the class of '95, and Louis J. Cooke, a pitcher who graduated in 1894. "Arlie" Pond later had a short but distinguished career with the Baltimore Orioles, winning 35 games and losing only 19 in slightly more than two seasons prior to his service in the Spanish-American War.

In May 1902 a baseball game between the medics and academics indicated that some of the old animosity continued into the twentieth century. The *Cynic* reported that "it was a pleasure indeed to see the old Hospital fence go up in smoke," but the reporter was happy at the "good feelings between the men of the Medical and Academic departments."[46]

Aside from outdoor exercise exemplified by football or baseball, some medical students got their exercise in other ways. Although the medical faculty purchased cadavers from sources outside of Vermont, occasionally it was necessary for students to take the time-honored path to success in the profession, which started in the local cemetery.[47] Dr. J. S. Richmond declared back in 1870 that "but a few years ago churchyards were ransacked and graves robbed of their dead," and in the past "the medical student received a large pecuniary credit for obtaining a subject."[48] Richmond believed that body-snatching was a thing of the past. Yet Winfield Scott Nay, of the class of '73, described how he and a classmate, Frank A. Packard, went to the Catholic cemetery at Milton and disinterred the body of Joseph Germain. The two students boxed and shipped the cadaver

43. *Burlington Free Press and Times*, July 15, 1890, p. 1, col. 2.

44. UVM Medical Faculty Minutes, July 6, 1892.

45. Ibid., June 21, 1894.

46. *University Cynic*, May 17, 1902, p. 18.

47. UVM Medical Department Cash Book, 1866–75 and 1875–90 (UVM Archives) includes notations that cadavers were purchased from William E. Bessey, a Montreal physician, and from A. N. White, of New York City. Bessey operated a "private asylum or retreat" for alcoholics and narcotic addicts, and perhaps it can be assumed that he sold the bodies of those who died under his charge and were not claimed by friends or relatives. See W. E. Bessey, *How to Cure Drunkenness* (Montreal, 1880).

48. Vermont Medical Society, *Transactions, 1869 and 1870* (Burlington, 1870), p. 111.

to Burlington "for use in the dissecting room." In that instance, friends of the deceased discovered the empty grave and came to Burlington in search of the body. When they identified and recovered the remains, Packard had to leave school "for parts unknown," until the excitement subsided. He returned before the end of the term, however, and he graduated with his class.[49]

Six years later A. V. Bowker, class of 1879, also described body-snatching while a student at the University. He and the janitor went one night to a local cemetery, and each of them earned five dollars for digging up a recently buried body. In that incident, Loggins, the janitor, patiently sawed the top of the coffin apart with a sharp knife before he could remove the body.[50]

It was more typical, however, for the faculty to procure their own cadavers. Bowker, for instance, who was Bingham's assistant, described how he was told to take the horse and wagon to the grocery store to pick up a "package" that came in the express car. The young man got the coffin onto the wagon. He got lost in the night but managed to find his way back to the Medical Building. In another case, Bowker told of a time when a "barrel of onions" arrived from New York by rail. When the barrel was opened, they found onions on top of the "main part of the package," which "had died of small-pox." All the students were vaccinated the following day.[51]

Anatomical material continued to be a problem for the Medical School, despite a state law that was passed to solve the problem. The 1884 act required overseers of the poor and superintendents of public institutions to deliver bodies to physicians, "for the advancement of anatomical science." The law, however, exempted the bodies of those who themselves or through relatives requested burial, as well as those of strangers and travelers "who had died suddenly" before their names were known, and those of former military men.[52]

In 1891 the medical faculty decided to take advantage of the law by directing Tinkham to negotiate with the poor-masters "in the principal towns and cities of Vermont for the bodies of paupers dying under their charge." Also, it was decided that if necessary an agent would be dispatched to other states to "negotiate for anatomical material for this college." The professors at the same time established a committee to investigate the cost of erecting "an ice-house for the preservation of anatomical material." When the committee recommended construction of a tank, A. F. A. King, the professor of obstetrics and gynecology, moved that a "brewing vat" be procured for preservation of subjects "in pickle."[53]

It is unclear whether Tinkham was successful in his search for cadavers, but in April 1893 the local newspapers reported that two "cut up and badly mutilated" bodies had been found in a box consigned to Burlington. The express company held up shipment in

49. Chapin, *History, University of Vermont College of Medicine*, p. 100. *Alumni Weekly*, March 25, 1925, p. 239.
50. Chapin, *History, University of Vermont College of Medicine*, p. 101.
51. Ibid.
52. *Vermont Statutes, 1894* (Rutland, 1895), pp. 833–834.
53. UVM Medical Faculty Minutes, July 8, 1891, July 13, 1891.

Jersey City, but the company received a telegram from Charlottesville, Virginia, informing it that death certificates were being forwarded. According to the *Burlington Dispatch*, "as the bodies were those of two negroes" it was likely that "they are dissecting material consigned to some medical students here." The package was addressed to "H. C. Turner," in Burlington, which apparently was Henry Crain Tinkham, the demonstrator of anatomy.[54] Since William Beverly Towles was professor of anatomy at both Burlington and Charlottesville, it is likely that he was shipping cadavers north for the next term of the University of Vermont Medical College. In July of that year, in fact, the medical faculty voted to pay $58 to Towles for expenses incurred in the loss of anatomical material shipped from Virginia.[55]

After the medical lectures ended each year, the students were subjected to final examinations. Those who had fulfilled the requirements for graduation then gathered in suspense while the professors determined the results. In 1893 it was reported that while waiting, the students sang a number of songs, including "In the Sweet Bye and Bye," "with evident enthusiasm." According to the *Cynic*, usually "a few 'sore-heads' have howled around more or less about the unfairness of this or that professor."[56] Normally about 10 or 15 percent of the class would "be plucked"—they failed the examinations and would not graduate. In 1895 seven of the fifty-three students were "plucked," but they included two who "came to Burlington about a week ago from some medical college in New York City." Those two students apparently had failed their examinations in New York and had come to Burlington hoping to pass there and receive degrees from the University of Vermont.[57]

Then the survivors of the examinations attended the commencement exercises. They would be subjected to one last lecture, one that would not be interrupted by tramping or practical jokes. In 1883 Rudolph A. Witthaus addressed the class. He said that if he adhered "to time-honored custom," he might suggest "that a coarse demeanor and a breath redolent of whiskey and tobacco are not conducive to your successful treatment of a delicate female patient." He continued to note that if he followed tradition, he "might show" the "immorality of seeking to increase your practice and importance by leading your patient to believe that he is standing upon the brink of a grave, from which you will rescue him." Witthaus decided instead to speak on the relation between science and art in medicine. He quoted Oliver Wendell Holmes, who had written that "if the whole materia medica, as now used, could be sunk to the bottom of the sea, it would be all the better for mankind,—and all the worse for the fishes." Witthaus noted that "the glories of the lancet and of calomel have departed," but he asked whether the profession was

54. *Burlington Independent*, April 22, 1893, p. 5, col. 2. See also undated newspaper clippings in Grinnell Papers.

55. UVM Medical Faculty Minutes, July 11, 1893.

56. *University Cynic*, June 27, 1883, p. 49.

57. *Burlington Free Press and Times*, July 6, 1895, p. 7, col. 2.

"better" as a result of it. "Every copy of every medical journal," he declared, "teems with *new remedies*, not one percent of which will be in general use a decade hence." Witthaus concluded by urging the graduates to be both "the practitioner of an art and the student of a science. The practitioner," he exclaimed, "who ceases to be a student becomes a mere animated machine, and like most machines in these days of activity, soon becomes antiquated and is superseded by some more perfect mechanism of later construction." According to the report in local newspapers, Witthaus' "sharp hits and slashing statements" "made a decided sensation; and were applauded by a considerable portion of the audience." [58]

After hearing the commencement address, the graduating class would present a gift to one of the professors. In 1856 the class presented Samuel White Thayer with a gold watch; the following year Walter Carpenter was awarded a cane. When the cane was presented to Carpenter, the *Free Press* described it in light of the recent "caning" of Senator Charles Sumner in the nation's capital. There was a "slight rustling, a turning about, and a fine looking fellow, whom we took to be a representative of the medical class, was seen approaching the speaker's desk with a *cane* in his hand. The scenes of the famous *cane* Congress rushed upon us in all their horrors, yet we were not alarmed for we felt conscious that the fatherly professor had said nothing which could rouse the ire, even of Southern blood." The cane turned out to be "a golden headed testimonial of respect from the class, to a loved professor." [59]

Then the diplomas would be awarded to the graduates. The *Free Press* of July 14, 1891, provided a fine description: "As their fingers closed over the long hoped for parchments and they faced about to descend," the students "were greeted with the hearty applause of the audience." Then, the graduating class, the faculty, and invited guests assembled in the large dining room of the Van Ness House, "where a long table loaded with ices, coffee, cake, fruits, etc., tempted the appetite. Refreshments were taken standing, while the orchestra played and boys and professors moved about in groups, shaking hands, congratulating, joking and unbending generally from the hard work and suspense of the past few days." Professor King called "for vocal music," and soon "the melodious strains of the medical students' favorite 'seeing Nellie Home' rolled through the hall, followed by the 'old Oaken Bucket' and other familiar songs." After "an hour's enjoyment the medical class . . . scattered to their homes, every man with a . . . light heart and a white looking scroll, three feet long, in his hand." [60] Then the students would prepare to practice medicine, although a handful of graduates would head for New York or elsewhere to take postgraduate courses which would in effect prepare them for specialization. During wartime a number of students went

58. Unidentified newspaper clipping, 1882 in UVM Medical Faculty Minutes, 1875–93, pp. 100–102.

59. *Daily Free Press*, May 30, 1856, p. 2, col. 1; June 20, 1857, p. 2, col. 2.

60. *Burlington Free Press and Times*, July 14, 1891, p. 4, cols. 4–5.

directly from their graduation to the battlefield. During the Civil War, for instance, at least 15 percent of the students served as surgeons in the Union army, according to the listing in the General Catalogue of the University, that is obviously an underestimate, as evidenced by the testimony of George H. Van Deuson, class of '61. He recalled that ten of the twenty men who graduated with him were commissioned as surgeons, and he listed the names of the men.[61] It can be assumed that during the "Great Rebellion," as many as 30 or 40 percent of the graduates went on to serve the nation as surgeons in the military.

The historian can certainly conclude that the graduates of the University of Vermont College of Medicine had enjoyed their student days. They had spent time at their studies, but they also found time for pranks, athletics, songs, and other amusements.

61. *General Catalogue of the University of Vermont, 1791–1900* (Burlington, 1901), pp. 255–256. *Burlington Free Press and Times,* June 2, 1885, p. 4, col. 1.

Chapter Eleven

The Flexner Report and Its Aftermath

THE MOVEMENT to reform American medical education was continuing; in 1903 the Council on Medical Education of the American Medical Association joined in the struggle to raise standards. Now it was a three-pronged attack. The Association of American Medical Colleges set standards, the A.M.A. inspected the schools, and the state boards of medical examiners continually increased licensing requirements. The colleges were in a difficult position. As standards increased, it become more costly to provide a medical education. Proprietary medical schools such as that of the University of Vermont were first to be affected. Although nominally a part of the University, the College was financed as a joint-stock company, supporting itself with student fees. It was only a matter of time until student fees would no longer be sufficient. In addition, it was expected that enrollment and student fees would decrease as standards were increased.

In 1905 the faculty compared its curriculum to the one recommended by the Association of American Medical Colleges, and discovered that the students at Burlington received 860 hours fewer than recommended. The program was revised, but it was still 316 hours too short.[1] Increased hours meant more teaching, but the professors were busy physicians who did not want to increase their teaching load. Therefore, more instructors had to be appointed. In Vermont, however, the question of paying additional instructors was not the immediate concern. The immediate problem was more directly related to the local situation. The 1903 fire had destroyed the Medical Building and the lack of adequate facilities resulted in decreased attendance.

In the 1903–04 session there were 225 students; the professors re-

1. UVM Medical
Faculty Minutes,
November 27, 1905.

ceived a dividend of $1600. In 1904–05 the enrollment decreased to 203, and the dividend was reduced to $1200. In 1905–06 only 169 students attended classes, which meant a reduction to $200. Yet while the enrollment was decreasing, the College's expenses increased from $15,070 to $20,400. It was no longer financially rewarding to teach in Burlington; several professors threatened to resign.[2]

Dean Tinkham tried to find a remedy. In a report to the faculty he took note of "the diminished number of students, consequent upon the loss of the medical building by fire, and the unsettled condition of the department since." He hoped to "relieve, to a certain extent, the distressing financial condition . . . without giving any reasonable cause for dissaffection among the various instructors, on account of the smaller salary." Tinkham proposed that since the enrollment had decreased, the number of recitation and laboratory sections could be reduced, saving about $2,000 in salaries. "With other savings," that would increase the compensation to $700 for each full professor.[3] As

2. Ibid., June 1, 1907.
3. Ibid., June 18, 1906.

FACULTY OF 1904

14. President Matthew Buckham with the faculty of the College of Medicine in front of Billings Library, 1904.

there seemed to be no other solution to the problem of decreasing salaries, the report was adopted. The savings would take effect the following year, however. In 1906 the faculty was forced to borrow $1,000 in order to pay $200 to each member of the executive faculty.[4]

During the following year A. O. J. Kelly, the professor of medicine, prepared a statement "embodying the educational and financial situation" of the Medical Department. He noted the decreasing enrollment, the increasing cost of medical education, and the "necessity of adding to our equipment and generally improving our course in medicine." Referring to the reduced dividend, Kelly declared that it was impossible to keep "the faculty of medicine together upon a basis of such a small salary."[5]

Kelly explained the problem of financing the modern medical school. "It is quite impossible to give a satisfactory education in medicine for the fees paid by the students." In addition he noted that the professors no longer could determine the curriculum, for every college had to accept the standards of the A.M.A. Council on Medical Education and the various licensing agencies. He cited a concrete example—the A.M.A. had recently recommended that no student be admitted who did not have one year of college level work. Kelly predicted that state licensing boards would soon require that standard of preliminary education. Thus the College would once again be forced to increase requirements, which would "tend, at least temporarily," to decrease the number of students. Kelly explained that the College had to comply with the new standards or the graduates would not be able to practice medicine in most of the states. Indeed, he noted that as a result of higher standards in those states, Vermont graduates "are debarred from Michigan, Colorado, and California."[6]

Kelly, who also taught at the University of Pennsylvania, noted that Pennsylvania and several other states had appropriated money to support medical education. That permitted the hiring of full-time professors of physiology, anatomy, and chemistry. He concluded by quoting the *Journal of the American Medical Association*: "the successful medical school of the future must receive aid. Whether such endowment shall come from the state or from private sources local conditions will determine, but that such support must come is self evident."[7] Kelly's report resulted in action. He and Tinkham were directed to request that the trustees "assume entire control" of the finances of the Medical College. They proposed that the Board appropriate at least $1000 a year to expand laboratory facilities, and that the professors be paid reasonable salaries. They also requested the Board to "follow the sensible suggestion" of President Buckham by appealing to the medical alumni for contributions to defray the "running expenses" of the College until a permanent endowment had

4. Ibid., June 26, 1906.
5. Ibid., May 28 and June 1, 1907.
6. Ibid.
7. Ibid.

been secured. Since the faculty was still considered "a semi-private money-making corporation," it was impossible for the professors to initiate such a fund-raising campaign. The trustees, however, responded in the least expensive manner, by appropriating $1000 a year to increase laboratory facilities, and by advising the professors to increase tuition to a total of "not less than" $125 per year.[8]

In 1908 the faculty once again appealed to the trustees to take over the finances of the Medical College. Enrollment had continued to decrease, to 165 in 1906–07 and to 155 the following session. Kelly once again prepared a proposal, which declared that "the laborer is worthy of his hire [and] for three years now [the professors] have conducted the Medical College almost without compensation." He insisted that if the trustees took action to make the medical department an integral part of the University, it "would probably serve to dissipate such popular prejudice as remains against the College of Medicine, borne of the belief that the College is what it should not have been, a private commercial enterprise." Moreover, if the Department were part of the University, it would "pave the way for appropriations from the State and for private endowments."[9]

After discussing the matter with President Buckham, the trustees agreed to release the faculty from its pledge to pay the interest on the $40,000 which had been borrowed to rebuild the College after the fire, and agreed also to apply for aid from the legislature. If the money were appropriated, the trustees would assume the financial management of the Medical School. The way was now clear for the financial takeover of the Medical College by the University. As a result, the faculty was able to vote a $500 dividend to each professor, and apparently in order to keep the out-of-state professors from abandoning the School, the Board appropriated an additional $1,000, to be equally divided between King and Kelly. Then the legislature appropriated $10,000 to support the School.[10]

In June 1909 Kelly presented another report detailing the faculty's recommendations for the financial operation of the Department. He included annual salaries of $2,000 for each professor. The trustees agreed to the entire package, except for reducing the salaries to $1500. This completed the financial takeover by the University.[11] Tinkham, overjoyed at the developments, exclaimed that "it is the beginning of a new epoch of prosperity" for the Department.[12]

While the faculty was moving toward closer ties with the University, Dean Tinkham tried to gain wider support for the Medical School. Even the alumni believed that the professors were becoming wealthy from the fees of the students, so a great deal of re-education had to be done. In addition, Tinkham was concerned that raising standards too fast would reduce enrollment to the point where maintaining the

8. UVM Trustee Minutes, June 24, 26, 1907. UVM Medical Faculty Minutes, July 12 and August 7, 1907.

9. UVM Medical Faculty Minutes, May 26, 1908.

10. Ibid., June 19 and 24, 1908. UVM Trustee Minutes, June 23 and December 4, 1908. *Vermont Medical Monthly*, 14 (December 15, 1908), 304.

11. UVM Medical Faculty Minutes, June 21, 1909. UVM Trustee Minutes, June 28–30, 1909.

12. *Vermont Medical Monthly*, 15 (August 15, 1909), 197.

School would no longer be feasible. In December 1906 he attacked the state board of medical registration for requiring every candidate for a license to have a four-year high school education. Since only ten or twelve of the high schools in Vermont could "turn out young men able to meet the requirements of this State Board," the University was forced to admit students who were required to make up deficiencies in various subjects.[13]

The dean also argued that those who set the standards tended to disregard the quality of teaching and at the same time overemphasized the physical plant and the financial situation of the School. For instance, the A.M.A. Council on Medical Education paid little attention to the success of graduates on state board examinations. Tinkham was upset that the A.M.A. put a premium on large endowments, which enabled some schools to construct modern laboratories, have full-time professors, and raise standards irrespective of enrollment. He declared that if the A.M.A. continued on its present course, "the medical schools which cannot secure endowments must cease to exist."[14]

Tinkham conceded that higher standards would result in better educated physicians, but he was convinced that they would also result in a shortage of practitioners in rural areas. He explained that when every physician had to devote four years to his premedical training, another four years to medical school, and additional time to hospital service, only a handful would be willing to practice in rural America, where patients had little money to pay for their medical care. Since Vermont was predominantly rural, Tinkham feared that the movement to increase standards would ultimately wreak havoc throughout the state.[15]

Though he argued against the emphasis on endowments, he recognized that the University's Medical School needed financial aid to meet the increasing standards of medical education. He was upset that the College was commonly considered to be a "profitable enterprise." He tried to explain that the College was far from being profitable. Once, when the faculty was small and expenses low, it was possible for the professors to "receive a fairly good income." Now, with the emphasis on laboratories and small recitation sections, more instructors were required and other expenses increased, but salaries decreased. Tinkham concluded that the solution was more financial aid. He hoped that the "friends of the University will not allow the Medical Department to suffer for the lack of an endowment."[16] In January 1908 he told the medical alumni that "in the interests of a square deal" he would not "legislate out of existence" a medical school whose graduates were maintaining a satisfactory standard on the state board examinations.[17]

13. Ibid., 12 (December 15, 1906), 269.

14. Ibid., 13 (June 15, 1907), 149–150; (July 15, 1907), 176–177.

15. Henry Crain Tinkham, "Preliminary Education," *Vermont Medical Monthly*, 13 (August 15, 1907), 185–187.

16. *Vermont Medical Monthly*, 13 (September 15, 1907), 227–228.

17. Ibid., 14 (February 15, 1908), 39–40.

Now that the financial situation was being alleviated by the trustees and the legislature, Tinkham could become more progressive. It became possible to "improve the Course in Medicine and to make it conform to the modern trend of medical education." First, the faculty voted to accept the requirements of the Association of American Medical Colleges, which included one premedical year in college.[18] The following year Tinkham proposed further changes, including fulltime men in anatomy, physiology, and chemistry, fulltime laboratory instructors, additional professors, and an added year to the course, which would in effect be the premedical college course in physics, inorganic chemistry, and biology. The proposal was presented to the trustees, who referred it to committee for further study.[19]

Although the College had substantially raised its standards since the resignation of Dean Grinnell, a bombshell was about to fall which would threaten to destroy the College before it had an opportunity to make further advances. In 1908 Abraham Flexner was commissioned by the Carnegie Foundation for the Advancement of Teaching to analyze the condition of American medical education. In May 1909 Flexner visited Burlington to investigate the situation at the University of Vermont College of Medicine. After having visited all the schools, Flexner published his report, and it was devastating. Vermont's Medical School was a typical college, but it was hardly in the class with Johns Hopkins or the handful of other top-flight institutions. Flexner reported that the University had low standards; it accepted students who had fewer than four years of high school. Although the leading institutions had appointed full-time faculty in the preclinical sciences, the University had only one full-time teacher, the demonstrator of anatomy. Flexner described the "attractive new laboratory building" as "adequate to routine teaching of anatomy, pathology, histology, bacteriology, physiology, and chemistry," but he noted that there was absolutely no research being done at the College. In addition, he declared that the College had no library, no museum, and "practically no teaching accessories." Finally, he noted that although the College had access to the Mary Fletcher Hospital, there was no regular bedside work and the dispensary had "small attendance."[20]

Flexner believed that the University of Vermont was beyond repair. Since it was not located in a large city, it could not possibly provide sufficient clinical material. Since it did not have an endowment, he believed that it would not be able to provide the necessary financial support. He developed a long-range plan for American medical education, based on an analysis of population growth in the various sections. He said that New England should only have two medical schools—Harvard and Yale. Darmouth and Vermont would offer

18. Ibid., 15 (August 15, 1909), 197. See also UVM Medical Faculty Minutes, June 21, 1909.

19. UVM Medical Faculty Minutes, June 25, 27, 1910. UVM Trustee Minutes, June 27, 1910.

20. Abraham Flexner, *Medical Education in the United States and Canada* (New York, 1910), pp. 313–314.

two-year programs, which would be the preclinical work. Students would then transfer to city institutions where clinical material abounded in the large hospitals.[21]

Flexner declared that New England was "badly overcrowded with physicians," having a physician-population ratio of 1:592. Since the population was increasing very slowly, he said that New England would "need no more physicians for years to come." Therefore, the clinical departments of Dartmouth, Bowdoin, and Vermont "would certainly be lopped off; there is no good reason," he exclaimed, "Why these institutions . . . should be concerned with medicine at all. The mere fact that they are all old schools is a poor reason for continuing them," he said, "if they fail to do justice to the student, and thereby fail to subserve the public interest." Responding to the argument that rural schools trained country doctors, Flexner declared that schools which could not train students in obstetrics, contagious diseases, and "the ailments that throng dispensaries" were not producing the type of physician needed in rural America.[22]

For the first time since the 1830's, the existence of the Medical College at Burlington was seriously threatened. Although the same ethos that motivated Flexner had motivated the faculty since 1900, Flexner's report was seen as a declaration of war against the College. Interestingly, Flexner had viewed Bowdoin, Dartmouth, and Vermont all in the same light, and each school responded in a different way. Bowdoin's medical department could not raise the funds needed to support a modern medical school, and it closed its doors. Dartmouth followed Flexner's suggestion and became a two-year college. Henry Crain Tinkham, however, would not let the University of Vermont College of Medicine disappear or become a two-year school without a fight.

Almost immediately upon publication of the Flexner Report, Tinkham intensified his attack. In July 1910 the *Vermont Medical Monthly* published an editorial apparently written by Tinkham, who was on the editorial board. Agreeing that many of the facts presented by Flexner were "undeniable," he insisted, nevertheless, that "Mr. Flexner has been unjust in many instances. The whole trend of his work seems to be an attempt to forcibly crush out the small colleges and build up the great institutions." The *Monthly* continued by noting that "the medical profession as it exists throughout the country today is largely the product of these small and privately-owned schools." "Many of our most illustrious doctors of today are products of just the conditions which Mr. Flexner so vigorously condemns. The proof of the pudding is the eating," the editorial insisted, and "so long as the small schools are able to turn out men" who can pass the state board examinations and succeed in medical practice, it will be "impossible to argue the small school into oblivion by the

21. Ibid., p. 147.
22. Ibid., pp. 261–263.

results of any such pedagogic investigation as this." The editorial concluded by comparing Flexner's support of the large city schools to the development of the large corporation. The journal predicted that the medical profession would "resist any attempt to regulate medical education by Standard Oil methods." [23]

Before the end of the year Tinkham tried to take a positive step toward respectability by having the College join the Association of American Medical Colleges. After an on-site examination, however, the officers of the Association concluded that the College could not become a member until it had concluded a thorough reorganization. The report was specific, and in many ways it was similar to Flexner's. It noted the deficiencies in the faculty. While the leading schools were appointing full-time professors in the preclinical fields, Vermont had only one full-time man, the demonstrator of anatomy. In addition, the professors of pathology, John McCrae, and physiology, John W. Scane, lived in Montreal and came to Burlington only one day a week. Others came from large cities to teach short courses in special subjects. The report insisted that the College needed "live, full time teachers in the first two years, who will make use of the many excellent facilities now provided." In addition, the Association recommended the use of local physicians to teach the specialties, rather than men with outside affiliations. [24]

The report went on to note other problems. The library, for instance, was catalogued "but does not exist." Also, the College had no charts or models; the investigator concluded that "such teaching accessories are evidently not held to be worth while." Finally, the report asserted that "vastly improved clinical facilities" were required. [25] In short, the Association had uncovered the same problems as had Abraham Flexner. But while Flexner had insisted that the College should cease to exist as a four-year institution, the Association made suggestions that might enable it to survive.

Less than a month after receiving the report of the Association of American Medical Colleges, Tinkham called a special faculty meeting to discuss the reorganization of the faculty. A committee was established, and on May 9, 1911, it recommended expanding the seven-man executive faculty to a total of eleven, including five full-time men who were "in no way engaged in the practice of medicine or surgery." Then the committee, which apparently had consulted with the candidates, made specific recommendations concerning the composition of the faculty. [26]

Since the committee had decided that it was necessary to have a full-time preclinical faculty, it had to recommend full-time men in anatomy, physiology, chemistry, pharmacology, and pathology. Apparently, none of the older and more experienced professors was willing to abandon a lucrative practice, so the new positions had

The Flexner Report

23. Vermont Medical Monthly, 16 (July 15, 1910), 173. It may be noted that several actions had been taken by the faculty after Flexner's visit in May 1909. It may be argued that this was in anticipation of and response to any criticisms. Yet the sources provide no evidence that this was the case. Flexner himself noted in his autobiography that his intentions were miscontrued by deans and professors, who called attention to their own deficiencies in the hope of receiving a grant from the Foundation.
24. See W. J. Means to Tinkham, Columbus, Ohio, March 25, 1911, A.A.M.C. Folder, Tinkham Papers. See also correspondence between Tinkham and Fred C. Zapffe, 1910–11, in the same folder.
25. Ibid.
26. UVM Medical Faculty Minutes, April 18 and May 9, 1911.

to go to relatively young physicians who either had not yet developed extensive practices or who could afford to accept a limited income. The committee's recommendations were accepted.

Dean Tinkham, who had been professor of anatomy, became professor of clinical surgery. Thomas Stephen Brown, a 33-year-old member of the class of 1904, was given the anatomy position. He had been instructor of anatomy and histology since 1907. John W. Scane, the Montreal practitioner who had been professor of physiology and microscopic anatomy, was replaced by Fred Kinney Jackson, a 37-year-old who had graduated in 1899. Jackson, the son of Professor J. Henry Jackson, had done postgraduate work at Cornell, Harvard, University College in London, and Edinburgh. He had served as instructor of physiology from 1901 to 1904 and as assistant professor from 1904 to 1911.

James N. Jenne, who had been professor of materia medica and therapeutics, was given the chair of therapeutics and clinical medicine. David Marvin, a 34-year-old member of the class of 1900, became professor of pharmacology and materia medica. He had been instructor of pharmacology and therapeutics for the past few years. Pathology, which had been taught as a special subject by John McCrae, was to be handled by Bingham H. Stone, a 37-year-old physician who had graduated in 1899 and done postgraduate work at the University of Vienna. Charles S. Caverly, a well known physician who had graduated in the class of 1881, became professor of hygiene and preventive medicine. He had done postgraduate work at New York's College of Physicians and Surgeons and had traveled extensively in Europe studying sanitation. The appointments of Stone and Caverly signified a closer relationship between the Medical College and the State Board of Health, for Caverly had been president of the Board since 1891, and Stone was director of the State Laboratory of Hygiene and bacteriologist of the State Board of Health.

Brown, Jackson, Marvin, and Stone, all relatively young graduates of the University of Vermont College of Medicine, became the full-time members of the executive faculty. The part-time professors included A. F. A. King, who taught obstetrics and diseases of women; Tinkham, who held the chair of clinical surgery; John Brooks Wheeler, professor of surgery; and Clarence H. Beecher, the adjunct professor of the theory and practice of medicine, who became professor of medicine when A. O. J. Kelly died in the winter of 1910 at the age of 40.[27]

The College, then, had four full-time professors. They all were Vermonters and they all lived in or near Burlington. Except for A. F. A. King, all members of the executive faculty were Vermont residents. Now, partly as a result of the College's response to the

27. For an obituary of Kelly, see *UVM Notes*, 12 (March 1911), 6.

College of Medicine

Dr. Lyman Allen

Dr. Clarence Beecher

Dr. Thomas Brown

Dean James N. Jenne

Dr. David Marvin

Dr. George Sabin

FACULTY — 1933

Dr. Charles Dalton

Dr. Charles Johnson

Dr. Ernest Buttles

Dr. John Wheeler

Dr. Fred Jackson

Dr. Patrick McSweeney

Dr. Charles Whitney

*15. Dean Jenne and
professors, College of
Medicine, 1933.*

*16. Henry Crain Tink-
ham, Dean of the Col-
lege of Medicine,
1898–1925.*

recommendations of the Association of American Medical Colleges, the faculty was inbred and relatively inexperienced.

The College continued to bring in "professors of special subjects" to give short courses and hold clinics on various specialties that could not be adequately covered by the permanent faculty. In the 1911–12 session, the first year following the reorganization, the special professors included Godfrey Pisek of New York City, who taught pediatrics; Fred H. Albee, also of New York, who demonstrated orthopedic surgery; Charles A. Peters of Montreal as professor of dermatology; Watson Lowell Wasson of Waterbury, Vermont, as professor of mental diseases; William Warren Townsend of Rutland as professor of genito-urinary diseases; Patrick E. McSweeney of Burlington as professor of gynecology; and Marshall C. Twitchell, also of Burlington, as professor of the diseases of the eye, ear, nose, and throat. In addition, Major J. A. Wilson of Fort Ethan Allen taught tropical diseases.[28]

By the fall of 1911 the reorganization was almost complete. Tinkham informed Fred C. Zapffe, the secretary of the Association of American Medical Colleges, that "we have all-time men in the subjects of anatomy, physiology, materia medica and pharmacology, and we shall have an all-time man in chemistry next year." He also noted that the College had five other full-time instructors. Finally, he emphasized the "important change in terms of professors of clinical medicine and clinical surgery," which signaled a change from the didactic teaching of the past to the bedside instruction of the present day.[29] Now, the chair of surgery was divided, with Wheeler being professor of surgery and Tinkham assuming the position in clinical surgery. Similarly, Beecher would be professor of medicine, while Jenne became professor of clinical medicine.

On January 30, 1912, William J. Means, chairman of the judicial council of the Association, wrote Tinkham he was "very much gratified to learn of the reorganization already made and to be made in the teaching faculty of the Medical Department of the University of Vermont. With these facts before us," he said, "I can see no objection to admitting the College to full membership."[30] The reorganization of the faculty had been successful. Just two years after the devastating Flexner Report, the College was accepted into the Association of American Medical Colleges.

In 1912, however, the College faced still another serious threat. The New York State Department of Education informed Tinkham that New York no longer would automatically license those graduates who were approved by the Vermont Board of Medical Registration. The decision resulted from the Vermont Board having licensed several graduates of the University who did have the required three years of high school training and who were given advanced standing

28. Taken from UVM College of Medicine, Bulletin, 1911.

29. H. C. Tinkham to Fred C. Zapffe, carbon copy in A.A.M.C. Folder, Tinkham Papers. UVM College of Medicine, *Annual Announcement, 1911* (Burlington, 1911), pp. 21–22, 23, 27, 42–43.

30. Means to Tinkham, Columbus Ohio, January 30, 1912, A.A.M.C. Folder, Tinkham Papers.

in spite of having failed all their subjects in their first year elsewhere. Tinkham responded that the University met the New York standards, and that "whatever may have been the condition of the records under the old regime," they were now in order. He concluded by suggesting that since the University's new president, Guy Potter Benton, had just arrived in Burlington, it was "an inopportune time to magnify minor evils or to dwell upon evils which have been done away."[31]

Although Benton was new on the scene, he immediately rushed to the defense of the Medical School. Both Tinkham and Benton went to Albany to meet personally with Augustus S. Downing, New York's Commissioner of Education. They convinced him that the errors of the past should be overlooked. Benton assured Downing that the College's officials would "be glad to cooperate with you in any way that you may suggest to guarantee the integrity of our entrance admissions for the future."[32] When Benton received a letter indicating Downing's decision to postpone consideration of the case, he immediately scribbled a note to Tinkham, which declared, "Hip, hip hurrah! Three cheers are in order!" Benton went on, however, to inform Tinkham that much more had to be done. "It is 'up to us' now to get busy and straighten matters out before May. I am with you heartily," Benton exclaimed, "to fight the thing through to final victory."[33]

Benton's euphoria was not to last. On February 21, the day after his happy note to Tinkham, Downing informed Tinkham that he had inspected the College's class lists and that he was disappointed at what he had found. "A cursory examination," he said, "leads me to believe that there are a number of these students who have been admitted on lower requirements than our statute demands." Downing would have to withhold registration until he was able to reach "an accurate and just conclusion." He suggested that he and Tinkham take the same train to the meeting of the American Medical Association, so they would have time to discuss the matter fully while en route to Chicago.[34] (Downing's assessment of the college standards, by the way, was correct.)

The threat to the Medical College was not the Dean's only problem. His daughter, Mabel, was in Colorado Springs, dying of tuberculosis. In April 1912 Benton assured Tinkham that his "first duty was to his only remaining child." He urged the Dean to go to "the bedside of his invalid daughter." Tinkham took the President's advice and departed for Colorado. Meanwhile, Benton informed Downing of the situation, and the Commissioner wrote Benton that "in view of the trouble that has overtaken Dr. Tinkham," he was willing to postpone a decision on the status of the School. It was easy to grant the request, for all the medical schools had to be reregistered as a result of the new A.M.A. requirement that every acceptable school have six full-time adequate-

31. See Tinkham to Downing, February 11, 1912, carbon copy in New York Department of Education Folder, Tinkham Papers.

32. Benton to Downing, February 20, 1912, carbon copy in New York Dept. of Education Folder.

33. Benton to Tinkham, February 20, 1912, Benton Folder, Tinkham Papers.

34. Downing to Tinkham, Albany, February 21, 1912, New York Department of Education Folder, Tinkham Papers.

ly paid instructors. As a result of the postponement, the College had time to prepare an adequate defense as well as to continue with the reorganization.

Unfortunately, Tinkham's daughter died on June 5. The Dean returned to Burlington in mourning.[35] Meanwhile, the faculty set out to raise standards. On June 3, for instance, the professors voted to require one year of college work in chemistry, physics, biology, and language, and to abolish the equivalency examination that had enabled poorly educated students to enroll in the past. In 1912 the University officially announced that one year of college-level work was required for admission to the Medical School.[36] Now the University satisfied the New York statutes.

In October 1912 Downing informed Tinkham that after careful consideration, he had decided to recommend that the regents approve the Medical School at Burlington, on condition that each autumn the Dean furnish a list of matriculants, "showing the credentials recognized for matriculation in order to affirm officially the standing" of the institution.[37] Downing's decision climaxed the College's second successful campaign to maintain its integrity. The first resulted in the reorganization required by the Association of American Medical Colleges, and the second increased admission requirements, as demanded by the New York Board of Regents.

Yet faculty reorganization and higher admission standards were only part of the overhaul needed to develop a first-rate institution. Perhaps most crucial was the need to increase the quantity of clinical material. Both the Flexner Report and the Association of American Medical Colleges had emphasized Burlington's lack of clinical facilities. Indeed, Flexner had concluded that the College should not even bother to offer the last two years' work; he believed that clinical teaching could only be effective in the municipal hospitals of the large cities.

In the hope of improving the clinical situation, the medical faculty appealed to the trustees of the Mary Fletcher Hospital to establish a maternity ward, which would enable the College to provide formal obstetrics training, and a free dispensary, which would substantially increase the number of patients available for teaching purposes. The directors of the Hospital, reluctant to finance a project that would primarily benefit the College, established a committee to negotiate with the trustees of the University, proposing that the "whole expense of establishing and maintaining the same be borne by the College."[38]

When the executive committee of the University Board of Trustees met on April 24, 1912, President Benton supported the faculty request for funds to establish a dispensary. The trustees finally voted to direct a committee to "cooperate with the hospital authorities in the

35. *UVM Notes*, 8 (June, 1912), 14–15. Downing to Benton, Albany, April 29, 1912, Benton Folder, Tinkham Papers.

36. UVM Medical Faculty Minutes, June 3, 1912. UVM Medical College, *Annual Announcement, 1912* (Burlington, 1912), pp. 24–25.

37. Downing to Tinkham, Albany, October 17, 1912, Department of Education Folder, Tinkham Papers.

38. UVM Medical Faculty Minutes, November 10, 1911. Mary Fletcher Hospital Board of Directors, Minutes, April 8, 1912, Medical Center Hospital of Vermont Administrator's Office.

establishment of a dispensary for the common use of the hospital and the Medical College."[39] By September, however, very little progress had been made; the directors of the Hospital refused to provide funds, and the trustees of the University were not willing to underwrite the entire cost of the dispensary. Finally, in what must have been a moment of great frustration, Dean Tinkham wrote a long letter to the president and the executive committee, reiterating the need for a "free dispensary where all forms of disease can be treated and demonstrated to students in just the same way that diseases of the Eye, Ear, Nose and Throat are now utilized by Dr. Twitchell." The dean predicted that the cost would be less than $1500, and that if ten cents were charged to each patient, it "would go a long way in meeting the actual expenses of the dispensary."[40]

The executive committee was less than enthusiastic when it finally reported to the full Board of Trustees. Although the committee "recognized the vital importance to the College of Medicine," it recommended that no action be taken as "no funds appeared available at present for the purpose suggested."[41] An obvious solution was to appeal to the legislature, which had appropriated $10,000 for the Medical College just four years before. As early as April 1912 there had been some discussion of a request to the legislature, but a great deal of opposition had developed within the University, especially from the deans of the other colleges. First, Joseph Hills, dean of the College of Agriculture, wrote to inform President Benton that he had "stepped to one side" in 1908 in favor of the Medical College, and that if absolutely necessary he was willing to do so again. He went on to note, however, that Middlebury College intended to ask the legislature for funds to teach agriculture, and he predicted that unless the University made the same request, it was likely that Middlebury would establish a competing school of agriculture. Dean G. H. Perkins of the College of Arts and Sciences and Dean J. W. Votey of the College of Engineering joined Hills in complaining that the Medical School was "absorbing an undue proportion of the income of the University."[42]

It seemed obvious that another request for an appropriation to support the Medical College would result in internal warfare: each dean would fight to protect his own school. After all, an appropriation to support one school was in effect a budget cut for the rest of the University. Benton recognized the political realities of the situation, and in June 1912 he included in his annual report the statement that although the Medical College must have larger support to survive, "we should not allow the life-blood of the other colleges of the university to be sapped simply for the sake of supporting a college of medicine."[43] A compromise was finally reached; the trustees request-

39. Executive Committee Report to the Trustees, April 24, 1912, UVM Archives.

40. Tinkham to President and Executive Committee of the Board of Trustees, 1912, Benton File, Tinkham Papers.

41. Executive Committee Report to Trustees, September 19, 1912, Executive Committee Folder, UVM Archives.

42. Hills to Benton, April 25, 1912, Trustee File, UVM Archives. UVM Trustee Minutes, June 24, 1912.

43. *UVM Notes,* 8 (June, 1912), 14–15. For an interesting counterpoint see Tinkham to Benton, July 23, 1912, Benton File, Tinkham Papers.

ed an appropriation to support the colleges of Agriculture, Medicine, and Engineering.

On March 11, 1913, the trustees once again voted to establish a committee to work with the directors of the Mary Fletcher Hospital in establishing dispensary facilities and a maternity ward at the Hospital. This time, however, the financial problems had been met by the legislative appropriation.[44] As a result of the negotiations between the Hospital and the University, there was a substantial improvement in clinical facilities at the College. A free dispensary was being established in rooms provided by the Hospital, and that would greatly increase the number of cases available for teaching. In addition, the directors of the Hospital consented to give the students greater access to the Hospital. Henceforth, a "large percentage" of the patients would be admitted as clinical cases; they would be "practically turned over to the College of Medicine" and would be under the "direct supervision" of the clinical professors. The appropriation enabled the Hospital to develop a free maternity ward with twelve beds. According to the 1913 College announcement, the ward "furnishes an ample supply of obstetrical cases for clinical teaching." Although that statement might have been somewhat exaggerated, the ward did represent a tremendous increase in the quantity of material available for teaching, especially since the College's previous obstetrical service had been performed at the patients' homes. Finally, the College had access to the Fanny Allen Hospital in Winooski, the State Hospital for the Insane at Waterbury, and two children's homes in Burlington.[45]

In the fall of 1912, when President Benton, Dean Tinkham, and others were lobbying for a state appropriation, a number of legislators began to ask whether better use could be made of tax revenues. Some suggested that since the state's common schools were inadequate, it was more logical to use state funds to improve elementary and secondary education, rather than continuing to support the University of Vermont, Middlebury College, and Norwich University. Benton, familiar with recent developments in "scientific" education, advised Governor Allen M. Fletcher to establish a commission to determine the educational needs of the state, and to make recommendations for the best way to allocate state funds. The educational survey was in vogue at the time; in 1911 a survey of Baltimore was completed, and in 1912 there were educational surveys of Virginia and North Dakota. Governor Fletcher was impressed with the idea, and on his recommendation the legislature adopted a joint resolution setting up the Vermont Education Commission.[46]

The members of the Commission decided to seek expert advice; they requested the Carnegie Foundation to make the survey. Since

44. Executive Committee Report to the Trustees, March 11, 1913, copy in Executive Committee Folder, UVM Archives. *Vermont Medical Monthly*, 19 (April 15, 1913), 96. The legislative appropriation was $18,500 for the schools of Agriculture and Medicine. See *Burlington Free Press and Times*, November 8, 1912, p. 1, col. 1; January 6, 1913, p. 2, col. 2; and February 20, 1913, p. 4, cols. 1–3.

45. *Vermont Medical Monthly*, 19 (April 15, 1913), 96. UVM Trustee Minutes, June 24, 1913. *Vermont Cynic*, October 25, 1913, p. 6, col. 1. UVM Medical College, *Announcement, 1913* (Burlington, 1913), pp. 20–21.

46. *UVM Notes*, 9 (April–May, 1913), 1ff. J. L. Hills, "History of the Medical College," p. 146.

the Carnegie Foundation had sponsored the Flexner Report, which had questioned the need for a medical school at Burlington, the decision to appoint the Educational Commission posed a new threat to the University. And rather ironically, President Benton had urged the Governor to establish the Commission! In any case, it did not take long for the investigators to determine that the Medical School still had low standards. In retrospect, the standards were understandable in the light of recent developments. In 1912, in response to the demands of the New York regents, the faculty had increased admission requirements to one year of college-level work. That, combined with the lengthening of the course to nine months, tended to decrease the number of applications. Only six students were qualified for admission to the freshman class! At that point, Tinkham was *really* in a quandary. If the freshman class consisted of only six students, it would be almost impossible to argue that the Medical School played a major role in educating physicians for the state, which meant that the legislators would almost certainly cut off state support. In order to keep enrollment at a respectable level, Tinkham decided to admit students who had failed their first year of medical school, either at Vermont or elsewhere. When asked to explain why half of the freshman class had not completed one year of college work, Tinkham could "innocently" declare that they had been admitted on the standards when they first enrolled in medical school. Regardless of his argument, however, the fact remains that the University had a first-year class of twelve men, half of whom did not meet the stated admission requirements.[47]

In 1914 the Carnegie Foundation issued its report, *Education in Vermont*, which was devastating not only to the Medical School but to the entire University. The report concluded that state aid should be increased to elementary and secondary education, and aid to higher education should be severely reduced. In terms of the Medical School, the report noted the "high order of devotion exhibited by the dean and by the professors. . . . who have put into their work great intelligence, sincere devotion to the student, and a high determination to give . . . the best education they can furnish." The report declared, however, that the question of medical education in Vermont had to be considered "entirely apart" from the devotion of the faculty. The study concluded that on the basis of the low enrollment, the state was wasting money trying to support medical education. The lack of clinical facilities was emphasized, especially in studying contagious diseases and obstetrics. The report noted correctly that "it has been the practice for medical students at Burlington" to take summer courses in obstetrics in New York City, where clinical material was more plentiful.[48]

According to the Carnegie Foundation, the cost of providing medi-

47. See Tinkham to Physicians of Vermont, October 21, 1912, form letter in College Campaign Folder, Tinkham Papers. Clyde Furst to Tinkham, New York, May 20, 1913, Carnegie Foundation Folder, Tinkham Papers.

48. Carnegie Foundation for the Advancement of Teaching, *Education in Vermont* (New York, 1914), pp. 174–175.

cal education was prohibitive, and the State of Vermont, with its limited resources, could not afford such a luxury. "When one considers the pressing need in Vermont for the development of elementary and secondary education and for placing the public school system under a fruitful administration," the report continued, "the expenditure of the large sum of money necessary to develop a medical school . . . is hard to justify." [49]

On January 29, 1914, President Benton summarized the report at a meeting of the Board of Trustees. According to the minutes, "several members of the Board expressed the opinion that notwithstanding the findings of the Foundation, the State could not afford to see the Department discontinued and that the Legislature would see to it that an adequate appropriation was made for its continuance." No decisions were made, but the Board agreed that since the legislature had voted to establish a hospital for feeble-minded children, it should be located in Burlington where it could be a "clinical adjunct to the Medical College." [50]

Shortly after publication of the report, the entire state seemed to rally behind the Medical College. Led by the *Burlington Free Press*, newspapers supported the School; Dean Tinkham provided them with ammunition, in the form of elaborate defenses of medical education in Vermont. [51] The *Vermont Medical Monthly*, with Tinkham as editor, naturally supported the College and condemned its "enemy," the Carnegie Foundation. In February 1914, for instance, the journal exclaimed that when the Foundation was established, it had promised to help colleges by providing pensions that would enable the schools to attract a better class of teacher, and by providing funds for construction or expansion. The first hint "of a possible fly in the ointment—a suggestion that the pretty bee might have a sting," came in 1910 with the publication of the Flexner Report. The editor declared that the Foundation was placing the colleges in "the position of a scared puppy kicked by a boot behind and coaxed by a bone in front." [52]

Joseph Hills, dean of the College of Agriculture, who had been so angry at the appropriations supporting medical education at the University, wrote to inform Tinkham that he would not *openly* oppose the continuation of medical education in Vermont—"Because of my warm regard for you," he said, and because of "indignation at the unfair light in which the College of Medicine has been placed before the public, and finally because I love a man who will fight to the last gasp for his own and for what he regards the right." Hills bade the dean "Godspeed on your errand and sincerely to wish you success." He believed that the Medical School should be closed because it was draining too much of the funding away from the rest of the University, but he decided not to voice his views "to anyone but the

49. Ibid., p. 176.
50. UVM Trustee Minutes, January 29, 1914.
51. See, for instance, *Burlington Free Press and Times*, February 3, 1914, p. 4, cols. 2–3; February 16, 1914, p. 4, cols. 1–3.
52. *Vermont Medical Monthly*, 20 (February 15, 1914), 39–40.

President and the other academic deans." He was loyal to the University; if the trustees decided to maintain the Medical College, he would not stand in their way.[53]

With the implicit support of the trustees, who at least did not vote to close the school, and with the sympathy of the academic community, Tinkham began a campaign to discredit the Carnegie Foundation, much as it had discredited the College. On February 18, 1914, he declared to the western Massachusetts alumni association that "there is a conspiracy on the part of several organizations . . . to put the smaller medical schools out of business." "The octopus," he said, "has practically squeezed out the existence of the Hanover Medical School in the past two years," and its next intended victim was the University of Vermont. Tinkham condemned the recent report of the Carnegie Foundation as "vicious" and "unfair" and insisted that it was based on "garbled statistics."[54] He said that the Foundation had enjoyed the second chance to discredit the Medical School, and he even declared that Henry S. Pritchett, president of the Foundation, had tried to convince the A.M.A. Council on Medical Education to reduce the rating of the University of Vermont, which "would aid in the squeezing out process."[55]

In the winter of 1914 Tinkham and B. H. Stone, professor of pathology, went to Chicago to defend the College before the Council on Medical Education. They managed to convince the members of the Council to continue the class A rating until the next inspection, in 1915. When Tinkham and Stone returned to Burlington, they were received as conquering heroes. The medical students held a smoker to celebrate the class A rating, and President Benton received "loud cheers" for his support of the School. He insisted, however, that the real credit had to be given to the Dean and Professor Stone, who had met the enemy in Chicago and returned in victory. Tinkham told the students about the "infernal workings of the 'Foundation'" and he urged them to "talk to all influential men, legislators and laymen and try to secure for the medical college the needed appropriations." Then Dr. Clarence Beecher gave his "usual spicy characteristic talk," and Dr. F. E. Clark "had the boys in a spasm of laughter every minute." The smoker ended with the singing of "Hail, Green and Gold," accompanied by an orchestra.[56]

The decision of the Council on Medical Education gave Tinkham additional time to improve the clinical facilities. He began by "fishing" for money to support the construction of a new hospital. The Dean told the members of the Burlington Merchants Association that the School needed clinical facilities consisting of 200 beds, along with an increase in the state appropriation to $50,000. Tinkham was hoping that some philanthropic business leaders would step forward to endow the new hospital, and he informed the merchants that the

53. Hills To Tinkham, February 17, 1914, Hills File, Tinkham Papers.
54. *University Cynic*, February 28, 1914, p. 5.
55. Tinkham to W. L. McCormick, March 6, 1914, McCormick Folder, Tinkham Papers. See *Burlington Free Press and Times*, February 21, 1914, p. 4, cols. 2–3, for another indication that Pritchett was trying to convince the A.M.A. to reduce the rating of the Medical College.
56. *Vermont Cynic*, March 7, 1914, p. 1. There had been persistent rumors that the College would close, and Tinkham set out to dispel the fears. See *UVM Notes*, 10 (July, 1914), p. 30; Walter H. Sisson to members of the pre-med class, August 24, 1914, Tinkham Papers, Applications Folder.

A.M.A. would change the rating to class B if the state appropriation did not increase by February.[57]

Meanwhile, Tinkham did what he could to increase the number of patients available for teaching. The free dispensary had been handling from twenty to thirty patients daily, and the Dean managed to convince the city's board of aldermen to assign the work of the city physician to the dispensary. That enabled the College to establish a second dispensary, at the foot of Pearl Street, which promised to at least double the daily caseload.[58] At the same time, Tinkham sought funds to increase the number of hospital beds available to the students. In July 1914 the executive committee of the University Board of Trustees voted to authorize the faculty to raise $50,000, and in August they voted to authorize the faculty to negotiate with the directors of the Mary Fletcher and Fanny Allen hospitals for improved facilities.[59]

The faculty directed Tinkham, Jenne, and McSweeney to proceed with the negotiations. Tinkham and Jenne asked the directors of the Mary Fletcher Hospital if they would be willing to increase the number of clinical patients available to the College if the University would grant $25,000 to the hospital. After some discussion, the directors indicated that they would increase clinical facilities, even without the $25,000. In effect they agreed to let the College use all the beds except those in the private ward. The same arrangement was earlier developed between Columbia University and New York's Presbyterian Hospital.[60]

Meanwhile, Tinkham, Benton, McSweeney, and Jenne met with Bishop Joseph J. Rice, who said that he was anxious to have the Fanny Allen Hospital "come into the city." He also declared that he was willing to do everything in his power to keep the Medical School in operation. After some discussion, the Bishop offered to build a hundred-bed hospital, and if the University would contribute $25,000 to the building fund, he would give the Medical School complete control of the hospital for clinical purposes.[61]

At first glance, it would seem that the Bishop's proposal signaled the success of Tinkham's campaign. With increased access to the Mary Fletcher Hospital and with the construction of a Catholic hospital in the city, the College would have access to more than the 200 beds required by the Council on Medical Education. Yet the situation was more complex. Since several men served at the same time on the boards of the University and the Mary Fletcher Hospital, the directors of Mary Fletcher soon learned that the College had pledged to donate $25,000 to help construct a Catholic hospital. They were outraged. They had always been "generous in their dealings with the College of Medicine," and had increased clinical access without demanding any payment, even after Tinkham offered $25,000.[62] Ob-

57. *Vermont Cynic*, March 21, 1914, p. 31. Tinkham to George L. Hunt, June 27, 1914, Benton File, Tinkham Papers.

58. UVM Trustee Minutes, June 23, 1914. UVM Medical College, *Announcement, 1914* (Burlington, 1914), pp. 20–21. *Announcement, 1915* (Burlington, 1915), p. 19. *UVM Notes*, 14 (December 1917), 5.

59. Executive Committee Report, July 23 and August 31, 1914, UVM Archives.

60. Tinkham to Benton, October 30, 1914, Benton Folder, Tinkham Papers. Mary Fletcher Hospital Board of Directors, Minutes, August 27 and October 19, 1914, Administrator's Office, Medical Center Hospital of Vermont.

61. UVM Medical Faculty Minutes, May 20, 1914. Tinkham to Bishop Rice, October 12, 1914, Bishop Rice Folder, Tinkham Papers.

62. Tinkham to Benton, October 30, 1914, Benton Folder, Tinkham Papers. UVM Trustee Minutes, October 30, 1914.

viously, it would not serve any useful purpose to alienate the directors of the Mary Fletcher by donating money to construct a competing institution. In addition, there was a serious question about the legality of the University providing aid to a sectarian institution, especially since the state was beginning to appropriate money regularly to support the Medical School. In order to prevent conflict, and perhaps because of some anti-Catholic sentiment on the Board of Trustees, it was decided to forget the $25,000 pledge to the building fund of the Catholic hospital.

The situation was once again starting to look grim. The College would not have access to the required 200 beds and in February the Council on Medical Education was planning to reevaluate the School. In addition to the problem of clinical facilities, the fund-raising drive had not been successful. Indeed, "owing to certain obstacles," possibly the question of supporting a Catholic hospital, "little progress had been made." The faculty decided to try its own fundraising, and it voted to have Tinkham approach the Merchants' Association, the Woman's Clubs, and the Board of Aldermen.[63]

Early in February 1915 Tinkham wrote to William J. Means, chairman of the executive committee of the Association of American Medical Colleges and an active member of the Council on Medical Education. The Dean said that he would meet with Means in Chicago on the 16th, and he insisted that the University "is not asking for favors—we do not ask or expect any special dispensation for ourselves; all we ask is a square deal." He continued by noting that as long as the graduates of the College compared favorably in their general standing with graduates of other schools, and as long as the College continued to serve the medical needs of Vermont, "it seems to me a reasonable assurance that the character of teaching here is at least reasonably good."[64]

When Tinkham returned from Chicago, he reported that the attitude of the Council on Medical Education was "very much changed, and very much more friendly." The members of the Council were obviously impressed by Tinkham's ability to bring about reform and by his earnest support of medical education in Vermont. On February 27 the University's trustees voted to request an appropriation of $35,000 for the Medical School, after the legislators had adopted a joint resolution expressing their support for its continued existence.[65] Finally, the Council on Medical Education voted to continue the University of Vermont in class A and to require no further examination for at least two years.[66]

In 1916 Dean Tinkham was able to make an optimistic report for the first time since 1903. Although the total number of students had been decreasing for years, the size of the first-year class had increased from eleven in 1913 to twenty-one in 1916. The College had made the neces-

63. UVM Medical Faculty Minutes, January 19, 1915.
64. Tinkham to W. J. Means, February 6, 1915, A.A.M.C. Folder, Tinkham Papers.
65. UVM Medical Faculty Minutes, February 20, 1915. UVM Trustee Minutes, February 27, 1915. *UVM Notes*, 11 (March 1915), 5.
66. *UVM Notes*, 11 (March 1915), 5.

sary advances and was maintaining a "satisfactory standard of medical education," and now enrollment was stabilizing. In addition, contracts had been developed with the Mary Fletcher and Fanny Allen hospitals, giving the School use of the wards for clinical teaching. Moreover, the Burlington Free Dispensary had treated nearly 6500 patients in the past year. He boasted that for the first time the College was actively involved in medical research. The College had given the state Board of Health a laboratory to investigate infantile paralysis, and under the capable direction of Charles S. Caverly, a pioneer in the study of polio, the research was continuing.[67] As a demonstration of the commitment to higher standards, the faculty voted to increase the College's admission requirements, so that two years of college-level work were required of every freshman.[68]

Finally, also in 1916, the future grew even more promising when it was announced that the Catholic diocese of Burlington had decided to erect a hospital as a memorial to Bishop Louis DeGoesbriand, the first Bishop of Burlington, who was born one hundred years earlier. The hospital was to be constructed on the corner of Pearl and South Prospect streets, diagonally across from the Medical School, on the site of what had earlier been an orphanage and then St. Joseph's College.[69] Unfortunately, the shortage of building materials resulting from the start of World War I prevented the construction of the building until 1923, when the DeGoesbriand Memorial Hospital finally joined the Mary Fletcher in providing medical care to the citizens of Vermont, and in providing clinical material for the Medical School.

67. Tinkham to Benton, August 10, 1916, Benton Folder, Tinkham Papers.

68. UVM Medical Faculty Minutes, October 16, 1916.

69. *UVM Notes*, 13 (November 1916), p. 3. See *Burlington Free Press*, January 16, 1917, for Bishop Rice's letter to the editor describing the failure of previous negotiations with the University trustees, and the urgent need for a new hospital in Burlington.

Chapter Twelve

From Tinkham to Jenne and Beyond

IN 1915, while desperately trying to raise standards, the faculty followed the lead of a handful of colleges by requiring five years for graduation. The fifth year was a hospital internship away from Burlington. With the start of World War I, however, the increased demand for physicians resulted in the suspension of that requirement in Vermont and elsewhere. In 1920, with the return to "normalcy," the faculty decided to restore the previous requirement. That decision was once again revoked when Nathan P. Colwell, of the A.M.A. Council on Medical Education, informed Dean Tinkham that "no medical college should require an internship for a degree unless it is going to establish for itself some method by which the interns' work can be supervised." In addition, Colwell indicated that the hospitals should be carefully inspected, for a large number of the nation's hospitals were totally inadequate for medical education.[1]

As early as 1920 the Dean recognized the need to correlate scientific and clinical teaching. He suggested that faculty meetings include extensive discussion of specific cases, with all the professors participating. In January 1921, after Tinkham opened the discussion on the liver and gall bladder, Thomas S. Brown commented on anatomy, Hovey Jordan on histology, and Fred K. Jackson on the physiology of the liver and gall bladder. Then B. H. Stone commented on pathology, James N. Jenne spoke on the diagnosis of liver ailments, Clarence Beecher described their medical treatment, and John Brooks Wheeler discussed the surgery of the liver. Similar discussions took place over the next two years, with the clinical and scientific professors being

1. Tinkham to Walter G. Bain, February 6, 1920, Intern Folder, Tinkham Papers; N. P. Colwell to Tinkham, Chicago, June 28, 1921, Tinkham Papers.

forced for the first time to consider the relationships between their subjects.[2]

Meanwhile, in 1922 and 1923 Tinkham attended conferences sponsored by the Council on Medical Education and the Association of American Medical Colleges. He was particularly interested in keeping abreast of trends, so that he could anticipate the needs of the future rather than having to make changes without adequate preparation. He heard other medical educators extoll the benefits of the "elastic" curriculum, and many speakers emphasized "better correlation between scientific and clinical branches."[3] Moreover, some of the better schools were giving their students introductory courses in clinical medicine as early as the first or second years. That was quite different from the situation at Burlington, where students did not get practical work until the fourth year. By 1923 Tinkham was fully converted to the idea of early clinical training, and he planned to introduce it during that year.[4] As a result of discussions at faculty meetings, he was convinced that it would be "a very easy matter" to begin clinical teaching of first and second year men.[5] Late in 1924, before the curriculum could be changed, Tinkham became sick and was forced to give up a major part of his medical practice. After over a year of declining health, he died.[6]

In retrospect, Henry Crain Tinkham was the most important member of the Vermont faculty since Benjamin Lincoln in the 1830's. Tinkham had been dean since 1899, and he had supervised the reorganization from 1910 to 1916. Samuel White Thayer and Walter Carpenter were significant for their work in revitalizing the College in the 1850's, but they were able to work together; Tinkham was virtually alone in his fight to prevent the College from being forced to close its doors. He was able to defend it against the devastating recommendations of the Flexner Report, and he was able to bring about reform when it was required by the A.M.A. Council on Medical Education, the Association of American Medical Colleges, and the New York State regents. Tinkham had served the College very well indeed.

On February 22, 1926, the faculty elected James N. Jenne, clinical professor of medicine, as acting dean, and on June 18 the professors nominated him to serve as the permanent dean.[7] Jenne could not have been expected to serve for a lengthy period of time; he was 66 years old at the time he assumed the deanship. He was elected because of a general feeling that he was in the natural line of succession, having served on the faculty for over a quarter of a century. Tinkham had managed to keep the School in operation; it would be Jenne's task to make certain that his predecessor's work had not been in vain.

2. UVM Medical Faculty Minutes, December 20, 1920, January 17, 1921, and succeeding meetings.

3. Ibid., March 20, 1922, March 19, 1923.

4. Tinkham to Zapffe, March 30, 1923, A.A.M.C. Folder, Tinkham Papers.

5. Ibid.

6. For obituaries of Tinkham in University publications, see *Vermont Alumni Weekly*, 5 (December 9, 1925), 149; (January 13, 1926), passim.

7. UVM Medical Faculty Minutes, February 22 and June 18, 1926.

Less than a year after Jenne's assumption of the deanship, a familiar crisis developed. The Council on Medical Education inspected the University in November 1926, and in February 1927 President Guy W. Bailey was informed that "the Council will not be justified in continuing the college among class A medical schools unless within the next two years decided improvements shall have been brought about." Clinical work did not begin until the senior year, and according to the report, third-year students "do not secure clinical instruction either in the outpatient department or in the hospital." The inspectors suggested that the number of lectures in the third year be severely reduced, and that students be given experience in the examination and care of patients. In addition to the need for more and earlier clinical teaching, the report indicated that there should be six more full-time teachers, including professors of anatomy and physiological chemistry. The most serious deficiency, however, was the same one that had plagued the School since the turn of the century: lack of clinical material. In the letter to President Bailey, Colwell declared that "the inspector could not evade the doubt whether a serious attempt has ever been made toward the enlargement of clinical teaching in the hospital and dispensary." "Because of this serious shortage of clinical material," he said, "a definite plan for a state hospital should be laid down. Through such a development, the medical school will be enabled to exert a wider influence for public welfare in the state."[8]

An appeal to the legislature was prepared as soon as the college was informed of the threat to its rating. The University requested an additional appropriation of $40,000 for the 1926–27 year and $30,000 for the following year, "to be used for the purpose of procuring additional clinical facilities, equipment," and so forth. President Bailey, rather than the aging Dean Jenne, led the fight for the appropriation. Statistics were developed to demonstrate the importance of the Medical School to the people of Vermont; 92 percent of the physicians, for instance, who began to practice in the state over the past ten years had been trained at the University of Vermont.[9]

Before making the appropriation, a number of legislators wanted to be certain that the graduates of the Medical School would indeed practice in the state and fill the desperate need for physicians in the rural areas of Vermont. As a result of this concern, an amendment was added to the bill which directed the College to establish a department that would "cooperate with the rural communities in aiding such communities in procuring physicians and nurses." In addition, the amendment required the students to sign an agreement to practice one year in the state for every year enrolled in the Medical School, or refund the difference between the tuition and the actual cost of education.[10]

8. Colwell to Guy W. Bailey, Chicago, February 23, 1927, A.M.A. Folder, 1927–28, Bailey Papers.

9. *Vermont Alumni Weekly*, 6 (March 23, 1927), 355–56; (March 30, 1927), 371.

10. Ibid., (March 30, 1927), 371. *Vermont Cynic*, March 25, 1927, p. 1. "Act 39," mimeograph copy in statistics folder, Dean's office Papers, 1934–1963, Box 13.

Interestingly, there are indications that the A.M.A. Council on Medical Education never intended to reduce the College's rating to class B, even if the College did *not* make any improvements. The correspondence of Thomas W. Huntington, who had received his bachelor's degree from the University in 1871 and his M.D. from Harvard in 1876, provides the key. Huntington was chief surgeon of the Western Pacific Railroad, a member of the clinical faculty of the University of California, and a trustee of the University of Vermont. On learning of the A.M.A. report, he wrote to the Council on Medical Education in defense of the College. The letter was forwarded to Colwell, who replied that he was "particularly pleased with the personality and force of character of President Guy W. Bailey," and that the Council certainly recognized that the University "has had a struggle" in the past. Colwell continued by noting that the School appeared "to be making fairly good use of what they have" in the form of clinical material. "It was believed, however that both the medical school and the state will be greatly benefited," he said, "if provision can be made for a hospital directly controlled by the University of Vermont whereby better courses of clinical instruction can be provided in the medical school." Colwell did not make any reference to the threat that was made to the University.[11] It appears from the letter that the Council on Medical Education did not intend to reduce the rating, but instead made its report in the expectation that it would provide ammunition for increasing the state appropriation for medical education.

Jenne was not troubled by the A.M.A. "threat." At a faculty meeting, when he was asked about Colwell's inspection, Jenne replied that "certain things should be done in order to remain in class A, after the next two years, especially in regard to improving the clinical facilities."[12] Yet Jenne took no action except to ask for more money. The only change made was not to increase but to reduce the number of teaching hours from 4,144 to 3,600, which meant that the total of curriculum hours would no longer be 15 percent more than the national average.[13]

In 1928, however, Jenne initiated a reform intended to provide students with field experience and at the same time demonstrate the satisfactions of general practice in rural areas. Jenne apparently was inspired while attending a meeting of the Association of American Medical Colleges at which the preceptor system was discussed by several delegates. Since Jenne had started his medical career by going the rounds with an Enosburg physician, the thought of returning to the preceptorship touched a sympathetic cord. In addition, he recognized that the shortage of rural physicians might be alleviated if the medical students had an opportunity to work with rural general practitioners. In any case, during the fall of 1928 students were assigned to six blocks of extramural service, five two-week periods in

11. See Huntington to Bevan, San Francisco, August 2, 1927; Colwell to Huntington, Chicago, August 6, 1927, Medical Folder, Bailey Papers, 1927–28.

12. UVM Medical Faculty Minutes, May 3, 1927.

13. Ibid., September 19, 1927, and March 19, 1928. The number of hours had been increased between 1910 and 1916.

state institutions and one month with a rural physician. They served as student interns at the Weeks State Industrial School in Vergennes, the Home for the Feeble-Minded in Brandon, Vermont State Hospital in Waterbury, the State Laboratory of Hygiene, the Vermont Sanatorium for Incipient and Early Tuberculosis, and the Caverly Preventorium for Undernourished Children, the latter two at Pittsford. The final month was spent with a general practitioner in the Vermont countryside.[14]

It is difficult to determine the actual benefits derived from the experiment in preceptorship which lasted from 1928 to 1938. According to the *Vermont Alumni Weekly*, the students were enthusiastic over the opportunity for practice before graduation. Moreover, the physicians enjoyed the "companionship of the young men who were sent to them"; in some cases the country physician learned new techniques from the students. According to Dean Jenne, several of the students had decided to become country practitioners and some had been faced with emergencies during their preceptorship and had given "a good account of themselves in meeting those emergencies."[15]

After a 1932 evaluation of extramural service, the faculty decided that the work should be continued, with provision made for the faculty to evaluate the work of the student through on-site visits by the Dean or his representative and through regular reports by the student and his preceptor. In addition, the committee urged that more work in the third year be done in preparation for the extramural service, since not all students were prepared to practice medicine after having learned by lecture rather than through clinical experience.[16]

The experiment in preceptorship was an attempt to provide clinical experiences lacking in Burlington and at the same time encourage students to become rural practitioners. Yet in 1935 the Council on Medical Education questioned the benefits of the program. When the two inspectors, Herman Weiskotten of the A.M.A. and John Wyckoff, dean of the New York University College of Medicine, came to Burlington, they inspected what they described as an inferior school. Contrary to the claims of the College, fewer than thirteen faculty members were devoting "full time to the work of their departments." Moreover, although the College budget was inadequate, it was enough to provide "much more adequate staffing of the preclinical departments." The library was cast aside as totally inadequate, and the inspectors declared that "there is little indication that it is used to any appreciable extent by the students."[17]

When Weiskotten and Wyckoff examined the professors, they found that very few were qualified. They said that "although interested in their work and apparently conscientious," several of the department heads "have had inadequate training" in their specialties. For instance, Thomas S. Brown, chairman of the department of anat-

14. Ibid., December 19, 1927. *Vermont Alumni Weekly*, 8 (October 31, 1928), 71. Hills, "History of the Medical School," pp. 169–171. UVM Medical College Bulletin, (July 1934), p. 19.

15. *Vermont Alumni Weekly*, 9 (October 23, 1929), 51, 60. Preceptor's Correspondence, 1928–34, UVM Archives.

16. UVM Medical Faculty Minutes, June 13 and 14, September 20, 1932.

17. AMA Council on Medical Education and Hospitals, Inspection of UVM, October 16–18, 1935, Medical College Reorganization Box, UVM Archives.

omy, had never had training in gross anatomy. Chester Newhall, of the same department, had "no graduate training in anatomy." The report went on to assert that the local practitioners who taught the clinical subjects did not have sufficient background in those subjects, although they were "fine men with high ideals in medical education" and "much interested in their work with the students."[18]

Weiskotten and Wyckoff emphasized the lack of clinical teaching. The report noted that third-year students had "no actual contact with patients except in connection with amphitheatre clinics in medicine and surgery." They reported that junior students had "a relatively enormous amount of didactic work," consisting of six recitations per week in medicine, four in surgery, and three in obstetrics. Despite the trend toward more practical work by students, and despite the fact that both Tinkham and Jenne had recognized the need to over-haul the program, nothing had been done except to develop the fourth-year extramural program. In evaluating the extramural program, Weiskotten and Wyckoff doubted "whether such assignments are justifiable during the undergraduate course in medicine, especially with the apparent lack of supervision that exists in this school."[19] Although the Dean or his representative was supposed to make on-site visits to observe the work of the students, Dean Jenne apparently neglected either to make the visits or to appoint a delegate to do so.

The report concluded that notwithstanding the "fine spirit of idealism and a desire to serve on the part of the faculty, there would seem to be little reason for the attempt to carry on medical education under the conditions" existing in Burlington. For the School to remain in class A, the preclinical departments had to be adequately staffed with men who had done graduate work in the sciences, rather than with physicians who had an interest in anatomy or physiology. Like the inspectors of the past, Weiskotten and Wyckoff emphasized the lack of clinical material in Burlington, and they questioned whether the city could furnish enough clinical material "for the proper conduct of even a small medical school."[20]

In December 1935 Dean Jenne was informed that "because of manifest deficiencies," the College was being placed on probation. "If satisfactory improvements" could be made "within a reasonable length of time," the probation would be removed and the College would retain its class A rating. Of course the report was confidential; the A.M.A. continued to list the University of Vermont College of Medicine as "acceptable."[21]

Jenne had seen the College faced with similar threats in the past, and he "tended to pooh-pooh the report." He declared that the College had "survived several of these before," and he was certain that it would "have no difficulty in getting off the probationary list this time."[22] Although he had been informed of the probation in Decem-

18. Ibid., pp. 16–18.

19. Ibid., pp. 6–14, 17.

20. Ibid., pp. 16–18.

21. William D. Cutter to James N. Jenne, December 17, 1935, Medical College Reorganization Box.

22. Interview with A. B. Soule, transcript in UVM Archives.

ber 1935, Jenne did not call a faculty meeting to discuss the situation until the following July. At that meeting he indicated that the A.M.A. recommended hiring full-time heads for the departments of physiology, anatomy, and chemistry, and he announced that Thomas S. Brown had resigned as chairman of the Anatomy Department, as had C. F. Whitney, chairman of the Chemistry Department. That was the substance of Jenne's response to the A.M.A. report. After having received a vote of confidence from the faculty, the Dean presented several questions for discussion—whether the premedical requirement should be increased to three years, whether the College should require its graduates to complete an internship before receiving the degree, and whether the College should establish a mandatory retirement age. No action was taken on Jenne's first two questions, but a committee was established to consider the need for a mandatory retirement age. Less than one week after having received its charge, the committee recommended that professors be required to retire at age 67, with one year appointments possible until 70 when they could benefit the College.[23] Obviously, Jenne was convinced that these relatively insignificant changes were sufficient to retain the class A rating.

In October 1936 the Dean was informed by the A.M.A. Council on Medical Education that unless the probationary period was ended before June 1939, "the Council will at that time review the standing of your school, and take appropriate action."[24] Less than one month later, Jenne received more bad news—the Association of American Medical Colleges had joined the A.M.A. in placing the School on probation, for reasons similar to those of the Council. Fred Zapffe, secretary of the Association, noted that heads of preclinical departments should be full time and that the preclinical departments did not have adequate personnel. He indicated that the extramural program was inadequate; the clinical faculty was "in part, nonresident," which meant that "it is not possible to have an effective teaching organization nor proper supervision of teaching." In addition, Zapffe declared that the scholastic records of the students indicated that they were not adequately prepared to benefit from a modern and scientific medical education. Indeed, he questioned "whether admitted students would have been acceptable by other medical schools." In conclusion he noted the "need for reorganization of faculty, teaching and clinical material if the school is to proceed along the lines of an acceptable medical school."[25]

Now the situation was serious. Not only had the A.M.A. Council placed the College on probation, but the A.A.M.C. had indicated that for the same reasons it was inadequate. Jenne continued to feel that the threat was minor, but now the faculty disagreed. Accord-

23. UVM Medical Faculty Minutes, July 1 and 8, 1936.
24. Cutter to Jenne, Chicago, October 21, 1936, Medical College Reorganization Box.
25. Zapffe to Jenne, Chicago, November 16, 1936, ibid.

ing to A. Bradley Soule, who was to play a major role in the eventual reorganization of the College, "there was a unified feeling among the faculty that we must recognize that the school was doomed unless radical steps could be taken to pull ourselves up by the bootstraps." On March 18, 1937, the faculty decided to establish a Committee on Reorganization, which would assess the situation, analyze the requirements of the A.M.A. and the A.A.M.C., and determine the potential for "making a come-back."[26] Jenne appointed Ernest H. Buttles, who taught pathology, C. F. Whitney, professor of chemistry and toxicology, and A. Bradley Soule, who was soon to become chairman of a new Department of Radiology. Less than one week later the faculty established two other committees, one to make arrangements for increased clinical facilities, the other to consider revision of the extramural program.[27] Because of the reluctance of Jenne to take action the faculty had taken matters in their own hands; they set the machinery in motion to effect sweeping changes.

The Committee on Reorganization began its work by interviewing the University president, Guy W. Bailey, to "see how far" the trustees "would be willing to go in backing us up on recommendations and in attempting to fund them." Bailey assured the committee that unless the total reached "astronomical figures," he would try to find enough money to hire more faculty members and improve facilities. The committee met with members of the faculty to determine how they might fit into the future of the College.[28] The first decision was the most important: reorganization of the faculty to increase the number of full-time professors and to staff each department adequately. After the faculty approved the specific plans, the Committee set out to locate qualified men who were willing to teach in a medical school that might be forced to close in the near future.[29]

The Committee did that job well. The Anatomy Department, for instance, underwent a major face-lifting. Chester Newhall, who had served as instructor from 1929 to 1935 and as assistant professor from 1935 to 1937, became the acting head of the Department on a full-time basis, after having agreed to do graduate work in anatomy. Three full-time instructors were appointed, all of whom had training in anatomy rather than in medicine. These included Walter Stultz, who had received a Ph.D. from Yale in 1932 and had taught at Trinity College in Connecticut, Mount Union College in Ohio, and the Medical College of South Carolina. Stultz had published extensively in the *Journal of Experimental Zoology* and the *Anatomical Record*. He was joined by Jean Piatt, another Yale Ph.D., who had published articles in the *Journal of Morphology* and *Proceedings of the Philadelphia Academy of Natural Sciences*. The third new anatomist was Fred W. Dunihue, who held a Ph.D. from New York University and had published arti-

26. Interview with A. B. Soule.
27. UVM Medical Faculty Minutes, March 18 and 23, 1937.
28. Interview with A. B. Soule.
29. UVM Medical Faculty Minutes, April 16, 1937.

cles in the *Biological Bulletin* and the *Journal of Experimental Biology*. As a result of the infusion of new blood, of men with graduate training in anatomy, the students would be taught by qualified scientists.[30]

C. F. Whitney became acting chairman of the Department of Physiological Chemistry, and he was joined by Harold B. Pierce, a full-time associate professor. Pierce had received his Ph.D. from the University of Rochester in 1928 and had taught there since 1927. He had published extensively in the *American Journal of Physiology, Science,* and the *Journal of Bacteriology.* Dr. Soule, a member of the Committee on Reorganization, marveled that Pierce was willing to leave a secure position at Rochester to join the faculty in Burlington when it was questionable that the College "would be able to survive."[31]

There were major changes in the Department of Physiology. Fred K. Jackson was joined by another product of the University of Rochester, Ray Gilbert Daggs, who had been on the Rochester faculty since receiving his Ph.D. in 1930. Daggs had published articles in the *Journal of Nutrition,* the *American Journal of Physiology,* and the *Proceedings of the Society of Experimental Biology and Medicine.* In addition to Daggs, Ferdinand Jacob Morris Sichel was appointed as an instructor in the same department. Sichel had received his Ph.D. from New York University in 1934, and he had taught at McGill, New York University, the University of Pennsylvania, and Howard University. Like the other new appointees, Sichel had published in scholarly journals in his field.

In pathology and bacteriology E. H. Buttles became professor and head of the department. He was joined by three new assistant professors, including Ernest Hartman, who had received a Doctor of Science degree from Johns Hopkins in 1926 and had previously taught at Kansas State College, the University of Illinois, and Lingnan University in Canton, China.

Three new departments were established in areas which previously had been special subjects taught by visiting lecturers. C. K. Johnson, who had received his medical degree from the University of Vermont in 1899, became a part-time professor of pediatrics. The first Vermonter to specialize in pediatrics, Johnson had done postgraduate work in New York, Philadelphia, and Boston. He had taught pediatrics as a special subject since 1912, and he had published in the *Boston Medical and Surgical Journal,* the *Vermont Medical Monthly,* and *American Medicine.*

A second new department, Ophthalmology, Otolaryngology, and Rhinology, was headed by E. G. Twitchell, on a part-time basis. Twitchell had received his medical degree from Queens University back in 1906, followed by postgraduate work at the New York Eye and Ear Infirmary. He had been a special lecturer at the University of Vermont for many years and had a large practice in Burlington.

30. Ibid., April 16, 1937. List of Faculty, 1935–36, and 1937–38, Buttles Reorganization Folder, UVM Archives. The following paragraphs are from these sources.

31. Interview with A. B. Soule.

The third new department was Radiology, headed by A. Bradley Soule, who had been instructor in pathology from 1929 to 1932, and had been a resident in radiology at the Massachusetts General Hospital. Soule had by then published one article, in the *American Journal of Roentgenology*.

The most traumatic experience of the Committee came in its attempt to reorganize the Department of Pharmacology. The professor involved was David Marvin, "who had virtually no training in the field except from self-learning." Marvin had been considered as a full-time professor in the past, but he had devoted a great deal of time to his position as president of the Essex Trust Company. Students commenting on the program were brutally frank in their treatment of Professor Marvin. Forty-six students said that he should be removed; their comments indicated that in their opinion he spent too much time banking and too little time teaching. One student declared: "We need a good pharmacologist who knows up-to-date methods and drugs." A second insisted that "Marvin has failed miserably to keep up with the progress made in Pharmacology." Another student said: "We might just as well take a correspondence course and come up once a month to take an exam."[32] It was obvious that Marvin either had to be removed from the Department or had to be considered as a part-time instructor, enabling the department to have a qualified full-time chairman, as required by the A.M.A. When the Committee on Reorganization listed Marvin as a part-time professor, he complained that he had been treated unfairly, and he hired an attorney. Marvin insisted that he was indeed a full-time professor and that his banking duties were minimal.

On May 18, 1937, the issue came before the faculty, with Marvin presenting his side of the case, and with Buttles, Soule, and Whitney insisting that Marvin "has in fact, not given to the College of Medicine, in teaching hours, research work, or otherwise, the time and service that might be expected from a man who 'has devoted his entire time to teaching and research' and who had had 'no outside interests.'" The faculty upheld the decision of the Committee, in effect firing Marvin as chairman and relegating him to a minor role in the College. After he resigned the following year, a full-time pharmacologist was appointed—Forrest Ramon Davison, who had received a Ph.D. from the University of Minnesota in 1926 and an M.D. from the University of Chicago in 1935.[33] Davison had previously taught at Rutgers University and the University of West Virginia and had published articles in the *Botanical Gazette* and the *Journal of Agricultural Research*.

Patrick E. McSweeney retired, and the Department of Obstetrics and Gynecology was divided into two sections. The new chairman of the Department of Obstetrics was Herbert A. Durfee, who had

32. Results of questionnaire given to students, 1937, Medical College Reorganization Box.

33. UVM Medical Faculty Minutes, May 18, 1937. See Interview with A. B. Soule. UVM Trustee Minutes, June 10, 1938.

received his medical degree from the University of Vermont in 1920 and had had postgraduate training at New York's Lying-in Hospital. The Department of Gynecology was headed by Oliver Eastman, who had graduated from the University in 1908 and had also trained at the Lying-in Hospital. For the first time the Department of Medicine had full-time members—Ellsworth L. Amidon, assistant professor, and Harold F. Stolz, an instructor who had received his medical degree from the University of Michigan in 1933.

These changes represented a drastic transformation. The reorganization resulted in the appointment of professionally trained scientists to the preclinical faculty, men who were not from Vermont. In addition the faculty agreed to subsidize the graduate training of several local physicians in order to qualify them to teach in the modern Medical School. Ellsworth Amidon, the assistant professor of medicine, for instance, completed his training at the University of Pennsylvania after agreeing to assume a position as a full-time member of the clinical faculty at the College. In another case Albert G. Mackay was given a leave and financial aid to complete a residency in surgery at the Boston City Hospital. Two other young faculty members were given leaves to qualify themselves in their fields. They were Arthur Gladstone, who did postgraduate work in surgery at the University of Pennsylvania, and B. F. Clark, who took a residency in obstetrics and gynecology at the Women's Hospital in New York City.[34]

When the members of the Committee on Reorganization turned to the curriculum, they noted that "there has been insufficient correlation between different departments, resulting in some unnecessary duplication of instruction and omission or inadequate consideration of some subjects." They also found that the chairmen had not supervised work in their departments, which resulted in poor teaching methods continuing over the years, and inadequate treatment of the subject matter. The Committee reported that "Didactic teaching has been overemphasized, and not always well done, and clinical instruction has been inadequate." The Committee made a series of recommendations, which included the appointment of qualified department chairmen, men who had received certification by the "American Board" of their specialties. In cases where no "American Board" existed in a subject, the professor had to be a member of "one or more of the best recognized societies" in that area. The Committee also recommended that didactic teaching be "decreased in quantity, and improved in quality," and that more clinical instruction be required. Extensive changes were needed in the curriculum, especially in the third year, where didactic work predominated, and in the fourth, where extramural services were almost totally unsupervised.[35]

At the same meeting of the faculty, Clarence Beecher reported on the progress made by the Committee on Clinical Facilities. That com-

34. Interview with A. B. Soule. Buttles to Cutter, Burlington, January 25, 1938, Medical College Reorganization Box.

35. UVM Medical Faculty Minutes, May 18, 1937.

mittee had made arrangements for the use of the 158-bed hospital at Fort Ethan Allen, just north of Burlington, and Herbert Durfee, the professor of obstetrics, reported that an arrangement was being made with the Berwynd Clinic in New York City for students to obtain obstetrical experience during the summer following their third year of medical school. The professors voted to appropriate the seven hundred dollars needed to pay the expenses of the program in New York, enabling students to take advantage of the obstetrical material that was so abundant there and so lacking in Burlington. The Committee had been working on a plan to make better use of the Free Dispensary, especially in teaching physical diagnosis. In addition, the Committee hoped to meet with Bishop Joseph Rice to work out plans for more extensive use of the DeGoesbriand and Fanny Allen hospitals, but because of illness the Bishop was not available at the time.[36] Beecher explained that the increase of local clinical facilities "makes unnecessary the continuing of some of the extra-mural services."

On September 3, with the reorganization of the faculty completed and with improvement in clinical facilities, the faculty voted to discharge the Committee on Reorganization.[37] Less than one week later, on September 9, 1937, Dean Jenne died at the age of 77. Dean for eleven years, he had not continued the enlightened leadership of Henry Crain Tinkham. Indeed, when the College was threatened with loss of accreditation, Jenne had played a minor role in bringing about the needed changes. Buttles, Soule, and Whitney, along with the two committees headed by Clarence Beecher, did the work of reorganization. Some observers indicated that perhaps Dean Jenne died at a time when younger and more dynamic leadership was required. In retrospect, perhaps it can be said that had Jenne died a few years earlier, younger and more dynamic leadership might have prevented the Council on Medical Education from making such a devastating report in 1935.[38]

After Jenne's death, the search for a new dean began. One of those close to the scene, A. Bradley Soule, believed that Buttles, who had served as chairman of the Committee on Reorganization, was offered the position but refused to assume the deanship. It was recognized that the College could not conduct a national search for a dean at a time when its future was still in doubt. The Council on Medical Education had not lifted the probation, and it was possible that the members of the Council might consider the reorganization to be inadequate. That decision would result in the closing of the School, for graduates of class B institutions would not be able to practice medicine in most states. According to Soule's analysis, when Buttles refused the offer of the deanship, he suggested that he *would* be willing to head another committee, as long as he could select its members. As a result, the trustees recommended, and the faculty

36. Ibid. See also September 3, 1937.
37. Ibid., September 3, 1937.
38. For obituaries of Jenne, see *Vermont Cynic*, September 21, 1937.

agreed, that the former Committee on Reorganization become a "committee on administration," acting in effect as dean until it was feasible to search for a permanent dean. Thus Buttles became chairman of a three-man committee that included Soule and Whitney, men who had demonstrated their administrative ability and their commitment to the College while members of the Committee on Reorganization.[39]

The members of the Committee were familiar with the A.M.A. guidelines, *The Essentials of an Acceptable Medical School*, and they decided that the College had to assume control of the medical staff of the Hospital. As a result, they urged the directors of the Mary Fletcher Hospital to appoint the chairmen of the College's clinical departments as chiefs of service. The Hospital trustees were reluctant to give up the right to select chiefs of service, but they agreed to the proposal when Buttles, Soule, and Whitney informed them that without the change "there was little likelihood that the college would survive." On January 17, 1938, the trustees voted to accept the recommendations of the A.M.A.; henceforth department chairmen at the College would also be chiefs of service at the Hospital. Although the directors of the Hospital insisted on maintaining the right to veto nominations by the College, they never used that power.[40]

In March 1938 the Committee on Administration recommended that a new dean be appointed; the reorganization was complete and all that remained was for the Council on Medical Education to remove the probation and return the College to its class A rating. The trustees of the University responded by asking the members of the Committee to continue in office, but they were reluctant to start a national search until the College's future was assured. Moreover, they were convinced that no respectable candidate would leave "a worth-while institution to accept a position" in Burlington until "he is firmly satisfied that the College of Medicine will be approved finally as a Class A institution."[41]

The committee had kept the A.M.A. and the Association of American Medical Colleges informed of the progress of the reorganization. Soule was the "leg man," attending meetings of those associations and trying to demonstrate that the School was making progress. In November 1937 Soule met with Fred Zapffe, secretary of the Association of American Medical Colleges, who had participated in the inspections for the Council on Medical Education. At that meeting Zapffe was informed of the plans of the committee, and he responded in very specific terms. For instance, he told Soule that he approved the retirement of Brown, Whitney, Jackson, and Marvin, and that Pierce and Daggs would be acceptable department chairmen. He also approved the plan to have Chester Newhall take postgraduate courses prior to becoming chairman of the Department of Anatomy.

39. UVM Medical Faculty Minutes, September 23, 1937. Interview with A. B. Soule.

40. Interview with A. B. Soule. T. S. Brown to E. H. Buttles, January 27, 1938, Buttles Reorganization Folder.

41. Committee on Administration to Guy W. Bailey, March 30, 1938, Medical College Reorganization Box. Bailey to Buttles, May 21, 1938, ibid.

Zapffe said that a local man should be dean, questioning whether the University could attract "the right type of man from outside." Finally, he declared that he was opposed to the admission of Jewish students, especially those from New York City.[42]

In 1938 Soule received quite a different response from Herman Weiskotten, who had inspected the College in 1935. Soule was at a meeting in Syracuse with representatives of the Council on Medical Education and the Association of American Medical Colleges. When he was in the middle of his presentation, Weiskotten entered the room and declared, "Oh, Why waste your time? There is no point in a medical school in a small town like Burlington, Vermont and the sooner you close it up, the better. You will never have enough clinical facilities to provide an acceptable training program, and you're just wasting your time and efforts!" Having dropped his bombshell, Weiskotten walked out of the room. Soule later described the aftermath: "Fortunately, several of the more kindly disposed members of the committee and Council hastened to reassure me that they were pleased with what we had done and that I shouldn't be discouraged."[43]

In October 1938 the Committee on Administration informed Zapffe that it wanted the College to be reinspected during the following year.[44] In December 1938 Zapffe visited Burlington for the A.A.M.C. In May of the following year he wrote to inform Soule that the Committee had "done a splendid piece of work" and had "gone far to rehabilitate the college. I am convinced," he said, "that you will attain the end you have in mind in doing your work." "So far as the preclinical years are concerned," he added, "you have ironed out that situation quite well."[45]

Indeed, Zapffe was so convinced that the College would survive that he recommended a candidate for the deanship, a fellow who, he said, was "very cooperative, circumspect, knows the game thoroughly, who is well prepared to serve your cause, a fine appearing fellow, extremely likeable, etc., etc." This was Hardy A. Kemp, a 37-year-old professor of bacteriology and preventive medicine at Baylor University College of Medicine in Dallas, Texas. Zapffe's recommendation was symbolic of the successful reorganization. Obviously he would never have made a recommendation if he had thought that the College was doomed to failure. The Committee on Administration interviewed Kemp, and the faculty unanimously voted to make an attempt to "engage him" as the permanent dean of the Medical College.[45] Kemp accepted the offer.

Kemp became convinced, however, that much more had to be done before he could confidently request the Council on Medical Education to reinspect the College. In his first action as dean, he asked for the formation of an Advisory Council consisting of all full pro-

42. Interview with Zapffe, November 22, 1937, notes in Medical College Reorganization Box.

43. Interview with A. B. Soule.

44. Soule to Bailey, October 31, 1938, Medical College Reorganization Box.

45. Zapffe to Soule, Chicago, May 4, 1939, Dean's Office Papers, 1934–63, Box 3.

fessors, the superintendent of the Mary Fletcher Hospital, the Commanding Officer of the hospital at Fort Ethan Allen, and representatives of the DeGoesbriand and Fanny Allen hospitals. This was an attempt to correlate the clinical resources and to bring the hospitals into a closer relationship with the College. Then Kemp proposed changes in the third and fourth year curriculum, including the development of clinical clerkships in the third year, the elimination of preceptorships in the fourth year, and increased local assignments in obstetrics and city services. Students would continue to have obstetrical experience at the Wesson Woman's Hospital, in Springfield, Massachusetts, and training in urology and venereal diseases at the Worcester City Hospital.[47]

Perhaps Kemp's biggest role was in bringing the Catholic hospitals into a closer relationship with the Medical School. He informed Zapffe on October 4, 1939, that the "Catholic hospitals have been closely worked into the teaching programs through suitable teaching appointments from their staffs." These appointments included L. G. Thabault as instructor of surgery, A. J. Crandall as instructor in clinical surgery, and Christopher M. Terrien and W. F. Rogers as instructors in medicine. All four men were affiliated with the Fanny Allen or the DeGoesbriand hospitals.[48] Symbolic of Kemp's attempt to improve relations with the Catholic community was his appearance at the St. Patrick's Day supper at the Burlington Memorial Auditorium in 1940. Kemp made a speech extolling the accomplishments of St. Patrick and declaring that he was proud to be three-fourths Irish![49]

In a short time Kemp made a number of other significant changes. The out-patient dispensary was moved to new quarters in the building occupied by the Howard Relief Society, a well-known and active charitable agency, and placed under the direct supervision of a full-time physician, Jesse Rust, a member of the faculty of the Medical College. Fourth-year students were assigned to a month's service at the dispensary, where they would work under the close supervision of Rust. A similar arrangement was made in obstetrics; Fletcher White, a recent graduate of the Medical School, was placed in charge of all "city cases." In addition, the preceptorships were abandoned, as were the internships in small and unaccredited hospitals. The third-year schedule was rearranged to allow for ward work four afternoons a week, which was "an innovation as far as Vermont is concerned." Teaching in anatomy and pharmacology had been reduced, as suggested by Zapffe.[50]

Dean Kemp was described in the *Burlington Daily News* as a "Texas whirlwind on two feet."[51] Although he was originally from southwest Missouri, he enjoyed his reputation as a Texan, playing the role by keeping six-shooters on his desk. In 1947, when he was being

46. Zapffe to Bailey, Chicago, April 28, 1939, Medical College Reorganization Box. UVM Medical Faculty Minutes, July 13, 1939. *Burlington Free Press*, September 16, 1939, p. 1, cols. 1–2.

47. UVM Medical Faculty Minutes, September 15, 1939.

48. Kemp to Zapffe, Burlington, October 4, 1939, Dean's Office Papers, 1934–1963, Box 3. Kemp to Zapffe, October 14, 1939, ibid.

49. *Burlington Free Press*, March 15, 1940.

50. Kemp to Zapffe, October 14, 1939, Dean's Office Papers, 1934–63, Box 3.

51. *Burlington Daily News*, October 12, 1939, Dean's Office Papers, 1941–47.

considered for the deanship of a midwestern medical school, the professors at Vermont were asked for their opinions of him. The responses noted that Kemp had "very strong will power, and this combined with the fact that he is not always the most diplomatic in his approach to the problem, occasionally would cause embarrassment to himself or others." One professor noted that "the combination of a loud-talking Texan and a bunch of conservative Vermonters can be pictured in your imagination." Others said that Kemp "occasionally ran over people rather roughshod," but they all agreed that he was hard working and that he had done a fine job completing the required reorganization.[52]

During the week of April 29, 1940, Fred Zapffe and Russell H. Oppenheimer, dean of the medical college at Emory University, came to reinspect the School. Kemp informed President Bailey that he knew Oppenheimer "as a man of eminent fairness and sympathy for the relatively smaller institutions."[53] That was encouraging, especially when one considers that it was Zapffe who recommended Kemp for his position in Burlington. The School would be inspected by men who were not unfriendly to their cause. Yet after the inspection, Kemp informed Bailey that although the inspectors were "very encouraging and friendly in their attitude," they "did point out a very large number of needed changes"—changes that seemed "rather staggering" to Kemp. The Dean said that the faculty was in for a "shock," as everyone had assumed that as a result of the reorganization "we have the full approval of the Association in the bag and that there is nothing more to be done."[54]

When the report was received from Zapffe, however, it made only suggestions, it did not criticize, and it seemed to be more of a formality than a critical evaluation. The inspectors spoke in general terms, quite unlike the earlier days. They suggested that the curriculum be revised to reflect current trends in medical education, with the number of lectures reduced to the "lowest possible minimum." In addition, they recommended lengthening the senior year from eight to eleven months, following the lead of "two schools" that had already taken that step.[55]

Although the suggestions were insignificant compared with the earlier criticisms, Kemp responded almost immediately. At the faculty meeting on June 4, 1940, after he described what had to be done, the professors voted to lengthen the fourth-year program to 44 weeks, "in order to utilize to the fullest extent the available clinical material." It was then voted to revise the third-year program to allow for more clinical and less didactic teaching.[56] Within a few months other changes had been made. Theodore H. Harwood was placed in charge of the out-patient dispensary, and surgery at the dispensary was handled by another full-time man, H. B. Levine. A number of full-

52. Dean's Office Papers, hospitals to preceptorships box.
53. Kemp to Bailey, March 18, 1940, Kemp Folder, Bailey Papers, 1939–40.
54. Kemp to Bailey, April 29, 1940, ibid.
55. Report of the visitation of Russell H. Oppenheimer and Fred C. Zapffe, April 21–26, 1940, Dean's Office Papers, 1934–63, Box. 3.
56. UVM Medical Faculty Minutes, June 4, 1940.

time clinical teachers were appointed, mostly young men who had just completed their internships and residencies. These included Ellsworth Amidon, Theodore Harwood, and Wilhelm Raab in medicine, Albert G. Mackay and H. B. Levine in surgery, David W. James in obstetrics and gynecology, and Dorothy Corbin in pediatrics. Dr. Corbin, incidentally, was the first woman member of the medical faculty.[57]

Finally, in November 1940, Zapffe informed Kemp that the Association of American Medical Colleges had removed the University of Vermont from probationary membership. No reinspection had been made by the A.M.A. Council, and "conditions made it uncertain when such inspection would be made."[58] The "conditions" referred to included World War II and the national preparedness program, which made it unlikely that a medical school would be closed in what would soon be a time of national emergency. In any case the faculty had been reorganized, the curriculum modified, and the clinical facilities increased.

57. Kemp to Zapffe, October 15, 1940, Dean's Office Papers, 1934–1963, Box 3.

58. Zapffe to Kemp, Chicago, November 1, 1940, A.A.M.C. Folder, Dean's Office Papers. See also UVM Medical Faculty Minutes, November 4, 1940.

Chapter Thirteen

The Forties

BY 1940 it was apparent that the University was suffering a severe financial crisis. During the Great Depression, President Guy Bailey had used the endowment to maintain salaries and finance needed repairs. Unable to continue that policy indefinitely, in 1940 he imposed some heavy budgetary restrictions. In July, Dean Kemp informed his faculty that it was necessary to "make certain adjustments in the money spent by the School for teaching purposes." Yet to meet AMA standards the College would simultaneously have to increase the number of full-time clinical professors. Funds were so limited that the Medical School would have to reduce salaries of the part-time staff to support newly appointed full-timers.[1]

After President Bailey died on October 22, Newman Keyes Chaffee, an elderly Rutland banker and long-time trustee, was appointed Acting President. Almost immediately the financial plight of the University became public knowledge, and in January 1941 the trustees voted to reduce all salaries by "an average of twelve and one-half percent" for the 1941–42 academic year. This setback made it even more difficult for the Medical School to recruit and maintain faculty, especially after United States entry into the Second World War.[2] As early as February 1941 the trustees, who recognized the problem, prepared a special report to the legislature requesting additional funds for the Medical School. They emphasized the continuing role of the College, especially in terms of training physicians and providing medical care for the people of the state. The report noted that in spite of the annual $60,000 appropriation for the Medical College, the University had been forced to transfer $46,476.39 from its general fund to

1. Kemp to Faculty, July 23, 1940, Kemp Folder, Bailey Papers, 1939–40. See also interview with A. B. Soule for information on Bailey's relations with the Medical School during the period.

2. UVM Trustees Minutes, January 11, 1941.

meet the School's deficit. The report went on to estimate that the School would have a $36,000 deficit for the 1941–42 fiscal year. The trustees declared that in the past these deficits had been paid "out of benefactions and capital funds," and this had "contributed largely to the University's present condition." The trustees concluded by requesting a supplementary appropriation of $40,000, to meet the current deficit. Perhaps to prevent dissension within the ranks, they requested another $25,000 for "salaries and expenses incident" to the operation of the College of Agriculture.[3]

Now that the trustees had once again decided to seek aid from the legislature, Dean Kemp tried to drum up grass-roots support for the appropriation. Kemp had managed to neutralize Asa Bloomer, a state legislative leader who had always been careful about how tax revenues were spent. In 1955 Kemp told Dean George Wolf that the secret was to get down to Rutland "some noon hour during a week end at home from the Assembly" and watch Bloomer "eat his bread and milk lunch there in his office." After Kemp had watched, he asked Bloomer "how to run the Medical College." From that time on, the Medical School did not face the relentless opposition of Asa Bloomer.[4]

Aside from influencing Bloomer and other legislators, Dean Kemp toured the state and spoke of the benefits provided by the continued existence of the Medical College.[5] The *Burlington Free Press* described the choice offered to the legislators: "The University absorbed increased costs" of medical education "as long as possible. Now the legislature must decide whether the medical college is worth to the state the $50,000 additional annually which is required to continue it."[6] Finally, the legislature appropriated a total of $150,000 for the schools of medicine and agriculture, and authorized a bond issue of not more than $675,000. The appropriation was contingent, however, upon approval of a sound financial policy for the University. Governor William H. Wills took two steps to investigate the entire situation. First, he authorized a complete audit of the University's financial records. Then he appointed Dr. Paul C. Packer, Dean of the College of Education at the University of Iowa and a representative of the Carnegie Foundation, to conduct an educational survey of the University.[7]

By that time, however, Kemp had been offered a position as dean of the Ohio State University School of Medicine. It was natural for him to consider his job in Burlington completed: the appropriation had been passed guaranteeing the continuation of the College, which was no longer in danger of being forced by the A.M.A. to close its doors. Kemp formally presented his resignation, effective September 1, 1941.[8]

When the audit requested by the Governor was completed, it was devastating. Rather than the surplus of $8,585.50 reportedly on the

3. Ibid., February 22, 1941.

4. Kemp to Wolf, Houston, Texas, March 30, 1955, Dean's Office Papers, 1934–63, Box 7.

5. See *Burlington Free Press*, March 14, 1941; *Brattleboro Daily Reformer*, March 1, 1941.

6. *Burlington Free Press*, April 8, 1941.

7. *Vermont Alumnus*, 20 (June 1941), 212.

8. Kemp to author, Prairie Village, Kansas, November 1, 1974, Kaufman Folder, UVM Archives. Also Trustee Minutes, June 7, 13, 1941.

books, the University had a deficit of $1,840,146 over the past five years. The report indicated that there had been extensive manipulations which were "contrary to good accounting practices."[9] Undoubtedly, Bailey had attempted to balance the budget, at least on the books, until the national economic picture improved the financial status of the University. Governor Wills made public the report of Dr. Packer. As part of a larger package, he recommended that the College receive an allocation equaling the actual cost of operation. Since the legislature had already appropriated $50,000 for the Medical School, this meant that it was being asked to increase that by $32,000.[10]

On July 12 the trustees appointed a three-man committee to manage the University and reorganize its financial and internal operations. The committee consisted of Dean Hardy Kemp, Paul Packer, and Roy Patrick, a member of the Board of Trustees.[11] According to Kemp, a number of trustees, several legislators, and leading alumni of the University began to urge his nomination as president. Since he had already accepted a position at Ohio State, he declined to be a candidate. Then, "to avoid adding to the existing situation," Kemp decided to leave Burlington as soon as possible. It was such a sudden departure that Kemp's secretary was shocked to learn one morning that the Dean had removed his belongings and vacated his office "almost overnight."[12] With the Dean gone, the old Committee on Administration was reactivated. C. F. Whitney had retired, however, and he was replaced by Clarence Beecher, who served as chairman. The other members of the committee were E. H. Buttles and A. Bradley Soule.[13]

In September 1941 the legislature passed what was known as the "University aid bill," resulting in a "wild celebration on campus."[14] A "spontaneous demonstration" began in the evening; some students heard the announcement in a local theater, and rushed up the hill to the University. They "routed out hundreds of others, fixed up banners, and they started a torchlight parade through the city." About a thousand students gathered in front of City Hall, where they heard speeches by several professors. Each sentence was reportedly "greeted with cheers." The mayor then told the students to "have fun but don't destroy property." The students formed a snake dance and celebrated through the night. The University had been saved by the action of the legislature![15]

Packer, who remained in Burlington through the crisis, prepared specific recommendations for the administration of the Medical School. He called Soule into his office one day, and informed the stunned professor that he was to be recommended as the new dean. Soule "was aghast at the prospect," being convinced that he "did not have the qualities of a good administrator." Moreover, he knew that Clarence Beecher "was anxious to become dean . . . to round out

9. *Brattleboro Daily Reformer*, July 9, 1941, in Newspaper Clipping File, UVM Archives.

10. *Vermont Alumnus*, 20 (August 1941, special issue), pp. 4, 11.

11. UVM Trustees Minutes, July 12, 1941.

12. Kemp to author, November 1, 1974, and reminiscences of Miss Cornelia Baylies, UVM Archives. In his letter to the author Kemp indicated that he had made a terrible mistake: in retrospect his two years in Burlington were the happiest of his life.

13. UVM Trustee Minutes, August 18, 1941.

14. Description in *Vermont Cynic*, September 23, 1941, p. 1.

15. Ibid.

his career, and that he would be grievously disappointed if he were not given this position." Packer suggested a compromise. He would recommend that Beecher be appointed dean and that Soule be assistant dean, "with the understanding that Beecher would retire at the end of the academic year" and Soule would replace him. Soule accepted, but "with great reluctance."[16] Packer's recommendation to the trustees included the provision that Soule administer the Medical School, so Beecher "may be free to devote a large part of his time to the Alumni Committee in raising funds for the University." In any case, Beecher became Dean of the Medical College. In terms of his service to the University, it was a very appropriate reward. He had received his medical degree from the University back in 1900, and from 1901 to 1941 he was a member of the medical faculty. In addition to his role as professor, Beecher had been active in local politics, having served as a member of the board of aldermen, board of school commissioners, and, from 1925 to 1929, mayor of Burlington.[17]

Meanwhile, Soule was having second thoughts about the agreement that would have had him assume the deanship in 1942. He "sensed" that he could not "handle a job of this sort," and so in the Spring of 1942 he requested that Beecher continue as dean for another year, "because of the shortage of radiologists."[18] Soule continued to feel that he was not the man for the job. He did a great deal of soul-searching, which included consideration of an "almost intolerable" financial arrangement with the Mary Fletcher Hospital that would have practically "frozen" his salary at about $5,000 a year. Eventually, Soule decided that he could not and would not assume the deanship. He tried to get a military assignment, but the Procurement and Assignment Service refused to take him off the essential list. Soule even went to the office of the Surgeon General, seeking a way to avoid having to become dean. Finally, he was given an assignment as chief of X ray at the 7,000-bed Halloran General Hospital on Staten Island, the largest hospital in the armed forces.

When the war was about to end, the University President, John Schoff Millis, went to Staten Island to talk with Soule about the possibility of returning as dean. Soule managed to convince Millis that his decision was "right for the University and for himself." As he later confided in an interview: "I was unconsciously recognizing the 'Peter Principle' and I feel certain that if I had gone back as dean, I would have made a mess of it." Therefore, after having demonstrated his commitment to the College and his administrative ability as a key member of the Reorganization Committee, Soule returned to the University, not as dean but as head of the Department of Radiology.[19]

Soule's decision to join the military was symptomatic of a serious problem facing the Medical School. As early as 1940 Dean Kemp

16. Interview with A. B. Soule. See Trustee Minutes, November 1, 1941, for Packer's recommendations.

17. *Vermont Alumnus*, 21 (December 1941), 51, 58.

18. Interview with A. B. Soule. Trustee Minutes, May 15, 1942.

19. Interview with A. B. Soule (composite of two separate interviews used in this analysis); see also Trustee Minutes, February 20, 1943.

had worried about the possibility of the faculty rushing off to war and wrote each member, urging him to remain at the University.[20] In spite of his plea, the University was unable to retain many of the younger professors, who insisted on participating more directly in the national war effort. By 1942–43 twenty-five members of the medical faculty had received leaves to join the service.[21] Unfortunately, that came at the precise time when changes in the program to provide a larger number of qualified military surgeons increased the need for faculty.

In December 1941, almost immediately upon United States entry into the war, Beecher and Soule requested permission to increase enrollment from 32 to 36 students and to graduate classes every nine months, without vacations. In that way the University would join other medical schools which were accelerating their programs to increase the output of physicians by compressing four academic years into three calendar years. The trustees approved, expressing a desire to "place the entire facilities of the University at the use of the country in its defense."[22] The faculty would have to work without the usual vacations; with the limited finances of the University combining with the larger number of professors requesting military leaves, there was a severe staffing problem. The College of Arts and Sciences was affected by the same problems, and in February 1943 a number of medical professors had volunteered to "help out in the emergency" by teaching in the academic program. Four members of the faculty volunteered to teach chemistry, including two full professors, Harold Pierce and Clifford S. Leonard, who had both taught organic chemistry in the past. Ferdinand Sichel, who was "essentially a physicist," volunteered to teach physics, and Hovey Jordan, Fred Dunihue, and Walter Stultz all offered to teach biology.[23]

On March 2, 1944, Fred Zapffe wrote to inform Dean Beecher that he had been urging the officers of the A.M.A. Council on Medical Education to "do something" about the probation that the Medical School had been placed on eight years earlier. Victor Johnson finally agreed, and he and Zapffe were planning to inspect the College in April. A week later Zapffe wrote to Beecher, this time with some interesting advice; "Please do not forget to have two copies of the budget ready for us. Clean up; sweep out the cobwebs; dust off the tables and other impedimenta in the laboratories; put clean shirts and collars on the faculty."[24] It must have seemed like the worst possible time for an inspection. The faculty was being depleted by the wartime emergency and low salaries; in addition, the course was accelerated and perhaps not up to the standards of the prewar period.

When Johnson and Zapffe made their report, they demonstrated that they had been serious about the evaluation of the faculty, the program, and the facilities. The inspection had *not* been a formality.

20. Reminiscences of Cornelia Baylies.

21. Notice of changes in Medical College Faculty and organization, 1942–43, Beecher Folder, Millis Papers. *Vermont Cynic*, January 5, 1943, p. 1.

22. Beecher and Soule to Millis and Trustees, December 15, 1941, Beecher Folder, Millis Papers. Trustees Minutes, December 20, 1941.

23. Beecher to Millis, February 11, 1943, Beecher Folder, Millis Papers.

24. Zapffe to Beecher, Chicago, March 2, 9, 1944, AAMC Folder, Dean's Office Box, UVM Archives. Inexplicably, in 1940 the Council on Medical Education had not joined the A.A.M.C. in removing the probation.

*17. Bishop deGoes-
briand Hospital in the
1940's.*

*18. The entrance of the
deGoesbriand Hospi-
tal.*

They analyzed the various departments; there were some bright spots, and others not quite so bright. The Department of Pharmacology, which was combined with Physiology, was definitely a bright spot. Louis S. Goodman, who took his medical degree at Oregon in 1932 and had been assistant professor at Yale since 1937, joined the faculty in 1943. He was active in research, and he was co-author of Goodman and Gilman's *Pharmacological Basis of Therapeutics*. According to the A.M.A. report, Goodman had a national reputation and was a solid addition to the faculty. Ferdinand Sichel, who was mainly responsible for physiology, was well qualified and moderately active in research and attendance at national scientific meetings. In biochemistry Harold Pierce was "Next to Dr. Goodman . . . more aware than other department chairmen of the indispensability of research."[25]

On the other hand, the Pathology Department was not at all satisfactory. The report declared: "There is no pretense of, or apparent interest in scholarly productivity." "Energy is dissipated," the report continued, by providing pathological services for nine Vermont hospitals. That meant that it was virtually impossible for the members of the department to devote any time to research, or even to adequate

25. A.M.A. investigation of UVM Medical College, 1944, p. 18, Dean's Office Papers, UVM Archives.

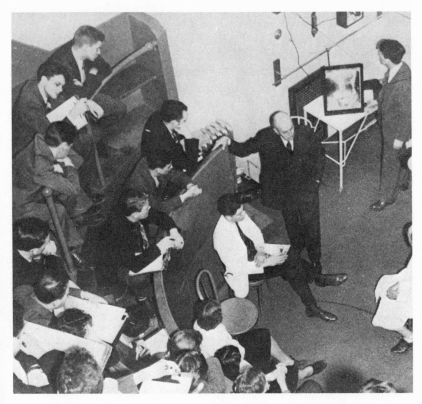

19. *Dean Beecher and Dr. E. L. Amidon in MFH amphitheatre, 1942.*

teaching.[26] Yet, when the investigators considered the basic science departments in light of the conditions of the past, when there had been little or no research, they recognized that the "present program represents tremendous advances. Should these advances continue," they declared, "the school can be a very creditable small medical school."[27]

When they analyzed the clinical program, Johnson and Zapffe noted that the criticisms of the past "have borne fruit." There still was too much didactic work, but the afternoons of third year students were free for work with patients. "These assignments to patients may still be regarded," however, "as timid moves in the direction of modern clinical instruction." The investigators noted that fourth-year students worked as interns, serving the hospitals during the wartime emergency. The students, however, were inadequately supervised, and the report continued to recommend that more students be assigned to the DeGoesbriand and Fanny Allen hospitals, and that their work be more closely supervised.[28]

They recognized that the clinical faculty had been "appreciably strengthened since the last survey," and Johnson and Zapffe especially commended Ellsworth Amidon, who was moderately active in research and appeared "capable of directing" the Department of Medicine. They also commented on the presence of Wilhelm Raab, who had been educated at Prague and Vienna, had spent one year at Harvard sponsored by the Rockefeller Foundation, and was world famous for his pioneering work on angina. They urged more support of his work and more encouragement. "Dr. Raab," they declared, "constitutes an asset to the school which seems to be not fully recognized."[29] Johnson and Zapffe recommended that although the clinical faculty showed great improvement since the last inspection, further improvement was needed. In general, they said, the faculty consisted of men "whose training and experience has been largely limited to the local scene. There is need for more 'new blood.'" They also noted that a full-time dean was desperately needed, to provide the "vigorous leadership" lacking at the time. They recommended an increase in the budget for research, as "medicine is an expanding, ever-changing science whose essence cannot be captured unless students have close contact with men who are contributing, however modestly, to that expansion and change." Since the School had a limited budget, Johnson and Zapffe thought it best to seek "young, promising, active men, even though it might appear unlikely that they could be retained a long time." That was better, they insisted, "than acquiring mediocre men with a view to retaining them permanently, which seems too often to have been the case in the past." Yet in spite of all the shortcomings, Johnson and Zapffe recommend-

26. Ibid., pp. 21–22.
27. Ibid., p. 24.
28. Ibid., pp. 27ff.
29. Ibid., pp. 32ff.

ed that since there had been "a decided improvement," the School "need not be considered to be on 'confidential probation.'"[30]

One of the recommendations was for the establishment of an executive committee, to advise the dean and to serve as "intermediary" between him and the faculty. Johnson and Zapffe may have felt that because the 67-year-old Beecher was not a vigorous dean, the faculty should play a greater role in decision-making. In any case, the trustees voted in May 1944 to establish such a committee, and in September Beecher announced that the committee consisted of Albert G. Mackay, Ellsworth Amidon, Harold Pierce, Walter Stultz, Louis Goodman, and E. H. Buttles.[31] The committee made several attempts to clarify its role, but "no real understandable explanation was offered by President Millis."

In November the members were stunned to learn through the press that a department chairman had resigned and a replacement named without their knowledge. Members had thought that their role was to make recommendations on personnel actions.[32] On November 17 the committee decided to take action. Not only was it disturbed by the lack of faculty participation in decision-making, but the entire situation in Burlington was becoming intolerable. During the past year resignations had reduced at least two departments to such an extent that they could not "carry on their minimal necessary duties. Several other resignations" were expected. This was due to low salaries, patriotic fervor, and the accelerated course, which increased the teaching load without added compensation. The executive committee had proposed an increased salary scale, but it had been rejected by the University administration. With such low salaries, it was impossible to find competent replacements for the men who had resigned. The result was "deep and widespread dissatisfaction" within the faculty. Since the executive committee occupied "an anomalous situation" and performed no useful purpose except possibly "to divide responsibility," Mackay, Amidon, Pierce, and Stultz resigned from the committee. This left only Buttles and Goodman, and Goodman was about to resign.[33]

In December 1944, President Millis' report to the Board of Trustees noted the "critical situation in the Medical College." He also reported that Soule had resigned as dean-elect and intended to return as professor of radiology. Furthermore, Beecher had submitted his resignation, effective "at the convenience of the Board." Finally, Millis recommended that the salary scale proposed by the executive committee be accepted, to raise salaries of the present professors and to result in more attractive salaries for prospective faculty members. Interestingly, Millis recommended an increase of $30,000 in the College budget, while Beecher and Mackay insisted upon $40,000. The trust-

30. Ibid., pp. 34–39.

31. Trustee Minutes, May 26, 1944. Medical Faculty Minutes, September 7, 1944.

32. Executive Committee Minutes, November 17, 1944, Advisory Committee Folder, UVM Archives.

33. Ibid.

ees accepted the faculty recommendation, and voted to appropriate $100,000 per year for the Medical School, rather than the usual $60,000.[34]

President Millis then wrote to inform Zapffe that Soule did not intend to return as dean, and that the College was about to search for a full-time replacement for Beecher.[35] Zapffe responded that in his opinion, Soule would "have been the man for the place." Zapffe asked if Millis would be interested in bringing Hardy Kemp back, for Kemp had returned from the military to a professorship at Ohio State rather than to the deanship. Zapffe also suggested Ellsworth Amidon as a possible candidate.[36] By this time Millis had responded to the resignation of the members of the executive committee by promising to consult with them on all matters of interest to the medical faculty, and he asked the committee for its reaction to the various candidates.[37] Finally, after getting a great many recommendations, Millis saw Dr. Alan Gregg, vice president of the Rockefeller Foundation. Gregg pulled out of his desk a group of index cards, his "potential dean file." One of the cards was for William Eustis Brown, who had been professor of preventive medicine at the University of Cincinnati and was about to be released from the United States Public Health Service.[38]

Millis investigated Brown, then offered him the position of dean. Brown accepted, and the College gained the vigorous leadership that had been lacking during the difficult days of the Second World War. To be fair to Beecher, however, it should be recognized that he expected to be dean for only one year, while Soule did the actual work of administering the College. When Soule had second thoughts about his commitment to replace Beecher, the Dean was forced to continue during several of the most difficult years in the history of the School. It is nevertheless interesting that while Beecher was dean, the College budget increased substantially, from $158,000 in 1941–42 to $220,000 in 1945–46.[39]

When William Brown arrived in the fall of 1945, he had three major objectives. First, he wanted to develop "an active medical center to serve the people in Vermont, New Hampshire, and Maine." At the same time, he wanted to increase the amount of clinical material available for teaching purposes.[40] Finally, he recognized the need for new blood on the faculty, especially in full-time clinical professorships. As soon as he was in Burlington, Brown began working to develop a medical center of Vermont. Late in July 1945, for instance, even before officially assuming his position, Brown outlined the recommendations made by Robin Carl Buerki regarding clinical needs of the Medical College and the Mary Fletcher Hospital. The Buerki report, which was in fact a survey of the Hospital, suggested that a Medical College Building be constructed adjoining the Hospital.[41]

34. Trustee Minutes, December 16, 1944.

35. Millis to Zapffe, December 18, 1944, Medical Deanship Folder, Millis Papers.

36. Zapffe to Millis, Chicago, December 26, 1944, ibid.

37. Trustee Minutes, April 21, 1945.

38. Ibid., June 1, 1945. Interview with John Schoff Millis, UVM Archives.

39. Medical Faculty Minutes, August 31, 1945.

40. Brown to Millis, Cincinnati, June 13, 1945, Brown Folder, Millis Papers.

41. Robin Carl Buerki, "Survey of the Mary Fletcher Hospital," M.F.H. Folder, Millis Papers.

This was the start of the planning of a new medical complex. At a meeting in August it was decided that a medical center should be established in Burlington, much like the New England Medical Center, which was affiliated with the Tufts Medical School.[42] The Hospital's planning committee was being expanded, with the University sending representatives and with the chairman of the state hospital survey commission, Laurence C. Campbell, an invited participant.[43]

At a meeting on September 29 the project was given an excellent start. Governor Mortimer Proctor, President Millis, Dean Brown, and Dr. Lyman Allen represented the University, Dr. T. S. Brown, Roy Patrick, and Lester Richwagen represented the Hospital, and four members of the state hospital survey commission were also present. The group unanimously endorsed Brown's plan, which promised to assist local hospitals by having the Medical College extend pathological, bacteriological, radiological, and other services to Vermont's smaller hospitals. Financial considerations were paramount. Millis noted that foundations were not interested in giving aid to individual institutions, but were enthusiastic about integrated systems of hospital and medical care. Furthermore, with the Hill-Burton Act working its way through Congress, it was likely that federal assistance would be possible if a plan were developed for a statewide system of hospital care.[44]

When the Vermont Hospital Association met in Montpelier on December 10, representatives of every group involved in planning the medical center were present. Dr. Samuel Proger, director of the Bingham Associates of Maine, described the operation of the Pratt Diagnostic Clinic of the Tufts Medical College. He also described the medical center in Maine, which had primary and secondary hospitals along with local health centers, all of which had proven successful since its founding in 1937. As Proger described it, the medical center strengthened the family doctor by making more facilities available to him. The patient knew that his physician had access to the best equipment and thus had more confidence in his skill.[45] It was a promising possibility for the state of Vermont.

Proger's testimony failed to dispel the fear that Dean Brown's proposal was an attempt to control medical care from Burlington, bypassing local physicians and surgeons in favor of members of the faculty.[46] A faculty committee suggested that in order to alleviate some of the suspicion, the medical center should be called a "diagnostic clinic," which implied that treatment would not be given in Burlington without permission of the referring physician. When the committee made this suggestion, however, Dean Brown declared that "the interests of the Medical School called for something beyond diagnoses alone," and he called attention to the importance of using the center for medical education.[47]

42. Planning Committee Minutes, July 20, 1945, MFH Folder, Millis Papers.

43. Minutes of Committee, September 15, 1945, Medical Center for Vermont Folder, Millis Papers.

44. Ibid., September 29, 1945. Medical Faculty Minutes, December 3, 1945.

45. Vermont Hospital Association, Minutes, December 10, 1945, Medical Center for Vermont Folder, Millis Papers.

46. Ibid., December 15, 1945.

47. Medical Faculty Minutes, December 19, 1945.

The Dean set out to educate the physicians of the state to the need for a statewide medical center; he requested meetings with the various county societies so that he could explain the project and assure local physicians that the Medical School was not trying to take business away from the rural practitioner or the local hospital.[48] After several years of discussion the proposal to develop a medical center was dropped, primarily because of continued opposition from physicians and surgeons who practiced outside of Burlington.[49]

Dean Brown continued the work of Hardy Kemp in bringing the DeGoesbriand Hospital into the Medical College program. Almost immediately after he arrived in Burlington, he received an emissary from Bishop Edward F. Ryan. When the Dean and the Bishop finally met, Ryan asked why Catholic hospitals were second and third rate institutions. Brown responded that Catholic hospitals traditionally selected their staff on the basis of religious affiliation rather than professional competence. Brown suggested that one way to upgrade the DeGoesbriand was for the Hospital to develop a closer relationship with the Medical School. If staff members were screened by the faculty and received faculty appointments, there would be a substantial improvement. As a result of the discussion, an agreement was drawn up giving the College the right to approve staff appointments at the Hospital.[50]

When Paul K. French became president of the Hospital's medical staff, he set out to change the by-laws to bring them into line with the newly developed College affiliation. Some staff members were bitterly opposed to any change. Some members of the Hospital staff were not qualified for college appointments, and there was a very real fear that the College men would ultimately push them out of the Hospital and take complete control. Since the staff was about evenly divided "for and against the revision of the by-laws," discussions at staff meetings went on until one or two in the morning. After three monthly staff meetings filled with animosity, French learned that the College group was planning to resign from the staff. He managed to convince them to remain, and the following month Mother Collins, the superior of the Hospital, gave French a letter from the Bishop to be read at the next staff meeting. The Bishop declared that the new by-laws were in force, and advised those who wanted to remain on the staff to sign the by-laws. "There was complete silence for a minute, then every person in the room arose, came to the secretary's desk and awaited his turn to sign." Frederick W. Van Buskirk, a radiologist on the staff, noted that one of the leading opponents of the affiliation with the College was first to sign. The Bishop had been forced to take action because the A.M.A. Council on Medical Education and Hospitals had refused to accredit the

48. John W. Brownlee to Theodore H. Harwood, Rutland, December 20, 1945, Chittenden County Medical Society, Correspondence, Wilbur Collection, Bailey Library, UVM.

49. Minutes, January 19, 1946, Medical Center for Vermont Folder, Medical Dean's Office Papers, 1934–63, Box 7. For the future development of such a medical center, see Chapter 14.

50. Interview with William E. Brown, transcript in UVM Archives.

Hospital unless there was substantial improvement. That improvement would come through affiliation with the College.[51]

It was agreed that the College would pay half the salary of the Hospital's director of medical education, who would be a full-time member of both the Hospital and the College staff. Harriet P. Dustan, a recent graduate of the Medical School, was appointed to the new position. She reorganized the teaching clinics and the ward rounds, assigned interesting cases to the students, and even scheduled student conferences to discuss the various cases. For the first time there was organized and coordinated medical education. Dustan remained on the job for two crucial years before going to the Montreal General Hospital and then to the Cleveland Clinic, where she distinguished herself in clinical and basic research in reno-vascular disease.[52]

Meanwhile, Paul French set out to overcome the animosity between the physicians and the Medical College. When he returned from military service, French found that the "Catholic DeGoesbriand staff and nearly all the doctors living outside of Burlington seemed to have real hatred of the Medical School and for the doctors associated with it." As the Chittenden County representative to the executive board of the Vermont Medical Society, French worked to overcome this. French and Dean Brown visited the various county societies, assuring them that the College wanted to cooperate with the local practitioners, rather than dominate them. Gradually, members of the state society abandoned much of their hostility.[53]

51. Ibid. See also interviews with Paul K. French and Frederick W. Van Buskirk.
52. Ibid.
53. Interview with Paul K. French, transcript in UVM Archives.

20. Drs. H. A. Durfee, Sr., E. H. Buttles, and T. S. Brown, 1943.

For developing a new faculty, Dean Brown was in a unique position. The staff was severely depleted by the War, and there was need for additional personnel in a great many areas, including orthopedics, neurosurgery, neurology, pediatrics, dermatology, thoracic surgery, ophthalmology, and otolaryngology. After the incapacitation of Herbert Durfee in 1948, a new head of obstetrics and gynecology was required. Moreover, since so many good young men were about to come out of the service, Brown was in the position of selecting from a number of top-flight candidates.[54] The Dean took advantage of the opportunity.

The position in orthopedics was filled by John F. Bell, who had worked with the Boston Children's Hospital on the polio victims of the 1918 epidemic. For neurosurgery Soule recommended R. M. Peardon Donaghy, who had trained in Boston, New York, and Montreal. After six months on the job, Donaghy was overwhelmed with his duties and needed help. Lester Wallman, a Yale graduate who had worked with Donaghy in the service, was appointed to work with him. Finally, when it was decided that the College needed a specialist in neurology, George A. Schumacher, who had been head of the department at Cornell, joined the faculty. The newly developed Department of Neurosurgery was crucial: patients with head injuries or other intracranial problems were flown either to Boston or Montreal, which entailed a great deal of needless expense and trouble. At last neurological and neurosurgical cases could be treated competently in Burlington.[55]

The position in pediatrics was filled by Robert J. McKay, who had taken his residency at the College of Physicians and Surgeons in New York City and had spent a year at Boston Children's Hospital. After some debate on whether the College needed a thoracic surgeon, it was decided to appoint Donald B. Miller, a graduate of Johns Hopkins who had extensive training in this specialty. Miller organized a division of thoracic surgery within the Department of Surgery. When E. G. Twitchell retired as head of ophthalmology, a number of professors recommended John C. Cunningham, a graduate of the University of Vermont who had completed a residency at the Eye Institute of Columbia University. After a while it was decided that the College needed a board-certified man in otolaryngology, and Rufus C. Morrow joined the faculty to fill that vacancy.[56]

The final position caused the most trouble. In the spring of 1946, Herbert A. Durfee, professor of obstetrics, was stricken with cancer of the bladder. After radical surgery, he attempted to continue practice and teaching but found that impossible. He arranged with William Slavin to take over his office, practice, and teaching while he struggled with his disease, hoping that it could be brought under control.

54. Brown to Millis, Cincinnati, August 22, 1945, Brown Folder, Millis Papers. Interview with William E. Brown.

55. Interview with William E. Brown.

56. Ibid.

Dean Brown, realizing the hopelessness of the situation, began a search for a promising young obstetrician and gynecologist to take Durfee's place in the teaching program. He visited John Van Sicklen Maeck, who had graduated from the College of Medicine in 1939 and was then a resident in obstetrics and gynecology at Woman's Hospital in New York City. Brown found him receptive to a return to Burlington after he had completed his training.

Maeck was a descendant of a Hessian surgeon who had settled in Shelburne after the American Revolution. After a two-year internship at Lenox Hill Hospital in New York City, he had served for four years at Fort Devens Station Hospital, working under the direction of B. F. Clark, a former member of the Obstetrics Department at the University of Vermont. His residency at Woman's Hospital began after separation from military service. In the spring of 1948 Maeck received, on the same day, three letters—from Dean Brown, Dr. Durfee, and Dr. Durfee's wife—all asking if he would be interested in joining the Department of Obstetrics and Gynecology.

In the meantime, Bishop Ryan had decided that in light of the affiliation with the College, it was a good idea to appoint a Catholic as head of the DeGoesbriand Hospital's Department of Obstetrics and Gynecology. Since the department head at the College would also be Hospital chief of service, the Bishop thought that if he appointed a chief of service, the Dean would be forced to appoint him as department head. In that case, for the first time since Patrick McSweeney, a Catholic would be "in charge of the College department." Since abortion was contrary to Catholic theology, it was natural for the Bishop to want the Hospital's department controlled by a devout Catholic. That was especially true now that the College approved staff appointments to the Hospital. If the Bishop did not find a Catholic obstetrician, he was afraid that the College would appoint someone who might permit abortions.

In any case, Frederick L. Good, a Catholic who had been professor of Obstetrics and Gynecology at Tufts Medical School from 1924 to 1947, recommended a Catholic candidate.[57] Good insisted, quite correctly, that religion should not be held against a qualified individual and that a tolerant professor could be objective in spite of his religious background.[58]

When it became public information that the Bishop was planning to appoint a chief of service without consulting the Dean, there was a great deal of turmoil in Burlington's medical circles. Rumors spread that the Bishop was going to "throw all Protestants off the staff" of the DeGoesbriand, that members of the Obstetrics Department of the Hospital "were going to be subject to a new czar," that the professorship at the University was "being stolen by the DeGoes-

57. Because the individual concerned was still alive in 1975, the author consented to a request to omit his name. In return, the author was granted complete access to the Diocesan Archives.

58. From materials in the Diocesan Archives.

briand," and that "a grand plot was under way to embarrass the University." A letter from the period of the First World War was "exhumed to prove that all non-Catholic doctors were unwelcome who did not send all their patients to the DeGoesbriand."[59]

In February 1949 Dr. Durfee died after a long and painful illness, and the chairmanship became vacant. The Bishop was concerned that if he did not announce the appointment of his candidate, the University would appoint someone who would be primarily on the faculty and only incidentally on the DeGoesbriand staff.[60] He was convinced that the faculty was "seeking someone else, anyone else," and that "the time is nearing, if not already arrived, when our hospital will have to have a show-down with the Medical College. Their policy, thus far, has been to treat the Bishop DeGoesbriand Hospital as a stepchild or to make it the tail of the kite to the Mary Fletcher." The Bishop knew that the College needed the Hospital for clinical material, and if the Bishop were to withdraw the use of the Catholic hospital, the College would almost certainly lose its class A rating. Political realities made it appear that the College would accept the appointment even though the faculty might not be happy that the decision was being made by the Bishop rather than by the Dean.[61]

Meanwhile, in January 1949 Dean Brown managed to find a reason to delay the appointment. The faculty had an old and forgotten rule that clinical professors had to reside in Burlington for a full year before they could be appointed to the teaching staff. Brown also made it clear that a faculty appointment had to be made by the College, and not by the Hospital.[62]

In May 1949 the obstetrician arrived in Burlington and assumed his position as chief at the Hospital. His credentials were impressive. He had experience as a professor, he was board certified, and at the time of his appointment he had twenty-six publications to his credit.[63] Yet, his credentials were immaterial. It was a matter of principle—would the College allow the Bishop to initiate the appointment? While Dean Brown gained time by citing the faculty regulation, he sought additional information on the Catholic obstetrician. Considering the developing confrontation with the Bishop, Brown must have been pleased when he was informed that the obstetrician had been dropped from a previous position "for just cause." The Pathology Department had discovered that "almost 90% of the ovaries, tubes, and uteri removed by this gentleman were found to be both grossly and histologically normal tissue."[64]

It did not take long for the DeGoesbriand, and for that matter the entire Catholic community in Burlington, to become involved in the situation. The obstetrician admitted in a letter to the author that he "was not in the habit of concealing under a cloak of modesty."[65]

59. Letter to Bishop Ryan, February 2, 1949, Diocesan Archives.

60. Bishop Ryan to Msgr. Flanagan, St. Petersburg, Florida, February 15, 1949, Diocesan Archives.

61. Bishop Ryan to Frederick Good, April 4, 1949, ibid.

62. Minutes, Dean's Advisory Committee, January 17, 1949, Advisory Committee Folder, UVM Archives.

63. See his curriculum vitae in Kaufman Correspondence File, UVM Archives.

64. Letter in Advisory Committee Folder, UVM Archives.

65. Letter to the author, December 17, 1974, Kaufman File. See also his oral history tape, UVM Archives.

According to Bishop Ryan, he was very egotistical; he "made himself a persona non grata" with all the doctors who had any dealings with him. The Sisters at the hospital "have come to dislike him very much," as he was very demanding and he continually insisted that not "enough consideration" was being given to "his dignity." Finally, a number of his colleagues became convinced that "he was performing too many operations and that, in many cases, they were needless." Indeed, the Bishop declared in a letter to Dr. Good that "word was being passed along by the women of Burlington . . . not to go to him, because if they did, they were sure he would operate on them." In addition, the Bishop had learned that the obstetrician was performing abortions at the hospital, in spite of the fact that this was contrary to Catholic doctrine.[66]

In a letter to the author the obstetrician insisted that the basic problem was jealousy: the others on the faculty of the College and the staff of the two hospitals were jealous of his extensive publication record.[67] It is difficult to determine the truth, especially when something as elusive as "jealousy" might be involved. In any case, it is clear that the Dean had correspondence indicating that the physician had been removed from a previous position "for just cause," and the Bishop became convinced that the obstetrician was egotistical, that he had alienated his colleagues, and that he was performing abortions and other "needless" operations. Yet in spite of the Bishop's insistence that the Catholic women of Burlington were afraid to go to the obstetrician, seventy-three women signed a petition in his support, declaring that they knew "from actual contact" that he was "an excellent Gynecologist and Obstetrician," that he had "helped many in moral as well as physical problems," and that he had successfully treated conditions that had "existed as long as twelve years."[68]

The facts of the eventual confrontation are missing from the sources. In 1950, however, he resigned from his position at the DeGoesbriand. By that time it was clear that he would not be offered a faculty position, and it seems that he had alienated even those who originally were his supporters. According to Paul French, who was friendly with both Bishop Ryan and Dean Brown, the Bishop apologized to Brown for the entire problem, declaring: "Just how stupid can a Bishop be?"[69]

On August 17, 1948, Maeck returned to Burlington. He took over Durfee's practice and practically all teaching in the department. Following Durfee's death in 1949, Maeck became acting chairman, and then chairman, of the Department of Obstetrics and Gynecology, a post he held until his retirement in July 1975.

In retrospect, the first six years of Dean Brown's tenure were suc-

66. Bishop Ryan to F. Good, September 25, 1950, DeGoesbriand Hospital Folder, 1950, Diocesan Archives.

67. Letter to the author, December 17, 1974, Kaufman File.

68. Petition included with letter, ibid.

69. Interview with Paul K. French. See also interview with John V. Maeck, Professor of Obstetrics and Gynecology.

*21. Dean Beecher dem-
onstrating William
Beaumont's surgical
kit to medics James A.
Sudbay, William E.
Schumacher, and
Joanna J. Metcalf,
Class of 1945.*

*22. Dr. Paul K.
French, professor of
medicine, conducting
bedside teaching in the
Old Men's Ward,
MFH, for (left to
right) resident P.
Kingston Larner,
M.D., '44; Ruth
Hunt, R.N.; and med-
ical students John H.
Perry-Hooker, '47;
John C. Patten '47;
and Edward B. Crane,
'47.*

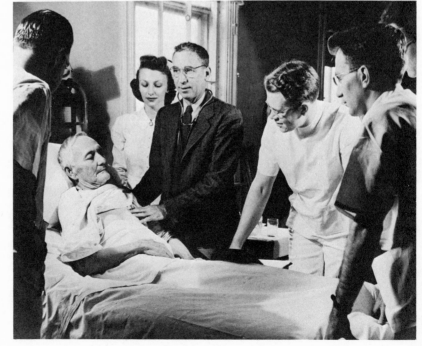

23. The Class of 1950
in the MFH am-
phitheatre.

24. Dean William E.
Brown and the faculty
of the College of
Medicine, 1951.

cessful. Although he was unable to develop the medical center of his dreams, he did substantially improve the faculty, increase clinical material through developing closer relations with the Catholic community, and, as will be seen, played a major role in planning a new Medical School complex for the University.

Chapter Fourteen

From Medical College to Medical Center

ALTHOUGH DEAN BROWN'S PLAN to develop a medical center had failed to gain the support he had envisioned, he was not one to abandon a dream. In 1948, when discussion focused on the need for new facilities, he insisted that there be ample "room to carry out a broad, far-seeking medical program." He did not want to construct new quarters that would soon be outdated or would prevent the future development of a medical complex.[1] Brown believed that a medical center could not be established without close cooperation between the two Burlington hospitals and the College. By 1950 he had taken a small first step, by reorganizing the residency training program at both hospitals. Under the new system, residents rotated through the Mary Fletcher and DeGoesbriand hospitals; that was especially beneficial for the DeGoesbriand, which, being smaller, was not able to provide extensive clinical experience for its residents. It was a step forward in cooperation.[2]

In 1952 Dean Brown reached retirement age, and it was necessary to replace him with another dynamic dean who, it was hoped, would be able to complete the medical complex. After a search, George A. Wolf, Jr., was appointed to the position. Wolf had received his medical training at Cornell; at the time of his appointment he was on the faculty of the Cornell Medical College and director of the outpatient clinic at the New York Hospital. When his name was presented to the faculty, the discussion centered on whether the thirty-seven-year-old physician would "be lured away after a short stay" in Burlington. Members of the search committee reported that Wolf had committed himself to remain through the construction of the new

1. Brown to Millis, March 6, 1948, Brown Folder, Millis Papers.

2. Brown to President William S. Carlson, April 14, 1950, Brown Folder, Carlson Papers. The College's Department of Medicine refused to participate in the plan.

*25. Professors emeriti,
1951. Left to right:
Benjamin Dyer
Adams, Fred Kinney
Jackson, Lyman Allen,
George Millar Sabin,
Thomas Stephen
Brown, Clarence
Henry Beecher, and
Oliver Newell
Eastman.*

*26. The City Physician, Murdo G. Mac-
Donald, M.D., '51
(right) with senior
medic Gerald Needle-
man, '53, leaving the
Burlington Free Dis-
pensary to make house
calls.*

Medical School, and with this assurance the faculty voted to endorse his appointment. Wolf had a summer place in Vermont and had already developed a "fondness" for the state. His wife, Marguerite Hurrey Wolf, subsequently wrote several books about her experiences in Vermont; including *Anything Can Happen in Vermont* and *Vermont Is Always with You*.[3]

Before the planning for construction could proceed further, Wolf recognized the need for closer relations with the DeGoesbriand Hospital. He did not want to plan the new medical complex near the Mary Fletcher if that would alienate those who controlled the Catholic institution. It would be self-defeating if the new building program resulted in the withdrawal of clinical facilities at the DeGoesbriand and Fanny Allen hospitals. In any case, with the departure of Harriet Dustan, "there was a tremendous void [at the Hospital], at least as far as teaching was concerned." Indeed, the physicians on the staff believed that "the medical school was running the hospital," and that the DeGoesbriand only received "a few crumbs that fell from Lazarus' table."[4]

The possibility for improved communication arose when Arthur Gladstone, a Jewish surgeon who was a member of the staff, was asked if he would become director of medical education for the two Catholic hospitals. Gladstone wanted the appointment initiated by the College as well as the Hospital, and he suggested that he be a "liaison officer" between the two institutions. Bishop Ryan, Dean Wolf, and leaders on the faculty agreed to the concept, and Gladstone was officially appointed for a three-year term, with the Hospital and the College each paying half of his stipend. The Dean was thus able to develop a major point of contact at the DeGoesbriand.[5]

Now that Wolf had demonstrated his good intentions by cooperating with the Bishop, he moved to formulate plans for the new Medical School complex. In 1955 a building committee was established to make specific recommendations, and the trustees authorized a campaign to raise enough money to qualify for matching grants under the Health Research Facilities Construction Act, then being debated in Washington. The trustees were not very optimistic at that point; it was noted in their minutes that if federal funds were not forthcoming, it was doubtful whether sufficient money could be raised for the project.[6]

When the faculty began to debate the proposed locations for the Medical College, the Dean's relationship with the Bishop seemed to be producing results. Gladstone prepared a memo for the faculty advisory committee indicating that Bishop Ryan was willing "to consider any plan for the benefit of the University of Vermont Medical Center, including two hospitals, even to the extent of considering changing the location" of the DeGoesbriand. At the meeting of the committee, Wolf indicated that the new building had to be surround-

3. Oral history interview with George A. Wolf, Medical Faculty Minutes, January 21, 1952. Trustee Minutes, February 23, 1952.
4. Oral history interview with F. W. Van Buskirk.
5. Minutes, Advisory Committee, January 15, 1954. See also Trustee Minutes, February 20, 1954.
6. Oral history interview with Harold B. Pierce. Trustee Minutes, June 10, 1955.

ed by enough space to enable the DeGoesbriand eventually to move next to it, without at the same time preventing further expansion of the Mary Fletcher. The Dean was directed to discuss the exact location with the directors of the two institutions.[7]

While this was occurring, James A. Hamilton Associates, who had been commissioned to make recommendations for the College's development program, completed its report. The report was totally unacceptable to the DeGoesbriand. And although Dean Wolf described it as an "honest and sincere attempt to help us and as such . . . a significant point of departure," he did so in a seventeen-page memorandum enumerating "some of the possible defects." The report recommended, for example, that the Medical College be relocated adjacent to the Mary Fletcher, along Colchester Avenue on Hospital Hill, a site Dean Wolf rejected as restricting future growth. More significant were Hamilton Associates' allegations that "the administration of the Bishop DeGoesbriand hospital has never cooperated completely with the College of Medicine in the overall teaching program." Dean Wolf noted that "evidence of lack of cooperation" was not presented, but this assumption permeated the report. Because the DeGoesbriand "does not permit the College of Medicine extensive control of its medical program," it should, the Report advised, be classified as a "medical center associated teaching hospital." The Mary Fletcher, which "has been closely integrated with the College of Medicine and does permit the College of Medicine extensive control of its medical program," should be "classified as a University of Vermont medical center teaching hospital." The DeGoesbriand, relegated to an associate status, "should not expect the College to duplicate on an equal basis every activity it promotes at the Mary Fletcher."[8]

Among the efforts of President Carl Borgmann and Dean Wolf to defuse the Report's potential divisiveness was an offer of land for the DeGoesbriand to relocate within the proposed medical complex. They recommended five acres of land near the present water tower, and, if the DeGoesbriand did not use it within five years, the option of land on the east side of East Avenue.

Early in January 1956 the situation was further complicated by a leak to the press which made it appear that the recommendations of the Hamilton report would be implemented. Dean Wolf and President Borgmann were placed in an awkward position. They objected to significant portions of the Report, had asked the University trustees to keep the report confidential, and had not even discussed it with the faculty. Arthur Gladstone was perhaps more embarrassed than either Wolf or Borgmann. Not only were his efforts as liaison officer between the College and the Hospital denigrated by the Report, but he had assured the Bishop that no decision would be made until after a series of meetings.[9]

7. Minutes, Advisory Committee, December 22, 1955.
8. See James A. Hamilton Associates, "A Development Program for the College of Medicine of the University of Vermont," November 28, 1955 (Confidential Report). Also George A. Wolf, "Comments Related to 'The Development Program for the College of Medicine of the University of Vermont.' By James A. Hamilton Associates," December 16, 1955, Confidential Memorandum, Wolf Papers. The quotes relating to the lack of cooperation are on p. 29 of the Hamilton Report. See pp. 21 and 30 for descriptions of teaching and associated teaching hospitals. The quotes from Dean Wolf's memo are from pps. 1 and 4.
9. See Advisory Committee Minutes, January 9, 1956, and Medical Faculty Minutes, January 27, 1956.

In February the situation grew even more complex. The Mary Fletcher had applied for a grant to establish a state rehabilitation center in Burlington; when the Bishop learned of this, he applied for the DeGoesbriand. After a hearing, the state department of health decided in favor of the Catholic hospital.[10] Now there was one more reason for the DeGoesbriand to remain at its present location. Planning for the rehabilitation center preceded the completion of the initial planning of the medical complex. Therefore, it had to be built in its present location, and, once constructed, it would be impossible for the DeGoesbriand to move without separating its facilities.[11] On February 16 the faculty advisory committee adopted a motion supporting the location of the new medical school "as close as possible and attached" to the Mary Fletcher, and it voted in favor of "a comparable location for attachment to the medical school building" for the DeGoesbriand.[12]

The DeGoesbriand medical advisory committee considered the advantages and disadvantages of the location adjacent to the new Medical College. Other than the location of the rehabilitation center, the basic reasons to remain in the present site were emotional. "*This is home*," the report declared. "Thirty years ago, ground was broken for the original building which is still in active service, and it stands as a symbol of courage and faith to those who were able to create a reality from a vision." In addition, in its present location the Hospital could maintain its identity as a Catholic institution, with fewer regulations from the Medical School. Finally, in case "differences should ever arise," it would be easier for the hospital to "divorce itself from the school." Of course, the construction of the rehabilitation center provided a material reason for remaining.[13]

Yet there were disadvantages to the present site. First, future expansion of the Hospital was limited. In addition, if the Mary Fletcher became the "primary teaching hospital," that would continue the "keen sense of competition" which "might be antagonistic rather than cooperative." Finally, the cost of providing modern medical service was increasing steadily; the Hospital would have to purchase expensive pieces of equipment, "trying to keep up with the Joneses" and realizing that "we cannot quite do it." The committee concluded that the Hospital should move to the new location and become part of the University Medical Center. The members of the committee believed that eventually "the barriers of prejudice" would be destroyed and through cooperation between the Medical School, a nonsectarian hospital, and the Catholic institution, the graduate would be "kind in his approach to patients, and well trained in medicine, a credit to all three participating units of the center."[14]

Yet in June of that year the DeGoesbriand executive committee unanimously decided to overrule the advisory recommendations— the hospital would remain where it was.[15] The following month Dean

10. Advisory Committee Minutes, January 6, 1956. Health Commission Minutes, February 2, 1956, copy in Rehabilitation Folder, Dean's Office Papers, UVM Archives. The Hamilton Report (p. 34) commends the Mary Fletcher for its "forward attitude" in planning to add a rehabilitation center building and then reported that the "Bishop DeGoesbriand Hospital in a published article in the local newspaper stated that it was not interested in adding a rehabilitation center." Dean Wolf's memorandum of possible defects in the Hamilton Report notes on p. 4 that the DeGoesbriand had filed a letter of intent to establish a rehabilitation center.

11. DeGoesbriand Hospital Medical Advisory Committee, report on the possibility of moving the hospital to the new medical school area, 1956, DeGoesbriand Hospital Folder, 1956–57, Diocesan Archives.

12. Advisory Committee Minutes, February 16, 1956.

13. Ibid.

14. Ibid.

Wolf received the results of the most recent evaluation of the College by the Council on Medical Education and Hospitals of the A.M.A. and by the Association of American Medical Colleges. Although the College had the complete approval of the two organizations, the "antiquated structure" of the Medical Building was described as "obviously inadequate both qualitatively and quantitatively for modern needs." The survey team suggested that a site for the new complex be found which would be acceptable to both hospitals.[16] At approximately the same time, the Dean suggested to President Borgmann that a liaison committee be established to discuss common problems of the three institutions.[17] He apparently hoped that through improved communication it might be possible to influence decisions on the location of the new medical center.

In September 1956 a fascinating exchange took place at the meeting of the faculty executive committee. By that time, Bishop Ryan had died and was about to be replaced by Bishop Robert F. Joyce, who had done his undergraduate work at the University. The discussion was on the possibility of establishing a completely new administrative structure, a medical center board of trustees, having representatives from the two hospitals and from the Medical School. Robert Coon, chairman of the Pathology Department, noted that there was too much competition between the hospitals. Ellsworth Amidon, Medical Director of the Mary Fletcher and Chairman of the Department of Medicine at the College, agreed. He declared that clinical material at the DeGoesbriand should be utilized more fully, and that they should "iron out duplication or triplication" of facilities. Amidon went on to assert that one research area would be sufficient. However reasonable that suggestion might appear, it was a direct threat to the prestige of the DeGoesbriand, for it would remove Wilhelm Raab to either the Medical School Building or the Mary Fletcher. Amidon went on to say that the Medical Department at the DeGoesbriand was "of the best caliber—active and productive." He liked working through the Hospital's chief of medicine, Christopher Terrien, rather than going to the Hospital himself.[18]

In response, representatives of the DeGoesbriand suggested that Amidon attend staff meetings at the Hospital, to demonstrate that he was truly interested in something other than the Mary Fletcher. Arthur Gladstone then entered the discussion. He said that the DeGoesbriand needed the impact of the chief of medicine. Amidon did not delegate authority to Terrien, Gladstone said, and Amidon needed to familiarize himself with the staff. Dean Wolf refused to be drawn into the discussion, saying that he preferred to look to the future rather than to the problems of the past.[19]

Early in 1957 the executive committee of the medical faculty dis-

15. DeGoesbriand Hospital Executive Committee Minutes, June 21, 1956, DeGoesbriand Hospital Folder, Diocesan Archives.

16. Wolf to Executive Committee, July 2, 1956, copy in Dean's Office Papers, 1934–63, Box 3.

17. Wolf to Borgmann, July 2, 1956, memorandum in Tri-Institution Committee Folder, Dean's Office Papers, 1934–63, Box 14.

18. Executive Committee Minutes, September 21, 1956.

19. Ibid.

27. *Dr. E. L. Amidon,
professor and chair-
man, Department of
Medicine, lecturing in
Hall A to the Class of
1955.*

cussed Arthur Gladstone's role as liaison officer between the College and the DeGoesbriand. His three-year appointment would expire in July, and Dean Wolf wanted to renew the contract. John F. Berry, administrator of the DeGoesbriand, agreed with Wolf, declaring that morale at the Hospital had markedly increased since Gladstone's appointment in 1954.[20]

After an extensive discussion which continued over two meetings of the committee, it was decided to authorize the Dean to continue the contract with Gladstone. In addition, the committee decided that there should be "a formal agreement with resulting tighter control over the staff" of the DeGoesbriand. Dean Wolf was directed to explore with Bishop Joyce "what steps can be taken to formalize and integrate the DeGoesbriand program with the College of Medicine."[21]

As a response to the ensuing discussion between the Dean and the Bishop, the trustees of the DeGoesbriand authorized Bishop Joyce, as their president, to propose a meeting of representatives of the boards of trustees of the two hospitals and the University "to study means of co-ordination and cooperation among the three institutions for the best interests of the sick and for the mutual welfare of the institutions."[22] This was the start of the "tri-institution committee" earlier proposed by Dean Wolf. Robert B. Aiken, State Health Commissioner, was strongly supportive of the idea and, by assisting in its organization, provided an early example of government interest in community planning.

The first meeting was held on May 3, 1957, with a discussion of the scope and area of the committee's work. If nothing else, the committee would provide a forum for representatives of the three institutions to discuss their plans, and perhaps to avoid future duplication and triplication of costly equipment.[23]

Meanwhile, the fund-raising campaign to support the construction of the new college buildings had started. According to Dean Wolf, "many people on the staff felt that it would be impossible to raise more than $4,000 or $5,000 from the alumni to conduct any project."[24] Although Dean William Brown had retired five years earlier, he played a major role in the campaign. In the first year of the drive, it was reported that the two men traveled over 20,000 miles each to contact alumni and foundations! Although neither Brown nor Wolf could interest foundations in the program, they had great success with the alumni. The personal approach was crucial for the success of the fund-raising campaign. Indeed, in one case Brown drank with his "victim" until "under the benign influence" of "bourbon and branch water," the two men were "soon building the new medical school building." "If the evening had been a trifle longer," he later wrote, "we would have it paid for!"[25] In all, he made at least fourteen trips on behalf of the College's building fund.[26]

20. Ibid., January 16, 1957.

21. Ibid., January 16 and 21, 1957.

22. Bishop Joyce to F. W. Shepardson, March 27, 1957, Diocesan Archives.

23. Hospitals— University Liaison Committee Minutes, May 3 and September 9, 1957, Tri-Institution Committee Minute Book, UVM Archives.

24. Interview with Dean Wolf.

25. Itinerary of Trip 4, William E. Brown Papers, UVM Archives.

26. See material in Brown Papers.

Although Dean Brown was able to maintain his enthusiasm and his sense of humor, Frederick W. McFarland, of Connecticut, had another response. The Stamford physician was fund-raising captain for the area, and he visited with every graduate in his territory. McFarland was upset that many who insisted that they could not afford to give had recently taken expensive vacations. "If I had any Religion of any kind," he exclaimed, "I would hope for retribution, so delightfully described in the Old Testament." He noted that physicians would be nothing without their diplomas but "they simply accept their good fortune as though it were theirs by divine right." In spite of McFarland's distress at having to "carry the freight for the slackers," he kept increasing his own donation.[27]

Contrary to McFarland's experience, Dean Wolf discovered that many of the alumni were grateful to the University and were glad to share their success with the College. Indeed, statistics demonstrate an enthusiastic response by most of the alumni, notwithstanding the rejections by some. In 1956, before the fund-raising campaign began, a total of twenty-five graduates had given a total of $21,180 to the University. In alumni support, that placed the University thirtieth of the seventy-nine medical schools.[28]

The following year, 1957, 797 graduates gave a total of $226,752.50, all for the building fund. Now the University ranked first among the nation's medical schools in the total sum contributed by alumni. In 1958, with the fund nearing its goal, 615 alumni gave a total of $151,442.04. In that year the University ranked second to Harvard in alumni support.[29] In two years the graduates gave a total of $378,000. To quote Dean Wolf: "There is no question at all that the title of 'alumni building' for Phase I of the College of Medicine was justly deserved."[30] It would not have been possible to obtain federal matching funds without the generosity of the alumni.

Early in 1958 Dean Wolf was offered a position as Associate Director of the Association of American Medical Colleges. Although it was a tempting offer, the Dean decided to remain in Burlington. His response was revealing: his "young and growing family" was happy in Vermont. "We have a horse, pigs, chickens, lots of land, a view, and our own home. All this contains a part of us," he said. "We are sweating out a tough mortgage for the view, shoveling manure, collecting eggs, hoeing the garden, and have done over the kitchen by hand, personally. We have a few more muscles left," Wolf declared, "some drive, and a lot of esthetic sense." In addition to the satisfaction of rural life, Wolf noted that the potential of the College was great. "In six years, the staff has increased in quality, grants have increased threefold, the state appropriation has increased by one third, alumni contributions increased from $5000 to $230,000, the curriculum has been revised and a new building

27. McFarland to Brown, Stamford, Connecticut, February 27, March 22, 1957, December 31, 1956, Phase I File, Brown Papers, UVM Archives.

28. Interview with Dean Wolf. "Physicians' Direct Contributions to Medical Schools, 1956," in American Medical Education Foundation Folder, Dean's Office Papers, UVM Archives.

29. Ibid., 1957 and 1958.

30. Interview with Dean Wolf.

31. Wolf to Ward
Darley, April 9, 1958,
Borgmann Papers.

started." He wanted to remain for the completion of the new building. Wolf did assert, however, that "in another year or so the time to leave will probably arrive," and he regretted that the offer came "at this particular time." [31]

In spite of his optimistic report, the problems of communication with the hospitals remained a difficulty. In a memorandum to the president Dean Wolf declared that at all levels the motives of the hospitals "are not trusted by the other," and that his motives were questioned by both. Wolf indicated that he had been "accused of

*28. President John T.
Fey in June 1958, laying the cornerstone of
the Medical Alumni
Building, with* (left to
right), *former Dean
Beecher, Dean George
Wolf, Jr., and former
President Carl W.
Borgmann looking on.*

playing politics, suspected of carrying information back and forth, and accused of influencing things in favor of the DeGoesbriand." "Unfortunately," he said, "each hospital feels that to build one up will tear the other down, and each expects the College of Medicine to help it." The Dean indicated that he detected "a feeling on the part of the Fletcher group that the DeGoesbriand is attempting to influence adversely their fund-raising campaign."[32]

The following month, possibly in response to Wolf's confidential note, President Carl Borgmann wrote a long letter for presentation at the June 12 meeting of the tri-institution committee. Since Borgmann had already resigned as University president, he felt that if he brought the situation into the open, perhaps it would be honestly discussed and overcome. Although the meeting was canceled, Borgmann sent copies of his letter to the members of the committee.[33]

In it Borgmann noted that one "real handicap" to the progress of the tri-institution committee was the "feeling by the hospitals that their planning must be kept confidential and not be disclosed to the other." Borgmann mentioned the "thunderbolt decision by the De-Goesbriand to 'grab' the Rehabilitation Center." Similarly, the Mary Fletcher was involved in fund-raising, but what it planned to do with the money was known only to the board of that hospital. Borgmann suggested that the problems would be overcome in the future, if they recognized that the existing situation was detrimental to all concerned, and if they abandoned their separation and banded together as the University of Vermont Medical Center and used the tri-institution committee "more actively as the guiding board to achieve this end."[34]

It did not take long for Borgmann's letter to become the center of attention. Arthur Gladstone told the representatives of the DeGoes-briand on the tri-institution committee that Borgmann's statement "could well serve as the basis for constructive negotiations."[35] Soon after the letter was circulated, other statements were prepared. A. Bradley Soule described the recent attempts to improve relations with the DeGoesbriand. His letter concluded by expressing gratitude to the former president for his "leadership and guidance" and for his "valedictory admonishments." "Let us hope," Soule declared, "that we will all be big enough men to meet these complex problems head-on, openly, intelligently and courageously and that we shall not be disheartened or defeated by past defeats." "As an incurable optimist," the radiologist looked "forward to great things yet to come."[36]

A number of people urged Bishop Joyce to reply, but he decided that "multiple letters circulating around will give the impression of a desire to stir up the past with confusion, instead of facing the future with determination of cooperation and just and equitable hospital-

32. Confidential Statement, May 15, 1958, Tri-Institution Folder, Dean's Office Papers, 1934–63, Box 14.

33. There is no evidence that the meeting actually took place.

34. Hospitals–University Liaison Committee Minutes, June 12, 1958, in Tri-Institution Committee Minute Book, 1957–63, UVM Archives.

35. Gladstone to members of the Tri-Institution Committee representing the DMH, June 23, 1958, DeGoesbriand Hospital Folder, 1953–62, Diocesan Archives. Trustees of the DeGoesbriand Hospital, Minutes, June 30, 1958, in DeGoesbriand Hospital Folder, 1958–59, Diocesan Archives.

36. Soule to Borgmann, June 16, 1958, Kaufman Folder, UVM Archives.

college relationships." In August the Bishop demonstrated his sincerity and his willingness to cooperate by donating five hundred dollars to the Mary Fletcher Hospital Development Fund, and by publicly announcing that the DeGoesbriand would not initiate a fund-raising campaign until the Fletcher had attained its goal of $1,250,000.[37]

In June 1959 Gladstone resigned from his liaison position, ostensibly because of illness. He revealed to the Bishop that the real reason was frustration at the continued refusal of Ellsworth Amidon to pay sufficient attention to the DeGoesbriand. Gladstone declared that "the progress we made caused some of our so-called friends to be uncomfortable." He went on to note that many of the Medical School "Giants who have been altar boys of prejudice and were distorting values became uncomfortable" as he "more clearly defined the situation." "They knew" that Gladstone was aware of the real problem, and they feared that he "was exposing them too much." Gladstone concluded with the hope that the DeGoesbriand would be able to replace him with "a man who will continue to carry the message of unity."[28]

At the next meeting of the tri-institution committee, Bishop Joyce made it clear that the staff at the DeGoesbriand "did not feel" that the Department of Medicine "was being fair to the hospital." He wanted that statement on the record, and he indicated that he would make positive proposals in the future.[39] Meanwhile, Gladstone had become convinced that the DeGoesbriand had to initiate its own planning and development, without waiting for guidance from the College. That conclusion was almost unavoidable, since the department chairmen were chiefs of service at the Mary Fletcher, and some indicated that they were too busy to take a more active role at the DeGoesbriand.[40]

It was not long before the Hospital was indeed initiating its own planning and development, especially in terms of staffing. A brilliant young researcher at the Rockefeller Institute and a UVM medical alumnus in the class of 1954, Thomas B. Tomasi, Jr., was willing to come to DeGoesbriand as acting head of the division of experimental medicine, but only if after two years he would become Chairman of Medicine at the Hospital. In effect, he would replace Terrien, but as a full-time chief.[41] Tomasi's appointment symbolized the continued emphasis on scientific research at the DeGoesbriand, for he was following the tradition of Wilhelm Raab and others with productive records as investigators.

Although the impulse to cooperate had faltered, the College's building campaign was totally unaffected by the problem. In 1960 the University was informed by the Health Facilities Research Construction Division of the United States Public Health Service that

37. Gladstone to Bernard J. Leddy, July 9, 1958, DeGoesbriand Hospital Folder, 1958–62, Diocesan Archives. *Burlington Free Press*, August 20, 1958.

38. Gladstone to Bishop Joyce, April 30, 1960, DeGoesbriand Hospital Folder, 1958–62, Diocesan Archives. See also Gladstone to Wolf, June 2, 1959, ibid.

39. Hospitals—University Liaison Committee, Minutes, June 5, 1959.

40. Gladstone to Boardman, August 6, 1959, DeGoesbriand Hospital Folder, 1958–62, Diocesan Archives.

41. Terrien to Bishop Joyce, August 20, 1959, DeGoesbriand Hospital Folder, 1958–59, Diocesan Archives. DeGoesbriand Hospital Department Chairmen Minutes, August 13, 1959, ibid.

29. Three deans: Drs. Beecher, Wolf, and Brown; the Medical Alumni Building on the way up.

$722,000 in matching funds would be available for Phase II of the new medical complex. Phase II consisted of a building to house the research necessary in the modern scientifically oriented institution. Dean Wolf set out to raise the additional $750,000. Earlier he had discovered while raising funds for Phase I that foundations were not at all interested in the University; now, there had been a dramatic change. Foundations "were very much impressed by the fact that the alumni had been so generous" in their support of the earlier campaign; for the first time there was a general feeling that "Vermont did exist and was on the move."[42]

Fortune was indeed shining on Vermont. After learning of Charles A. Dana's philanthropies from a *Time* Magazine article in the December 21, 1959, issue, Dean Wolf wrote him. Dana, who headed a corporation which supplied parts for the automotive industry and had established the Dana Foundation, had already given substantial financial help to small colleges that not only had proven their needs but also had taken steps to help themselves. His philosophy was to give one third to one half of the amounts needed by the schools with the understanding that the colleges or communities in which they were located would raise the rest. After receiving Wolf's letter, Dana wrote back expressing interest in the College's plans. Wolf then went to visit with him and returned with a challenge grant of $150,000 toward Phase II of the building program. Dana's grant was contingent upon UVM receiving similar amounts from other foundations, and Dana then proceeded to intervene on behalf of UVM with other foundations. The most important of these interventions was with the Avalon Foundation, which provided a grant of $350,000, almost half of the nongovernment monies required.

Sceva Speare, who operated department stores in Nashua, New Hampshire, and Haverhill, Massachusetts, and had established a foundation at Crotched Mountain in Greenfield, New Hampshire, for the care and treatment of the handicapped, donated $50,000. The Century Club of the Medical Alumni Association provided $50,000 and individual alumni pledged another $135,000.[43] The College was thus able to complete the second part of its building program, once again thanks to the generosity of the alumni but this time with a great deal of support from the Avalon and Dana foundations. The construction program, planned at the precise time when federal support for medical research increased, was able to take advantage of the availability of government funding.

The government was to play another role in encouraging cooperation between the College and the hospitals. In November 1960 the state health commission informed both hospitals that there had to be coordinated planning, so that future requests for Hill-Burton funds would not force the commission to be "a referee or umpire

42. Trustee Minutes, April 16, 1960. Interview with Dean Wolf.

43. Wolf to Fey, July 26 and August 8, 1960, Wolf Folder, Fey Papers. Correspondence between William Brown and Sceva Speare, Brown Papers, UVM Archives.

to decide which one of two similar requests was the more worthy."[44] This type of planning was becoming more important, and officials of the College and the hospitals knew it from experience. The DeGoesbriand had "won" the rehabilitation center, but it soon learned that it had "won a white elephant, because it was a very expensive proposition." The income of the center was limited to patient fees and a grant from the Federal Office of Vocational Rehabilitation, and income from patient fees was low because of the small caseload. The federal government would not support the center indefinitely; neither the University nor the state could support it; and the DeGoesbriand was being drained of needed funds.[45] It was obvious that planning for the rehabilitation center had been either inadequate or nonexistent.

In 1962 the College would have new leadership. Upon the completion of Phase II Dean Wolf accepted a position as vice president of Tufts University and Director of the New England Medical Center. Brown and Wolf had developed some cooperation with the DeGoesbriand, and they were responsible for the fund-raising and planning of Phase I and II of the building campaign. After a lengthy and often frustrating search, the committee succeeded in attracting Robert J. Slater, a pediatrician and director of research at the Hospital for Sick Children at the University of Toronto. He had previously served at the Rockefeller Institute for Medical Research.[46]

A short while after Slater assumed his position, he received a report from Herbert Martin, Acting Director of Medical Education at the DeGoesbriand Hospital. Martin described a grim situation, including poor communication between the Hospital and the College, "unclear and improperly utilized lines of communication" between the Hospital and several department chairmen, and "insufficient interest in" and failure to support programs designed to improve the "academic stature" of the Hospital. Martin suggested that Dean Slater and President John T. Fey, who had replaced Borgmann, be appointed to the board of the DeGoesbriand, to improve relations with the College. He also suggested that department heads "neutralize their positions" by using the Medical School rather than the Mary Fletcher as their "seats of operation."[47]

In June 1963 the tri-institution committee was the scene of an interesting meeting, which once again demonstrated the need for a complete merger of services in the hospitals. The DeGoesbriand planned to install a cobalt radiation therapy unit and Milford D. Schulz, a radiation therapist at Harvard Medical School and the Massachusetts General Hospital, was called in to evaluate the need for two such units in Burlington. Schulz reported that since the unit at the Mary Fletcher operated at a deficit and at less than 50 percent capacity, there was no need for a similar one at the DeGoesbriand. President

44. See DeGoesbriand Hospital Trustee Minutes, January 23, 1961, Diocesan Archives. Mary Fletcher Hospital Board of Directors Minutes of Annual Meeting, November 16, 1960, MCHV Administrator's Office.

45. Interview with John T. Fey. Rehabilitation Center Folder, UVM Archives.

46. Trustee Minutes, February 25 and April 15, 1961. Search Committee Papers, Fey Papers, UVM Archives. Slater assumed his position on January 1, 1962, after Donald Melville served as acting dean from July 1 to August 19, 1961, and Chester Newhall replaced him in that capacity from August 19 to December 31, 1961.

47. Hospitals Folder, Dean's Office Papers, Box 2.

Fey, Dean Slater, and Professor Soule, the Chairman of Radiology, all agreed with Schulz, but the representatives of the DeGoesbriand insisted that the unit was needed. As long as patients were transferred to the Mary Fletcher for radiation therapy, there would be a tendency for direct referral to the Fletcher. Thus the unit meant more to the Hospital than statistics about patient load or financial cost might suggest. The investment would be great, but failure to install the unit would threaten the existence of the DeGoesbriand if the Hospital could not perform this needed service.[48] The cobalt unit was purchased and installed at the DeGoesbriand.

Unless it were possible to develop the Medical Center and formalize relationships between the three institutions, the duplication of services would undoubtedly continue, regardless of the expense involved. In August 1963 President Fey told the members of the University Board of Trustees that he wanted to plan a meeting with the boards of the two hospitals to "discuss the development of the medical center and the relationships of the institutions involved." The meeting was set for October 18, 1963.[49]

Meanwhile, on Amidon's recommendation, Slater and Fey invited Dean Chester S. Keefer of Boston University to survey the Department of Medicine, which was the focal point in the failure of the three institutions to develop a unified program. Keefer was on campus from September 29 to October 2, 1963.

His written report did not recommend Amidon's resignation, but according to Fey, Keefer presented a supplementary oral report on the personality problems in the College.[50] On December 31, Slater wrote President Fey explaining why Amidon had to relinquish the chair of medicine he had held since 1942. The basic reasons were problems of leadership, "fragmentation of the department, and the fact that the department was the only one "persisting in a separatist program in which residents do not exchange between the two hospitals."[51] Slater concluded that Amidon had to be replaced with a department head acceptable to all three institutions, one who was not considered an advocate of one institution, one who could develop a unified program utilizing both hospitals. But the Dean lacked formal authority to remove any department head, let alone, in this case, one with forty years of dedicated service. This could be done only by the president.

Early in February 1964 Amidon met with the President, who, according to Amidon, "beat about the bush," indicating that many colleges were changing chairmen, and then recounted Amidon's many accomplishments. Amidon, who was well aware of the reason for the meeting, told Fey that he had decided to step down, and that if the President would state the conditions for his continuing

48. University—Hospitals Liaison Committee Minutes, June 26, 1963. Mary Fletcher Hospital Board of Directors Minutes, July 24, 1963.

49. UVM Trustee Minutes, August 24, 1963.

50. Chester S. Keefer, Survey of the Department of Medicine, Keefer Folder, Dean's Office Papers, Departments Box 2. Oral history interview with John T. Fey.

51. Slater to Fey, December 31, 1963, Amidon Folder, Dean's Office Papers, Departments Box 2.

as chairman, he would respond. Fey indicated that Amidon had to be Chief of Medicine at both hospitals and be a full-time chairman. Amidon decided to resign rather than to remain under those conditions. He was offered a position as associate dean in charge of postgraduate education, but he declined the offer.

He later noted that it was with "considerable disappointment" that he looked back on his "association with the University. The chameleon-like nature of the administration predicated somewhat by social and political pressures" made the positions of all concerned, "including the president and dean, unstable."[52] In the last analysis Amidon had done a fine job as Chairman of the Department of Medicine. During his tenure the Department had grown from six professors to a staff of fifty, and the faculty became increasingly involved in research. Not only was he respected by the medical students, but his residency program attracted many bright young men and women who became devoted to their professor. One expression of this was the development of the Amidonian Society, made up of former residents who still meet periodically for seminars and reminiscences.

The basic problem was that he was completely identified with the Mary Fletcher, being Medical Director of that hospital. His excellent work at the Fletcher only alienated those affiliated with the DeGoesbriand. Amidon had wanted the Mary Fletcher to house research and special treatment facilities, with the DeGoesbriand continuing its work as a community hospital. Naturally, that upset those who wanted the DeGoesbriand to be equal to the Mary Fletcher, even if this meant an expensive duplication of facilities and equipment. It was felt by many that his obligations to the Mary Fletcher were in conflict with his work as department chairman. For the hospitals to join the College in the development of a medical center, Amidon had to be replaced, if only to alleviate the fears of those controlling the DeGoesbriand.

President Fey wrote to Robert Patrick, president of the board of directors of the Mary Fletcher, informing him that Amidon would continue as Professor of Medicine and as Medical Director of the Hospital. The presidents of the board of each hospital were asked to serve on the committee that would search for Amidon's replacement, and Fey assured Patrick that the "candidate must be fully acceptable to the College of Medicine and to both hospitals." Moreover, Fey assured Patrick that in the future there would be "the closest cooperation" in planning and development, and in the movement toward the establishment of a medical center.[53] The search committee finally settled on William Allan Tisdale, who had graduated from Harvard in 1951 and had done graduate work at Yale. Tisdale had spent the past four years at Dartmouth and was well known as

52. Interview with Ellsworth Amidon. For specifics of Dr. Amidon's feelings, see also his letters, Kaufman Folder, UVM Archives.

53. Fey to Patrick, February 13, 1964, Department of Medicine Folder, Fey Papers.

an "outstanding clinician." Perhaps most important, he had no ties with either the Mary Fletcher or the DeGoesbriand.[54]

In May 1964 President Fey met with the directors of the Mary Fletcher. "Unless we are able to really turn these three institutions into a medical center," he said, "the cost is going to increase out of proportion" and eventually it was likely "that the State will feel it impossible to support a Medical School." Fey predicted that within the next five years the College would have full-time department chairmen, who would "be objective and not allied to either hospital." He insisted that there was a need for "a three headed, decision-making body to operate a diffused medical center." He described examples of the past failure in cooperation, including the rehabilitation center and the cobalt unit of the DeGoesbriand.[55]

Robert Patrick replied that "he saw no reason why the Mary Fletcher will not be large enough in the future to be the only hospital needed by the College of Medicine," and he mentioned the Hamilton report, which had recommended that it be the primary teaching hospital. Fey replied that the College needed "all of the clinical work it could get in this area and that the University could not sever relations" with the DeGoesbriand. He suggested developing an affiliation agreement as the first step toward ending costly competition between the hospitals. After Fey's presentation and the question period, the directors voted to appoint a special committee to develop an affiliation agreement.[56]

The development of formal affiliation agreements was important for completion of Phase III of the College's building program. Phase III had a projected cost of $8,700,000, with the federal government expected to provide matching funds. Having an affiliation agreement with the Mary Fletcher would enhance the College's chances for federal money, since federal agencies seemed to favor schools with agreements with local hospitals. A fund-raising campaign began in the hope of raising the $4.5 million needed to qualify for a matching grant. By June 1964 donations from four out-of-staters gave the fund a dramatic start. The Henry B. Shattuck Fund provided $343,000; Sceva Speare, who had given $50,000 toward Phase II, now donated $232,000; David Baird of New York City gave $100,000; and Peer Johnson, a Massachusetts surgeon who had graduated from the University and had also served as trustee, donated $50,000. The medical alumni and faculty contributed almost $750,000; another $300,000 was raised in Chittenden County; and the campaign was on the road to success.[57]

In November the fund received an anonymous gift of $500,000, and then the Given Foundation provided two million. After less than one year of fund-raising, the goal was less than $500,000 away. In

54. Executive Committee Minutes, February 12 and April 9, 1955. Interview with Albert G. Mackay, chairman of the search committee.

55. Mary Fletcher Hospital Board of Trustees Minutes, May 27, 1964, MCHV Administrator's Office.

56. Ibid.

57. For local fund-raising progress, see *Free Press*, April 21, May 28, June 9 and 19, 1964, and Trustee Minutes, October 3, 1964. Shattuck's home was in Underhill, Vermont.

March 1965 the University was informed by the Division of Research Facilities and Resources of the National Institutes of Health that the grant of $1.9 million for research facilities was approved. The following month the Medical College and the Mary Fletcher Hospital were awarded $4,635,353 in federal funds toward completion of the third phase of the medical building program and a new wing for the Hospital.[58]

Significantly, the building plan was phased according to the availability of federal matching funds, not necessarily the prime needs of the School. When Health Research Facility construction funds became available, Phases one and two were constructed as the matching private money was raised from first the alumni and then the foundations. Phase three was begun after matching funds for the construction of health educational facilities were authorized by Congress in the early 1960's. The sequence of passage of federal legislation to provide matching funds for first the construction of research facilities and then teaching facilities coincided with the planning and fund-raising for the new Medical College Building. Earlier passage of Hill-Burton legislation resulted in the prior expansion of both hospitals, starting in the early 1950's.

By 1965 the successful development of the affiliation agreements encouraged discussions on the possibility of merging the hospitals into a medical center. The boards established the joint hospital committee, which decided at its first meeting that merger had to occur before consolidation of services could either be planned or be effected. The Arthur D. Little Company was selected in May 1966 to develop a plan and proposal for the merger of the hospitals and the College into a medical center.[59]

In spite of this positive step, there was still a long way to go before the traditional animosity could be overcome. For instance, a report to the board of the Mary Fletcher stated that the DeGoesbriand wanted one board to "dominate" both hospitals, because the DeGoesbriand officials "are very anxious to turn over their operating problems to us." Some of the directors thought that the board of the Mary Fletcher could very well become the "one dominating" board of the Medical Center.[60] At a meeting held on January 21, 1966, representatives of both hospitals agreed that "amalgamation . . . is desirable under a single governing" body, but the Mary Fletcher insisted that it "could not accept a 50–50 Board." It insisted that "the larger hospital, with twice the number of admissions" should have the majority on the new board. Discussions continued, however, and a report to the Mary Fletcher board noted that "the attitudes and atmosphere of the meetings . . . had been remarkable with participants showing their confidence and trust in each other."[61]

58. *Free Press*, November 7 and 16, 1964; March 24 and May 26, 1965.

59. Report of the Joint Hospital Committee, August 10, 1966, Merger Folder, Dean's Office Files, Committees, Hospitals Box.

60. Mary Fletcher Hospital Board of Directors, Minutes, September 22, 1965.

61. Reported ibid., January 26 and July 27, 1966.

One major question was the role of the sisters. It was agreed that they might withdraw at any time, or the Hospital could ask them to withdraw. About half of the sisters at the DeGoesbriand were "actually practicing their professions." Those who would be "useful as professionals" would "be of service in the new hospital." "Those not capable of professional service" would "be taken care of by the church." Finally, it was agreed that there would be "no attempt to carry the religious atmosphere such as through images and symbols, into the new situation." [62] All of this reflected concession on the part of the DeGoesbriand, which was a "sisters' hospital" with a tradition of religious piety.

In November 1966 the work of the joint committee was reported in the local newspapers as part of a public relations campaign to explain the need for merger. [63] The reports provoked a number of letters to the editor from members of the Catholic community who were deeply disturbed that there no longer would be a distinctively Catholic hospital in the city. For instance, one writer declared that "soon the little crosses on the walls, that reminded us of God's love and the cross we must carry to follow Him will soon be taken, will be stripped from our walls. How much more must we give to be united?" Another insisted that the only possible response was opposition if merger meant "the removal of our Chapel, our priest, our nuns, our crosses on the walls and our statues in our halls." [64] William S. Cowles, Jr., chairman of the joint hospital committee, tried to allay the fears of those who were upset at the statement in the report that "evidence of religious affiliation will disappear." He noted that "the continuing participation of the Sisters" was "anticipated and hoped for." [65]

At least one physician, Martin J. Cannon, was concerned that the merger would result in a deterioration of patient care at both institutions. In a letter to the *Free Press*, Cannon declared that in the future there would be "no room for a doctor whose primary interest is patient care." He was also afraid that the physician would "lose more and more control of the care of his patient to the Medical College. The patient will no longer be treated as an individual, but as a piece of material on an assembly line geared to either teaching or research." Robert Patrick, president of the Mary Fletcher, and T. R. Wright, chairman of the board of the DeGoesbriand, publicly responded by assuring everyone that "the decision for merger was made solely on the basis of improving patient care and teaching." [66]

The *Free Press*, in the same issue that carried their joint reply, printed a bitter letter from a former supporter of the DeGoesbriand. He sarcastically congratulated the College, the State of Vermont, and the Mary Fletcher Hospital, which would get a multi million dollar estab-

62. Ibid., July 27, 1966.

63. See numerous issues of the *Free Press*, index in Wilbur Collection, Bailey Library.

64. *Free Press*, November 30 and December 7, 1966.

65. Ibid., December 7, 1966.

66. Ibid., December 13 and 22, 1966.

lishment," the DeGoesbriand, "absolutely free." "If the diocese is so well off," he exclaimed, "it doesn't need my money in the collection basket and I can surely find some charitable use for it. It would have been nice," he concluded, "to have received some reimbursement from these properties to use for charitable works among the truly poor of the world."[67]

In spite of this opposition, the merger was completed on December 15, 1966, when the boards of the two hospitals met in special session and voted in favor of establishing the Medical Center Hospital of Vermont, which would have two units, the Mary Fletcher and the DeGoesbriand. On January 17, 1967, the two boards formally and officially established the Medical Center. A dinner was held at the Hotel Vermont to commemorate the occasion, with Governor and Mrs. Philip Hoff as guests of honor and with more than 300 invited guests.[69]

A merger-planning committee was established to study ways to effect the efficient integration of services. The first areas to be merged were those related to the business activities of the Hospital. For instance, by October the committee was able to report that dietary, pharmacy, purchasing, printing, buildings and grounds, accounting, fund-raising, personnel, public relations, data processing, admitting, postal service, and telephone and information services had already been merged. The clinical services were handled by a special medical committee, which developed a master plan for that aspect of the merger.[70]

Lester E. Richwagen, administrator of the Mary Fletcher since 1944, became executive director, while John F. Berry, who had been administrator of the DeGoesbriand, became the administrator of the Medical Center Hospital of Vermont. Late in 1967, after Richwagen decided to step down, he was replaced by Herluf V. Olsen, Jr., who had been administrator of the University of Florida Teaching Hospital.[71] By the spring of 1968 the trustees had approved the plan to consolidate clinical services.[72]

The third phase of the College's building plan was completed while the merger was well under way, late in 1968. On October 4 and 5 the Baird Building, the Given Medical Building, and the Marsh Life Sciences Building were all dedicated. After an invocation by Bishop Joyce and greetings by Senator George D. Aiken, honorary degrees were presented to David Graham Baird, Sr., of Montclair, New Jersey; Charles Anderson Dana, of Wilton, Connecticut; and Laurence Rockefeller, of New York City—all of whom had been major contributors to the building program.

The Given Building was named after Irene Heinz Given and John LaPorte Given, whose foundation granted two million dollars, repre-

67. Ibid.
68. Medical Center Hospital of Vermont, Minutes, December 15, 1966, in Minute Book, 1967–72, MCHV Administrator's Office. See also January 17, 1967, ibid.
69. *Burlington Free Press*, January 14, 1967.
70. Medical Center Hospital of Vermont, Minutes, February 22, March 16, and October 14, 1967. *Burlington Free Press*, September 26, 1967.
71. Interview with Lester E. Richwagen.
72. *Burlington Free Press*, April 27, 1968, April 18, 1969.

73. *Dedication of the
Buildings, October 4
and 5, 1968,* pamphlet in Medical
Alumni Files, UVM
Archives. *UVM Medical College Bulletin*
(1968–69), p. 20.

74. *UVM Medical
College Bulletin*
(1966–67), p. 24.

senting the largest building gift ever received by the University. The
Building would house most of the teaching and research space of the
College, and it also contained the 280-seat Carpenter Auditorium.
The two-story Dana Medical Library, which connects the Alumni
building with the Given building, was named in honor of Charles
A. Dana of the Dana Corporation. The library contained eight times
the area of the old library, and it more than tripled the book capacity.
The Baird Building, in the Mary Fletcher Unit, represented the major
part of the Hospital's development program.[73]

With the completion of Phase III the College possessed an ample
physical plant. Equally important, the merger would eliminate the
costly duplications and alienations that had plagued the medical community. Dean Brown's dream had become a reality.

Chapter Fifteen

Students and Student Life in the Twentieth Century

UNTIL WELL INTO the twentieth century the students at the Medical School were almost exclusively white males. Dean Tinkham was not unmindful of that fact, and as early as 1912 or 1913 considered admitting women, who could not only supply desperately needed tuition income but also help solve the crisis in rural medical care by serving as general practitioners. Despite these substantial benefits, efforts to convert to a coeducational Medical College were postponed.

The color line had been more easily crossed, and over the years a small number of blacks had been enrolled. In 1912, for instance, Claude Carmichael, a Texan who had completed almost three years at Howard University, transferred into the third year at Burlington.[1] Black students, however, had a difficult time being accepted by the local citizenry. There was a general feeling that they should minister to black patients, and there were so few blacks in Vermont that black medical students were often sent south for their hospital training. In 1922 Dean Tinkham noted in a letter that "what few colored students" there were at the University had been referred "to the South for hospital service," since "it is not logical to have a colored man acting as an intern in a hospital where the patients are practically all white."[2]

That did not deter a few black students who wanted better training than they could get at the all-black institutions. In 1923 the University yearbook, *The Ariel*, mentioned David Gladstone Morris, of Miami, who had been an undergraduate at Florida Baptist Academy and Lincoln University. According to the *Ariel*, "Dave shone especial-

1. E. T. Rose to Tinkham, Edna, Texas, November 18, 1912. Tinkham to Rose, November 25, 1912, Rose File, Tinkham Papers. For information on student life prior to 1900, see above, Chapter 10.

2. Tinkham to S. W. Prowse, January 2, 1922, University of Manitoba File, Tinkham Papers.

*30. Members of classes
of 1960 and 1961 in
the hallway of the
Medical School.*

31. Dean Wolf and the
medical faculty, 1960.

32. The Class of 1936
whooping it up at a
beer party several days
before their gradua-
tion.

ly" in the pharmacology laboratory, where he always "let on when the professor had missed a trick" and he invariably knew the right answers. "His incomparable smiles, his ever-ready responses and his scholarly attributes" gained him the respect of his classmates.[3] The following year, the *Ariel* mentioned another black, Jack Ward Gray, who had done his premedical work at Dartmouth.[4]

James Lyons Kingsland, Jr., a black student originally a member of the class of 1938, was referred elsewhere for his clinical work, and he graduated from Howard University Medical School.[5] Six years later, when Elizabeth Gourdin applied for admission to the class that was beginning in September 1944, she was informed that "this College did not have the clinical facilities for teaching negro students," and it was suggested that she apply elsewhere.[6]

Despite the advice tendered Elizabeth Gourdin—a black and a woman—the College did not adopt a policy relating directly to black admissions. Blacks seldom applied, and those accepted usually elected to attend elsewhere. This was hardly a concern of the College. Its interests were on other matters. As the increasing dependence upon state support brought a corresponding commitment to state service, the educational mission of the College was directed toward the training of Vermonters and physicians to serve Vermont. No black Vermonter ever applied for admission to the University of Vermont College of Medicine, and in accordance with the belief that black physicians should minister to black patients, they were not needed in Vermont.

During the 1960's the situation changed. In 1959 Moses Alfred Haynes joined the faculty as a member of the Department of Preventive Medicine. Haynes, with a B.S. from Columbia and an M.D. from the State University of New York, became the first black medical college faculty member. He remained in Burlington only a few years, but in 1962, a year before he left, a second black, Jackson J. W. Clemmons, was recruited, and in 1966 a third black, H. Lawrence McCrorey, arrived. Clemmons came to the Department of Pathology with a Ph.D. in biological chemistry and an M.D. from Western Reserve; McCrorey to the Department of Physiology and Biophysics with an M.S. degree from the University of Michigan and M.S. and Ph.D. degrees from the University of Illinois. Outstanding instructors and popular with students (the class of 1970 named McCrorey Teacher-of-the-Year), these two professors emerged as campus leaders urging greater minority representation throughout the University. Their very special concern was for medical students.

Students had also become concerned about the "all-white nature of the medical student body" at Vermont. That was to be expected, for Martin Luther King's drive for integration had been the leading reform movement on college campuses from coast to coast, and some

3. *Ariel*, 36 (1923), 151.

4. Ibid., 37 (1924), 154.

5. Discussion in Department Chairman Minutes, April 2, 1970, Dean's Office Files.

6. C. H. Beecher to J. S. Millis, July 29, 1944, Beecher Folder, Millis Papers.

undoubtedly had become committed to the cause while undergraduates. When the problem was discussed by the Student Council in December 1968, it was suggested that a special five-year program be developed for students who could not get adequate premedical training, especially those who had graduated from all-black colleges, but no specific action was taken.[7] The concern of the students was reflected by the administration, and in April 1969 University president Lyman S. Rowell informed the Board of Trustees that there was a need to recruit black students into the medical programs of the University because "trained medical personnel among the Negroes is desperately needed." That fall the Student Council established a committee to examine the possibility of increasing the number of black medical students.[8]

In February 1970 Assistant Dean Stanley Burns proposed to the Department chairmen that the College recruit minority students. The chairmen concluded that there would have to be either a "scholarship mechanism or reduction in admission requirements." An increase in scholarships was rejected on the ground that "it would only tend to rob Howard and Meharry," and they certainly did not want to help destroy the few all-black institutions by enticing their students with offers of financial aid. After a long discussion, the chairmen agreed that it would be justifiable to reduce admission requirements for blacks by using the same standards for them as those applied to Vermont residents.[9]

For a number of reasons the professors were hesitant to take this action. The majority seemed to feel that minority representation was not nearly "as important as protecting the serenity" of the campus. "Many were worried about black students as potential rioters." Others feared the development of a program "which might graduate second class physicians." Finally, it was argued that the clinical facilities in Burlington were inadequate. Eventually the faculty began to move toward developing a two-way exchange program with the Meharry Medical College.[10] Very little happened, however. Late in 1972 the Student Council once again expressed its concern over the all-white student body, but this time the students offered to help by actively recruiting blacks, Puerto Ricans, and Native Americans, and by providing tutorial help. In 1975 there were three black students in the College. It was difficult to recruit qualified applicants willing to come to a school in a "small town in a rural state," and especially one with a very small minority population.[11] The largest potential source of minority students was from New York State, which under a recent tuition arrangement reimbursed the College for New Yorkers who attended. Even in this instance, however, the grade and medical board scores required for admission disqualified most minority applicants. Ironically, at the insistence of the New York authorities the

7. Student Council Minutes, December 11, 1968, Dr. David Tormey's Office. For the development of the Council, see p. 228.

8. UVM Trustee Minutes, April 5, 1969. See also Student Council Minutes, September 15 and October 29, 1969.

9. Department Chairmen Meeting, February 5, 1970.

10. Ibid., April 23, 1970, and Executive Committee Minutes, April 30, 1970, Dean's Office Files. The quotation is from an analysis of this manuscript prepared by Dr. Lester Wallman. See Kaufman Folder, UVM Archives.

11. Student Council Minutes, January 26 and December 13, 1972, and March 12, 1973. See also letter from Dean David M. Tormey to the author, April 16, 1975, Kaufman Folder. The 1976–77 College of Medicine flyer asserts that the College "actively encourages applications from members of minority groups" but because "our faculty is a relatively small one it is not possible to offer formal preparatory or remedial programs at this time."

standards were slightly higher than Vermont would otherwise have imposed.

There were no female medical students at the University until 1920. In 1918, when so many physicians had been called into military service, Tinkham decided that it was time to admit qualified women. He asked President Benton to bring the matter to the Trustees, but meanwhile, the Dean asked for a legal opinion from Edmund C. Mower, an attorney who was a member of the board.[12] Mower provided Tinkham with a legal argument for the admission of women when he concluded that since the Medical School was part of the public school system of the state, "it would seem . . . rather hazardous to take the position that its doors are closed to any citizen of the state properly qualified to pursue the study of Medicine."[13]

In March 1920 a committee of the medical faculty reported in favor of the admission of women, noting that fifty of the seventy-two class A schools had female students, as did twenty-six of the thirty-two state medical colleges.[14] Before the Trustees could come to a decision, however, the debate flared into print in the *Vermont Cynic*, the student newspaper. Through an anonymous letter a premedical student insisted that women did not possess the "mental temperament or physical capabilities which are essential to the successful physician." Furthermore, the student said, "practically the entire class" was opposed to the plan and "there has been considerable talk of transferring to other institutions." Two letters were printed in response, including one which noted that women had been admitted to Johns Hopkins since 1890 without reducing standards or destroying the reputation of that school.[15]

In the fall of 1920, with very little opposition, the first female student, Dorothy Lang, was admitted to the Medical School. This was fifty-one years after Lida Mason and Ellen Hamilton entered the College of Arts and Sciences, back in 1871, and forty-seven years after they became the first women in the nation elected to Phi Beta Kappa. It was twelve years after Alma Carpenter graduated as the first female agricultural major, in 1908.[16] As the years passed, a small number of women continued to enroll in the Medical School. In 1933 Dean Jenne told an interviewer from the *Cynic* that the Medical College had nine coeds in that year and that no female student had ever failed to graduate. He said that women did well in pediatrics, dermatology, and special subjects, and poorly in surgery and anatomy. The reporter spoke to the coeds, who said they were treated fairly well. "Of course they don't treat us like men," one declared, "but they really are awfully good sports."[17]

Dean Jenne's 1933 observations regarding female academic performances persisted through the ensuing decades. Female enrollment was more erratic. The 1933 class graduated four women, a total that

12. Tinkham to Benton, November 4, 1918, Benton File, Tinkham Papers.

13. Mower to Tinkham, November 18, 1918, ibid.

14. UVM Medical Faculty Minutes, March 22 and May 3, 1920.

15. *Vermont Cynic*, April 24, 1920, p. 4; May 1, 1920, p. 4.

16. UVM Trustee Minutes, June 15, 1920; Hills, History of The Medical College, pp. 156–159. *Burlington Free Press*, April 12, 1920.

17. *Vermont Cynic*, January 6, 1933, pp. 1–2.

was not reached again until 1949, when five graduated. In some of the intervening years there was only one female graduate, and in 1942 there was none. The class of 1950 included nine women among its thirty-five graduates, the highest percentage of female graduates to date. After that date enrollment again declined, but, unlike the minority student situation, there has never been a time since Dorothy Lang first enrolled that the Medical College was without some women students. In the 1970's the number and percentage of women began to increase as more applied—because of increased awareness of the opportunities within the medical profession and because of a conscious effort to recruit female students. Eighteen percent of the class of 1974 were women (14 of the 75 students), as were 22 percent of the class that enrolled in 1975.[18]

Although women students initially encountered a general feeling that female physicians should minister to female patients, that view did not remain as firmly entrenched as the view that black physicians should minister to black patients. Furthermore, half the patients were female. Nor did Dean Tinkham's solution to the crisis in rural medicine fully materialize. Almost from the beginning, internships for women UVM graduates were obtained at hospitals comparable to those of their male counterparts. They were also, like male physicians, attracted into specialization, although more than 25 percent were attracted to rural medicine.

To a large extent the medical students at the University reflected the educational and financial realities in Vermont. For instance, in 1914 23.5 percent of all the medical students in the country had bachelor's degrees but only 5 percent of the UVM graduates fell into that category. Five years later, in 1919, the situation had not changed. By then the national percentage of graduates with bachelor's degrees had increased to 48, while that of UVM had doubled to 10 percent.[19] Until the 1950's and 1960's, with their renewed emphasis on quality education for the masses, many towns in Vermont could not provide an adequate secondary education, and relatively few students went on to complete college. That made it difficult for the Medical College to insist upon the standards possible in the more educationally advanced states. The problem was compounded by financial reality. As the cost of medical education increased, the College began to accept large amounts of state aid, in return promising to train Vermont residents.

The College had always drawn students from other states, and it was obvious that with even optimum educational opportunities for Vermonters it must continue to do so. There were simply too few Vermonters to support the school their University had become. If, for example, between the years 1950 and 1972 there had been no out-of-state students and every Vermonter who applied to the

18. Chart in Medical Faculty Minutes Folder, Dean's Office Files. The classes of 1949 and 1950 had unusually high percentages of women: 25 percent of the class of 1950 was female (9 of 36 graduates). See chart in Kaufman Folder.

19. *Journal of the American Medical Association*, 63 (August 22, 1914), 684; 83 (August 16, 1919), 503.

Medical College had been accepted, the College would have had fewer students than actually attended and the state would have had more physicians than it could utilize. The College's commitment to train Vermont residents, its obligation to raise professional standards, and its responsibility for prudent financial management were not easily reconcilable. The matters were inexorably related, and there was really no way to deal with any of them in isolation.

Especially since the release of the Flexner Report, the faculty's principal emphasis has been on standards; students had to be well prepared to benefit from the modern scientific medical education. In addition, with the advent of state and national licensing boards, those unprepared would not be able to pass the examinations that were required to practice medicine. For instance in June 1930 the faculty adopted a rule requiring special permission before anyone who had failed more than 25 percent of his work could continue at the College, and directed Dean Jenne to consult with the other deans "with a view to requiring higher grades than at present for admission to the College of Medicine."[20] The professors were in a quandary. They wanted to maintain high standards, but they recognized their commitment to educate Vermonters and to solving the medical care problems in the state.[21] Considered in this context, the admission of women, though an ideological reform, was doubtless stimulated by expediency. Women were hardly as educationally disadvantaged as blacks, and to admit them would significantly increase the pool of qualified Vermonters. Some of the same reasons for admitting women, however, operated to the disadvantage of blacks—a dilemma left unresolved by the onset of federal aid, affirmative action programs, and the New England Higher Education Compact.

The compact was facilitated by the New England Board of Higher Education, a regional agency formally established in December 1955 to coordinate educational activities in the six states.[22] It had become increasingly apparent that the fortunes of the New England states were intertwined and that in many instances cooperation could work to mutual advantage. Medical education was one such instance. Three of the six states, Maine, New Hampshire and Rhode Island, did not have four-year medical colleges, and with three private medical schools, Massachusetts was reluctant to establish a state school to augment its numerically insufficient supply of physicians. Vermont, on the other hand, had a state-supported medical school and no obligations to educate residents of other states. Since there were not enough potential medical students from Vermont, however, the College relied upon out-of-state students to maintain its enrollment. A 1954 study of educational costs concluded that Vermont was making "a valiant effort to carry more than its share of the burden of supplying physicians," and that since she provided a great service

20. UVM Medical Faculty Minutes, June 3, 1930.

21. Ibid., June 6, 1966.

22. Draft of New England Compact and Borgman to David Anderson, December 30, 1955, Borgman Papers.

to her sister states by training residents of Maine and New Hampshire, those states should help share the expense of medical education in Burlington.[23] UVM President Carl Borgmann, who had seen interstate cooperation work while in Colorado, encouraged it in New England, and that same year contracted a medical-college admissions agreement with New Hampshire.

Through subsequent NEBHE negotiations that concept was expanded to include other New England states. In 1957 it was agreed that each compacting state—and all but Connecticut eventually joined the compact—would pay $2,500 to the Medical School for each of its students registered up to a number determined between the School and that state. The students would pay tuition at the instate rate. The University took advantage of this financial arrangement by admitting the established quota of students from contract states, and in so doing restricted the admission of other non-Vermont applicants. In 1959, however, New Hampshire and Massachusetts fell behind in their payments, and the University threatened to terminate the agreement unless the money was appropriated. The New England Board of Higher Education tried to resolve the problem, but some UVM medical professors suggested that to end the arrangement altogether would enable the College to raise standards by picking only the best students nationwide. The professors thought such an approach might improve the ability of the College to receive grants from national foundations. Dean Wolf, however, was considering the possibility of negotiating similar agreements with states outside of New England.[24]

By 1960 representations to the New England governors were proving successful, primarily because of the realities of the situation. The shortage of physicians was becoming apparent, and it was much more costly to construct a medical school than to help support medical education at the University of Vermont. Governor Foster Furcolo of Massachusetts even managed to convince his state legislature to appropriate enough money to increase the number of subsidized medical students from 48 to 70.[25] Rhode Island and Maine each contracted for ten places. New Hampshire still owed $56,000, however, and Governor C. Wesley Powell, committed to an austerity program, opposed any appropriation to compensate Vermont for the past few years. Powell often provoked outrage, and this was one such occasion. The University of New Hampshire's student newspaper, for instance, censured him for making "New Hampshire the world's leading clown." Powell had made national headlines by calling John F. Kennedy "soft on communism" during the 1960 presidential campaign and then had threatened freedom of the press by demanding an investigation of the student newspaper. Now he was adversely affecting the state's medical needs "because of this moribund poverty

23. Edward E. Palmer and Sidney C. Sufrin, *Educational Costs in Vermont* (Syracuse, 1954), pp. 5, 23–24.

24. UVM Medical Faculty Minutes, September 16, 1959.

25. UVM Trustee Minutes, February 20, 1960. *Burlington Free Press*, April 13, 1960.

consciousness."[26] Despite Powell's opposition, in April 1961 the legislature passed an appropriation bill that included compensation to UVM and enabled New Hampshire to rejoin the medical tuition plan.[27]

During the 1960's instate tuition ranged from $550 to $600, and out-of-state tuition rose from $1,500 to $2,000. As the cost of medical education continued to increase, the annual payment per student went up from $2,500 to $5,000, and the differential paid by the New England states became an important source of revenue helping to finance medical education at the University. By 1975, however, costs had escalated to where the Medical College (and Vermont) was again heavily subsidizing *all* students and the University trustees directed that compacts be renegotiated so that contracting states would more fully assume actual educational costs. Rhode Island and Maine renegotiated under these new guidelines. Massachusetts withdrew as the University of Massachusetts Medical School opened at Worcester, and New Hampshire, which had begun withdrawing in 1971, elected not to reenter. The loss of students from the two latter states was compensated for by a contract with New York and a quota of eighty students from that state.

Costs to students showed only modest rises between 1927 and 1967 but rapidly escalated between 1967 and 1977. Tuition for Vermont residents increased from $600 in 1967 to $2,200 in 1977, while nonresident tuition increased from $1,800 to $4,500 during that same period. Students from compact states, of course, paid in-state tuition rates. In 1959, largely due to the efforts of David B. Pitman of the class of 1933 and Ralph Sussman of the class of 1938, the UVM Medical Alumni Association developed the Century Club, whose principal objectives were to promote educational resources for the College and to establish a low-interest, revolving student-loan fund. By 1977 nearly half a million dollars had been allocated to student loans, enabling many needy students to meet the escalating costs of medical education.

During the early years of the twentieth century, medical students regularly participated in undergraduate activities, and in some they played major roles. In 1904, for instance, the *University Cynic* suggested having the "whole Glee Club" of both the academic and medical departments get together for a "sing or smoker" in order to increase college spirit.[28] Three years later the *Cynic* happily reported that the medics "have taken their places right beside" the academic students "for the good of the University," by voting to pay a three-dollar tax to support the Athletic Association of the University.[29]

In March 1910 the medics held a smoker which, according to the *Cynic* was "one of the most enjoyable and successful of the year. The

26. UVM Trustee Minutes, December 10, 1960. *New Hampshire*, January 19, 1961, p. 4 (in Wolf Folder, Fey Papers, 1961).

27. *Burlington Free Press*, April 8, 1961.

28. *University Cynic*, March 5, 1904, p. 216, col. 2.

29. Ibid., January 12, 1907, p. 154; February 16, 1907, p. 200.

room was filled, the medics were first-rate hosts, the cheering was good, the speakers were numerous but brief and snappy and . . . the band gave us lots of good music." Nearly every speaker emphasized the need for cooperation between the medical and academic departments of the University. The *Cynic* editorialized that the smokers offered a chance for the medical and academic students to meet each other "for the inter-change of ideas and the discussion of current college topics of interest, such as baseball, for example." The smoker was held in the Medical College Building in the hope of inducing more medics to participate, but there were more "academs" in attendance.[30]

In 1913 a junior medical student wrote to the *Cynic*, defending the medics against the charge that they lacked enthusiasm and "true Vermont spirit." He admitted that the medics did "not enter into all the spheres of college activity with as great ardor as the men on the 'other side' but," he declared, "like Grape-Nuts, 'there's a reason,'" He indicated that medical students were carrying a heavy course load, leaving little time for diversion, then noted that since the medics were preparing for a profession in which "a human life may be the price of an error," they had to devote more attention to their studies. Furthermore, the expense of medical education was high (tuition was $130), and most of the medics had "to scratch gravel pretty industriously during our few spare moments gathering in what shekels we may." Yet, despite all of these problems, the medics were "doing very well indeed in furnishing almost half of the football and baseball material, as well as a good number of men for the musical clubs." He went on to note that those who were not "present when the athletic ability was passed around" did not participate in sports for good reason; they were in class or studying over forty hours a week, sleeping occasionally and spending the rest of the time "figuring out how we are going to invest all the money we make after we get into practice; perhaps."[31]

In spite of such concerns, the medical students continued to participate in University activities. In March 1919, for instance, the medics sponsored a smoker in the gym, with an elaborate program that included music by the "All-Medic 16 piece orchestra led by Markoff" of the class of 1919, songs by the Senior Medic Quartet, Hawaiian dancing, and refreshments. The smoker was to bring medics and academics closer together, to promote baseball and to support the student union.[32] That year the baseball team was led by Roy G. Hamilton, a third-year medical student; Karl C. McMahon, a freshman medic, was the cheerleader "who energetically drew cheers from the overflowing wooden grandstands."[33]

In 1920 the *Ariel* noted what it supposed to be "the beginning of a new era, a period of co-operation" between the two departments of

30. Ibid., March 24, 1910, pp. 1, 4.
31. Ibid., March 22, 1913, p. 7.
32. Ibid., March 1 and 8, 1919, p. 1.
33. Ibid., May 31, 1919, p. 4.

the University. In the past, according to the article, there had been "open warfare, Medic versus Academ." The "old Medical Building was the only safe harbor for Docs, while their opponents kept close to their dormitory and ventured out only in force." Gradually, that feeling had subsided. One reason for the change in attitude was that as the Medical School began to require premedical college training it was inevitable that a number of medical students would have attended undergraduate college at the University, where they were able to develop the "true Vermont spirit." When they entered the Medical School in some numbers, they helped to bring the two departments closer together. On occasion medics served as officers of their undergraduate fraternities, but even more important were athletes who continued to participate in college sports. Having classmates on the varsity teams encouraged school spirit among those medics who had no "Vermont spirit" when they first enrolled.[34]

With the development of football as a major intercollegiate sport, a new area for intra-University harmony developed. In the fall of 1920, for instance, the medics held a smoker on the eve of the big game with Norwich. By that time there was no question about the school spirit of the medics, and the *Cynic* noted that as long as the word "medic" was prefixed to the word "smoker," "almost every man in college knows that pep, more pep, action, harmony, music, and refreshments will be forthcoming." All the spirit, however, did not help the team, which lost by a score of 16 to 7.[35]

The medics' 1925 "smoker-pep raiser" for the football game against Middlebury featured Jerry Buckley, a junior medical student as cheerleader, and there were speeches by Dr. E. Douglas McSweeney, former manager of the football team, and Dr. Thomas S. Brown, the anatomy professor and superintendent of the Mary Fletcher Hospital who was known as the "first man to ring the bell at the Old Mill following the win over Dartmouth." Coach Henry O. Dresser commented on the fact that so many medics "were able to play on the team and still do their 'stuff' on the other side." He cited the case of Walter S. "Speed" Denning, a 166-pound tackle who practiced regularly in spite of a heavy course load. Denning, incidentally, was also captain of the hockey team.[36]

In 1927 Hazen "Noisy" Fogg, a pitcher, was elected captain of the College baseball team. At the time he was a freshman medic, but he had been on the team for three years. Two years later, in 1929, the varsity opened its season against the medics, and the medics won, 7 to 2. Everyone in the "doctors' line-up was credited with at least one hit, while Fogg kept the Varsity down to four scattered safeties." "Big Bill" Morse, who played for Portland of the New England League several summers earlier, got three hits for the medics.[37] The Medic band performing at the game was described by then sophomore med-

34. *Ariel*, 33 (1920), p. 312.
35. *Vermont Cynic*, November 3 and 10, 1920, p. 1.
36. Ibid., November 21, 1925, and February 13, 1926. For lists of medical students who played football, see November 21 and December 12, 1925.
37. Ibid., March 25, 1927, and May 7, 1929.

ic Albert G. Mackay as having so few men that it had to march on the field single file. Frederick Crump, dressed in a top hat and silk pajamas, was followed by a bass tuba and two trombones, and they in turn were followed by four men carrying a black casket marked "VARSITY." Whenever there was an injury, the four pallbearers would run onto the field and stay there until the academic students got them to take their casket back to the stands.[38]

As indicated in Chapter 10, there were several medical fraternities that provided social as well as intellectual stimulation. Delta Mu (which later became a chapter of Nu Sigma Nu), Phi Chi, and Alpha Kappa Kappa continued to be active on campus. The male fraternities spawned a female counterpart in 1924, when the five female students established their own "fraternity," Alpha Gamma Sigma.[39] The fraternities provided students with inexpensive housing, dances, and other social events, and even academic assistance. Chester Newhall recalled that when he was a member of Delta Mu, the older brothers would drill the freshmen in gross anatomy and the fraternity kept a file of examinations.[40]

In 1910 an honorary medical fraternity, Cap and Skull, was organized, and every year a few senior honor students were initiated into it. During its early years Cap and Skull served an important academic purpose. In 1913, for instance, each member read an original paper on "some of the latest topics of interest to the medical profession." Toward the end of the 1930's Cap and Skull was disbanded, "largely through the efforts of the committee on administration of the medical school, which felt the society performed no useful purposes and, in fact, had engaged in some rather questionable financial ventures."[41]

In 1932 an academically oriented medical society was established at the University, the Osler Clinical Society, which was designed to provide extracurricular instruction through lectures and seminars conducted by some of the leading physicians of the time who were brought to campus specifically for that purpose.[42] The Osler Clinical Society continued to be active until about 1937, when it evolved into a social organization. In 1952 a local chapter of the national honor society, Alpha Omega Alpha, was organized, and it continues to prosper. In 1970, when the pass-fail replaced the numerical grading system, however, it appeared that the chapter might succumb to curriculum reform. With traditional means of identifying outstanding students no longer available, a point system based on departmental evaluations along with student participation was designed instead. Continued scholarly production on the part of AOA graduates serves to justify the selection process.

One of the more interesting University events attended by medical students was the annual Kake Walk, first held on December 7, 1894. According to the *Cynic*, it showed promise, but the students got so

38. Interview with Albert G. Mackay.

39. *Vermont Cynic*, April 19, 1924.

40. Interview with Chester Newhall and A. B. Soule.

41. *Vermont Cynic*, March 24, 1910; May 31, 1913. Interview with A. B. Soule.

42. In 1933, for instance, W. Russell McAusland, head surgeon of the Carney Hospital in Boston, spoke on "Ankylosis of Joints and its Treatment," and Walter Alvarez of the University of Minnesota lectured on "The Art of Medicine." His presentation was followed the next month by that of Philip D. Woodbridge of Boston, a noted authority on anesthesia, and in December 1933 Edward S. Welles, of the Trudeau Clinic of Saranac Lake, New York, spoke on "Surgical Treatment of Pulmonary Tuberculosis." *Vermont Cynic*, January 13, February 10, March 10, and December 5, 1933.

carried away that "they could not refrain from destroying property." On November 12, 1897, the first "Kullud Koons Kake Walk" was held as a charitable affair, raising a total of $165 for the football team. The students put on skits and, blackfaced and in costume, delighted the crowd by "stepping high" in time to music while "walkin' fo' de Kake." From 1898 to 1970, when it was discontinued after a lengthy dispute as to whether it was racist, the Kake Walk was an annual event on the University calendar.[43]

Held on Washington's Birthday, the Kake Walk began with a "Peerade," with colorful floats being dragged around the old gymnasium, now the Royall Tyler Theatre. The "Peerade" was followed by a number of skits, with each fraternity having fifteen minutes to set the stage, complete its stunt, and remove its props. Then came "walkin' fo' de Kake." Two men representing each fraternity appeared, blackface and in costume, "stepping high" to the strains of "Cotton Babe." They were quite a spectacle. "Kakes" and cups were given to the winners.[44]

In 1910 the Briggs Cup for the best Kake Walk specialty went to the Delta Mu Medical fraternity for a stunt entitled "Dr. Fulenmall-Osteowalk." In what was later described as an "admirably executed satire of osteopathy," the "doctor" delivered an amusing lecture extolling the benefits of osteopathy and then performed a series of "hair-raising cures." In one case he examined a "country girl" and decided that "her neck needed lengthening." She was placed on the operating table, and the "doctor" and his assistants stretched her neck "about a foot." "Unfortunately," according to the *Cynic*, "she did not survive the operation."[45]

In 1914 Delta Mu once again won the award for the best stunt, this time with one entitled: "A Day at the Rockefeller Institute in 1920." In the skit, a professor with a "strong Yiddish accent" gave a lesson in surgery. "The patient's inner workings" were "taken out, cleaned and repaired." Then the parts were replaced with the doctor's assistants producing a skeleton "piece by piece from a chest." Finally, after the "bones had been placed together as they should be, the students gathered round the table and rubbed them to restore the circulation. In due time there was a stir beneath the sheet, and a real flesh-and-blood patient sat up." Again according to the *Cynic*, the patient's appearance made the "feminine part of the audience gasp, for his costume was exceedingly brief."[46]

As the years passed and the curriculum was greatly expanded, the students devoted more time to their studies and less to the extracurricular events that continued to interest undergraduates. In part this was because the activities themselves held less attraction for them. In tightening its admission requirements the Medical College insisted upon three and later four years of undergraduate work, thus widen-

43. For the history of Kake Walk, see *Vermont Cynic*, January 27, 1917, and the *Burlington Free Press*, October 9, 10, 11, 24, 29, 30, 1969, and February 20, 1970.

44. *Vermont Cynic*, December 15, 1933.

45. Ibid., February 24, March 3, 1910.

46. Ibid., February 28, 1914. For other Delta Mu stunts, see ibid., February 26, 1916, February 24, 1917, and February 25, 1922.

ing the age difference between medics and undergraduates. Athletic eligibility requirements were also made more stringent, disqualifying some who might otherwise have participated in college sports. By the late thirties medical student participation in undergraduate activities lessened visibly and was not resumed after the Second World War. There were, of course, some exceptions, mostly by former UVM undergraduates. John Costello was a director of Kake Walk in 1942; Phi Chi's team of Malcolm Paulsen and Jim Bulen won the cup in 1946 and 1947 as the last medics to compete. John "Bob" Jake, '49, and James E. "Bud" Riley were the last medics to play varsity sports, and neither continued after his freshman year. Medics sought other amusements.

There were times, however, when students had almost no time for amusements. For instance, medical education at Burlington and elsewhere was profoundly affected by the two World Wars. Interestingly, even before the United States entered the first World War, the College was forced to respond to the international situation. After President Wilson called up the national guard during the Mexican Crisis of 1916, the faculty decided to suspend the rules regarding advancement from one year to another so that the students in the militia would not be penalized. Twelve medical students were in the Hospital Corps of the First Vermont Regiment, and they were rushed to the Mexican border in June 1916. While in Texas they encountered natural phenomena unknown to Vermont: sandstorms, tropical downpours, and a hurricane, which destroyed two barracks. For recreation the men went to Eagle Pass, a town of 8,000 which "afforded new experiences that were not exhausted" until the men learned that they were being sent back to Vermont.[47]

When it became obvious that the United States would soon enter the first World War, the Council for National Defense asked the nation's medical schools to participate in the preparedness program. On January 6, 1917, the colleges agreed to add to their curriculum a course "especially adapted to medical, sanitary and surgical training for the army and navy." In April the Council urged the medical schools to eliminate all vacation periods in an attempt to train as many military surgeons as possible. At the same time, the departments of the army and navy recommended that the colleges graduate seniors who had maintained an 85 average, so they could enlist in the service at once. The Vermont faculty agreed to both requests.[48]

By May, however, it had become apparent that it would be inadvisable to eliminate vacations. First, the shortage of surgeons disappeared when seven hundred young physicians enlisted for military service. Furthermore, hospital administrators complained that early or late graduation would make it impossible for hospitals to maintain their services because they required interns at definite intervals. It

47. UVM Medical Faculty Minutes, June 23, 1916. *Vermont Cynic*, October 7, 1916.

48. *UVM Notes*, 13 (January 1917), 1–2. UVM Medical Faculty Minutes, April 11, 1917. UVM Trustee Minutes, April 13, 1917.

also appeared that the elimination of vacations at the medical schools would disrupt the continuity of education in high schools, colleges, and medical colleges. Finally, students who graduated in fewer than four years might have difficulty getting licensed in states that required a four-year medical course. As a result of these factors, early in May it was decided that the colleges would close for the summer as usual.[49]

Almost as soon as the scheduling problems had been solved, a serious question developed over the conscription of medical students. After a great deal of lobbying by the American Medical Association and the Association of American Medical Colleges, the provost marshal agreed to let medical students enlist in the reserves until after graduation.[50] The result can be seen from statistics from the University of Vermont. In the 1917–18 academic year, 17 of the 22 seniors were in the reserves, 4 had been rejected for medical reasons, and one was an alien and not eligible for the draft. Sixty-nine of the 104 students were in the reserves, 5 had failed to pass the physical, 3 were aliens, and the rest were either women, or men under 21 or over 30 and thus not eligible for the draft.[51]

Although at times the situation threatened to become serious, it was not necessary to accelerate the course or alter the schedule; neither did the wartime emergency result in the wholesale conscription of medical students. During World War II, however, the colleges *were* disrupted. As early as December 1942, the Association of American Medical Colleges recommended that in order to train a sufficient number of military surgeons, the colleges should admit students with two years of premedical training. The Vermont faculty responded by voting to suspend the three-year rule for the remainder of the war.[52]

In June 1943 the Army Specialized Training Program (ASTP) went into effect in most of the American medical schools. Students were inducted into the service; within 48 hours they were back in school to complete their medical education. They were assigned uniforms and housed in barracks on campus. The development of ASTP removed the students from "the red tape of local draft boards" and put them "under direct army control." Since the students were privates who received military pay while completing their education, the program provided them with needed financial aid, for the colleges began to accelerate their programs and eliminate summer vacations, which also eliminated the opportunity for summer employment.[53] According to the *Cynic,* the "classrooms and halls of the UVM Medical School have finally succumbed to the rhythmic clomp, clomp, clomp of GI shoes; the classrooms have taken on a very regular color scheme." The *Cynic* went on to note that the men marched to and from classes, and did physical training in the mornings. Upon graduation, the students got their diplomas and their commissions; the

49. *Vermont Cynic,* May 5, 1917, p. 3.

50. Material in Selective Service Folder, Tinkham Papers.

51. List of students in Enlisted Medical Reserve Corps, 1917–18, Student Folder, Tinkham Papers.

52. UVM Medical Faculty Minutes, December 7, 1942.

53. See A.A.M.C., Memorandum to Deans of Medical Schools, April 27, 1943, Beecher Folder, Millis Papers. *Vermont Cynic,* June 10, 1943. UVM Trustee Minutes, June 19, 1943.

54. *Vermont Cynic,* June 24, 1943, and June 4, 1945.

navy men became ensigns, and those in the army became second lieutenants.[54]

As indicated, in response to the military emergency, the course was accelerated. For the duration of the war freshman classes began every April and September, and vacations were eliminated. The faculty was overburdened by an excessive teaching load, and, as noted earlier, that combined with patriotism to convince a number of professors to go into the service. When the professors finally had an opportunity to vote on a timetable for deceleration, they unanimously voted to admit no freshmen until the fall of 1946, and to stop the acceleration of all classes as of April 3, 1946. The seniors would graduate on that date, and the other students would vacation until September 1946, when the School resumed its normal schedule.[55]

The transition to postwar normalcy was highlighted by campus overcrowding, with large veteran enrollment and older and more disciplined students becoming the rule rather than the exception. Frequently married with very young families, such students were no less likely than those before the War to congregate near Centennial Field. In 1946, however, it was not necessarily to witness some big game; an acre or so of land adjacent to Centennial Field had become the site of a large student trailer camp. And with family obligations also determining social hangouts, Greer's launderette superseded the fraternity house as the most important gathering place. The veteran phenomenon pervaded the entire campus, but for the Medical College it proved a harbinger of change rather than an interlude. Even after the supply of veterans was exhausted and campuses resumed leisurely patterns, medical students tended to maintain their more rigorous routine. In part a product of the expanded curriculum, no single factor can adequately explain this. Increased competition for Medical School admissions certainly contributed. In the 1930's as an incentive to attend undergraduate college beyond the two years required for admission to Medical School, the UVM College of Arts and Sciences awarded a baccalaureate degree to its three-year students upon successful completion of the first year of Medical College.[56] Soon after the War, and despite a three-year minimum requirement that is still in force, the Medical College increasingly insisted upon a completed baccalaureate for admission. After 1956 a fair percentage of entering students had also earned advanced degrees, usually an M.S. and occasionally a Ph.D. in a physical or biological science or in education.[57] Although this in itself would have produced an older and more thoroughly schooled student body than before the War, other factors also conditioned behavior. Not the least important of these were changes in the medical profession itself. Expectations of completing four years of Medical College and a perfunctory one-year internship and then embarking upon a private practice were rendered

55. UVM Medical Faculty Minutes, September 18, December 3, 1945.

56. See, for example, University of Vermont Catalog, 1976–77, p. 71.

57. Unless specifically indicated otherwise, student aggregate profiles have been compiled from Medical College Catalogs.

obsolete by greater specialization and an intern-residency track. Without a prestigious internship, a "good" residency was unlikely. Graduation from medical college had become merely the prerequisite for an M.D. degree; superior performance was the ticket to a prestigious internship. Concern for quality internships did not immediately manifest itself. In 1947, for example, the placement pattern was quite similar to that of the class of 1935, whose internships were widely scattered, with nine in the Burlington area and most of the others in New England and New York community hospitals. By 1957, however, a radical change was evident. Seven graduates remained in Burlington at the Mary Fletcher and DeGoesbriand hospitals. Almost all the others interned in either teaching hospitals affiliated with medical schools and universities or in large Army or Navy institutions like Walter Reed General Hospital, where they fulfilled their military commitments. At this same time the Burlington hospitals and the Medical College also began developing teaching programs. A few years later when the DeGoesbriand and Mary Fletcher merged to become the Medical Center Hospital of Vermont, this process was accelerated and attracted graduates from leading colleges and universities around the country as well as from the University of Vermont. Thus by 1976 graduate education in the College and Hospital encompassed a House Staff of approximately 130 interns, residents, and fellows training in fifteen clinical disciplines. These, when added to approximately fifty students in Masters' and Ph.D. programs, constituted almost 40 percent of the Medical College's student population.

Given these factors, it is not surprising that recent medical students have been heavily profession-oriented, with organized extracurricular activities centering upon internal educational reform. Through adaptations of the increasingly popular concept of participatory democracy, they have been able to assert a direct and continuing influence on Medical College and University decision-making. Although the students established a senate as early as 1926, it quickly atrophied.[58] In September 1944 the students proposed a new system of student government. The faculty approved of the plan, and in the fall of 1945 the Student Council was formally established.[59] The minutes of the medical faculty contain only two references to the Council until the 1960's. In 1950 it was reported to have acted in the matter of freshmen students "playing with apparatus," and in 1953 Dean Wolf reported that it was meeting every month and that students had complained about some professors who failed to meet their classes.[60]

Student influence was clearly not being exercised by the Student Council; other student organizations, however, were more effective. Chief among these was the medical fraternity Nu Sigma Nu, which in

58. *Vermont Cynic,*
October 22, 1926.
59. UVM Medical Faculty Minutes, September 7, 1944. Student Council Folder, Dean's Office Papers, 1934–63, Box 13.
60. UVM Medical Faculty Minutes, May 4, 1950, and February 16, 1953.

1954 established an annual award to a member of the faculty for excellence in teaching.[61] This soon became known as the "Teacher of the Year Award," with the members of the graduating class selecting the recipient. E. L. Amidon was the first to receive the award, and C. Alan Phillips, professor of Medicine, and John P. Tampas, professor of Radiology, have been so honored twice. Dallas Boushey, then Demonstrator in the Department of Anatomy, was the choice of the class of 1972. Boushey, whose formal education ended with eighth grade, had, largely through self-training, acquired an encyclopedic knowledge of gross anatomy which he dispensed with a natural aptitude for teaching. Mainly through the efforts of William J. Young, professor and chairman of the Department of Anatomy, Boushey was

61. See Figure 33, a listing of Teacher-of-the-Year recipients.

33. *Teachers of the
Year, 1954–1977.*

subsequently promoted to an assistant professorship and granted tenure, an action unprecedented at the University of Vermont.[62]

Although Teacher of the Year awards are cherished as recognition of teaching excellence, in a few instances they seemed to express student protest against the failure of the College to retain teachers for various reasons, including refusal to grant tenure or promotion.

Protests of this sort constituted the most fervid expressions of dissatisfaction the medical students openly manifested, as occurrences such as the Novikoff incident serve to illustrate. Alex Benjamin Novikoff was an associate professor of biochemistry and an active researcher who in 1953 was summoned before the Senate Internal Security Committee. Rather than testify on alleged past Communist affiliation, Novikoff invoked the Fifth Amendment and was subsequently relieved of his teaching duties while a faculty-trustee committee investigated the situation. Acknowledging his right as a citizen to invoke the Fifth Amendment, they were concerned over the un-

62. Department of Anatomy Files, Boushey Folder, Young to Luginbuhl, April 27 and June 2, 1972.

34. *Dr. John H. Bland, Teacher of the Year, 1977.*

35. *Drs. R. J. McKay, Jr., professor and chairman, and Carol F. Phillips, professor of pediatrics, holding the award granted by the national Ambulatory Pediatrics Association and the UVM silver shovel, both for departmental excellence in teaching, 1977.*

favorable publicity he had generated for the Medical College and the University. Furthermore they insisted that status as a faculty member at a state-supported institution implied obligations beyond those imposed upon private citizens. In June at the Board of Trustees meeting, Governor Lee E. Emerson, an ex-officio member of the Board, moved that Novikoff be indefinitely suspended as of July 15 unless he was willing to appear before the Senate committee and "answer fully and freely any questions." The Governor's motion was adopted by a vote of 11 to 5.[63] Novikoff, alleging that University tenure regulations had not been followed, requested a hearing before a board of review. The trustees agreed to the board and directed four attorneys to prepare specific charges to be considered by its members. After a day-long meeting, the board concluded that Novikoff should be dismissed, and the trustees implemented its recommendation.[64]

Apart from being the only instance of McCarthyism at UVM resulting in faculty dismissal,[65] the incident also reflects student non-involvement, for despite intense conflict among the faculty and community, there is no recorded response from the students. Medical students made no effort publicly to condemn or support their professor. Undergraduates also professed no concern.

The political climate had changed considerably by 1970. Yet in May of that year when rage over the shooting deaths of four students at Kent State University shut down most academic activities at UVM and elsewhere, the Medical College was able to continue operating. The shooting had served to fuse opposition to the government's foreign policy, a matter over which medical students shared a deep concern, and Dean William Luginbuhl urged his faculty to "remain flexible and recognize" it was "a very delicate issue." The students' "sincerity and dedication to non-violence," ultimately enabled the Medical College to proceed with final examinations while the rest of the campus experienced considerable disruption.[66]

Less concerned with protest than with having their views solicited by established authority, the medical students wanted to participate in College decision-making, and their goal was achieved during the sympathetic administrations of Dean Edward C. Andrews and his successor, William Luginbuhl. During the late 1960's Assistant Deans Stanley Burns and David Babbott began admitting students into active membership on major faculty committees. Chief among these were the formerly sacrosanct faculty areas of admissions and curriculum. Both committees subsequently proposed changes that were implemented by policies permitting the enrollment of more Vermonters and a pass-fail grading system. Students helped to design both.

A 1969 A.M.A.–A.A.M.C. evaluation team took special note of this involvement. Specifically commending Burns and Babbott for their work with the student body, the evaluators linked the drop in stu-

63. UVM Trustee Minutes, April 10, June 12, 13, and 20, 1953.

64. Ibid., August 14, September 5, 1953.

65. Hearings before the Subcommittee to Investigate the Administration of the Internal Security Act and Other Internal Security Laws of the Committee on the Judiciary, United States Senate, Eighty-Third Congress, First Session, on Subversive Influence in the Educational Process, Washington, D.C., 1953.

66. Executive Committee Minutes, May 5, 1970.

67. A.M.A.—
A.A.M.C. Liaison
Committee on Medical Education, Survey of UVM College
of Medicine, January 13–15, 1969,
Dean's Office. For
more information on
student participation in decision-making, see Executive Committee
Minutes, January 30,
1969, Dean's Office;
Student Council
Minutes, June 2,
1969, and January
28, 1970; Executive
Committee Minutes,
August 28, September 18, and 30, 1969;
UVM Medical Faculty Minutes, October
3, 1969.

dent attrition ("from one of the highest rates in the country a few years ago to the national average of 10%") to their efforts. "Student participation and constructive criticism are encouraged and these have resulted in changes in admissions policies and curriculum." The evaluators went on to note that "student morale seems high due to the relatively small student body and faculty and to easy communication channels and receptive faculty and administration attitudes."[67]

Since then, students have routinely exercised an ever-expanding role in the College decision-making process; one that was not even vaguely anticipated twenty years ago. Interestingly, they have asserted their greatest influence not through Student Council or other student organizations but rather as individual members of faculty-student committees and in similar situations. Perhaps the ultimate reflection of this participatory democracy occurred in March 1972 when Miss Cajsa Nordstrom, a sophomore medic, became the first student elected to the University of Vermont Board of Trustees.[68]

Chapter Sixteen

Only Yesterday

THE MEDICAL COLLEGE budget for 1947 was under $290,000—and all but $21,000 went for instruction. Nonetheless, with tuition set for instaters at $650, tuition and fees accounted for less than 25 percent of the College's operating costs. Possessing few other significant sources of income, the College relied heavily upon state support, and Vermont chafed under the burden. This was of considerable concern to Dean Brown. He recognized that if UVM were to maintain accepted standards in teaching and research, costs would continue to rise.

Faculty recruitment was particularly troublesome. Full-timers numbered 26; an additional 76 physicians held part-time status. In 1947 there was nothing equivalent to full-time clinical appointments, and all clinical instructors were part-time. Even Ellsworth Amidon, Chairman of the Department of Medicine, received only $4,000 from the College; his income was supplemented by patient fees and a salary as Medical Director of the Mary Fletcher Hospital.[1] The conflicting responsibilities this arrangement engendered has been chronicled elsewhere and in all probability were not fully perceived at that time. More readily apparent were indications that such economic arrangements precluded ever attracting a wide range of clinical specialists and researchers to the Medical College.

As long as clinical instructors were directly dependent upon patient fees from their private practices, the Burlington area could support relatively few specialists, certainly not in the quantity and variety required by a modern medical school. Even those who were attracted to Burlington frequently held their appointments in some specialty while pursuing more general practices. Given the financial realities

1. The dollar figures have been extracted from University of Vermont financial reports for the years ended June 30, 1947, and June 30, 1948. The faculty count is from Dr. A. Bradley Soule's analysis of the 1947–48 Medical College Bulletin.

in Vermont, with no endowment and limited state resources, opportunities for recruiting a qualified clinical staff and providing it with teaching and research incentives were limited.

Dean Brown and his successor, Dean George Wolf, viewing the situation with grave concern, attempted to add young clinicians to their faculty under conditions which left them relatively free from dependence upon patient fees. Contracts were negotiated individually and not guided by formal policy, but the general pattern was for the College to offer salaries in the range of $6,000 and full-time faculty benefits. Those who accepted (Ethan A. H. Sims, 1950, and Arthur Kunin, 1957, were two such individuals) were expected to provide expertise and conduct research in areas not otherwise represented by the UVM faculty.[2] From the view of the Medical College administration, another virtue of this arrangement was that the principal responsibilities of those appointed in this manner were to the Medical College.

Although the arrangement was to the College's advantage, it was only a temporary expedient. To an important extent these new faculty members had been appointed in the expectation that they would attract outside funds to finance their research and other costs to the College, and during the 1950's and 1960's federal largess made this possible. In the 1950's, however, direct federal funding to medical colleges was limited almost exclusively to research. Ironically, it was during that time that medical colleges modified their teaching mission increasingly toward graduate medical education, a teaching commitment requiring more extensive and more specialized clinical instruction, and usually in a hospital setting. Simultaneous with the escalation in graduate medical training the necessity for a full-time clinical staff became accepted within the profession, and it was anticipated that eventually the Council on Medical Education and the A.A.M.C. would require that every school have one. None of this was lost on Dean Wolf, who reasoned that despite the lack of an endowment and limited state resources it might be accomplished at UVM, through group practice plans under University control.

The Radiology and Anesthesiology departments had already established their own group practices. Following the Second World War, they had developed contracts with the various hospitals they served for a percentage of the gross billings. The University supported these services in a limited way with small stipends to the chairmen (who were also chiefs of service) for administrative duties. Although the other group members all held clinical appointments at the College, none received compensation from the University. Their salaries were determined by their departments and paid through departmental earnings. Surpluses, if any should occur, were disposed of at departmental discretion; usually by adding to the staff, raising salaries,

2. See, for example, Dean George A. Wolf, Jr., to Dr. Arthur Kunin, October 19, 1956, Wolf Folder.

purchasing new equipment, or making donations to the Medical College. The arrangements supported the two departments and enabled them to serve the Medical College more effectively than previously, but also permitted greater autonomy than envisioned by advocates of full-time staffs. Furthermore, it was believed that arrangements suitable for hospital services could not be adopted without modification by primary care physicians.[3]

The first of these to show interest in group practice were obstetricians. In 1954 they initiated discussion but dropped the matter after a survey revealed that most Burlington physicians opposed anything other than private practice. The matter rested until 1958 when John Maeck, Chairman of the Obstetrics Department, reopened the discussion. In June 1959 Maeck and three other department chairmen joined Dean Wolf on a tour of Southern medical schools that had recently developed group practice on a large scale. Their observations and discussions with the faculties and administrators of Virginia, North Carolina, Duke, Emory, and Bowman-Gray convinced them of the advantages of group practice in a medical school setting. At these schools, group income was divided according to a predetermined formula, to supplement the base salary, to compensate the University and the hospitals for space and facilities, and to support research and department budgets. It was a practical solution to the problem of how to support a clinical staff. Group practice would increase the financial support of the Medical School and enable it to attract promising clinicians by guaranteeing them a base salary along with teaching and research opportunities.[4]

The chances for working out similar arrangements at UVM seemed favorable. Many private practitioners had been attracted to Burlington because of the Medical College and their interest in academic pursuits. Their dedication to the College was evidenced by sometimes distinguished and almost always financially unrewarded service. Working out the details of group practice proved, nonetheless, exceedingly complex. Some clinicians with large practices feared they would be required to sacrifice substantial income. Others feared that if they surrendered control of their practices to the University, they would be induced to cut back on academic activities in order to maintain the flow of patient fees which would now constitute income.

Plans without University participation seemed less threatening, and following the Radiology and Anesthesiology models, the Pathology Department began consideration of a private agreement. This move made Dean Wolf and President John T. Fey apprehensive over the Medical College's future. It seemed to them that eventually every department might develop its own practice plans, with the University having no voice in determining the level of practice and with income divided among the physicians and the hospitals, rather than helping

3. Wolf Folder, Fey Papers, June 1959.
4. Hospitals—University-Liaison Committee Minutes, October 13, 1949, Tri-Institution Minute Book, 1957–63, University Archives. Medical Faculty Minutes, June 11, 1959.

to support the Medical School. Of potentially greater significance was that under such arrangements, the Medical Center might not always exercise direct influence over the appointment of new group members or possess leverage with which to negotiate terms of service to the College. The clinical faculty would, in effect, continue to consist of physicians whose only formal affiliation with the University would be a product of geographic propinquity. Some might locate in Burlington to be near the Medical College; others would be associated with the College merely because they practiced in close proximity. Whatever the circumstances, the administration would be exercising less quality control of its clinical faculty than it thought advisable. Sufficiently alarmed at these prospects, Fey, at a meeting of the University Board of Trustees, suggested that group practice plans be developed only by tripartite agreement, so that the hospitals and the College could cooperate.[5] The Trustees concurred, and in December 1960 Fey reported an agreement with the pathologists, limiting additional compensation to 25 percent of the base salary. The remaining funds would be used to finance the internal operations of the Department and to support departmental research. The faculty members in the group would be considered full-time faculty, eligible for tenure and fringe benefits.[6]

At a faculty meeting in May 1961, A. Bradley Soule, the veteran radiologist, proposed an amendment to the by-laws of the College which set the ground rules for group practice at the University. For a professor to qualify for tenure, he had to devote an average of at least thirty hours per week to teaching, research, or administration. Clinicians would be able to pursue other professional activities, with the level of their additional income determined by the trustees. The clinicians, however, could not have office practice outside of college facilities.[7] Although the faculty approved the amendment, there appears to have been no formal response by the trustees until 1954, when they appointed a planner.[8]

A May 1965 faculty report urged the trustees to approve a practice plan for full-time clinical faculty. The Medical School, it asserted, could not support the large number of faculty required in "what is essentially a tutorial system in the clinical years." Furthermore, since the students intend to practice medicine, and since they learned "by precept," their preceptors "should be primarily in the practice of medicine." Because some patient care was essential for teaching and for the development of academic excellence, and because fees were available to the physicians for those services, the money should be used to support full-time clinical faculty. The report continued that if the full-time faculty were to have the time and freedom to meet their academic responsibilities, "monetary incentives must be limited and the motivation for practice based on the necessity for continued academic growth in patient care, teaching, and research."[9]

5. UVM Trustee Minutes, June 10, 1960. Lester Wallman to the author, August 17, 1975, Kaufman Folder.

6. UVM Trustee Minutes, December 10, 1960.

7. UVM Medical Faculty Minutes, May 8, 1961.

8. UVM Trustee Minutes, June 5, 1964.

9. Suggestions for policies governing the private practice of medicine by full-time clinical faculty at the UVM College of Medicine, May 6, 1965, College of Medicine Folder, McCune Papers, UVM Archives.

On October 9, 1965, the Trustees approved development of practice plans for the clinical departments. The various departments recruited more and more of the clinical faculty and developed their own plans. Thus the University was relieved of the financial burden of having to subsidize departmental budgets totally.[10] The appointment in the Department of Medicine of William A. Tisdale as successor to E. L. Amidon exemplified this trend. Major subspecialties were fleshed out with the recruitment of a new breed of medical academician, the physician-investigator. His training like that of his academic predecessors was firmly grounded clinically, but he also possessed several years of laboratory or clinical research training in his respective subspecialty. He was expected to organize and administer expert and up-to-date clinical units and in addition obtain federal financial support for research.

The Medical College had emerged from World War II with its primary mission intact: to educate physicians. As was clearly evident from its 1947 budget, research *per se* constituted a minor commitment. As federal policy made research grants more available, however, the College eagerly applied for these funds, and with a great deal of success. By 1970 research expenditures exceeded those for undergraduate medical instruction. Once the federal government had become the major source of revenue, it was inevitable that the College's mission would evolve to reflect federal influence in other ways as well. A most obvious area in which this occurred was in redefining the College's public service role, particularly regarding health care delivery. The clinical faculty was instrumental in affecting this change.

The University had initially assumed that its only commitment to health care delivery was in training students to practice medicine. In the 1920's, when it became apparent that there was a shortage of physicians in rural areas, money was made available by the state with the understanding that students would practice in Vermont after graduation or repay their share of state support. This did not result in an appreciable increase in the number of doctors in the state, and Dean Jenne instituted a preceptorship program which was short lived. Dean Brown continued the preceptorship, believing the experience to be useful not only to recruit students for rural practice but also to introduce the student to the family and social aspects of medicine.[11]

In 1953 Dean Wolf felt that because of the state support of the Medical School, it would be useful to establish a Citizens' Advisory Committee to promote understanding between the College of Medicine and the citizens of the state. This Committee, although interested and well meaning, offered support for the College of Medicine but not the consumer input that was expected, and so it was abandoned. In the meantime, Wolf by chance met Leon Lezer, an alumnus who had

10. Press release, from Deans Slater and Andrews, College of Medicine folder, McCune Papers. Interview with John T. Fey.

11. See above, pp. 155–156, for a fuller discussion of Dean Jenne's preceptorship plan.

12. G. A. Wolf, Jr.,
"Progress at the
University of Ver-
mont College of
Medicine in the field
of rural medical
care," May 10, 1954,
Wolf Folder,
Borgmann Papers,
UVM Archives. For
Lezer's personal ac-
count of the Ver-
mont experience see
his *Community
Medicine: Organiza-
tion and Application
of Principles* (New
York, 1977).
13. *Burlington Free
Press*, October 17,
1950. For extensive
information on the
role of the regional
medical needs pro-
gram from 1955 to
1961, see Mary L.
Phillips, John H.
Mabry and Charles
S. Houston, *Eager
Communities and Re-
luctant Doctors* (Bur-
lington, 1967). Over
the life of the board,
Lezer dealt with
more than fifty
communities, half in
Vermont, and one
quarter each in New
Hampshire and
Maine, and he
helped to establish
eight community
health centers from
1957 to 1959.

practiced medicine in Chelsea, Vermont, and had made the acquaintance of former Governor Stanley Wilson. Although then an administrator at Massachusetts General Hospital, Lezer had retained his ties
to Chelsea and had developed a plan for providing medical care for
that town which included consumer participation, community involvement, and organizational concepts that were especially attractive to physicians, such as time off for continuing education, a small
initial investment without subsidy by the community, the elements
of group practice, and the use of physician assistants. Wolf then invited a group of out-of-state and in-state doctors and an executive
of the Commonwealth Fund to meet to discuss the problems of delivery of health services in the rural setting, emphasizing Vermont's
small population and the good relations between the Medical College
and the doctors in the state. Their interest and suggestions led to the
plan to hire Lezer to start a new Department of Preventive Medicine
in the College of Medicine, and the Commonwealth Fund provided
the start-up funds.[12] Among Lezer's first steps was to take over the
Burlington Free Dispensary, which for many years had been run by
the Department of Medicine of the Medical School. This clinic took
care of the indigent in the clinic and in the home. The plan was to
turn it into a family-care clinic so that it could pursue some of the
current interest in comprehensive versus episodic care for the poor.[13]

The next step was to import a group of professionals from other
universities representing the disciplines of sociology, social work,
nutrition, public health, Indian Health service, statistics, and nursing.
These individuals were to address the problems of health in rural
communities from the standpoint of total health care, not simply the
provision of one physician for each town.

This approach led to the obvious next step which was the development of the regional concept. Lezer designed and had passed in the
states of Maine, New Hampshire, and Vermont legislation creating a
Regional Medical Needs Board with representation from the state departments of health, state medical societies, and medical schools. Its
purpose was to study and consider solutions to the rural medical
problems in the region.

The implementation of studies involving areas and regions was
fraught with problems, most of them reflecting individual or state desire for autonomy. Moreover, at that time the only funds available
were Hill-Burton funds for hospital construction, the expenditure of
which was the business of the state department of health. Thus planning had no impetus. In 1959 the Commonwealth grant terminated
and Lezer had resigned. In 1962 the department was reorganized as
a Department of Epidemiology and Community Medicine by Kerr
Lachlan White, a medical graduate of McGill who recently had been
engaged in social medicine research in London Hospital in England.

White spearheaded plans for two related activities. First, he advocated development of a regional health services research center for northern New England, which would form the basis for an ongoing study of the problems of supply and demand for health services in the tri-state region. He also wished to establish a small number of community health centers, associated with regional hospitals, to be used as demonstration units for teaching medical students, residents, nurses, and other medical personnel. Rolf R. Struthers, of the University of Toronto, came to the University to initiate the planning for the two projects, and the Council of the Vermont State Medical Society agreed to help finance them.[14]

Even before the programs were effectively mounted, it became apparent that the Federal government would be moving more broadly into health care delivery. Until 1965 the Federal contribution had been channeled through Hill-Burton funds and directed mainly toward the construction of hospital facilities. On March 7, 1964, however, President Lyndon B. Johnson appointed a commission chaired by Dr. Michael DeBakey to develop a plan to reduce the loss of human and economic resources from heart disease, cancer, and stroke. The final report of the DeBakey Commission, issued in December, proposed the "establishment of a national network of Heart Disease, Cancer, and Stroke Centers for clinical investigation, teaching and patient care," and also that a "broad and flexible program of grant support be undertaken to stimulate the formation of medical complexes whereby university medical schools, hospitals, and other health care and research agencies and institutions work in concert."[15]

On January 19, 1965, Johnson proposed the DeBakey recommendations to Congress. It appeared likely that Congress would enact the recommendations which would result in federal grants dwarfing all previous state and foundation support. Dean Slater moved rapidly. Seeing an opportunity for Vermont and northern New England to "become a prototype for areas of lesser population," with the University of Vermont College of Medicine as its core, he immediately sounded out Governor Philip Hoff on the matter. Hoff was supportive and arranged a meeting of Medical College and State Health administrators in his office the following week. After a series of meetings, they designed a statewide planning organization for a regional medical complex associated with the Medical College. Along with a $10,000 planning fund, it was approved by the state legislature. The bill passed with the endorsement of the Vermont Medical Society and the Vermont Hospital Association four full months before a federal program was enacted into law.[16] When on October 6 the Regional Medical Program did become law, Slater had already established himself as a leading proponent of the program. He had testified for the bill before Congress and organized his state and college in anti-

14. Executive Committee Minutes, August 23 and December 13, 1963. UVM Faculty Minutes, January 17, 1964. In 1964 White resigned to accept a position at Johns Hopkins.

15. President's Commission on Heart Disease, Cancer and Stroke, Report to the President. *A National Program to Conquer Heart Disease, Cancer and Stroke*, I (Washington, 1964), 23, 32, 34. See also Catherine Morris Lloyd, "History of the Regional Medical Program in Vermont, 1965–1971," unpublished M.A. thesis, UVM, 1972. The account below is generally derived from Ms. Lloyd's thesis.

16. Draft Minutes of Meeting, February 5, 1965, College of Medicine Folder, McCune Papers.

cipation of its enactment, and was prepared to discuss specifics on how it might be implemented. At a November 1964 White House Conference on Health he delivered a paper entitled "Regional Medical Programs." The paper, concerned largely with technological adaptations to link medical centers with regional hospitals, was well received. In December, Slater was invited to become a member of the U.S. Public Health Service National Advisory Council on Regional Medical Programs. He was the only medical college dean to serve on the Council.[17]

Also in December, Governor John Volpe of Massachusetts called a meeting of New England Governors to consider development of a New England program that involved forming a nonprofit corporation to handle applications from the area. Although the New England states all sent representatives, the idea of centralized regional planning was not well received outside of Massachusetts. Most representatives feared that they would become satellites of a regional plan emanating from Boston. As early as the previous May, Dean Slater had articulated his concern that Vermont "might become a satellite of one of the larger adjacent urban areas and thus lose the advantage of our own initiative, decreasing our capability for growth, and more directly, our capability for patient care."[18]

Other New England states shared this concern—there is the story of a Maine hospital administrator who supposedly commented that if he threw a rock in Penobscot Bay it would float back with a Bandaid from Boston—and the first meeting produced little but evidence that the rest of New England would not accept membership in a Boston-centered regional complex. Furthermore, it seemed evident to Dean Slater and others that Vermont's plans were "much more developed than the nebulous ideas that now center in Boston." A second Governor's Conference meeting in January adopted a Vermont-proposed resolution that there be independent planning by Medical Centers, essentially giving approval to a University of Vermont Regional grant application for what eventually became the Northern New England Region—one of four semi-autonomous regions established in New England.

Vermont's efforts were rewarded in June 1966 when the College of Medicine became one of the first five institutions to receive a three-year grant to plan a regional medical program for heart disease, cancer, and stroke. Before the grant could be implemented, however, Slater announced his resignation from UVM to become Executive Director of the Association for the Aid of Crippled Children.[19] It is difficult to assess the significance of the departure of Dean Slater to the subsequent fortunes of the Northern New England Regional Medical Program. By far the Medical College's most enthusiastic and influential proponent of the RMP concept, Slater left its administra-

17. White House Conference on Health, November 3, 4, 1965, McCune Papers.

18. *Burlington Free Press*, May 6, 1965. See also UVM Medical Faculty Minutes, January 7, 1966.

19. Dean Slater submitted his resignation to the Board of Trustees effective December 31, 1966, on October 15.

tion to successors—Edward Andrews and William Luginbuhl—who were far less convinced that the federal legislation was well conceived and who were less personally identified with the Vermont project. That the Vermont project (NNE/RMP) failed to achieve success cannot be attributed to the College's lack of energy or commitment. RMP was a disappointment in most instances, and eventually it was abandoned by Congress as unworkable.

The NNE/RMP focused upon the development of a health planning data base, a regional management approach to disease control, and a continuing education program. This largely nonproject orientation was of concern to Washington. NNE/RMP was not, Washington alleged in 1970, carrying "out the types of projects in the delivery of health care that had been envisaged in the federal legislation. Its largest project, the data base, was yet to be employed; and democratic participation remained undeveloped." University, state, and other medical officials attempted to meet these criticisms by merging the NNE/RMP with Vermont Comprehensive Health Planning, another federal health project that had been established at about the same time as the RMP. The restructuring did not lead to any apparent improvements in health care delivery, and in 1974 the Medical College and the RMP decided upon a "friendly divorce." Dean Luginbuhl subsequently labeled the entire Regional Medical Program a "misadventure at a federal level." Former Dean Wolf concurred.[20]

In addition to the development of group practice and attempts to improve the quality of rural health care, recent years have also witnessed strenuous efforts to modernize the curriculum. The 1950's was a period of curriculum reform throughout the country. Colleges had responded to the development of specialism by adding to the curriculum, but by then it had become apparent that "the apparatus that had worked so well up through World War II was beginning to creak." In 1953 Dean George P. Berry of Harvard, observing the need to examine medical education critically, suggested a series of teaching institutes (subsequently sponsored by the Association of American Medical Colleges). Berry hoped to eliminate unnecessary material and develop a curriculum designed around a scientific core, so that more time could be devoted to the relevant social and behavioral sciences. The first real change took place at Western Reserve, with a reduction of time in the common core and a corresponding increase in electives. During the same period Johns Hopkins, Northwestern, and Boston University all experimented with an integration of the premedical and medical courses.[21]

Although UVM's most sweeping curriculum adjustments took place after Dean Brown had retired and took forms he could not have envisioned, it was under his administration that the College mobilized for curriculum reform. As early as 1948, with the financial

20. The expression "friendly divorce" is from Dr. John Mazuzan, whose arduous efforts to keep the NNE/RMP with the College by meeting federal objections to its operation were unsuccessful. He is the principal source for post 1971 information. Dean Wolf's and Dean Luginbuhl's evaluations of RMP are from personal interviews.

21. John Field, "Medical Education in the United States; Late Nineteenth and Twentieth Centuries," in C. D. O'Malley, ed., *The History of Medical Education* (Berkeley, Los Angeles and London, 1970), pp. 519–520. See also P. V. Lee, *Medical Schools and the Changing Times*, (Evanston, 1962).

22. UVM Medical Faculty Minutes, March 23, 1948. *Vermont Cynic*, April 7, 1948.

23. UVM Medical Faculty Minutes, October 31, 1952; Curriculum Committee Minutes, December 30, 1952, Curriculum Committee Folder, 1945–53, Committee Box 2, Dean's Office Papers, UVM Archives. Upon arriving at UVM, Dean Wolf interviewed every senior medic. His primary objective was to learn something about UVM students and "compare them with their Cornell counterparts." In the course of those interviews he discovered that the students thought there was too much didactic and theoretical material in the third year, and that the transition from the junior to the senior was too abrupt. In addition, the students wanted better correlation between preclinical and clinical work, and they declared that the emphasis should not be on rarities, but rather on methods of approach and interpretation of data. Wolf passed this in-

help of the Lamb Foundation, Dean Brown had initiated an experimental attempt to bring back into medicine "certain things which older doctors have" which were "as important to the patient as drugs." To help the student recognize that the patient's "comfort and apprehension should be taken into consideration," Brown invited practitioners throughout the state to visit the School, confer with students, lecture them, and make hospital rounds with them. The physicians in the program included Clarence Beecher, reputed to have been among the best teachers in the history of the School, John E. Woodruff of Barre, Frank J. Hurley of Bennington, and Frank C. Angell of Randolph. [22]

Of even greater long-range importance, however, was the work of preclinical and clinical study committees appointed by Dean Brown. When these "fact-finding" committees submitted their reports, Dean Brown was about to retire, and it was decided to wait for the arrival of George Wolf before proceeding. In 1952 Wolf, shortly after his arrival in Vermont, established a five man "action committee" with clinical and preclinical members to implement the recommendations. Fred Dunihue and George Schumacher assumed leadership roles. [23] They advocated major changes in the third year, with the elimination of the lecture method of teaching and an emphasis on patient-centered work in small groups. There would be only one formal lecture each day, and the students would be divided into groups for modified clinical clerkships at the two local hospitals. The daily lecture would deal with the modern status of the various phases of medicine, with the departments cooperating in the presentations. In August 1953 the faculty approved their plan. [24]

The following year the committee recommended a reorganization of the fourth-year program. The thirty-two-week year would be divided into eight four-week periods, with students rotating services. The services included out-of-town hospitals, work with general practitioners, psychiatric work at the Vermont State Hospital, medical and surgical service at that same institution, tuberculosis service at Sunmount or Trudeau, and work on the city service and the free dispensary and at the out-patient departments of the Mary Fletcher and DeGoesbriand. [25]

In addition, the committee recommended a drastic change in the second-year curriculum. There would be three basic courses to introduce students to clinical work much earlier than previously had been the case. The first course was entitled Morphology, Physiology, and the Chemistry of Disease, which included pathology, pharmacology, bacteriology, clinical pathology, anatomy, and public health. The second course was called Elicitation of Data from Patient, and it consisted of an introduction to history taking and diagnostic examination. The third and final course was an Introduction to Clinical

Medicine, with basic work in medicine, surgery, obstetrics, and pediatrics. In June 1954 the faculty adopted the changes, which went into effect in the fall of that year.[26]

As a consequence of these innovations, the second year had become a transition period between the didactic first year and the clinical third. The third year lost its didactic emphasis and became a time of modified clerkship. The fourth year was better organized than ever before.[27]

Matters remained in that stage until 1958, when Dr. George E. Miller, then of the University of Buffalo Project in Medical Education, visited the College to study teaching practices in Burlington. He concluded that the College was a typical medical school. The faculty tended to encourage and be receptive of student differences, although some of the professors did reject student questions. Most teachers were totally oblivious of the physical setting; they did not correct poor lighting, they did not reduce the heat, and they did not raise their voices to overcome the ever-present noise of the bulldozers working on the extensive construction going on at the University at the time. Miller reported that relations between professor and student were generally friendly, the teachers calling the students by name and sharing occasional jokes. He noted, however, that there was not a high degree of "challenge" at the College. The instructors "told" the students, rather than encouraging them to think, learn, or discover.[28]

Dean Wolf responded the following year by establishing a new curriculum study committee. Since he did not want the curriculum analyzed by men who were active in the earlier changes, and might be committed to the existing curriculum, Wolf selected newly arrived professors who had worked under other programs and had some basis for comparison. John Rice, who had come from Yale, therefore became chairman.[29] The committee submitted a very substantial report in August 1960. Its principal recommendations were geared toward promoting greater coordination between preclinical and clinical training.[30] They were never seriously considered. They had been proposed at a particularly inauspicious time: before they could be acted upon, Dean Wolf resigned.

In 1962 Dean Slater appointed his own committee to reevaluate the curriculum, and Edward Andrews, Jr., a member of the Pathology Department who was raised in Vermont and received his medical education at Johns Hopkins, was named chairman. He was clearly the most influential individual involved in curriculum development at that time. Both he and Slater advocated extensive faculty participation in the reevaluation process, and toward that end scheduled a faculty retreat. To avoid distractions it was held at the relatively isolated Woodstock Inn, and only male faculty were invited to at-

formation on to the action committee.

24. UVM Medical Faculty Minutes, June 10 and August 21, 1953.

25. Ibid., April 12, 1954.

26. Ibid., April 12 and June 10, 1954.

27. Advisory Committee Minutes, April 1, 1955. Also Wolf to Schumacher, July 13, 1959, Curriculum Committee Folder, 1959–61, Dean's Office Papers, Committee Box 1.

28. See Medical Education Study Folder, Box 7, Dean's Office Papers, 1934–63.

29. Wolf to Schumacher, July 13, 1959, Curriculum Committee Folder, 1959–61, Committee Box 1, Dean's Office Papers.

30. Report of the Curriculum Study Committee, August 1960, Curriculum Study Committee Folder, Committee Box 1, Dean's Office Papers. The committee urged the development of "some rapport" between the practicing physician and the first-year student, perhaps through a one-hour-per-week course on the clinical aspects of the first

year subjects. The committee also recommended that the second year program be changed so that students would not totally lose contact with their preclinical teachers. In the fourth year program, the committee noted a lack of cooperation between the divisions of internal medicine at the DeGoesbriand and the Mary Fletcher hospitals, and recommended that senior students attend the Saturday morning Grand Rounds at the De-Goesbriand, which were "so excellent that time [should] be allotted to them throughout the senior year." Finally the committee recommended the teaching of medical history, to provide the "necessary cultural background for a physician" and to "dramatize the rise and fall of concepts, the pathways that have led to important discoveries."

31. Educational Policy Study Committee, Minutes, March 23 and 28, 1962, in Woodstock Retreat Folder, Curriculum Study Committee Box.

tend.[31] Over two thirds of the active faculty attended the retreat. The principal speaker was George E. Miller, who had by then moved to the University of Illinois. Miller had given the entire faculty and student body the Hutchins Environment Inventory Test, and the Woodstock retreat provided him with the opportunity to reveal the results. His analysis of those results disclosed that the UVM faculty and student body held their School in lower esteem than counterparts at any of the other twenty-eight medical schools tested.[32] His discouraging report provoked frank discussion.

Following the meeting, the faculty continued curriculum discussions, and for the first time they thought not solely in terms of medical science, but also in terms of the learning experience. In the aftermath of the retreat, committees were established to study student affairs, teaching methods, and examinations. In the fall of 1963 it was decided not to imitate experimental programs at other schools, for the pilot programs elsewhere lacked "adequate controls," and there was "no instrument for measuring their accomplishments." It was also determined that the faculty should study the curriculum "as a body," working together to develop needed changes.[33]

In December 1965 the faculty held another retreat at the Woodstock Inn, which resulted in a "clear mandate" to develop an entirely new curriculum. The result was in line with national trends, which basically were movements away from the traditional programs and toward more vocational relevance.[34] Before the Flexner Report, medical schools had tried to train general practitioners. Flexner ushered in the new scientific age, which was characterized by attempts to train physician-scientists. Over the years since 1910, as medical knowledge has increased, schools responded by increasing the number of hours and eliminating electives. In effect they tried to provide each student with intensive courses in every medical specialty, most of which were irrelevant to the student's future work as a medical specialist.

The curriculum committee at the College attempted to develop a flexible curriculum suitable for training general practitioners, specialists, and teacher-investigators. The program was divided into three segments. First, there was a basic core of science which would provide "that body of knowledge common to all types of medical practice and to avoid minute details which are relevant only to individual medical specialties." In the second half of the sophomore year students began the clinical science core, which consisted of twelve weeks of instruction in medicine, twelve in surgery, and eight weeks each in pediatrics, psychiatry, and obstetrics and gynecology. During that phase of their education, which extended into the first part of the junior year, they would work in the hospitals, and instruction was patient centered at all times. The student would conclude his training with a major program of his choosing. Those interested in family practice would pursue one course of study, while those interested in surgery, obstetrics, or psychiatry, for instance, would pursue another. In the third year there would be a review of the basic sciences most relevant to the student's major, after which he would sign for blocks of related clinical work.[35]

The changes in the curriculum were developed through intensive discussion by the entire faculty, a technique possible only in a small medical school. Leadership came from two individuals, however, both of whom would continue to play major roles in the history of the University: Edward C. Andrews, Jr., and William H. Luginbuhl. In 1964 Andrews, then Associate Professor of Pathology, was appointed to the new post of Associate Dean of the Medical School. When Dean Slater resigned in 1966 to become Executive Director of the Association for the Aid of Crippled Children, Andrews was appointed dean. In December 1967, when the trustees approved the establishment of the Division of Health Sciences, bringing together into one administrative unit the College of Medicine, the School of Nursing, and the newly founded School of Allied Health Sciences, Andrews was named Dean of the Division, remaining Dean of the Medical School. In 1970 he became President of the University. Luginbuhl, who had received his medical degree from Northwestern University, was also a pathologist. In 1967 he became Associate Dean, and when Andrews was named University president in 1970, Luginbuhl replaced him as Dean of the Medical School and Dean of the Division of Health Sciences. Luginbuhl had been chairman of the curriculum development committee while Andrews was Associate Dean of the College. The two men, working together, were primarily responsible for planning the change in the curriculum which went into effect in 1967 for the incoming class of 1971.[36]

By 1970 it appeared that the College had moved toward lasting solutions to its major problems. Its financial situation had stabilized, despite the increasing costs of medical education. The development of group practice plans and cooperative agreements with other states had further relieved the burden on Vermont taxpayers, who in effect were supporting a school that was educating many out-of-state students. Since Castleton had closed its doors in the nineteenth century and Dartmouth was only a two-year school, UVM was, in fact, attempting to provide medical and health services to the entire northern New England area. The College appeared able to obtain the clinical material needed for medical education, and lack of material had not been a serious problem since the 1930's. Developments of the 1970's were to demonstrate, however, that problems waxed and waned but did not disappear.

As costs continued to escalate during the late sixties and early

32. See, for instance, the report of the Curriculum study committee, Committees Box 4, Dean's Office Papers. See also Educational Policy Study Committee Minutes, October 8, 1962, and report of the retreat, Curriculum Study Committee Box.

33. UVM Medical Faculty Minutes, October 18, 1963.

34. See Field, "Medical Education in the United States," p. 521.

35. UVM Medical College Bulletin, 1966–67, pp. 18–19. Also William H. Luginbuhl and Edward C. Andrews, "A New Curriculum: Its Evolution, Design and Implementation," *Journal of Medical Education*, September 1967.

36. For a defense of the new program, see Luginbuhl to Executive Committee, June 14, 1967, Curriculum Development Committee Box, 1966–67. Also *Burlington Free Press*, September 2, 1967.

seventies, Congress entered the financial picture. In response to the shortage of physicians and to the severe problems of financing medical education, it voted to support America's medical schools on a capitation basis, providing $1,800 per year per student. Schools, to qualify, had to expand their classes by 10 percent if their first year classes numbered fewer than one hundred students. To qualify for federal funding, the Vermont Medical School had to admit 83 students, an increase of 8 over the previous years. When the faculty voted to increase enrollment, about $550,000 was added to the College's income, virtually eliminating the anticipated $600,000 deficit of the School.[37] The changing sources of funding can be seen through an analysis of the college budget. In 1970–71 state funds provided through the University budget amounted to 33.6 percent of the Medical School's finances. By 1973–74 they had decreased to 22.2 percent, and then to 13.0 percent in 1975–76. At the same time, federal funding increased from 37.2 percent in 1970–71 to 48.5 percent in 1975–76, and income from practice increased from 13.4 percent in 1970–71 to 18.8 percent in 1975–76.[38] State funds, then, have been substantially reduced over the years, corresponding with an increase in federal grants and practice income.

This appeared to be a fortunate development, but with the increase in enrollment the problem of clinical material reappeared. Given the national trend toward shorter periods of hospitalization, the shortage of clinical material would have become a problem even without increased enrollment, but the problem was compounded by the demands of the additional students. Late in 1971 and early in 1972, Dean Luginbuhl made plans to ensure that education would not suffer because of the added students. Consideration was given to approaching medical centers in Hartford, Portland, Providence, and Springfield, in the hope of solving the problem by developing training centers outside of Burlington. Plattsburgh, New York, across the lake from Burlington, seemed a logical location for added clinical facilities, and the physicians and hospital authorities there were pleased to affiliate with the School and provide teaching resources. In addition, the house staff at the local hospitals was reduced, thus providing more clinical material for students.[39] The newly developed ambulatory care center offered some opportunity for increased student-patient contact, but these were merely holding actions, and the effect of the nationwide trend toward shorter periods of hospitalization was readily apparent in Burlington. The problem of clinical material, which had threatened to force the College out of existence in the first four decades of the century, reemerged as a major concern.

In addition to the continuing quests for financial support and clinical material, the need for even more general practitioners was increasing. Indeed, in 1974 a new Department of Family Practice was

37. Medical Faculty Minutes, January 14, 1972, Dean's Office Files. Material from David Tormey, in letter from A. B. Soule to author, November 20, 1976, Kaufman File, UVM Archives.

38. See Kaufman Folder for specific budgetary information, made available through A. Bradley Soule, 1977.

39. College of Medicine Advisory Council, Minutes, November 4 and 30, 1971, February 8 and July 6, 1972. Medical Faculty Minutes, May 18, 1972. Student Council Minutes, March 1, 1972, Dean's Office Files.

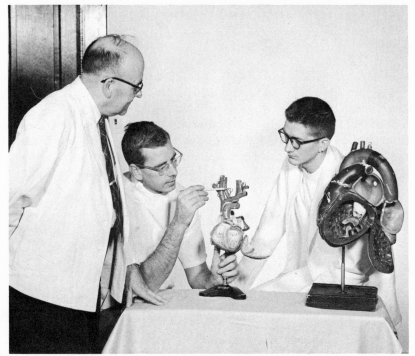

36. *Dr. Ferdinand J. M. Sichel, professor of physiology and biophysics, with members of the Class of 1962.*

37. *Dr. Chester A. Newhall, professor of anatomy (left), in his laboratory.*

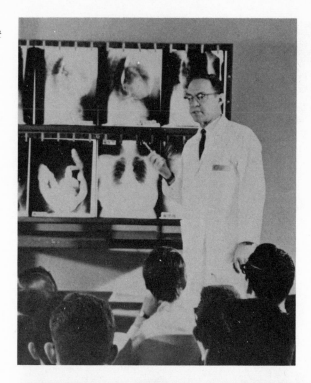

38. *Dr. Albert G.
Mackay, professor of
surgery, in Austin
Auditorium, Mary
Fletcher Hospital,
about 1965.*

39. *Dr. Wilhelm Raab,
professor of experimen-
tal medicine, with as-
sociates Gigee and
Herrlich.*

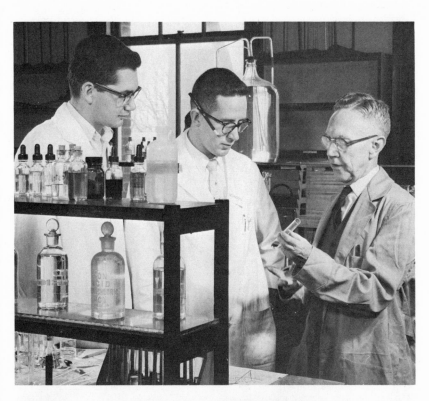

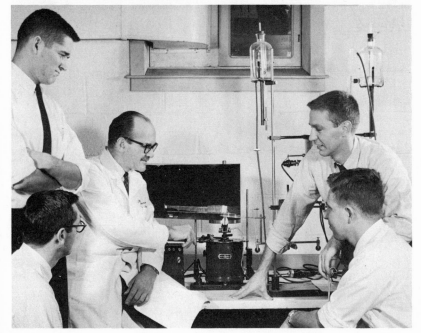

40. *Dr. Harold B. Pierce, professor of biochemistry* (right), *in his laboratory.*

41. *Dr. Durwood J. Smith, professor of pharmacology* (center), *in his laboratory with members of the Class of 1961.*

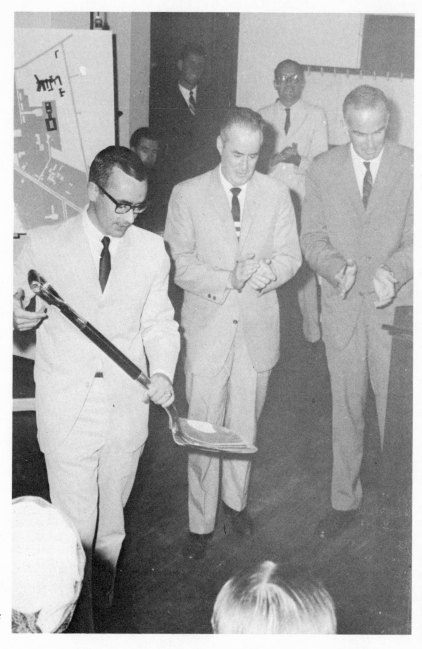

42. *"Breaking ground"*
for the Given Build-
ing, 1965. Ceremony
was held in Hall A be-
cause of rain. Left to
right: James E. Em-
mons, '68, president of
the freshman class,
which would be the
first to occupy the new
building; UVM
President Shannon
McCune; Dean Robert
J. Slater.

developed, with emphasis not only on medicine, but also on epidemiology, health care delivery, and the interrelationships between the family practitioner and the community. Once again, this development was in line with national trends, and to some extent in response to the realization that federal funding would be dependent on an emphasis on family practice.[40] The historian, of course, cannot evaluate these recent developments in terms of their success. It is likely, however, that the graduation of specialists in family practice will do little to alleviate the continuing problem of health care delivery in rural America unless some way can be found to guarantee that students will practice where they are most needed.

The curriculum continued to evolve in the 1970's. In the late sixties the College had begun to employ the pass-fail system in the basic sciences, to eliminate the intense competition for grades and with the hope that the result would be development of an atmosphere in which students would work together as colleagues rather than competitors.[41] In 1972 discussion of an accelerated program toward the M.D. degree culminated in the decision to graduate selected students after three years of study, as long as they continued as interns at the Medical Center Hospital of Vermont. Once again this was in line with national trends: a number of medical schools were developing three-year programs in order to increase the number of physicians and at the same time better utilize facilities. The Vermont approach was to select students on the basis of a careful evaluation of their ability to perform as primary physicians with a minimum of supervision. Of the nine members of the class of 1974 who were given the opportunity to graduate in 1973, five accepted the offer. The others decided to remain in the undergraduate program for another year, apparently because they "felt the need for the additional electives of the Senior Major Program, particularly in order to better deal with a career choice.[42] In effect, the students who were selected for early graduation had completed their Clinical Core, and their senior major program was condensed from sixteen to five months.[43]

In retrospect, although the College had seen times of progress and innovation liberally interspersed with days of stagnation and depression, it had come a long way since the time of John Pomeroy. In one respect, its history has been the history of American medical education, for it has had to encounter the same obstacles that faced other medical institutions. Yet the University of Vermont College of Medicine was unique in many ways. First, it was the home of the foremost reformer of the 1820's, Benjamin Lincoln, who tried so desperately to improve an outrageous situation that ultimately resulted in the discontinuance of lectures in the 1830's. The School was also unique in its willingness to fight to preserve medical edu-

40. College of Medicine Advisory Council, Minutes, February 28, 1974.

41. For student comments on the effectiveness of the pass-fail system, see *The Pulse* (1971), pp. 66–67.

42. College of Medicine Advisory Council, Minutes, January 3, 6, 1972. Medical Faculty Minutes, January 14, February 18, April 7, and November 10, 1972. For student comments, see *The Pulse* (1973), p. 105.

43. *The Pulse* (1973), p. 105.

*University of Vermont
College of Medicine*

*43. Air view of the
campus, 1975. (1)
deGoesbriand Memo-
rial Unit, (2) Dewey
Building, (3) Rowell
Building, (4) Given
Building, (5) Medical
Alumni Building, (6)
Mary Fletcher Unit.*

cation in rural America. While other institutions, like neighboring Dartmouth, accepted the findings of the Flexner Report, the University, led by the resolute Henry Crain Tinkham, refused to accept defeat. Although it was costly and although it meant raising standards beyond the reach of many Vermont students, Tinkham managed to keep the College alive during the most difficult time in its history, with threats from the A.M.A. and the A.A.M.C. Indeed, almost the same scenario could be seen during the turbulent 1940's, when a complete reorganization was necessary, this time led by E. H. Buttles, A. Bradley Soule, and Clarence Beecher. The faculty managed to make the needed changes and to convince the accrediting agencies, the A.M.A. Council on Medical Education, and the A.A.M.C. that the college was worth preserving.

*44. Dr. Bruce R. Mac-
Pherson '67, assistant
professor of pathology,
lecturing to the Class
of 1979 in Given E
214.*

Finally, the history of the College was unique in demonstrating that it was possible for a small, rural state to support the ever-increasing cost of medical education, at least until the federal government came to the rescue in the 1960's and 1970's, relieving the state's financial burden. The evidence of the value of the College can periodically be seen in figures indicating that Vermont has one of the highest ratios of physicians per capita. Indeed, the University has been an example for other rural states; its archives include numerous letters from governmental officials, medical societies, and University administrators asking how Vermont supports a medical school.

Some day, a future historian will continue where this work has concluded. Present and future deans, professors, students, and alumni are part of a long tradition that began with the work of John Pomeroy, continued with Benjamin Lincoln, Walter Carpenter, Samuel White Thayer, Ashbel P. Grinnell, Henry Crain Tinkham, Clarence H. Beecher, E. H. Buttles, William E. Brown, and scores of others who devoted their lives to the success of the School. If future deans, professors, students, and alumni maintain that tradition, follow that example, the future will remain bright.

Bibliography

Primary Sources

MANUSCRIPT COLLECTIONS

Bowdoin Medical Faculty Records, 1880–1890. Bowdoin College Library, Brunswick, Maine.

Citizens of Burlington to the Faculty, Woodstock Medical College, March 25, 1834. Vermont Historical Society, Montpelier.

Diocesan Archives. Burlington, Vermont. Includes extensive material on the DeGoesbriand Hospital, and miscellaneous material related to the appointment of a new chief of obstetrics and gynecology in 1949.

Harvard Medical Faculty Minutes, 1833–1840. Countway Library, Harvard Medical School, Boston, Massachusetts.

Kaufman Folder. UVM Archives. Includes correspondence related to this study, and material accumulated which was not previously in any archive.

Mary Fletcher Hospital Board of Directors, Minutes, 1876–1967. Administrator's office, Medical Center Hospital of Vermont, Burlington.

Medical Society of the University of Vermont, "List of Books Belonging to the Library," 1831. UVM Archives.

———Original Act of Incorporation, 1825. UVM Archives.

———Record Book, 1822–1831. UVM Archives.

Murdock, James, Letters. Dartmouth College Archives, Hanover, New Hampshire.

Pomeroy, John N., "Sketch of the Life of John N. Pomeroy," UVM Archives.

Regional Medical Needs Board, Minutes, 1955–1961. Regional Medical Needs Box, UVM Archives.

Rehabilitation Center Folders. UVM Archives.

Root, Erastus, "A Journal of the Most Remarkable Proceedings, Studies, and Observations." Pomeroy Papers, Wilbur Collection. Bailey Library, UVM.

Ruston, Thomas, Papers. Library of Congress, Washington, D.C.

Shattuck, George C., Papers. Massachusetts Historical Society, Boston.

Third Medical Society of Vermont, Minutebook. Wilbur Collection, Bailey Library.

Tri-Institution Committee, Minute Books, 1957–1963. UVM Archives.

Troy Medical College, Original Correspondence. Trustees' File, UVM Archives.

UVM. Papers of the Presidents.

    Guy Bailey Papers, UVM Archives.

    Carl Borgmann Papers, UVM Archives.

    William S. Carlson papers, UVM Archives.

    Daniel Haskel Papers, UVM Archives.

    John T. Fey Papers, UVM Archives.

    McCune Papers, UVM Archives.

    James March Papers, UVM Archives.

    John Schoff Millis Papers, UVM Archives.

    John Wheeler Letters, Dartmouth College Archives.

Presidents' Annual Reports to the Trustees. Trustees' File, UVM Archives.

Trustees, Executive Committee Papers. UVM Archives.

————Minute Books. UVM Archives.

UVM Medical Department, Cash Book, 1866–1875, 1875–1890. UVM Archives.

————Curriculum and Development Committee, Papers, 1966–1967. UVM Archives.

————Deans and Professors Papers.

    F. N. Baylies Papers. UVM Archives.

    George W. Benedict Papers. UVM Archives.

    William E. Brown Papers. UVM Archives.

    E. H. Buttles Reorganization Folder. UVM Archives.

    Ashbel P. Grinnell Papers. UVM Archives.

    Benjamin Lincoln Papers. Countway Library, Harvard Medical School.

    John Pomeroy Papers. UVM Archives.

    Arthur L. Porter Papers. Dartmouth College Archives.

    Nathan Smith Letters. Dartmouth College Archives.

    ————Yale College Library, New Haven, Conn.

    Nathan Ryno Smith Letters. Yale College Library.

    Henry Crain Tinkham Papers. UVM Archives.

————Dean's Advisory Committee Papers, 1944–1950's. UVM Archives.

————Dean's Office Files. Dean's Office, UVM Medical College. Includes Faculty Minutes, 1962– ; Department Chairman Minutes, 1969–1971; Executive Committee Minutes, 1965–1971.

————Dean's Office Papers, 1934–1963. UVM Archives. Boxes 2, 3, 7, 13, 14, and Committee Box 1, 2, and 4 were most useful for this study.

————Dean's Office Papers, 1941–1947. UVM Archives.

————Ledgers, 1879–1890. UVM Archives.

————Medical College Reorganization Papers, 1930's. UVM Archives.

————Preceptor's Correspondence, 1928–1934. Box in UVM Archives.

————"Statement of the Condition of the Medical College (so called) & Its Properties," August 1, 1836. Trustees File, UVM Archives.

————Student Council Minutes, 1960– . Dean Tormey's Office, UVM College of Medicine.

UVM Medical Faculty, Letter to the Corporation, August 12, 1824; Reply from the Corporation, October, 1824. UVM Archives.

————Minutes, 1875–1961. UVM Archives.

———"Report of Committee Appointed May 31 to Investigate Conduct of
    Prof. Grinnell." Grinnell Papers, UVM Archives.
Vermont Medical Society Minutes. Wilbur Collection, Bailey Library.
Whitney, Isaiah, "Notes Taken from Lectures Given by Dr. Nathan Smith,"
    1822. UVM Archives.

ORAL HISTORIES AND REMINISCENCES

Oral History interviews. Tapes and transcripts in UVM Archives.
    Ellsworth Amidon   Chester Newhall
    William E. Brown   Harold B. Pierce
    John Cunningham   Lester E. Richwagen
    John T. Fey   A. B. Soule
    Paul K. French   Frederick W. Van Buskirk
    Albert G. Mackay   George A. Wolf
    R. James McKay, Jr.   Jonas W. Wolf
    John Schoff Millis
Reminiscences of Cornelia Baylies. UVM Archives. Miss Baylies was secre-
    tary to the deans from the 1930's to the 1960's, and her reminiscences
    cast light on the personalities of various recent leaders of the College.

ARTICLES

Lewis, H. Edwin. "The Medical Department of the University of Vermont,"
    Vermont Medical Monthly, 8 (June 25, 1902), 154–156.
Luginbuhl, William H., and Andrews, Edward C. "A New Curriculum: Its
    Evolution, Design, and Implementation," *Journal of Medical Education*,
    42 (September 1967), 826–832.
Sweetser, William Jr. "On the Treatment of Cynancha Trachealis," *New
    England Journal of Medicine and Surgery*, 9 (January 1820), 11–15.

BOOKS AND PAMPHLETS

Association of American Medical Colleges. *History of Its Organization*. De-
    troit, 1877.
———*Report of the Committee on Syllabus*. Chicago, 1895.
Bessey, W. E. *How to Cure Drunkenness*. Montreal, 1880.
Calkins, Marshall. *An Introductory Address Delivered before the Medical Class
    of the University of Vermont, Thursday, March 8th, 1877*. Burlington,
    1877.
Carnegie Foundation for the Advancement of Teaching. *Education in Vermont*.
    New York, 1914.
Collier, Peter. *Opening Address Delivered before the Medical Class of the Uni-
    versity of Vermont, Thursday, March 9th, 1876*. Burlington, 1876.
Dedication of the Buildings, October 4 and 5, 1968. Burlington, 1968.
Erni, Henry. *Introductory Lecture, Delivered before the Medical Class of the Uni-
    versity of Vermont, May 12th, 1857*. Burlington, 1857.
Flexner, Abraham. *Medical Education in the United States and Canada*. New
    York, 1910.

Gallup, Joseph A. *Sketches of Epidemic Diseases in the State of Vermont, from Its First Settlement to the Year 1815*. Boston, 1815.

Jackson, J. Henry. *An Introductory Address Delivered before the Medical Department of the University of Vermont, March 1st, 1883*. Burlington, 1883.

Lezer, Leon R. *Community Medicine Organization and Application of Principles*. New York, 1977.

Lincoln, Benjamin. *An Exposition of Certain Abuses Practiced by Some of the Medical Schools of New England*. Burlington, 1833.

———*Hints on the Present State of Medical Education and the Influence of Medical Schools in New England*. Burlington, 1833.

Mary Fletcher Hospital Training School for Nurses. *Announcement, 1882*. Burlington, 1882.

Palmer, Edward E., and Sufrin, Sidney C. *Educational Costs in Vermont*. Syracuse, 1954.

Proceedings of a Convention of Medical Delegates, Held at Northampton (June 20, 1827). Boston, 1827.

Stiles, R. Cresson. *An Introductory Lecture to the Course of Instruction in the Medical Department of the University of Vermont, February, 1858*. Burlington, 1858.

Thomson, Samuel. *A Narrative of the Life and Medical Discoveries of Samuel Thomson, Containing an Account of His System of Practice, and the Manner of Curing Disease with Vegetable Medicine, upon a Plan Entirely New*. 5th edition, St. Clairsville, 1829.

———*Thomsonian Materia Medica*. 12th edition, Albany, 1841.

Two Hundred Vermonters. *Rural Vermont*. Burlington, 1931.

University of Vermont. *Catalogue of the Officers and Students, 1855–1856*. Burlington, 1855.

———*Catalogues, 1823–*. Files located in UVM Archives and in Wilbur Collection, Bailey Library.

———*General Catalogue of the University of Vermont, 1791–1900*. Burlington, 1901.

Vermont, State of. *Acts of Vermont, 1804*. Montpelier, 1804.

———*Acts of Vermont, 1828*. Montpelier, 1828.

———*Vermont Statutes, 1894*. Rutland, 1895.

Wheeler, John Brooks. *Memoirs of a Small-Town Surgeon*. New York, 1935.

Wright, Frances. *Views of Society and Manners in America*. New York, 1821.

NEWSPAPERS

Brattleboro Daily Reformer, 1941.

Burlington Clipper, 1886, 1899.

Burlington Free Press, 1831–1836, 1856–1859, 1878–1903, 1912–1917, 1920, 1940–1941, 1958–1970.

Burlington Gazette, 1814–1816.

Burlington Independent, 1886, 1893.

Burlington Mercury, 1796–1797.

Burlington Sentinel, 1830–1838.

Democratic Sentinel, 1877.

Northern Sentinel, 1818–1826.

Vermont Centinel, 1809.

Vermont Cynic, 1883–1975. Also called *University Cynic* at various times over the years.

American Journal of Sciences, 1896.
Bulletin of the American Academy of Medicine, 1899–1905.
Journal of the American Medical Association, 1890–1894, 1914, 1919.
Medical Record, 1876.
New England Journal of Medicine and Surgery, 1820–1825.
Popular Science Monthly, 1883.
Proceedings of the American Medical College Association, 1879–1880.
Transactions of the Vermont Medical Society.
Vermont Medical Monthly, 1899–1902, 1908–1914.

UNIVERSITY PERIODICALS

Alumni Weekly, 1925–1930.
Ariel, 1905, 1920–1924.
UVM Notes, 1911–1917.
Vermont Alumni, 1941.

Secondary Sources

MANUSCRIPTS

Hills, J. L. "History of the Medical College." UVM Archives.
"Legislative History of the University of Vermont." UVM Archives.
Lloyd, Catherine Morris. "History of the Regional Medical Program in Vermont, 1965–1971," unpub. M.A. thesis, UVM, 1972.
Tinkham, Henry Crain. "History of the Medical Department of the University of Vermont," Tinkham Papers, UVM Archives.

ARTICLES

Atwater, Edward. "The Development of the Medical Profession in a Frontier Economy: Rochester, New York (1812–1860)," paper presented before the American Association for the History of Medicine, Montreal, May 4, 1972.
Bassett, Tom. "Training Medics in Early Vermont," *Chittenden*, 4 (July, 1973), 27–30.
Bell, Whitfield J., Jr. "The Medical Institution of Yale College, 1810–1885," *Yale Journal of Biology and Medicine*, 33 (December 1960), 169–183.
Berman, Alex. "The Thomsonian Movement and Its Relation to American Pharmacy and Medicine," *Bulletin of the History of Medicine*, 25 (September–October 1951), 405–428; (November–December 1951), 519–538.
Chandler, John Loche. "Medical Education," *Buffalo Medical Journal*, 11 (September 1855), 218–219.
Edwards, Linden F. "Resurrection Riots During the Heroic Age of Anatomy in America," *Bulletin of the History of Medicine*, 25 (March–April 1951), 178–184.
Field, John. "Medical Education in the United States; Late Nineteenth and

Twentieth Centuries," in C. D. O'Malley, ed., *The History of Medical Education*. Berkeley, Los Angeles, and London, 1970.

Grinnell, A. P., and Lewis, H. Edwin. "History of Medical and Surgical Practice in Vermont," in William T. Davis, ed., *The New England States: Their Constitutional, Judicial, Educational, Commercial, Professional, and Industrial History* (Boston, 1897), pp. 1452–71.

Jordan, Philip D. "The Secret Six: An Inquiry into the Basic Materia Medica of the Thomsonian System of Botanic Medicine," *Ohio State Archaelogical and Historical Quarterly*, 52 (October–December 1943), 347–355.

Kaufman, Martin, and Hanawalt, Leslie L. "Body Snatching in the Midwest," *Michigan History*, 55 (Spring 1971), 23–40.

King, John W. "Dr. John Pomeroy and the College of Medicine of the University of Vermont," *Journal of the History of Medicine*, 4 (Autumn 1949), 393–406.

Lewis, H. Edwin. "The History of the Medical Department of the University of Vermont," *Vermont Medical Monthly*, 5 (September 1899), 264–276.

Miles, Wyndham D., and Kuslan, Louis. "Washington's First Consulting Chemist, Henry Erni," in *Records of the Columbia Historical Society of Washington, D.C., 1966–1968* (Washington, D.C., 1969), pp. 158–162.

Miller, Genevieve. "Medical Apprenticeship in the American Colonies," *Ciba Symposia*, 8 (January 1947), 502–510.

Smiley, Dean F. "History of the Association of American Medical Colleges, 1876–1956," *Journal of Medical Education*, 32 (July 1957), 512–525.

Stookey, Byron. "Origins of the First National Medical Convention: 1826–1846," *Journal of the American Medical Association*, 177 (July 15, 1961), 123ff.

Waite, Frederick C. "Grave-Robbing in New England," *Bulletin of the Medical Library Association*, 33 (July 1945), 272–294.

Wallman, Lester. "Benjamin Lincoln, M.D. Vermont Medical Educator," *Vermont History*, 29 (October 1961), 196–209.

———"Early History," in *Vermont Society Handbook: Vermont, 1813–1963* (Rutland, 1963), 13ff.

BOOKS

Bishop, James A. *The Day Lincoln Was Shot*. New York, 1955.

Chapin, William A. R. *History: University of Vermont College of Medicine*. Springfield, Massachusetts, 1951.

Cowen, David L. *Medical Education. The Queens-Rutgers Experience, 1792–1830*. New Brunswick, New Jersey, 1966.

Davis, N. S. *Contributions to the History of Medical Education and Medical Institutions in the United States of America, 1776–1876*. Washington, D.C., 1877.

———*History of the American Medical Association, from its Organization up to January, 1855*. Philadelphia, 1855.

Dock, Lavinia L., and Stewart, Isabel M. *A Short History of Nursing*. New York and London, 1938.

Gazetteer of Vermont Heritage. Chester, 1966.

Grinnell, A. P. *History of the Medical Department of the University of Vermont, An Introductory Address Delivered before the Medical Class, Thursday, March 4th, 1880*. Burlington, 1880.

Grob, Gerald N. *Edward Jarvis and the Medical World of Nineteenth Century America*. Knoxville, 1978.

Haggard, Howard W. *Devils, Drugs, and Doctors*. New York and London, 1929.

Hemenway, Abby Maria. *Vermont Historical Gazetteer*. Burlington, 1867.

Jamieson, Elizabeth M., and Sewall, Mary F. *Trends in Nursing History*. 4th ed., Philadelphia and London, 1954.

Kaufman, Martin. *American Medical Education: The Formative Years, 1765–1910*. Westport, Connecticut, 1976.

———*Homeopathy in America*. Baltimore, 1971.

Kett, Joseph F. *The Formation of the American Medical Profession*. New Haven and London, 1968.

Lee, P. V. *Medical Schools and the Changing Times*. Evanston, 1962.

Lindsay, Julian Ira. *Tradition Looks Forward*. Burlington, 1954.

Myer, Jesse S. *Life and Letters of Dr. William Beaumont*. St. Louis, 1912.

Perkins, Nathan. *Narrative*, Rutland, 1964.

Phillips, Mary L., John H. Mabry, and Charles S. Houston, *Eager Communities and Reluctant Doctors*. Burlington, 1967.

Rothstein, William G. *American Physicians in the Nineteenth Century*. Baltimore, 1972.

Sandberg, Carl. *Abraham Lincoln: The War Years*. New York, 1939.

Shryock, Richard H. *Medical Licensing in America*. Baltimore, 1967.

———*Medicine and Society in America, 1660–1860*. Ithaca, 1962.

Thompson, Zadock. *History of Vermont, Natural, Civil, and Statistical*. Burlington, 1842.

Waite, Frederick C. *The First Medical College in Vermont: Castleton, 1818–1862*. Montpelier, 1949.

Williams, Samuel. *The Natural and Civil History of Vermont*. Burlington, 1809.

Index

Accelerated program, 251. *See also* World War II.

Accreditation, 130–151, 154–168, 170, 173, 175, 194, 231–232

Adams, Charles, 12

Admission requirements and standards, 23, 30–32, 113–115, 132–133, 135, 142–143, 146, 151, 158, 217, 224–225, 227

Agassiz, Professor, 51

Agriculture college, 65, 77, 144, 147–148, 170, 216

Aiken, George D., Senator, 209

Aiken, Robert B., 196

Albee, Fred H., 141

Allen, Ethan, 1–2

Allen, Heman, 1

Allen, Ira, 1–3

Allen, Lyman, 115, 118, 125, 179

Alpha Delta Sigma, 122

Alpha Gamma Sigma, 223

Alpha Kappa Kappa, 122, 223

Alpha Omega Alpha, 223

Alumni, 79, 82, 83, 96, 100, 132–134, 148, 171–172, 196–197, 202, 206, 220

Ambulatory Care Center, 246

American Medical Association, 130, 132, 134, 148–150, 152–153, 159, 163–165, 168, 173, 175–176, 180–181, 194, 226, 231, 234, 254

American Public Health Association, 63

Amidon, Ellsworth L., 162, 168, 176–177, 194, 200, 204–205, 229, 233, 237

Amidonian society, 205

Anatomical material, source of, 26, 45–50, 53, 125–127. *See also* Clinical material, source of.

Anatomy, Department of, 4, 11–12, 16–17, 21–23, 37, 39, 51–52, 62, 68–70, 74–75, 83, 119, 138, 156–160, 164

Anatomy, public lectures in, 47

Anatomy, teaching of, 11–12, 22, 26, 28, 56

Anderson, William, 31

Andrews, Edward C., 231, 241, 243, 245

Anesthesia, experiment with, 11

Anesthesiology, Department of, 234

Angell, Frank C., 242

Angell, James B., 61

Antiseptic treatment, 70

Apprenticeship, 4–5, 36. *See also*

Admission requirements and standards.

Ariel, 96, 211–212, 221

Arms, Willard, 13

Army Specialized Training Program (ASTP), 226–227

Association for the Aid of Crippled Children, 240, 245

Association of American Medical Colleges, 77, 102–105, 109, 111–112, 130, 135, 137, 141, 143, 153, 158–159, 164–165, 167–168, 197, 226, 231, 234, 241, 254

Athletics, 123–125, 220–225

Atwater, Hiram, 92

Avalon Foundation, 202

Babbott, David, 231

Bailey, Guy W., 154–155, 159, 167, 169, 171

Baird, David G. Sr., 206, 209

Baldwin, Gilman E., 102

Beaumont, William, 8

Beecher, Clarence H., 138, 148, 152, 162–163, 171–173, 177–178, 242, 254–255

Bell, John, 22

Bell, John F., 182

Bell, Luther V., 42

Bell, Whitfield, 31

Bellevue Hospital Medical College, 65–66, 104

Bellevue Hospital Nursing School, 92

Benedict, G. G., 65, 71, 93

Benedict, George W., 22–23, 31–42, 50

Benton, Guy Potter, 142–147, 216

Berkshire Medical Institution, 26, 30, 57

Berry, George P., 241

Berry, John F., 196, 209

Berwynd Clinic, 163

Biddle, John B., 102

Bingham Associates, 179

Bingham, Leroy M., 68–73, 90, 92, 126

Biochemistry, Department of, 175

Bliss, Levi W., 50–52

Bloodletting, 13, 26, 27. *See also* Medical Practice.

Bloomer, Asa, 170

Body-snatching. *See* Grave-robbing.

Borgmann, Carl, 192, 194, 199, 203, 219

Boston University, 58, 204, 241

Botany. *See* Materia Medica

Boushey, Dallas, 229

Bowdoin Medical College, 18, 22–23, 30–32, 36, 57, 108–109, 113, 136

Bowker, A. V., 126

Boylston Prize dissertation, 22–23

Boynton, Charles S., 75

Bradish, James, 5

Bradley, Harry, 87

Brown, Thomas S., 138, 152, 156–158, 164, 179, 222

Brown, William E., 178–186, 189, 196–197, 233–234, 241–242, 255

Buckham, Matthew, 65–67, 70, 78, 81–82, 84, 89, 92, 96, 100, 114, 132–133

Buell, Ozias, 41

Buerki, Robin Carl, 178

Buildings and facilities, 11–13, 17, 20–21, 23, 33, 38, 41–42, 51, 54–55, 86–100, 191–194, 196–198, 200–203, 206–207, 209–210

Bulen, James, 225

Burke, William, 46

Burlington, description of: before settlement, 1; in 1820, 15–16; grave-robbing in, 46; medical profession in, 7, 19–20; support of UVM by citizens of, 20, 55, 150, 206

Burlington Free Dispensary, 143–145, 149, 151, 163, 238

Burns, Stanley, 215, 231

Butler, L. C., 105

Buttles, Ernest H., 159–161, 163, 171, 177, 254

Calkins, Marshall, 63, 66, 117

Campbell, Laurence C., 179

Cannon, Martin J., 208

Cap and Skull Society, 223

Carmichael, Claude, 211

Carnegie Foundation, 135, 145–148, 170
Carpenter, Alma, 216
Carpenter, Walter, 52–53, 59, 61, 66–68, 72, 86, 89, 120, 128, 253, 255
Carr, Ezra L., 51
Castleton Medical College, 9–13, 14, 21, 26, 29, 31–32, 33–35, 46, 49, 51, 54, 58, 60, 245. See also Selah Gridley.
Catlin, Moses, 15
Caverly, Charles S., 122, 138, 151
Caverly Preventorium, 156
Cazier, John LeComte, 11–13
Century Club, 220
Chaffee, Newman K., 169
Chandler, Benjamin, 4, 8–9
Chandler, Moses, 19
Chemistry, professor of, 11–12, 16–18, 21–22, 39, 51–52, 61, 64–66, 74, 84, 86, 116–117, 158, 160
Chemistry, teaching of, 9–12, 56
Chittenden, Thomas, 2–3
Civil War, 58, 128–29
Clark, B. F., 162, 183
Clark, F. E., 148
Clark, S. S., 105
Clemmons, Jackson J. W., 214
Clinical material, lack of, 135, 143–151, 154, 157, 162–163, 165, 178, 245–246. See also Anatomical material.
Clinical surgery, professor of, 138, 141
Clinical teaching, 55–56, 64, 84–85, 107, 111, 117, 135, 141–146, 153–157, 176, 233–237, 242–243
College of Physicians and surgeons (New York), 11, 50, 58, 63–64, 69, 104, 122–123, 138, 182. See also Columbia University
Collier, Peter, 61, 64–65, 116–117
Collins, Mother, 180
Columbian University (Washington, D.C.), 62–63, 79
Columbia University, 11, 58, 65, 149, 183. See also College of Physicians and Surgeons.

Colwell, Nathan P., 152, 154–155
Commencement exercises, 127–128
Commonwealth Fund, 238
Conant, David Sloan, 57, 59
Connor, Leartus, 104
Cooke, Louis J., 125
Coon, Robert, 194
Cooper, Elijah, 19
Corbin, Dorothy, 168
Cornell Medical College, 65, 138, 182, 189
Costello, John, 225
Coté, Cyril, 33
Council for National Defense, 225
Cowles, William S., Jr., 208
Crandall, A. J., 166
Crosby, Alpheus B., 58–59, 61
Crosby, Dixi, 58
Crump, Frederick, 223
Cunningham, John C., 183
Curriculum, 24–25, 56, 64, 73, 75–76, 101–112, 130, 135, 152–153, 155, 157, 162, 166–167, 176, 241–245
Cynic. See University Cynic.

Daggett, John F., 46–47
Daggs, Ray G., 160, 164
Dalton, John C., 64
Dana, Charles A., 202, 209–210
Dana Foundation, 202
Darling, William, 62–64, 68, 85, 107, 119, 121
Dartmouth, 2, 17, 18, 22, 30–31, 38, 42, 45, 49–50, 52, 57–58, 104, 108, 113, 122, 124, 135–136, 148, 205, 222, 245, 254
Davison, Forrest Ramon, 161
Deans, 61, 64–65, 76–81, 153, 163–165, 170–172, 176, 178, 189, 203, 240–241, 245
DeBakey Commission, 239
DeGoesbriand Hospital, 151, 163, 166, 176, 180–186, 189–196, 198–200, 202–209, 228, 242
DeGoesbriand, Louis (Bishop), 151
Degrees, 8–9
Delameter, John, 33–34
Delta Mu, 122, 223–224

Deming, Eleazar, 15
Denning, Walter S., 222
Depression, Great, 169–171
Dermatology, professor of, 64, 141
Dimock, Susan, 91
Dissection, 11, 26, 56
Donaghy, R. M. Peardon, 182
Downing, Augustus S., 142–143
Dresser, Henry O., 222
Dunihue, Fred W., 159–160, 173, 242
Dunster, Edward S., 58–59, 61
Durfee, Herbert A., 161–163, 182–
    184
Dustan, Harriet P., 181, 191

Eastman, Oliver, 162
Emerson, Lee E., 231
Englesby, E. T., 23
Enrollment, 18, 20–21, 33–37, 39,
    53–54, 60, 77–78, 87, 92–93, 110,
    124, 130–133, 146, 150–151, 173,
    246
Epidemiology and Community
    Medicine, 238–239
Erni, Henry, 51–52, 56, 116

Faculty (*1801–14*), 8–12; (*1822*), 16–
    18; (late *1820's*), 23; (*1850's*), 51–
    54; (*1854–70*), 57–60; (*1870–86*),
    61–73; (*1897–99*), 74–85; (*1902*),
    112; (*1940's*), 172–173, 182–183,
    223–237; conflict within, 64–73,
    76–85; qualifications of, 156–157;
    recruitment of, 233–237; reorgani-
    zation of (*1911*), 137–141; (*1937–
    39*), 159–162, 169; research by (af-
    ter World War II), 237; trustees
    conflict with, 68–85; views of col-
    lege by, 244
Family medicine, 237–238, 246,
    251
Fanny Allen Hospital, 145, 149, 151,
    163, 166, 176
Farrand, Daniel (Judge), 12
Federal Government grants, 191,
    200, 202–203, 206–207, 234–241,
    245–246, 251
Fees, 23–24. *See also* Tuition.
Female faculty members, 168

Female medical students, 115, 211,
    216–217, 223
Fey, John T., 203–206, 235–236
Fifield, Benjamin F., 81
Final examinations, 59–60, 66, 105–
    107, 127
Finances, 6–7, 12, 14, 16, 24, 33–37,
    39–42, 50–55, 60, 64, 75, 77–78,
    81–82, 86–87, 89, 93–94, 96, 100,
    102, 130–134, 144, 156, 169–171,
    177–178, 218–220, 233–237
Fires, in 1824, 20–21; in 1903, 94–96
Flanders, L. W., 118
Fletcher, Allen M., 145–146
Fletcher, Mary, 89–93. *See also* Mary
    Fletcher Hospital.
Fletcher, Thaddeus R., 89
Flexner, Abraham, 135–137
Flexner Report, 135–137, 143, 146,
    153, 218, 244, 254
Fogg, Hazen, 222
Foote, Alvan, 16
Fort Ethan Allen, 141, 163–166
Foundations, support by, 202, 206,
    209–210, 238, 242
Fowler, George P., 64
Fraternities, 122–123, 223–224
French, Paul K., 180–181, 185
Full-time professors, 132, 135, 137–
    138, 141, 154, 156, 158–159, 169,
    178, 233–237
Fund-raising, 87, 196–197, 199–200,
    202–203, 206, 209–210. *See also*
    Burlington, support by.
Furcolo, Foster, Governor, 219

Gallup, Joseph, 21–22, 29, 58
Geddings, Eli, 102
Genito-urinary diseases, professor
    of, 141
Gerrish, Henry, 108
Given Foundation, 206, 209–210
Given, Irene Heinz, 209
Given, John LaPorte, 209
Gladstone, Arthur, 162, 191–192,
    194–196, 199–200
Good, Frederick L., 183
Goodman, Louis S., 175, 177
Gourdin, Elizabeth, 214

Government. *See* Federal Government, Vermont legislature.
Grading system, 112
Graduate medical education, 228
Graduates, 9, 19–20, 39, 52–54, 102
Graduation requirements, 8–9, 20, 24, 30–31, 34, 102, 106–110, 114
Grave-robbing, 26, 45–48, 125–127
Gray, Jack Ward, 214
Gregg, Alan, 178
Gridley, Selah, 9–11, 13, 58
Grinnell, Ashbel P., 64, 66–69, 71–72, 74, 76–87, 89–90, 92–94, 106–107, 115, 118, 121, 124, 135, 255
Griscom, John H., 11
Gross, Samuel, 102
Group practice plans, 234–237
Gynecology. *See* Obstetrics and gynecology.

Hamilton Associates, 192, 206
Hamilton, Ellen, 216
Hamilton, Roy G., 221
Hanover, N.H., 2, 18. *See also* Dartmouth College.
Hare, William, 46
Hartman, Ernest, 160
Harvard Medical College, 1–3, 6, 18, 22, 30–31, 47, 50–51, 58, 109, 113, 115, 135, 138, 155, 176, 197, 203, 205, 241
Harwood, Theodore H., 167–168
Haskel, Daniel, 16, 20
Hatch, Horace, 42
Haynes, Moses A., 214
Health Sciences, Division of, 245
Heineberg, Bernard, 38–39
Henry, F. J., 120
Hickok, Henry P., 50
Hickok, Samuel, 15
Hill-Burton Act, 202, 207, 239
Hills, Joseph, 77, 96, 113, 144, 147–148
Hoff, Philip, 209, 239
Holmes, Oliver Wendell, 127
Holton, Henry Dwight, 63–64, 67–69, 71–73, 90, 102, 106–107, 121
Home for the Feeble-Minded, 156

Hopkins, Lemuel, 5
Hospitals in Vermont, 60, 89–93, 143–151, 155, 178–186, 189–196, 198–200, 203–210. *See also* De-Goesbriand Hospital, Fanny Allen Hospital, Mary Fletcher Hospital.
Howard, Benjamin, 63
Howard, John P., 87, 89
Howard Relief Society, 166
Huntington, Thomas W., 155
Hurley, Frank J., 242
Hygiene and Preventive Medicine, professor of, 138

Illinois Board of Health, 109
International Medical Congress (*1890*), professors at, 75
Internships, 152, 227–228
Introductory lectures, 116–117

Jackson, Fred Kinney, 138, 152, 160, 164
Jacksonian democracy, effect on medical profession, 43
Jackson, J. Henry, 69, 74, 76, 79, 81–82, 84, 106–108, 117, 121, 138
Jake, John, 225
James, David W., 168
Jarvis, Edward, 47
Jefferson Medical College, 22, 102
Jenne, James N., 75–76, 79–80, 82, 84, 122, 138, 149, 152–159, 13, 216, 237
Jewish students, AMA official opposed to admission of, 165
Johns Hopkins, 135, 160, 182, 241, 243
Johnson, C. K., 160
Johnson, John, 16
Johnson, Lyndon B., 239
Johnson, Peer, 206
Johnson, Victor, 173–177
Jordan, Hovey, 152, 173
Joyce, Bishop Robert F., 194–196, 199–200, 209
Jurisprudence, teaching of, 52, 58–59

Kake Walk, 223–225
Kane, Edward, 52

Keefer, Chester S., 204
Kelly, A. O. J., 84–85, 132–133, 138
Kemp, Hardy, 165–171, 173, 178, 180
Kennan, Jairus, 10–12
Kennedy, John F., 219
Kent State shootings, effect on UVM, 231
King, A.F.A., 62, 68–70, 74, 78–80, 82–84, 90, 93–94, 100, 107, 121, 126, 133, 138
King, Edward, 62
King, Gideon, 15
King, Martin Luther, 214–215
Kingsland, James L., Jr., 214
Kinsella, L. I., 125
Knight, E. A., 59
Kunin, Arthur, 234

Laboratory work, 112, 132–133, 135
Lamb Foundation, 242
Lang, Dorothy, 216–217
Leonard, Clifford S., 173
Levine, H. B., 167–168
Lewis, Frank C., 118
Lewis, H. Edwin, 112
Lezer, Leon, 237–238
Library, 33, 135, 137, 156, 210
Lincoln, Abraham, Professor King at death of, 62
Lincoln, Benjamin, 23, 28, 31–42, 47, 50, 153, 251, 255
Lincoln, Theodore, 41
Linsley, Jo Hatch, 70, 75, 80–81
Little, Arthur D., 207
Little, James L., 63–64, 68–69, 71, 85, 90, 106–107, 121
Luginbuhl, William, 231, 241, 245–246
Lund, William B., 92
Lyman, John, 19

McCarthyism, 230–231
McCrae, John, 137–138
McCrory, H. Lawrence, 214
McFarland, Frederick W., 197
Mackay, Albert G., 162, 168, 177, 223
McKay, Robert J., 182
McMahon, Karl C., 220
MacNevin, William J., 11

McSweeney, E. Douglas, 222
McSweeney, Patrick, 119, 141, 149, 161, 183
Maeck, John V. S., 183, 185, 235
Mann, Horace, 51
Markoff's orchestra, 221
Marsh, James, 38
Marsh, Joseph, 38–39, 42, 49
Martin, Herbert, 203
Marvin, David, 138, 161, 164
Marvin, Ebenezer, 4
Mary Fletcher Hospital, 15, 68–70, 89–93, 111, 135, 143–145, 149, 151, 164, 166, 172, 178–179, 189–196, 198–210, 222, 228, 233, 242
Maryland, University of, 22, 32–33, 35
Mason, Lida, 216
Massachusetts Anatomy Act, 47
Massachusetts General Hospital, 92, 161, 203, 238
Massachusetts Medical Society, 22, 30
Materia medica, professor of, 16, 21, 39, 52, 58–59, 63, 72, 74–75, 84, 138; teaching of, 56
Means, William J., 141, 150
Medical Center Hospital of Vermont, 178–180, 189–196, 198–200, 203–210, 228, 251
Medical colleges, admission requirements at, 36; competition between, 25–26, 29–37; finances, 6–7; preliminary education of students at, 113. See also Northampton Convention.
Medical education, reforms of, 102–105, 109–112. See also Benjamin Lincoln, Northampton Convention.
Medical licensing, 7, 9–10, 30–31, 44, 77, 104–105, 114–115, 130, 132, 134
Medical practice, 13–14. See also Medicine, Thomsonianism.
Medical professor, in colonial period, 4–8; popular views of, 45–48
Medical societies, in Chittenden county, 7, 9, 19; in Vermont, 7, 9,

19, 29, 44. *See also* Vermont State Medical Society.

Medical Society of the University of Vermont, 27–28

Medical specialism, effects on medical education, 64, 227–228, 233–234, 241

Medical textbooks, 4–5, 9–10, 13–14

Medical treatments, 13–14

Medicine, Department of Theory and Practice of, 12–14, 19, 21–22, 26–27, 39, 51–52, 66–67, 74, 83–85, 138, 162, 176, 204–205

Medicine, practice of, 4–6; teaching of, 56

Meharry Medical College, 215

Mental diseases, professor of, 141

Mexican crisis of 1916, 225

Microscopic anatomy, professor of, 63, 66, 74, 117, 138

Middlebury College, 3, 19, 22, 124, 144–145, 222

Miller, Donald B., 182

Miller, George E., 243–244

Millis, John Schoff, 172, 177–179

Milton, Vermont, 125–126

Mitchell, Alfred, 108

Moody, John, 19

Moore, Elisha, 19

Morris, David G., 211

Morrow, Rufus C., 183

Morse, William, 222

Mott, Valentine, 49, 63, 117

Mower, Edmund C., 216

National Medical Convention, 50

Nativism, 23, 39

Naylor, James H., 125

Nay, Winfield Scott, 117, 125

Negro cadavers, 127, 211–215; faculty members, 214; medical students, 115

Nelson, Horatio, 52–53

Neurology, professor of, 68

Neurosurgery, Department of, 183

New England Board of Higher Education, 218–219

New England Higher Education Compact, 218

New England Medical Center, 179, 203

Newhall, Chester, 157, 159, 164

New York Post-Graduate Medical School, 63–64, 68, 74, 80

New York State Department of Education, 141–143

New York State Legislature, 21–22

New York University, 49–50, 52, 62–65, 68–69, 104, 159–160

Nightingale, Florence, 92

Nordstrom, Cajsa, 232

Northampton Convention (*1827*), 30–31, 44, 102

Northern New England Regional Medical Program, 240–241

Norwich University, 145

Novikoff, Alex B., 230

Nurses, training of, 91–92

Nu Sigma Nu, 223, 228

Obstetrics and Gynecology, Department of, 39, 52, 58–59, 62–63, 74, 83, 138, 141, 161–162, 183–185, 235; teaching of, 56, 145, 163

Olcott, Mills, 18

Olsen, Herluf V., Sr., 209

Ophthalmology, otolaryngology, and rhinology, Department of, 64, 141, 144, 160, 182

Oppenheimer, Russell H., 167

Ordronaux, John, 58–59, 61, 63–64

Orms, Cornelius, 33

Orthopedic surgery, professor of, 141

Orthopedics, Department of, 182

Osler Clinical Society, 223

Packard, Frank A., 125–126

Packer, Paul C., 170–172

Paddock, William, 16–17, 19, 22

Paine, Martyn, 49–50

Parker, Willard, 63

Pathology, Department of, 57, 63, 72, 80, 116, 137–138, 160, 175, 235–236; teaching of, 56

Patrick, Robert, 205–206, 208

Patrick, Roy, 171, 179

Pattison, Granville Sharp, 49

Paulsen, Malcolm, 225
Pease, Calvin, 55, 86
Peaslee, Edmund R., 57
Peck, Edward S., 101
Pediatrics, Department of, 64, 141, 160, 182
Pennsylvania, University of, 57–58, 62, 84, 109, 132, 160, 162
Perkins, George H., 96, 144
Perkins, Joseph, 58–59
Peters, Charles A., 141
Pharmacology, Department of, 138, 161, 175
Pharmacy, professor of, 16, 21, 39, 51–52; teaching of, 56
Phelps, Abel Mix, 74–76, 78–79, 82–83, 85
Phelps, Edward Elisha, 38–39, 42, 49
Phi Chi, 122, 223, 225
Phillips, C. Allen, 229
Physiology, Department of, 12, 16–17, 22–23, 39, 52, 57–58, 63, 66, 69, 74, 84, 116–117, 137–138, 160; public lectures on, 23; teaching of, 56
Piatt, Jean, 159
Pierce, Harold B., 160, 164, 173, 175, 177
Pisek, Godfrey, 141
Pitman, David B., 220
Platt, James Kent, 19, 21
Polio, research on, 151
Pomeroy, Cassius, 8, 12
Pomeroy, John, 4–16, 19–20
Pomeroy, John N., 11–12, 50
Pond, E. A., 125
Porter, Arthur L., 16–22
Powell, C. Wesley, 219–220
Powell, Truman, 9
Pratt Diagnostic Clinic, 179
Preceptorship program, 155–156, 166, 237
Preliminary course, 56–57
Presbyterian Hospital (New York), 149
Preventive medicine, Department of, 238
Pritchett, Henry S., 148. *See also* Carnegie Foundation.

Proctor, Mortimer, 179
Proger, Samuel, 179

Quizzes, 62, 119–120

Raab, Wilhelm, 168, 176, 194, 200
Radiology, Department of, 161, 234
Ranney, Ambrose L., 68–69
Regional medical needs board, 238
Regional medical planning, 238–241
Rehabilitation center, 193, 199, 203, 206
Revolutionary War, 1–2, 5
Rice, John, 243
Rice, Bishop Joseph J., 149, 163
Richmond, Ernest, 125
Richmond, J. S., 125
Richwagen, Lester, 179, 209
Riley, James E., 225
Roberts, Stephen M., 64
Rochester, University of, 160
Rockefeller Foundation, 176, 178
Rockefeller Institute, 203
Rockefeller, Laurence, 209
Rogers, W. F., 166
Root, Erastus, 13
Roosa, D. B. St. John, 64, 90
Rowell, Lyman S., 215
Ruback, Jacob, 5–6
Rural medical care, 134, 136, 154–156, 217, 237–239
Rush, Benjamin, 13, 27
Rust, Jesse, 166
Ruston, Thomas, 6
Rutgers Medical School, 22, 161
Rutherford, Jacob C., 75, 121
Rutland Herald, 3
Rutland, railroads in, 78, 87
Ryan, Bishop Edward F., 180, 183–186, 191–192, 194

Sanders, Daniel C., 6, 14, 16
Scane, John W., 137–138
Schulz, Milford D., 203–214
Schumacher, George A., 182, 242
Shattuck Fund (Henry B.), 206
Shattuck, George C., 18, 23, 32–35
Shattuck, George C., Jr., 34, 37
Sichel, Ferdinand J. M., 160, 173, 175

Silliman, Benjamin, 18, 51–52
Sims, Ethan A. H., 234
Sisters of Providence Hospital, 60
Slater, Robert J., 203–204, 239–240, 243, 245
Slavin, William, 183
Smith, Nathan, 16–19, 21–23, 26, 38
Smith, Nathan Ryno, 16–17, 19–22
Smith, Orrin, 51
Smith, Worthington, 50
Smokers sponsored by medics, 220–222
Soule, A. Bradley, 159, 161, 163–165, 171–172, 177–178, 199, 204, 236, 254
Spanish-American War, 76, 125
Speare, Sceva, 202, 206
Specialism. See Medical specialism.
Special subjects, lecturers of, 64, 68, 75, 111, 137, 141
State support, 246. See also Vermont legislature.
Stiles, R. Cresson, 57, 59, 116
Stolz, Harold F., 162
Stone, Bingham H., 138, 148, 152
Struthers, Rolf R., 239
Students: boycott by, 70–73; characteristics of, 227–228; council, 215, 228, 232; geographical distribution, 20, 113–114, 218–220; college life, 113–129, 220–232; organizations, 27–28, 223–224; role in decision-making, 77–80, 228, 231–232
Stultz, Walter, 159, 173, 177
Sumner, Charles, Senator, 128
Sunmount, 242
Surgery, professor of, 4, 12, 19, 21, 23, 37, 39, 51–53, 57–58, 63–64, 68–75, 84, 138–141; teaching of, 56, 111
Surgical practice, 13–14
Sussman, Ralph, 220
Sweetser, William, Jr., 22–23, 27–28, 31–32, 34–36

Tampas, John P., 229
Taylor, Robert W., 64
Teacher-of-the year awards, 214, 229, 230

Teaching hospital, 89–93, 164, 166, 178–184, 189–210. See also De-Goesbriand Hospital, Mary Fletcher Hospital, Medical Center Hospital of Vermont.
Teaching methods, 56–57, 117, 137, 141, 162, 243–244
Terrien, Christopher, 166, 194, 200
Thabault, L. G., 166
Thayer, Charles P., 68
Thayer, Samuel White, 49–53, 56–57, 61, 66–68, 90, 106, 128, 153, 255
Therapeutics and clinical medicine, professor of, 138
Thomson, Samuel, 42
Thomsonians, 42–44, 48
Tinkham, Henry Crain, 68, 70, 75–76, 80–84, 96, 100, 118, 120, 122, 126–127, 131–150, 152–153, 157, 163, 211, 216–217, 254–255
Tisdale, William A., 205, 237
Tomasi, Thomas B., Jr., 200
Towles, William B., 68–69, 74–75, 127
Townsend, William W., 141
Transportation, 4–5, 11, 113–114
Tri-institution committee, 196, 199, 203–204
Tropical diseases, professor of, 141
Troy Medical Institution, 21–22
Trudeau, 242
Trustees, 6–10, 12, 14, 16–18, 22–23, 37–39, 41–42, 49–51, 54, 63, 65, 67, 68–73, 78, 81–85, 86–87, 89, 93–94, 132–133, 135, 144–145, 147–149, 151, 159, 164, 169–171, 173, 177, 204, 216, 231–232, 236–237, 245
Tufts Medical College, 179, 183, 203
Tuition, 220, 233. See also Fees
Twitchell, E. G., 160, 182
Twitchell, Marshall C., 141, 144

Underwood, Levi, 87
University Cynic, 68–69, 77, 87–88, 93, 118–120, 122, 124–125, 127, 216, 220–221, 223, 226
University of Vermont: in early

nineteenth century, 16; finances, 17, 20, 55, 169–171; founding of, 1–4; medical teaching begins at, 4, 8. *See also* Finances.
Upton, E. F., 106–107

Van Buskirk, Frederick W., 180
Van Deuson, George H., 129
Van Ness, C. P., 16
Van Ness House, 62, 128
Vermont Academy of Medicine. *See* Castleton Medical College.
Vermont Alumni Weekly, 156
Vermont Comprehensive Health Planning, 241
Vermont: constitution of, 1–2; diseases in early, 21; early history of, 1–3
Vermont Education Commission, 145–147
Vermont Hospital Association, 179, 239
Vermont Laboratory of Hygiene, 80, 138, 156
Vermont Legislature, 3, 9, 18, 44–45, 126, 133, 135, 144–145, 147–150, 154, 169–171, 246
Vermont Medical Monthly, 83, 94, 96, 112, 136, 147
Vermont, medical practice in, 26–27
Vermont Sanatorium for Incipient and Early Tuberculosis, 156
Vermont, settlement of, 1–2
Vermont State Board of Health, 63, 138
Vermont State Hospital for the Insane, 145, 156, 242
Vermont State Medical Society, 9–10, 19, 21, 29–31, 44, 59–60, 66, 101–102, 105–107, 181, 239; relations with UVM, 101–102, 105–107
Vermont, University of. *See* University of Vermont.
Vienna Exposition (*1875*), 65
Virginia, University of, 68–69, 74–75, 126, 235
Volpe, John, 240
Votey, J. W., 144

Waite, Frederick, 25, 32
Waite, Laura, 92
Wallman, Lester, 182
War of *1812*, effect on University, 10, 13, 17
Warren, John H., 63
Washington, George, 2
Wasson, Watson L., 141
Webb, W. Seward, 78, 81, 84
Weeks State Industrial School, 156
Weiskotten, Herman, 156–157, 165
Wells, John Doane, 23
Wentworth, W. P., 89
Wesson Woman's Hospital, 166
Western Pacific Railroad, 155
Western Reserve University, 214, 241
Wheeler, John, 42, 50
Wheeler, John B., 64, 75, 84, 90–91, 111, 115, 120, 138, 141, 152
Wheelock, Eleazar, 2
White, Fletcher, 166
White, Horace L., 84
White House Conference on Health (*1964*), 240
White, Kerr L., 238
Whitney, C. F., 158–161, 163–164, 171
Whitney, Isaiah, 26
Willard, A. J., 92
Williams, Samuel, 3, 7
Williams Science Hall, 93
Wills, William H., 170–171
Wilson, J. A., 141
Wilson, Stanley, 238
Wilson, Woodrow, 225
Winthrop, John, 3
Witthaus, Rudolph A., 65–66, 70, 74, 76, 78–79, 81–83, 85, 93–94, 106–108, 110, 121, 127
Wolf, George, 170, 189–192, 194–199, 203, 219, 234–235, 237, 241–243
Wolf, Marguerite Hurrey, 191
Woodruff, John E., 242
Woodstock Inn, retreats at, 243–244
Woodstock Medical college, 25, 29, 31, 34, 39, 45, 52, 54, 59, 60
Woodward, Adrian T., 103

Woodward, Julius Hayden, 74–75, 100
Woodward, Theodore, 33, 35–36
Worcester City Hospital, 166
World War I, 152, 225–226
World War II, 168, 172–173, 176–178, 226–227
Wright, Frances, 15
Wright, J. Williston, 68–69, 71, 74, 85
Wright, T. R., 208
Wyckoff, John, 156–157

Yale, 1, 17, 18, 31, 38, 51–52, 54, 57, 61, 113, 122, 135, 159, 175, 182, 205, 243
Young Men's Christian Association, 120
Young, William J., 229

Zakrzewska, Marie, 91
Zapffe, Fred C., 141, 158, 164–168, 173, 175–178

Library of Congress Cataloging in Publication Data

Kaufman, Martin, 1940–
    The University of Vermont College of Medicine.

    Bibliography: p.
    Includes index.
    1. Vermont. University. College of Medicine—History.
I. Title.
R747.V52K38   610'.7'1174317   77-78882

(2) deGoesbriand
Memorial Unit

(4) Mary Fletcher

(1) Dewey Building

(3) Laboratory, Vermont
State Department of Health